THE PARLIAMENTARY DIARY OF
ROBERT BOWYER, 1606-1607

THE
Parliamentary Diary of
ROBERT BOWYER
1606-1607

Edited by DAVID HARRIS WILLSON

1971

OCTAGON BOOKS
New York

Reprinted 1971
by special arrangement with the University of Minnesota Press

OCTAGON BOOKS
A Division of Farrar, Straus & Giroux, Inc.
19 Union Square West
New York, N. Y. 10003

Library of Congress Catalog Card Number: 72-120677

ISBN 0-374-98636-3

Manufactured by Braun-Brumfield, Inc.
Ann Arbor, Michigan

Printed in the United States of America

To My Mother

PREFACE

ONE cannot follow the history of the English Parliament from the death of Queen Elizabeth to the opening of the Civil Wars without becoming aware that great things were taking place. The all-important question whether King or Parliament should be the sovereign power in the state was at issue during these years, and at their close the answer was no longer doubtful. Parliamentary government, with all that it has meant for England and for the rest of the world, was being fought for and won. This period is the high-water mark of modern constitutional history.

But the history of early Stuart Parliaments has in the past been written from very meager sources and must be written once more from the new material that has been brought to light in recent years. Historians in the past were perforce content with the *Commons Journals* as their chief source, supplementing it where they could with bits from scattered manuscripts and from a handful of well-known diaries kept by private members. The *Commons Journals* is and will always remain a fundamental source. Yet the hasty and jotting character of this record of the Clerk leaves only too much to be desired as a source for the history of the House. He wrote so rapidly that his notes were short and frequently unintelligible, usually consisting of little more than the mere titles of bills, the barest outlines of speeches, and the formal resolutions of the House. Nor did he regard it as part of his duty to record the proceedings of committees. Moreover, considerable portions of the Journals have been lost. It was the custom for the Clerk to take notes in the House and later, after the session was over, to rewrite his journal in a fuller and more presentable form. For most of the early Stuart period this perfected journal has been lost, and only the original and unofficial jottings of the Clerk remain. Thus the *Commons Journals*, though used by every historian, is at best a meager and unsatisfactory record.

The new sources through which future scholars must study the debates of early Stuart Parliaments are the recently discovered diaries of private members. Certain diaries have been known and used by historians for a considerable period, but most of them have been but recently brought to light and are as yet unavailable in printed form. Private members took notes in much the same way as the Clerk, jotting down what they could in the House and later filling in the gaps or rewriting their diaries altogether. As sources, their accounts compare most favorably with that of the Clerk. They constantly noted things that he did not, and their accounts are fuller and frequently more reliable. They are less formal; they give speeches in more detail; they report the work of committees. Thus the diaries complete and at times supersede the account of the *Commons Journals*.

But they do not exist in any numbers until the Parliaments of the 1620's. Little has been discovered dealing with Elizabeth's reign, except what is included by Sir Simonds D'Ewes in his parliamentary history of that reign. And for the period from 1603 to 1620 there are but two diaries of any length, that edited by Mr. Samuel R. Gardiner for the Camden Society dealing with the year 1610 and that of Robert Bowyer covering the sessions of 1606 and 1607. Thus Bowyer's account is the earliest long diary unearthed so far and while it perhaps lacks the interest that attaches to more stirring sessions, it nevertheless throws light on the beginnings of antagonisms and conflicts that must be studied to make later Parliaments understandable. It deals with sessions that have never been portrayed in adequate detail. For these reasons, if for no others, Bowyer's diary possesses considerable interest for students of seventeenth-century Parliaments.

The attention of the present editor was first called to Bowyer's diary by Professor Wallace Notestein of Yale University, who has made the whole subject of early Stuart Parliaments peculiarly his own. It is therefore due to Professor Notestein that this edition was undertaken. For errors of fact or judgment in its execution the editor alone is responsible.

The little that is known concerning Bowyer's life can be told in a few words. He came of a well-to-do family of some prominence in Sussex local history, his grandfather having been mayor of Chichester in 1532 and 1546. His father, William Bowyer, was admitted to the Middle Temple in 1553 and later became Keeper of the Records in the Tower, a position that led him to make a "perfecte Kallendar of all the Records" under his care.[1] He is probably

---

[1] Harl. MSS 94, ff. 41–48. He probably secured the office in 1564. St. P. Dom. Eliz. XXXIII, 2. In 1567 the Rolls of Parliament and the Chancery Rolls were transferred to his care. *Ibid.* XLII, 43, 74; XLIII, 4, 5; Lansd. MSS 133, ff. 103–112.

also the author of a "Study of the Laws of the Realm" for the use
of legal students, a manuscript dated 1571.[1] William Bowyer married Anne, daughter of Sir John Harcourt of Stanton, and had two
children, Robert Bowyer being the only son.[2]

In 1579 Robert Bowyer received the degree of B. A. from the
University of Oxford, and after a short term of study at Clifford's
Inn, was admitted to the Middle Temple in 1580. His connection
with the Temple proved to be a long one, for he was allowed to
keep his chambers after business took him to other parts of London[3] and did not surrender them until 1606, by which time he
had become a master of the utter bar. From 1594 to 1597 he made
an unsuccessful attempt to secure the clerkship of the House of
Lords. His friend Lord Buckhurst, later the Lord Treasurer and
the first Earl of Dorset, wrote to Sir Robert Cecil in his behalf, and
Bowyer personally petitioned the Queen and also satisfied the former Clerk by offering to "give something for the transfer." Another candidate, however, one Thomas Smith, also wrote Cecil
requesting the position for himself and adding, "I think there is or
will be one Bowyer a suitor for the place by the means of my Lord
of Buckhurst, who may be well worthy, perhaps, of some other and
greater preferment, but I may be bold to say (without any ill affection to the man) that he is not fit for this place, by reason of a
great imperfection he hath in his speech." Smith secured the post
and Bowyer was forced to remain satisfied with a grant of the office
in reversion.[4]

About this time, or at least by 1599, Bowyer became secretary
to Lord Buckhurst, a position that he continued to fill through
1607 and probably till Buckhurst's death in 1608.[5] Bowyer begins

---

[1] Lansd. MSS 98.

[2] *Harleian Society*, XV, 94; *Sussex Archaeological Collections*, XXV,
113–116; XLII, 32. William Bowyer left the manuscript of a thirteenth-
century chronicle to his son. *Hist. MSS Com. 11th Rep.* Pt. VII (Inner
Temple MSS), 229.

[3] C. H. Hopwood, *Middle Temple Records*, I, 238. "Mr. Bowyer shall
not forfeit his chamber by reason of his attendance upon the Lord High
Treasurer." *Ibid.* I, 395.

[4] *Cal. Hatfield House MSS*, IV, 467; V, 55; VII, 299; St. P. Dom. Eliz.
CCLI, 26; *Cal. St. P. Dom. 1595–1597*, 505, 509.

[5] For Bowyer as secretary, see *Cal. Hatfield House MSS*, X, 286; St. P.
Dom. Eliz. CCLXXXIIIa, 84. Naunton (*Fragmenta Regalia*, ed. of 1808,
p. 279) says that Buckhurst was very careful about his secretaries.

certain passages in his diary by saying that he came into the House following his "attendance upon my Lord Buckhurst." He first entered the House of Commons in 1601 as member for Steyning Borough, Sussex. In this Parliament he was an insignificant figure, though upon one occasion he startled the House by denouncing the common practise of pulling members by the sleeve in close divisions, so as to induce them to vote with one side rather than the other. "A Gentleman," said Bowyer, "that would willingly go forth according to his Conscience, was pulled back: Though I much reverence my Masters of the Temple, and am bound to our Benchers of the Middle-Temple, yet if it will please the House and you Mr. Speaker to command me to name him, I will." Sir Walter Raleigh replied that this was but a small offense "for so have I done my self oftentimes. (And great loud Speech and stir there was in the House.)"[1]

Bowyer's more important part in Parliament during the sessions of 1606 and 1607 rested largely upon the fact that in 1604 he, together with Henry Elsyng, with whom he shared chambers in the Temple,[2] secured the clerkship and the keeping of the Rolls of Chancery and all other records and rolls in the Tower.[3] This brought Bowyer into contact with all those desiring to secure material from the records under his care. He received numerous letters asking him to copy records or to allow others to do so, to lend books and manuscripts, to hunt for precedents, or to give general information about the Rolls.[4] He was also asked to make searches for the House of Commons or to assist members sent by that body. Fees made the office a valuable one and brought Bowyer a good, if somewhat variable, remuneration. He and Elsyng, for example, in return for their assistance to Ferdinando Pulton, who was pre-

---

[1] D'Ewes, *Journal of all the Parliaments during . . . Elizabeth*, 683–684. Bowyer is mentioned once again in this session, when he swooned in the House. *Ibid.* 688.

[2] *Hopwood*, I, 388. Elsyng had married Bowyer's niece Blanche.

[3] *Cal. St. P. Dom. 1603–1610*, 178. In the same year Bowyer received the minor office of Door-Keeper of the Exchequer and Keeper of the Council Chamber of the Star Chamber for life. *Ibid.* 124.

[4] These letters cover the years 1604 to 1620. St. P. Dom. James I, L, 31; *Hist. MSS Com. 12th Rep.* Pt. I (Cooper MSS), 55; *11th Rep.* Pt. VII (Inner Temple MSS), 239–240; *3rd Rep.* (House of Lords MSS), 14, 17; Spedding, *Letters and Life of Francis Bacon*, IV, 129.

paring an edition of the statutes, were to receive a division of the profits accruing from the work. But apart from the income it yielded him, the office greatly increased Bowyer's importance and position in the world.[1]

In the fall of 1605 Bowyer was returned to Parliament from Evesham Borough, Worcester, and for the next two years he kept the diary that is published in this volume. There are records of some eleven of his speeches. His legal training led him to speak concerning bills involving points of law; he spoke also on matters relating to Oxford; he attacked the Catholics and defended the Puritans; and the offices that he held induced him upon most occasions to support the measures desired by the Crown. But his position in the House depended largely upon his knowledge of the records in the Tower and upon his control over them. He was frequently asked to bring precedents and read them to the House. He was placed upon many committees because he could readily obtain desired documents or make easy the access to them of other committee members. He served upon some twenty committees during these sessions, including the important Committee of Privileges and Returns and also committees appointed to confer with the Lords on the questions of union with Scotland and of dealing with Catholic recusants.[2]

In 1610 Bowyer became Clerk of the House of Lords—the place he had attempted to secure in 1597—taking the oath before the Lord Chancellor on January 30 and allowing his place in the Com-

---

[1] *Hist. MSS Com. 11th Rep.* Pt. VII (Bridgewater MSS), 139. Sir William Cecil wrote to Thomas Heneage in 1569: "Boyar [William] was want to tell me that over his charges, he gained not some yere above 26£. 13s. 4d., but yet in some other tyme he had for some speciall serch 13£. 6s. 8d. at once, which was not common." *Ibid.* Finch MSS, I, 6. Bowyer could expect to receive a compensation from his successor when he wished to vacate the office. Sir Thomas Knyveton wrote Cotton in an undated letter, "I doe heare that two are in hand with Mr. Bowier for his office in the Tower and that they are like to go thorough for yt." Cott. MSS, Julius C III, f. 228. *Ibid.* Vespasian F IX, f. 252.

[2] *Commons Journals* for 1606 and 1607 (especially pp. 284, 296, 384, 1032, 1055) and his diary, *passim. Hist. MSS Com. 3rd Rep.* 13; St. P. Dom. James I, XXI, 17. It is impossible to state the exact number of committees upon which Bowyer served, since there were other Bowyers in the House. Of thirty-three committees, Robert Bowyer certainly served on thirteen and in all probability on a number of the others.

mons to be filled by a new election. His fees were substantial, £40 a year from the Crown and many fees from members who paid when they were absent or when they desired copies of bills or information about parliamentary business.[1] He also supplied Salisbury and other ministers with parliamentary documents, thus continuing the kind of work he had been doing as Keeper of the Rolls. While he was Clerk he copied or abridged the Lords Journals of some earlier Parliaments of Mary, Elizabeth, and James I.[2] He undoubtedly had some control over the celerity with which bills went through the upper house. Petitioners wrote him concerning pending legislation, asking him to "show . . . what lawful favour he could to further" a bill, or "to take his word [the writer's] for fees and let the Bill go on," or to see that a certain bill "may be read to-morrow." In one instance a letter dated April 16, 1610, asking him to favor a certain bill, was followed by its first reading on April 18, its second on April 19, and its third on April 29.[3]

On March 12, 1621, in the House of Lords "the Lord Chancellor declared, That (Mr. Bowyer) the Clerk of the Parliament was so dangerous sick, that he might not come to the House, without Peril of his Life; and therefore was an humble Suitor, that he might make Henry Elsyng his Deputy, who hath also a Patent of the Clerk's Place in Reversion."[4] To this the Lords agreed. Bowyer died in 1622, leaving most of his property to the children of his friend Elsyng.[5] He himself had never married.

The attitude of Bowyer toward the struggle of the King and the

---

[1] *Hist. MSS Com. 3rd Rep.* 12–14. One of these letters is addressed to Bowyer at his house on Tower Hill. In another, Lord Say and Sele writes to his "cousin" Bowyer: "On Monday or Tuesday at utmost will bring him his fees, and bestow a piece of venison on him." See also St. P. Dom. James I, LVII, 12.

[2] E. Jeffries Davis, "An Unpublished Manuscript of the Lords' Journals for April and May, 1559," *English Historical Review*, XXVIII, 531–542 (July, 1913). Lansd. MSS 496, f. 2, mentions "a Calendar made by Robt. Bowyer (who succeeded Sir Thomas Smyth as Clerk of the Lords) of the severall acts in the office with the assistance of his servant Owin Reignolds."

[3] *Hist. MSS Com. 3rd Rep.* 12–13; *4th Rep.* (House of Lords MSS), 119; *Lords Journals*, II, 578, 579, 583.

[4] *L. J.* III, 41. Bowyer offered a precedent of Edward IV for his request. *Hist. MSS Com. 3rd Rep.* 20.

[5] Bowyer's will is at Somerset House.

Commons presents a certain contradiction. As Dorset's secretary and a minor officeholder, Bowyer was obviously connected with the "Court" party and was spoken of in Parliament as "my Lord Treasurer's man."[1] In 1606 he warmly defended the financial proposals of the government before a hostile House, saying that he was "in some sort tied by special duty" to do so. But though he was usually found acting with the royal faction, there are passages in his diary which indicate that on many questions its writer was strongly drawn toward the popular cause. He was intensely interested in the history of the House and in those elusive precedents of its ancient liberties. He was also interested in the rules by which it conducted its business and defended itself from the Crown. He noted with extreme care any new rules or any deviations from the usual methods of procedure, as if he were collecting precedents for use in future sessions. In 1607 he spoke against a bill suppressing illegal assemblies although he knew the government greatly desired its passage. He sympathized strongly with the Puritans, devoted much space to their grievances and demands, and lamented that a certain bill in their behalf was so lacerated by amendments of the Lords that the Commons threw it out as useless. It was in his opinion "a very good bill" and the amendments of the Lords "very strange." He said that he wrote it out in full at the end of the second (lost) book of his diary. Thus Bowyer, while a member of the "Court" faction, was one of those "mutineers" who embarrassed the government by their occasional defection.

There are two manuscripts containing Bowyer's diary: the one the original in Bowyer's own hand in the library of Lord Braye at Stanford Hall, Yelvertoft, Northants, near Rugby, and the other a copy in the British Museum (Harleian MSS 4945). The copy is in an unknown hand, but one that appears also on certain of Bowyer's papers among the Petyt MSS in the Library of the Inner Temple. Neither the copy nor the original is complete. Bowyer originally wrote his diary in three books: the first running from January 21 to March 24, 1606, the second from March 25 to May 27, and the

---

[1] At a committee on May 8, 1607, there "was a bone cast in about Escuage . . .: but that was offered only by my L. Treasurer's man, Mr. Bowyer, for others to take hold of, but neither he nor any other apprehended it or prosecuted it." St. P. Dom. XXI, 17. D'Ewes, *Journal of all the Parliaments during . . . Elizabeth*, 688.

third from November 19 to July 3, 1607. Only Books I and III are now preserved at Stanford Hall. Fortunately, however, the second book is contained in the copy. The copyist began by merely taking down brief extracts, but by the time the end of Book I was reached he was making an almost perfect copy. It may therefore be presumed that the Harleian MS is a very faithful reproduction of the lost second book, the omissions being slight, if indeed they exist at all. Book III is contained in both manuscripts. For the first part of this book (covering the period from November 19, 1606, to May 18, 1607) the editor has used the British Museum copy, since this portion of the diary had already been set up in print before the original was placed at his disposal and since the differences between the two manuscripts were too immaterial to warrant change. For the remainder of Book III (covering the period from May 19 to July 3, 1607), the diary is printed from the original Stanford MS. The following diagram may clarify these relationships:

DIVISION OF DIARY	STANFORD MS (Original)	HARLEIAN MS (Copy)
Book I (January 21–March 24, 1606).	Printed (pages 1–90).	Contains only extracts from the original. Not printed.
Book II (March 25–May 27, 1606).	Lost.	Printed (pages 91–184).
Book III (November 19, 1606–July 3, 1607).	Printed from May 19 to July 3, 1607 (pages 295–368).	Printed from November 19, 1606, to May 18, 1607, where it ends (pages 184–294).

Once the Stanford and the Harleian MSS were placed in their proper relationship, the arrangement of the text presented few difficulties. Bowyer's hand is a good one and the diary is unusually simple and straightforward in arrangement. This is equally true of the copy. Each day is carefully dated, though there are a few inaccuracies. The spelling is much better and more consistent than in most seventeenth-century manuscripts, and it has been retained except for abbreviations (such as *ye* for *the* and *Lds* for *Lords*), which have been spelled out in modern form. This has involved a small number of words many times over rather than a large number of different words. The original capitalization has also been kept. The capital and the small *s* are almost identical and therefore, where it has been impossible to make any distinction between them, the small *s* has been used. The punctuation in both manuscripts, though bearing little resemblance to modern usage, is quite full and understandable and hence has been retained without change. Throughout, the manuscripts have been altered as little as possible, in order to preserve the atmosphere of the original as much as can be done in a modern edition.

Although Bowyer's diary is for the most part an entirely independent account, there are occasional passages that bear a marked similarity to corresponding passages in the *Commons Journals*. These seem to be mere paraphrases of the record of the Clerk. Moreover, Bowyer begins his account of many days with formal lists of the bills read, such as are contained in the *Journals*,[1] and incorporates into his diary two long documents that are also to be found in the Clerk's journal.[2] Concerning one of these, a message from the King on June 2, 1607, Bowyer says that the Speaker read it to the Commons and then "delivered it to the clerke of the howse whereof the coppie followeth." It is clear, likewise, that Bowyer did not write his diary in the House itself, but took notes and later wrote them up in final form. One must therefore suppose that occasionally he had the account of the Clerk before him as he wrote the finished draft of his diary, supplementing his own notes by reading over the Commons Journals. On the other hand, there is evidence that the Clerk at times consulted Bowyer's notes or completed diary in writing his own perfected journal. When a certain Sir William Seaton described to the House the trial in Scotland of an Englishman named Barrow, the Clerk did not take down the speech but wrote in the margin of his rough notes, "*Quaere de* Mr. Bowyer for the Relation."[3] Thus Bowyer and the Clerk at times

---

[1] When these lists of bills add nothing to the lists in the *Commons Journals*, they have not been reprinted in this volume.

[2] Harl. MSS 4945, ff. 224–226; Stanford MS, ff. 34b–35a. A third such document is found in the Harl. MSS 4945 (ff. 208–214), but it is not in the original Stanford MS. Since these three documents or "separates" are in the *Commons Journals*, they have not been reprinted.

[3] C. J. I, 1046.

borrowed from each other, though it must not be presumed that this took place with any regularity.

In compiling the notes to this volume the editor has attempted primarily to present as full a picture as possible of what took place in the House of Commons during these years, directing the reader to both published and manuscript sources and printing as much of the latter as was practicable. This has been his chief care and to it other considerations, such as identifying every minor name, have been somewhat subordinated. A word of description may be added concerning certain of the manuscript sources. Apart from Bowyer's diary the most important unpublished materials for the history of Parliament during these years are the numerous letters of the time. These are found chiefly in the great collection of state papers in the Public Record Office and among the manuscripts of the Marquis of Salisbury, which, when printed, will add so tremendously to our knowledge of the first years of the reign of James I.[1] The parliamentary notes of Sir Robert Harley for April and May of 1607 form another valuable supplement to Bowyer's account. These notes, contained in a little notebook, were scribbled down while debates were actually in progress in the House.[2] There is another very brief account in the Cottonian MSS, Titus F IV, a journal that was written up after the sessions, leaning heavily upon the Commons Journals to fill out the personal recollections of the writer. A few notes have been made from the manuscript of the Commons Journals, which is in the Library of the House of Commons, since the Clerk frequently crossed out or changed portions of what he had written and these alterations do not appear in the printed *Journals*.[3] Besides these sources there are in the great

---

[1] Copies of the Hatfield House MSS for the years 1603 to 1612 are in the Public Record Office awaiting publication by the Historical Manuscripts Commission. The Marquis of Salisbury has graciously allowed about a score of them to appear in this volume.

[2] The manuscript containing these notes is among the Harley Papers in the library of the Duke of Portland at Welbeck Abbey, Worksop, Notts. The Duke of Portland has graciously allowed these notes to be printed here. There is another short manuscript among the Harley Papers containing notes taken by Sir Robert Harley in 1610. The editor hopes to publish this manuscript in a small volume along with certain other documents dealing with the sessions of 1610.

[3] For these notes the editor has to thank Professor Wallace Notestein, who kindly placed them at his disposal.

depositories of England many scattered manuscripts bearing on these sessions. Such "separates" are brief documents containing perhaps a single speech, the proceedings at a conference, or the debates on a single issue. In most cases there is no indication of their purpose or author, nor is there any absolute assurance of their accuracy. A member might write out a speech and then never deliver it or he might touch it up after it was given, in order to impress his friends or constituents. A few of these "separates" or extracts from them have been printed in the following notes, though for the most part it has been impossible to do more than point out their existence.

In editing the documentary material in the notes the same rules have been followed as in editing the text, except that where no punctuation appears in the manuscripts and the sentences run into each other without periods or capitalization, it seemed advisable to make the necessary sentence division by supplying periods and capital letters and thus relieve the reader of a task he would otherwise be forced to perform painfully for himself.

To a number of persons and institutions the editor must express thanks for assistance and courtesies in the preparation of this volume. First of all, his thanks are due to Lord Braye for allowing the photographing and publication of the diary. He also wishes to thank the Marquis of Salisbury, the Duke of Portland, and the Benchers of the Inner Temple for permission to publish other manuscripts. He must acknowledge his deep indebtedness to Professor Wallace Notestein, through whose assistance and friendship this work has been made possible. He wishes to thank Professor Frances H. Relf of Wells College for informing him of the existence of the original of the diary in the library at Stanford Hall, which she discovered there while editing Bowyer's notes as Clerk of the House of Lords. He wishes also to thank Professor John E. Neale of the University of London for his assistance. He must express his sincere gratitude to the University of Minnesota Press for undertaking the responsibility of publication. He wishes to thank his brother, the Reverend Hugh Latimer Willson, for transcribing much of the diary from photographs of the Harleian MSS. He is grateful to Mr. Francis R. D. Needham, librarian at Welbeck Abbey, for valuable suggestions in deciphering the extremely difficult hand of Sir Robert Harley. For the kindness and consideration he has received he must thank the Library of the University of Minnesota, the Library of Cornell University, the Library of the Inner Temple, London, the Library of St. John's College, Cambridge, and above all the British Museum and Public Record Office. The consideration that is shown the American student who crosses the sea to work in English libraries should always be gratefully acknowledged.

* * *

Certain of the broader and more general aspects of the relations of the Crown and Parliament in 1606 and 1607 may perhaps be briefly sketched. Before 1603 the Crown had controlled the Commons. This control was due chiefly to Elizabeth's dominant personality, her able and flattering speeches, her frequent concessions, and her occasional display of regal authority. It was due also to the fact that certain of her chief Privy Councilors were members of the lower house and wielded a very real influence over that body. But the opposition was rising, and the Queen and her ministers managed the House with ever increasing difficulty. It was obvious that whoever became sovereign in 1603 would have trouble with his Parliaments.

In James's first Parliament circumstances combined to weaken the forces of the Crown. While James was not the fool that court historians have painted him, he lacked the knowledge and the ability to handle his Parliaments successfully. His long and scolding speeches, his too frequent interference in the details of parlimentary business, his lack of dignity and tact, his extravagance, his references to the divine right of kings, all lowered the prestige of the Crown. At the same time the Councilors were less able to make their influence felt in the lower house.[1] Most of them were now peers, and in the sessions of 1606 and 1607 there were but two members of the Council who were also members of the Commons. In fact, for the first few weeks of 1606 there was but one, Sir John Herbert, a man of very mediocre ability. The government was therefore forced to rely upon lesser officials to represent its interests in the House: Sir Henry Hobart, the Attorney, Sir Ed-

---

[1] The editor is working upon a monograph dealing with the influence of the Privy Councilors in the House during the early Stuart period. See Wallace Notestein, "The Winning of the Initiative by the House of Commons," *Proceedings of the British Academy, Raleigh Lecture on History, 1924.*

ward Phelips, the Speaker, Sir Henry Montague, the Recorder of London. The subsidy of 1606, wrote Sir Edward Hoby, was first "propounded by Sir Thomas Ridgeway, and seconded by such like (for I must tell you, that I think the State scorneth to have any privy counsellors of any understanding in that House) . . ."[1] And the act that contained what little of union with Scotland the King could persuade the Commons to accept was introduced in 1607 not by a Councilor but by Phelips the Speaker. Thus the government was poorly represented in the Commons. A way of escape might have been found in the employment of Sir Francis Bacon, the greatest figure in the House, and Bacon was used to a considerable extent, especially in the matter of the Union, in which he was a "principal instrument," but he was a servant rather than a counselor and did not have the influence that he would have enjoyed had he been admitted into the inner secrets of the state.

The minister who was responsible to James for continuing the Elizabethan control over the House of Commons was Sir Robert Cecil, now the first Earl of Salisbury.[2] As the chief adviser of the Crown, James looked to him to secure the passage of royal measures and to prevent the Commons from obtaining their demands for a modification of the Elizabethan settlement of church and state. Salisbury realized his responsibilities fully and devoted much time and labor to parliamentary business. He attempted to prepare public opinion before a session began; he influenced such by-elections as he could; he carefully instructed his lieutenants and agents as to the part they should play in the House. He kept himself constantly informed of the course of events in the Commons and though, as a peer, he could not address the entire lower chamber, he spoke to large numbers of the House in conferences, urging with force and ability the measures desired by the Crown. He was the Tudor statesman attempting to carry on the Elizabethan tradition of a dominant Council controlling a subservient House of Commons.

But in this he failed. In James's first Parliament the aggres-

---

[1] Hoby to Sir Thomas Edmondes. March 7, 1606. Thomas Birch, *Court and Times of James I*, ed. Robert F. Williams, I, 59–60.

[2] For a fuller discussion see "The Earl of Salisbury and the 'Court' Party in Parliament, 1604–1610," *American Historical Review*, XXXVI, 274–294 (January, 1931). The editor is working on a short biography of Salisbury.

siveness of the Commons increased, and the popular party of opposition grew continually in strength and effectiveness until it presented a united and powerful majority that became the despair of Salisbury and the King. Parliamentary privileges were reverenced and defended with an almost religious fervor. Government policies were criticized and attacked with a freedom that the Queen and her ministers would never have tolerated. Leaders and debaters appeared among the Commons who could hold their own with any comer. As yet, however, there was little or no organization among the opposition. Revolt was individual and unplanned, and the close coöperation and studied method found among the leaders of the opposition after 1620 had not yet appeared. Even in the question of the Union in 1607, in which the Commons were practically unanimous, they did not oppose the King under the organized leadership of political chiefs but by a sort of obstructionist policy, by making objections at every point, by mincing every word and balking at every advance. Opposition was rife, but it was not organized.

There was one man who approached the parliamentary leader of later sessions. This was Sir Edwin Sandys. His wisdom and moderation, his power of debate and wide experience of affairs won him the unqualified confidence of the House. He very definitely opposed the King. On March 8, 1606, he moved that a bill concerning purveyors should be pushed forward by the House in spite of a royal message of prohibition, a bold step by which the Commons won a decided victory. In 1607 Sandys played the most important part of any member in opposing the Union, both in committee work in the House and in conference with the Lords. On April 28 he brushed aside the articles suggested by the government and moved for a complete union of the laws and legislatures of the two countries, a point towards which debate in the House had been for some time tending. This "digression," as the government called it, may be regarded as a turning point in these debates, for after it the government gave up the hope of naturalizing the Scots by act of Parliament or of bringing about a commercial union and contented itself with a measure for the repeal of hostile laws and for the trial of criminals committing outrages along the Border. Sandys was highly important in the commercial considerations of the Union and, in fact, in all matters concerning trade and commerce. Yet this Parliament cannot be summed up in the name of Sandys as later Parliaments can be summed up in the names of other leaders.

Bacon's position was a rather anomalous one. On most points he stood for the Crown and spoke in the House with the purpose of gaining favor at Court. Yet at the same time he enjoyed the confidence and regard of the Commons in a high degree and was constantly employed by them upon committees and in conferences. He was therefore not a leader but rather a mediator, forever seeking a compromise between King and Commons.

The rising tide of opposition was less clear in 1606 than in any other session of James's first Parliament. The escape from the Gunpowder Plot drew the King and the Commons together, and both were agreed on framing stricter measures against the Catholics. The Commons were "much more temperate than they were at the first session," and Salisbury could write that in granting supplies they "had carryed themselves very lovingly and dutifully to his Majesty."[1] Although purveyors were attacked and both economic and religious grievances presented without result, the Commons in this session showed a fairly cordial attitude toward the Crown. The session of 1607 was much more turbulent, since the question of union with Scotland aroused suspicions and animosities and produced a wide and fundamental divergence of opinion between James and his people. The struggle was embittered by irritating points of parliamentary privilege and by the resentment of the Commons at the constant meddling of the King. In the House itself the defense of the government's proposals was intrusted principally to Bacon, who played his part with skill and sincere conviction. Yet the Union had small chance of success. The Commons won the victory, though in this their conduct calls forth less praise than in their struggles for the larger principles of constitutional freedom.

As to details, the following debates must speak for themselves.

DAVID HARRIS WILLSON

UNIVERSITY OF MINNESOTA
MAY 1, 1931

---

[1] Earl of Shrewsbury to Sir Thomas Edmondes. Feb. 12, 1606. *Court and Times*, I, 52. Salisbury to Sir Henry Wotton. March 19, 1606. St. P. Dom. XIX, 59.

THE PARLIAMENTARY DIARY OF ROBERT BOWYER, 1606-1607

BOOK I

[STANFORD MS]

f. 1. a]   21 JAN. 1605.[1]

BEING the first daie of this cession of parliament was redde a
Bill for sale of certaine lands late parcell of the possessions of
Sir Jonathan Trelawny deceased: wherein the parcells weare
particularly mencioned, the sale to be by the Earl of Salis[bury]
Master of the wards·Sir H[enry] Neveill Sir W[illiam] Killigrew *et
aliis* or anie fowre of them for paiment of the debts of the said Sir
Jonathan: for that his soon and heir being then within age and in
warde to the King provision could not otherwise be made for
paiment of the said debts: *prima vice lecta:*

A long unnecessarie weake speache by SIR W[ILLIA]M MORRICE[2]
a welshman: for the Union: next to perswade provision for soldiers:

---

[1] The session opened on Nov. 5, 1605, but was prorogued from Nov. 9
to Jan. 21 because of the Gunpowder Plot. For proceedings in the House
from Nov. 5 to 9, see *Commons Journals*, I, 256–257 (hereafter cited as *C.
J.*); Williams, *Court and Times of James I*, I, 39–40 (hereafter cited as *C.
& T.*); *Cal. St. P. Venetian, 1603–1607*, 294; *Journal of Roger Wilbraham*
(*Camden Misc.* X), 71–75. The King's speech of Nov. 9 is to be found in
Lords Journals, II, 357–359 (hereafter cited as *L.J.*); Lansd. MSS 513,
ff. 4–14; *Harleian Miscellany*, III, 5–14; McIlwain, *Political Works of
James I*, 281–289. The speech of the Lord Chancellor on Nov. 9 is described in a letter from M. Dujardin to M. de Villeroy, Jan. 24/Feb. 3,
1606. "Il y fut proposé trois poinctz par le Chancellier au nom du Roy,
qui estoient que le Roy leur remettoit le jugement des traitres qui avoient
attenté contre sa personne et la lair, et qu'il les prioit d'en faire une example semblable au delet qu'ilz avoient conunis, la seconde estoit qu'il de-
mundoit un subside, et la troisiesme qu'il desiroit que l'union fust retiffiée
de la façon que les Commissaires qui avoient esté deputez cydevant pour
ladicte union avoient acordé." Paris Transcripts, Public Record Office.
For Jan. 21, see *C.J.* I, 257; *C. & T.* I, 45–46.

[2] The Clerk made a note on Jan. 21, which he later crossed out, "Sir
Wm. Morrice answereth the objections of against the name of (*d.* the)
King of Great Brittaine. 1. name. no newe but a restitucion of the old.
2. (*d.* Brittane) name more dearer (*d.* of) then of our lives. 3. Brittaine
[*blank*] the name of Englands and continueth a long speech to little purpose a repeticon sermon." *C.J. MS, Jac.* I, II, f. 8.

NOTE: In quotations from the C.J. MS deleted words are placed between parentheses and prefaced with a *d.*

1

Then for a good sound sufficient round subsidy to be graunted to
the King with a voluntary contribucion besids, viz. such as might
paie all the King's debts which he ougheth either as dew by Queen
Elizabeth or himselfe and to fill his resce[ipt] and theis to be doon
now in the beginning before anie other thing be delt in: Lastlie
Touching the Annexacion of lands to the Crowne.[1]

Then Sir Rob[er]t Wroth, delivered a bill to the Speaker to
be reade which he withall declared to be that all young men passing
over (as I understoode him into spayne, according as some others
conceaved, generally over the seas)[2] might take the oath of
Supremacy, with some addicions which he did not make knowen:
This bill Mr. Speaker receaved and put in his pocket, using a few
woords with a low or soft voice, which I herd not more then that
the Speaker affirmed plainely and Confidentlie that within one
yeare last past more then two thowsande youthes, of which none
exceeded sixteene yeeres of age had passed over into Spaine:[3]
And so he arrose and the howse for that tyme broke upp, After
dinner the same daie the howse did meete againe, but my selfe
having no notice therof was not present:

22 Jan:

Was readde an act that all youthes aged 14 yeeres and upwards
passing over the seas shall take the oath of Supremacie with certaine addicions unlesse licenced under the King's hand or sixe of
the Counceill. 2° *lecta:*

An act for reliefe of the poore: *primo lecta:* The effect was that
of every 20 quarters of graine transported one quarter should be
taken by officers there appoint[ed], att prises in the said act also
sett downe for the poore:

f. 1. b]   Sir H[enry] Montague[4] Recorder of London moved that
the Committees formerly appointed to receave and consider of all

---

[1] A bill was drawn for this purpose entitled "A Bill for assurance
of lands, tenements, and other hereditaments surrendered, forfeited, or
escheated to the Crown." *Cal. St. P. Dom. 1603-1610,* 284. It was not
passed.

[2] The bill was general to all parts of Europe.

[3] "They say that when the proposal to compel all children of Catholic
parents to be educated as Protestants was made known a vast number of
children were sent over to Spain." *Cal. St. P. Venetian, 1603-1607,* 322.

[4] Cf. *C. & T.* I, 46.

articles which anie man should exhibite against Recusants and so
to frame ther uppon a Lawe might allso receave all such Articles
as should be exhibited and likewise to frame accordingly a law for
preservacion of the King's Majesties person, which Mocion was
granted. Hereuppon MR. WENTWOORTH, moved as a matter though
not parcell nor member of the former yet as a necessarie thing to
breede the safety of the King's person and the state that for the
trew instructing of the people in the knowledge of God and dutie
towards his Majestie the said Committees might allso receave
articles and frame a lawe for an able sufficient and Resident Ministry: Thes three points he shewed veary schollerlike to be both
possible and necessary and offered rather then there shold want
maintenance for such churchmen him selfe would give the tenth
parte of his estate towards it: SIR RICH[ARD] LOVELACE moved
that in this busines moved by Mr. Wentwoorth, a Conference
might be with the Lords before anie proceeding in it, but the howse
reiected that course and resolved to deale in the matter (as Mr.
Speaker termed it) Substantively: Uppon SIR RO[BERT] WING-
FIELDS mocion a speciall Committee[1] was appointed for Mr.
Wentwoorth his mocion viz. Mr. Wentwoorth Sir Edw[ard]
Montague Sir Fra[ncis] Hastings Sir Ro[bert] Wingfield on the 23
of January at 2 of the clocke in the Temple Hall.

An act for the better execucion of penall lawes: 2° *lecta* and
committed uppon MR. GORE his mocion: And SIR EDWYNE
SANDYS moved that the same Committees, manie of them being
learned in the Law, might allso consider what penall lawes are
needelesse and fitt to be abrogated: this mocion was allso allowed,
And friday following att 2 of the clocke in the chequer chamber
appointed for their meeting.

A bill for the iointure of Dame Elionor Cave 2° *lecta:* and uppon
declaracion by SIR RO[BERT] WINGFIELD that the heir being hir
sonne is within age and beyond the sea, and he moving that
consideracion be had that hir iointure might not be over greate
wherby a competent maintenance should not be left to the heir the
said bill was Committed.

f. 2. a]   23 JAN:

Mr. Speaker at the first sitting of the howse declared that he had

---

[1] See *C.J.* I, 257–258.

receaved a Letter from Sir John Payton, declaring that whereas the Knight at the beginning of this parliament was a member of the howse and since was made sheriffe and so yet continueth, he desiereth to understand their pleasure whether they woulde forbeare his attendance or enioyne his presence to which was aunsweared that [*blank*].[1]

Sir Edw[ard] Montague,[2] in a speach well penned, but not affected did declare how greate a deliverance his Majestie and the Realme latelie had from the entended treason: and moved that the same having happened through Gods greate favor there may be some provision wherby the rememberance of his goodnesse in this behalfe be continued to posterity: this he perswaded to be necessarie, by declaring that God having provided for the continuance of his Churche by the preservacion of Noe, and his family commanded a rememberance therof, and to that purpose placed the Raine bow in the firmament and so discended to Gods other blessings towards his church and people in auncient time and their thanckfull rememberance of the same by building of Alters and other like signes which he particularly and breife did mencion or rather touche: and in conclusion offered a bill intituled An act for a publique thankesgivinge unto God every yeere on the 5th of November *primo lecta* and herin he wished the howse would proceede before anie other matter. Mr. Speaker taking this bill began with himselfe to peruse it and soddainly staied, and moved the howse that a private bill might be readde whilest he overlooked this so delivered by Sir Edw[ard] Montague, wherunto the howse assented, and then was readde An bill intituled, An act to enable John Houther the father and John Houther the soon to make a iointure to the wife of John the soon: *primo lecta:* Then was the foresaide bill of thankesgivinge, offered as afore by Sir Edw[ard] Montague, readde, and presentlie the howse requiered the same to be readde the second time which was doon, and then allso committed and the Committees directed by the howse foorth with to repaire into the Committee chamber: whether they immediately went accordinglie where they continued together untell halfe hower after 12 of the clocke at which time the Speaker sent

---

[1] "Resolved, He shall attend." *C.J.* I, 258.
[2] Cf. his speech in *C.J.* I, 258. Also see *C. & T.* I, 46.

the Serieant to wish them to come away if they weare ready, for
that the howse had staied longer then their other occasions requiered beyond the ordinary hower for them, but for that they
returned aunswere that they had not concluded of all points in
such sort as they desiered, but requested to be forborne and
f. 2. b] that they might meete the next day in the same place before
the setting of the Court the howse yelded therunto and so arrose.
But in the Interim betweene the departure of the said Committee out of the place and this sending unto them by Mr. Speaker,
was readde An act for confirmacion of Leases against patentees of
Enheritance[1] 2° *lecta:* which is the bill offered by Mr. Fra[ncis]
More the daie before.

Sir Rob[er]t Jonhson offered to Mr. Speaker certaine clauses
or Articles in wrightinge to be added to this bill left as he saied with
him by Sir Ro[bert] Wingfield whome he named not, when the said
Sir Rob[er]t Wingfield with other the Committees of the last mencioned bill went foorth of the howse: The howse differing whether
the clauses should be readde as Sir Ro[bert] Jonhson requiered or
referred to the Committees of this bill of Confirmacion of Leases,
Mr. Speaker delivered the Order of the howse to be that clauses
offered as motive to enforce the passing of the bill weare to be
given to the Committees of the bill, but if the same did containe
addicions to the bill then to be readde openlie in the howse:
howbeit, it was concluded that this paper tendered by Sir Rob[er]t
Johnson, should be referred and given to the Committees of the
bill.

The parson of Radipole his bill *secundo lecta:* And in committing of this bill exceptions was taken to such as had spoken against
the bill, and some doubt being touching committees Mr. Speaker
began to move, and having spoken a few woords, Saied to this
effect (If I should not offend I would move) where the howse inter-
upting him, desiered he would proceede in his mocion, which he
did to this effect that the bill might be committed to some gentlemen of the countie: which was thought fit to be, unto the knights
and certaine others of that countie:

---

[1] This act stated that leases of lands made by Elizabeth or James
should stand good in law against any new assignee to whom James had
granted the lands notwithstanding any breach of condition or other
defect. Lansd. MSS 487, f. 21*v*.

A bill for the Allmeshowse and schole called Godshowse in
Thetforde 2° *lecta:* this Allmeshowse etc. by Sir Edw[ard] Cleere
or his exec[utors] desiered to passe in performance of the last Will
of Sir Richard Fulmerston deceased: wheruppon it was moved that
warning might be given to Sir Rich[ard] Fulmerstons heir, viz. the
soon of Sir Edw[ard] Cleere by Sir Rich[ard] Fulmerstons daughter,
which was thought fitt: and heruppon Mr. Speaker moved that a
Letter should be wrightten as from the howse to warne the said
heir of Sir Rich[ard] Fulmerston, according to a course thought fit
and appointed in like cas[1] the last Cession of parliament: wherof
the howse well liked and ordered accordinglie.

f. 3. a]   24 JAN: 1605.

An act that Youthes passing over the seas being above the age
of 16 yeeres shall take the oath of Supremacy with some addicions:
2° *lecta:*

MR. JOHN HARE[2] in a good comly speech, did put the howse in
mynde of the labor which the howse the last parliament did take
for redresse of the oppression by purveiors: and how they weare
supported by such as shoulde specially have suppressed them.
Allso of the Kings gracious favor and inclinacion to our releife,
Then of the wrong offered to the howse by somme of the cheife
officers of the Greenecloath who enformed the King that the howse
had falsely enformed his Majestie: that yet within 2 daies it
appeared uppon examinacion to be trew which the howse alleaged.
Lastly he put the howse in mynde that the Lords had promised
that consideracion should be had of the greavances complained on,
and aunswere given to the howse:[3] He moved that the tyme of
consideracion so requiered as afore being past and no aunsweare
yet given that Mr. Speaker would move the howse to declare
whether they woulde have the Lords conferred withall for aunsweare, or that a bill shoulde be preferred for reformacion of the
misdemeanors of purveiors which he saied was readdy: which

---

[1] See *C.J.* I, 202, 203.

[2] Cf. *C. & T.* I, 46.

[3] This was in April, May, and June of 1604. See *C.J. passim.* The
astounding evidence given by the purveyors for their own justification
is found *ibid.* I, 215–217. See account in Spedding, *Letters and Life of
Francis Bacon,* III, 181–190.

question being propounded it was ordered by the howse that the bill so prepared shoulde the next daie be brought into the howse:

Mr. Sollicitor[1] brought in againe the bill of thankesgiving before offered by Sir Edw[ard] Montague, with some alteracions in forme agreed on by the Committees, which alteracions weare readde: which bill so altered by consent of the howse was put to engrossing.

Mr. Speaker desier[ed] such as stoode in the enterance of the howse to take their places affirming that it is against the order of the howse to stand on that sort in troopes.

Sir Tho[mas] Holcraft[2] moved that by peticion the howse should desier of the King that the persons now to be arraigned for the late greate treason entended by blowing upp the parliament howse might be tried in the parliament.

Sir Ro[bert] Wingfield seconded this mocion adding that some more greavous death might be by the parliament appointed to the said traitors then the law inflicteth. But after a speach by Mr. Sollicitor against theis mocions the howse deferred to proceede away herein untell the Lawe had passed against the offendors:

f. 3. b]   25 Jan. 1605.

An act what fees shalbe paied by the p[lain]t[iff] and def[endan]t for coppies out of anie court of Recorde:

In this bill was requiered that all coppies should be made in paper called ordinary paper, 18 lines to be on every sheete and 22 sillables in every line, In the starre chamber to be taken Sixe pence the sheete in the Chauncery and other courts 4d. the sheete the party offending to forfeite 20s. for [*blank*] and to suffer one moneth imprisonment: *primo lecta.*

Mr. Sollicitor declared that himselfe and other the particuler Committees for a lawe against popish Recusants had thought good, first to draw their conceipt into articles, and then to move the howse that those articles maie be delivered over to the generall Committees for that busines and upon consideracion so had of the same a bill to be framed wherof the howse allowed and appointed the afternoone in the same place:

---

[1] Sir John Doderidge.
[2] Cf. debate in *C.J.* I, 259.

An act for publique thanksgiving to allmighty God every yeere on the fift daie of November being engrossed was brought backe by the Committees engrossed and readde the third tyme: Uppon a question first moved by Mr. Speaker viz: whether the woord (owr) should be passe[d] or be made (their) it was ordered by the howse uppon often reading over of the sentence that the said woorde (Our) should be wholy left or blotted out, for that as was conceaved the sence best so served. Then it was moved that the said bill should be sent up to the Lords by Sir Edw[ard] Montague who preferred the same, but it was overruled that Mr. Secretary Herbert should deliver it, first for that it seemed fit that this being the first bill should be presented by the best of the howse, And then it was held indecorus that a privie Councellor should go up and stande by whilest anie other should deliver the bill.

An act to assure certaine lands lieing in Middlesex unto Sir Tho[mas] Lake and Mary his wife *primo lecta*.

Mr. Fuller moved that the heir of Sir Hugh Losse who sold the lands should be warned and have a tyme given: but notwithstanding his speach the bill was committed:

Mr. Speaker asked the pleasure of the howse touching the two prisoners which yesterday the Serieant tooke by their warrant, viz. John Carew and Tho[mas] Percy: wheruppon the Prisoners weare brought to the barre and their Accusers called into the howse: and for that it appeared that John Carew had the daie before neere the howse stroken and abused one of the accusers, he was iudged to be whipped, and for that it was only easely laied to the charge of Percy that in or after the affray he aided Carew therfore with an admonicion to forbeare the like misdeameanor he was dismissed:

Sir Fra[ncis] Evers offered a bill for the better observinge of the Saboth day with a speach to enforce it: which the Speaker receaved and whilest he perused it with him selfe the Clerke did reade a Act prohibitinge resiance of married men with their wives and familyes, within Colleges cathedral churches etc., which beinge now 2° *lecta* was committed. Temple Hall this day Senight.

f. 4. a] The Court adiorned untell tuisday to the entent so manie of the howse as thincke good maie be at the Arraignement:

28 Jan. 1605.

Because the howse was not full Mr. Speaker caused a private bill[1] to be redde:

Mr. Fuller moved that no man shoulde name above two committees to a bill affirming that such is the order of the howse: which was denied and his mocion reiected as frivolous.[2]

This after noone the Committees that shoulde have mett on Satterday to meete about the greate bill of theis Traitors:

An act touching bonds made for assurance of lands and Tenements preferred by Mr. Fuller: 1 *lecta:* the effect was that the obligees maie assigne such bonds to the purchasors of the lands:

Dayes weare appointed for Committees to meete for severall bills. *daies for Committees*

The bill against Recusants,[3] Allso that for a learned ministry this day in the place allso for the Supremacy:

The bill against resiance of heads of collegs etc: on monday in the Temple hall:

Mr. James moved that consideracion might be had of a bill concerning the Spanish company: wherunto was said that the said bill was preferred the last cession and not readde this Cession and that in the last Cession the committees mett about this bill and sent for the Governor[4] of the saide companie, who comming before them desiered respect and time to conferre with the said companie: which was granted, and so long the said Governor protracted the tyme that the parliament was adiourned, heruppon the names of the said Committees weare readde and some more added,[5] and it moved that the said gentlemen should meete and consider what course is to be holden viz. whether by bill, or Peti-

---

[1] The bill for naturalizing Daniel Godfrey, of the Parish of St. Buttolphes without Algate. *C.J.* I, 260.

[2] Yet such an order was passed in May, 1621. "P" (manuscript diary, shortly to be published by Professors Notestein and Relf), f. 178.

[3] "The afternoon spent in the committee about order to be taken for papists." *C. & T.* I, 47.

[4] Thomas Wilford. *Cal. St. P. Dom. 1603–1610*, 112. This was before a committee of the House of Lords. See W. R. Scott, *The Constitution and Finance of English, Scottish, and Irish Joint Stock Companies to 1720*, I, 124; Astrid Friis, *Alderman Cockayne's Project and the Cloth Trade*, 155–156.

[5] See names in *C. J.* I, 183, 261.

tion, and so ordered, for which purpose their meeting was appointed heere this daie senight.

f. 4. b] Mr. Leucknor a burgesse of the howse complained that him selfe and divers others of the howse did yesterday repair to the hall to heare the arraignement of Rockwood, Winter, Sir Evered Digby and other Traitors that by the wardein of the Fleete[1] they weare brought in to a Scaffell prepared for the members of this howse, and that they paied 10s. a man for their standing and that the wardein or his people did presentlie admitt so manie of the baser sort for 4d. and 3d. a peece that they of this howse stoode at greate disease not without much danger, he moved that the parties offending might be sent for and that the wardein who caused them to stand in litle ease might be committed to litle ease: The misdemeanors in the premisses of them who kept the scaffells was iustified by Sir Herbert Croft Sir John Lake Mr. Duncombe and others but by cause the offendors names weare not knowen Mr. Speaker moved that 2, 4 or 6 att the most might be appointed to examine the cause and to certifie the howse therof: but in conclusion it was thought good that such a nomber as before should be appointed to examine the premisses, but the fault not to be punished by this howse because this howse had no enterest in westminster hall and therefore as that scaffoll was by my Lord Chamberlaine[2] in honor and favor appointed for the howse, and the same so signified by Mr. Secretary Herbert, therefore the gentlemen appointed to examine the cause shoulde attend Mr. Secretary and declare to him what they founde and his honor to acquaint my Lord Chamberlaine therewithall to whose honorable and grave wisdome the punishment of the parties offending was by the howse referred:

29 Jan. 1605.

purveiors   An act for the better execucion of sondry statuts against Purveiors and Cartakers *primo lecta:*

The preamble sheweth the present abuses to be *inter alia:* That the commissions made to purveiors do containe divers matters contrarie to the statuts of Purveiance now in force and do omitt sondry things appointed by the said statut lawes.

[1] John Trenche.
[2] Thomas Howard, Earl of Suffolk.

That divers subiects are called before the officers of the Greenecloth uppon pretence that the said statut lawes are not in force
against the King, wherby the subiect cannot know how to give
his obedience in case of Purveiance, but are often tymes wrongfullie imprisoned by the said officers of the Greenecloth not knowing the law in that behalfe:

Wheruppon this present act is recited to be made and ordained
of and by the Kings Majesties most gracious and voluntary goodnes for releife of his subiects in case of Purveiance and Cartaking.
f. 5. a] By which act First all former statuts touching Purveiance
and cartaking are confirmed.

Then *inter alia* it is therby provided, that

No warrant for or to the purpose aforesaid be made in the Kings
Majesties name but such as is warrantable by the statuts, and
nothing to be omitted in such warrants which is by anie statut
law required.

Redy mony to be paied for wag[e]s of cartes and carriages in
such sort as in the act is at large set downe.

The Justices of peace in every county to rate yeerely the prices
to be paied for cartes and carriages by lande or by water at the
Quarter cessions next after easter.

The order how the subiect shalbe paied either by the hands of
the Maior bailiffe or hed constable or in other case by the Coferer
of the King's howse, is at large expressed.

The apprisers of things to be taken, shalbe swoorne to deale
indifferently betweene the King and the subiectes.

Every Purveior to be swoorne before the Lord stewerd, the
Treasurer or Controller of the howse, to the truth of his complaint
which he shall make against anie subiect, before anie subiect be
called or se[n]t for to appeare before the officers of the Greenecloth: and theruppon warning to be sent and left for such party
against whome such complaint shalbe, two daies before he be to
come upp: to the ende he maie come upp prepared with witnesses
to iustifie himselfe. And if the Complaint be founde false then such
complainant to be punished as periured according to the statut of
5: Elizabeth.[1] This act to continue 3 yeres after the ende of this
cession and from the ende of that three yeeres unto the ende of the
next cession then followinge:

---

[1] An act against perjury. 5 Eliz. c. 9. *Statutes of the Realm*, IV, 436.

Fees The bill formerly exhibited by Sir John Parker touching Fees for coppies was called for, wheruppon Mr. Speaker desiered leave to acquaint the howse with a petition delivered unto him by manie finding them selves greeved with this bill, the effect whereof he declared to be briefely but this, viz. that they might be hard heare at the barre by their Counceill. Which mocion was yelded as reasonable, and Saterdaie given for that purpose. Wheruppon Sir John Parker stoode up and commended the bill, adding that he thought the petition of the parties greaved reasonable, and the order of the howse iust: he shewed that Lawyers weare uppon iust and good cause left out of the bill: for in regard they spent much time and charge in their studies and for that whatsoever was given them was voluntary he thought not fit to abridge them, but the Clerks for copies do expect theis greate Fees against the suiters will. He desiered that such Lawyers as be of accompt in the howse would prepare them selves against Satterday to defend the bill, and affirmed that such councell as the clerks shall bring can alledge or pretende no law for their defence but would and must stande only on custome, which as he saied was no stronger for them to do this wrong by extorcion then for such as robbe on s[h]ooter[?] hill.

Mr. Speaker declared that the Kinge commaunded him to request not to commaund, the howse with all speede convenient to proceede in the bills for Service of God and preservacion of his roiall person: wheruppon the howse deferred all other committees, and appointed the committees for theis bills to meete this afternoone in howse of parliament.[1]

f. 5. b]   30 Jan. 1605.

An act for bringing in of a fresh streame of runninge water from the river of Lee neere Ware and the river of Uxbridge to the north parte of the cittie of London: *primo lecta:*

An act for the true making of linen cloth and sackcloth *primo lecta.*

The howse cried away with it.

Uppon Mr. Fullers demaunde, it was ruled that a man maie speake against a bill to dashe it at the first reading:

[1] Cf. *C. & T.* I, 47–48.

Mr. Speaker asked if it weare the custome to reade every bill twise before it be cast away: SIR Ro[BERT] JOHNSON affirmed that he remembered a bill sent from the Lords engrossed, and heare cast forth at the first.[1] The same was iustified by an other of the howse and theruppon ruled in the affirmative: Wheruppon Mr. Speaker affirmed that he knew but three questions: viz

1. Whether the bill should be committed:
2. Whether the bill shalbe engrossed:
3. Whether the bill shall passe:

and therefore he desiered to be directed what question shall now in this case be made: and it was resolved and by Mr. Speaker asked in this sort: As many as will have the bill reiected without farder readinge say yea: and then: As many as will not have the bill reiected without farder readinge say no: and the Yea: was much greater:

MR. SOLLICITOR before the rising of the court brought in the act and articles against Recusants:[2] etc. and declared that for as much as himselfe was this after noone to attende the Lord Chief Justice[3] for the King's service therefore that the howse woulde deliver the said act and articles unto Mr. Fuller, Sir Fra[ncis] Bacon or Mr. Recorder of London:[4] being likewise committees therin: and Mr. Fuller only being then present the howse requiered him (though unwilling) to receave the same, and bycause he seemed unwilling the howse therfore did notwithstanding his receiving the said bill and articles commaunde the Serieant to seeke Sir Fra[ncis] Bacon and Mr. Recorder and bring them up into the howse, and uppon some diversitie of opinions, it was ruled and directed that the Serieant should seeke and bring the said Sir Fra[ncis] Ba[con] and Mr. Recorder without taking his mace with him:

31 JAN. 1605.

SIR THO[MAS] BEAMONT delivered in a bill which was the last

---

[1] D'Ewes, *Journal of all the Parliaments during . . . . Elizabeth*, 335, contains an example of a bill being rejected at the first reading.

[2] From the Grand Committee for Religion appointed on Jan. 21. The Gunpowder Plot insured severer laws against the Catholics. See *Cal. St. P. Venetian, 1603–1607*, 285, 320–321.

[3] Sir John Popham, Chief Justice of the King's Bench.

[4] Sir Henry Montague.

parliament twise[1] red viz. An act for abatinge and restraining the new ereccion of Weares Kyddell etc. on greate and navigable rivers. *primo lecta:*

An act for the assurance of the mannor of Cruby in county warwick to Geo[rge] Ognell: *primo lecta* and ordered by the howse that Otho Nicholson and one other whom in like sort it doth concerne shall on monday next be herd in the howse by their Counceill: f. 6. a] SIR RO[BERT] WINGFIELD moved the howse to know what opinion they would hold of a member, that since the last cession had ben at Masse:[2] and before anie aunsweare was made, SIR WILL[IA]M MAURICE stoode up and tooke notice that the last mocion was entended of him: and theruppon declared that when the greate Constable of Spaine[3] was heare and laie at Somerset howse, he was by a frende perswaded to go into the howse and accordingly he went into the Gallery and anon among others came in a fellow whome, saied Sir W[illia]m, I knew not to be a priest for he was not balld and mombled I know not what so as belike quoth he Masse came to mee I went not to Masse, and therfore the gentleman that last spake needed not heruppon to have accused mee of flim flam: and so with like iesting woords concluded. This aunswere of his was by divers misliked. Her uppon it was thought good that sixe ientlemen[4] of the howse should examine the matter and certifie the howse how they found it: others would that Sir W[illia]m Morrice should aunswere it at the barre and Sir Tho[mas] Cornwallys the Groomeporter who was vouched for author, as having affirmed to divers that he had seen Sir W[illiam] Maurice come forth from Masse should be also sent for: to iustifie what he knew in the cause: R[OBERT] B[OWYER] standing up saied that he conceaved that the howse ment not to examine whether Sir W[illia]m Maurice had ben at Masse for quoth he

---

[1] *C. J.* I, 245.

[2] See this incident in *C. & T.* I, 48–49.

[3] Juan Ferdinand de Valasco, Duke of Frias, who was in England in 1604.

[4] In the manuscript of the *Commons Journals* a list of names is given at this point: "Sir H. Neville, Sir Rob. Wingfield, Sir Dan. Dun, Sir Thos. Holcroft, Sir Nath. Bacon, Sir Roger Wilbraham, Sir Hen. Neville, Sir Rob. Mansell, Sir John Scott." These names are crossed out and the words "No Committee" follow. The House had later determined not to use the committee. C.J. MS, Jac. I, II, f. 25v.

Habetis confidentem reum, but that the circumstances be examined whether *casu* or *concilio:* and Mr. Speaker saied he, I pray you let the gentleman that hath confessed him selfe guiltie declare heare to the howse how often he hath ben at Masse since the beginning of last Cession: Afterwardes some spake in excuse of Sir W[illiam] Maurice commending his forwardnesse against recusants. In conclusion, the howse ordered that on monday next Sir W[illiam] Maurice should aunsweare at the barre and the Groomeporter to be sent for to be then present, but uppon the Speakers mocion it was directed that Mr. Speaker should wright to him to be then present:

Mr. Speaker declared to the howse that the King's Majestie commaunded him to move the howse that whereas Sir John Fortescue and Sir Fra[ncis] Goodwyn weare the last cession by the King's pleasure signified and uppon order of the howse separated from the howse, that now they both maie come as chosen into new places since voide: this mocion was willing[ly] embraced: wheruppon Mr. Lawrence Hyde with all reverent regard towards his Majestie affirmed that without trobling the King, yea and without the privitie of the howse those two gentlemen might be chosen into anie places voide since the last Cession: for they weare not disenabled to be of the howse, but both forbidden to serve in that place which they so labored for: And quoth he I am a litle ielous what maie follow if wee receave Burgesses by his Majesties comendacions: afterwards without farder replie it was agreed that the said too parties should and might come in uppon new elecions[1] but herof no enterance to be made by the clerke of the howse:[2]

---

[1] Cf. *C. & T.* I, 48. Both Fortescue and Goodwin secured seats. *List of Members,* I, 442, 444.

There were a number of vacancies at this time. See Winwood, *Memorials,* II, 141. The Government was determined to influence by-elections where it could. "The King . . . . is well aware how much his neglect of the elections cost him last year." *Cal. St. P. Venetian, 1603–1607,* 267–268. See also *ibid.* 270, 509; Lodge, *Illustrations of British History,* III, 171. Mayor and Burgesses of Portsmouth to Salisbury, Jan. 12, 1607. Mayor and Burgesses of Kingston-upon-Hull to the same, March 12, 1607. Salisbury MSS. See *American Historical Review,* XXXVI, 277–278 (January, 1931).

[2] The Clerk had already made an entry but he crossed it out. The manuscript of the *Journal* reads thus: "Mr. Speaker (*d.* moveth) informeth

f. 6. b] Sɪʀ H[ᴇɴʀʏ] Pooʟᴇ[1] in a labored speech, and preamble
somewhat farre fetched and premeditated moved that some honor
might be doon to the Lord Montegle who was the cause and evidence of our greate deliverance saieing that the course and order
of such honor to be doon to the said Lord he would leave to the
howse, but contrary to his promise in conclusion he wished that
a clause might be added to the greate bill of Recusants maie be
inserted mencioning the said Lords desert. This mocion was seconded by an other *sed nihil venit vide.*

ᴘʀɪᴍᴏ Fᴇʙʀ. 1605.

An act to restraine purveiors that they exceede not the limites
of their commissions. *primo lecta:* note that on satterday before

that (*d.* their) his Majestie (*d.* is) desireth to make the House acquainted
and their leave for the Admittance yf they shalbe elected of Sir Fr. Goodwyn and Sir Jon Horshom, yf they be elected in another place." This note
was then crossed out and in the margin was written, "Thought not to be
entered." C.J. MS, Jac. I, II, f. 26.

[1] Thomas Wilson, a servant of Salisbury's in the House, wrote him
an account of this speech. "Ther hath litle hetherto passed in the
lower house worthy of your Lordships knowledg, matters being yett
but in the mowldinge and therefore ther relacion fitter to be reserved
untill they have receyved perfecter forme. Only this daye ther were two
thinges which I thinke fitt to report whilest they be fresh albeit they be
of noe great moment; the one by cause your Lordship was named in it,
the other for the extrordnarynes of it. The first was a motion made by
Sir Edw. Pole. That whereas this late fowle practise by gods enimies and
ours had begotten divers motyves in mens mynds apt to be the seedes of
many good lawes which are nowe in hand in parlament; as first concerninge
thanksgeving to God for soe admirable deliverance, Secondlye prevention
of such dangers heerafter, Thirdly for takinge awaye the causes efficient,
& forthly for refourming the causes deficient; by which 4 pointes he
intimated the act passed the lower howse alredy for the celebracion of the
5 of November yerlye, 2dly the act for the preservacion of the kings
person & his posteritye, 3dly that which is to be done against recusants,
& 4Thly for providing a lerned & dilligent ministrye. Soe he wold crave
to add a fift for gratuitye and that was that somethinge might be done
by consent of parlament in the honor of the Lord Montegle who by your
Lordships report had done the most notable service that ever any man did.
His words were thes 'The renowned Erle of Salisbury that worthy Counsellor of this state said of this noble man that we were all happie that ever
he was borne.' " St. P. Dom. XVIII, 55. See also *C.J.* I, 262 and St. P.
Dom. XVIII, 54.

viz. *ultimo Januarii* SIR RO[BERT] JOHNSON after he had commended the greate bill now depending in the howse against Purveiors and Cart takers so well labored by MR. HARE and so profitable for the Common wealth, adding that he doubted lest it would not passe, to be a lawe, desiered that the bill last mencioned which was moved the last parliament might be brought into the howse and readd to thentent that if wee cannot passe the one bill wee maie passe the other, which was doon.

Sir Tho[mas] Cornwallys came to the barre uppon such letters as formerly he had receaved from Mr. Speaker, to satisfie the howse of his knowledge touching Sir W[illiam] Maurice going to Masse: and standing at the barre Mr. Speaker declared unto him that the howse desiered to be enformed what he knew of Sir W[illiam] Maurice going to Masse: wheruppon Sir Tho[mas] desiered to know who charged him to be able to accuse Sir William and in what particuler he should declare his knowledge, which was by Mr. Speaker denied as unfit to be opened unto him: it is a strange course said Sir Tho[mas] to call mee to accuse anie man in this sort, Nay saied the Speaker it is not strange that you or anie man should speake uppon your alleageance to the King and duitie to the state what you know of this nature. Then he saied that one daie in his private chamber at dinner hearing some saie that Sir W[illiam] Maurice was earnest against Recusants I quoth he replied if It should be told him that I saw him come foorth of the Spanish Ambassadors from masse it would amase him, and concluded that once and neaver at anie other time nor offener he saw him so come foorth of the howse where he thought masse had ben saied and so veary unmannerly he departed without salutacion or reverence to the Speaker or anie other: whereat some tooke exceptions and would have had him called backe which was spoken alowde but confusedly and not pursued by anie:

f. 7. a] It was moved that Sir Will[ia]m Maurice should forbeare the howse and avoide, whilest this matter should be disputed concerning him: which mocion SIR THO[MAS] HOLCRAFT earnestlie with much passion gaine said, affirming that Sir Will[ia]m was cleered and no reason he should be sequestred: some others weare of his opinion but the Speaker thought otherwise and the howse uppon divers presedents vouched Namely My Lord of Moungo-

meryes case the last parliament and other civill causes did over
rule that much more in this criminall cause the accused should
avoide and forbeare the place during the dispute untell he should
be called to heare the opinion of the howse: yet the howse was
pleased before his avoidance to heare him speake: which being doon
he was by SIR THO[MAS] HOLCRAFT and others of his opinion
directed to go upp into the Committee chamber but the howse
requiered him to go foorth of the doore of the howse into the outter
roome where the clerks sett: and all others resort: which he did.

Then SIR THO[MAS] HOLCRAFT moved that insomuch as he
thought the howse did cleere Sir W[illiam] Maurice of the matter
complained that therfore the gentleman that accused him might
make him amends: which mocion was seconded by SIR RO[BERT]
MAUNSELL and SIR EDW[ARD] GREVEILL: Wherunto SIR RO[BERT]
OXENBRIDGE affirmed that he could not assent, for quoth he albeit
Sir Tho[mas] Cornwallys hath heare openly affirmed that he could
saie no more but that once and no oftener he saw Sir W[illiam]
Maur[ice] come foorth of the howse where he thought masse was,
yet quoth he I know a gentleman of vearie good woorth who herd
and will iustifie that Sir Tho[mas] Cornwallys saied that he had
seen Sir W[illiam] Maur[ice] five severall times come foorth of the
Roome where masse was saied and I will name him if the howse
commaund mee but the howse tooke no hold of that speech: Then
SIR EDW[ARD] HEXT: against the opinion and mocion of Sir Tho-
[mas] Holcraft etc: saied he saw no reason that the gentleman who
first gave notice of the matter against Sir W[illiam] Maur[ice]
should anie waie be questioned or that Sir William should have
anie amends for quoth he if informacion be given against anie
person in anie Court able to punish though the complaint be not
uppon profe thought or iudged iust yet no amends is given to the
partie. Otherwise where the informacion is given in a court not
having power of coercion: but in this case there was no accusers
but Sir Will[ia]m him selfe: and the gentleman that first gave
notice to the howse did but his duitie and could do no lesse, seeing
there was so greate presumptions of so high a fault and Mr.
Speaker saied he a gentleman of good sort told mee that Sir Tho-
[mas] Cornwallys saied he had seen Sir W[illiam] Maur[ice] five
times come from Masse and the gentleman's name is captaine
[*blank*]. Whereuppon the howse ruled that the accused should

have no amends. Then was SIR W[ILLIAM] MAWRICE called in who took his place and gave thancks to the howse for so honorable hearing his cause in publique and for cleering him: [*the following words are crossed out*] acknowledging iust cause of suspicion.

f. 7. b] An act for explanacion of a statut made A° 8 Elizabeth[1] but the title not named: *primo lecta:*

MR. SOLLICITOR delivered to Mr. Speaker certaine articles drawne by the Committees for the bill of Recusants: which articles weare redde and afterwards appointed to be distinctly readde on monday next in the howse, where the companie promised to be present by eight of the clocke: but first the Articles weare once readde which as I could take from the Clerks mouth weare as followeth[2] in effect:

1. The King to choose either to have of every popish Recusant 20£ *per mensem* or 2 partes of his lands leases etc: bycause 20£ *per mensem* is to the greate Recusants a small punishment:

2. The Church wardens and Constables monthly to present the names of all Recusants within their parish:

3. [*blank.*]

4. Every Recusant conformed shall receave the Communion in such sort as is there appointed:

5. A new oath wherof the forme is sett downe, to be ministered at the quarter cessions by the Justices to every Recusant conformed.

6. The law to be explaned that the husbande shall aunswere the penaltie for his wives recusancye:

[*Written in margin.*] this sixth article was afterwards let slip and not put to the question:

7. Recusants to keep no armor municion nor weapons but only for their persons, and their other weapons to be taken from them and kept by the Justices, neverthelesse such Recusants to be charged to buy and provided armor and the same to be kept by the Justices at the Recusants charge.

---

[1] An Act for the Incorporation of Merchant Adventurers for the Discovery of New Trades. *Statutes of the Realm*, IV, 482.

[2] See scattered lists of these articles in *C. J.* I, 262–264. They are also contained in St. P. Dom. XXI, 41.

Cf. the statutes as passed. *Statutes of the Realm*, IV, 1071–1082.

8. The bringinge in or printing of superstitious bookes prohibited under a paine. Which 5 February was made 40s. a booke.

9. If anie person shall discover anie papist to have receaved anie Jesuites etc. or to have herd masse: [*blank*] shall have the third parte of such goods as the offender shall forfeite, the poore a 2d. third parte and the King the residew: so agreed 5 February.

10. Every popish recusant shall bring his child to be Christened within such tyme and to such place as is there limited: viz. the parish church or some chappell or other place lawfull and by a lawfull minister on paine of 100£ resolved 5. February.

11. No Recusant [*blank*] shall practise the commen or civill law or phisicke or beare anie office in anie court of Justice on paine of [*blank*][1] a tyme and be disabled to beare anie publique office in the commen wealth: resolved 5. February.

12. Every recusant shalbe disabled to present to anie church during his recusancy and the two Universities to have the nominacion during that time, Proviso that the Universityes present none that have anie benefice before. resolved 5. February.

13. Every popish Recusant *ipso facto* disabled as a person excommunicated untell his conformity, resolved so: 5 February:

[*Written in margin.*] On the 5 of February the 6 article beinge left out the rest *usque* 14 resolved to be in one bill the rest referred untell the next setting to be examined for an other bill.

14. Every popish recusant man disabled and excluded to be Tenant by the Curteisy and every woman recusant barred of hir dower or freebancke,[2] and of anie parte of hir husbands goods. resolved 5. February:

15. The children of able Recusants to be taken from their parentes at the age of [*blank*][3] yeeres and to be brought up by the Justices of the peace at the charge of their parents. And their parents to have no power to alien above the one halfe of their lands from such children so brought upp, uppon anie consideracion other then such as the Lord Chauncellor and 2 chief Justices or two of them shall allow.

16. No popish Recusant to be gardein in chivalry in Soccage etc. to anie person:

---

[1] £100 in the act as passed. *Statutes of the Realm*, IV, 1079.

[2] Free Bench, dower in copyhold lands.

[3] Nine years.

f. 8. a] 17. If anie child of anie popish Recusant shalbe sent or passe over sea without the Kings speciall licence, or licence under the hande of six of the Counceill wherof the principall Secretary to be one, he shalbe disabled to enherit untell he shall returne and take the oath in thes articles set downe and the next of Kinne being a protestant to enherit in the meane tyme:

18. If anie person except merchants and marriners shall go over and not take the oath to incurre a punishment there limitted:

19. Treason to be hereafter reconciled.

20. It was by Mr. Sollicitor affirmed that one other article concerninge such as go over as soldiers is not yet perfected:

21. Mr. Fuller moved that whereas the statut[1] now in force doth charge the master to pay 10£ *per mensem* only for his servant which shalbe an obstinate Recusant: and no man can be saied an obstinate Recusant except he be first requiered to come to churche: which seldome happeneth there that consideracion might be had for an article to be in that behalfe devised: which mocion was approved by the howse:

For that the tyme was past Mr. Speaker moved that the consideracion of the foresaid Articles might be deferred untell monday at which tyme every Article to be severally readde and considered by the whole howse and so to be agreed which articles shalbe inserted in the bill and which not and theruppon it was resolved that the howse would meete by eight of the clocke on monday:

It was moved by Mr. Wentwoorth that every member of the howse that would in the meane tyme send for the coppy of the articles might have the same: which Mr. Speaker and the whole howse affirmed to be dew by the orders and custome of the howse:

3 Febr: 1605.

Then weare the Articles[2] offered which the Committees had devised for a bill against Recusants: viz. so manie as the tyme served and would permitt. The effect wherof was as followeth:

1. The King to choose whether he will have 20£ *per mensem* or two partes of the Recusants lands:

In the discussing of this article Sir John Boys moved that it shoulde be added that the Justices of peace may make proclama-

---

[1] 35 Eliz. c. 1. *Statutes of the Realm*, IV, 842.
[2] Cf. debate in *C.J.* I, 262–263.

cion as they might by the statut of 29[1] which was omitted in 23 Elizabeth.[2]

Allso provision woulde be made for the parte dew to the poore as was in the second statut.

Mr. Speaker asking leave to speake, said that the first point moved by Sir John Boys, is materiall and may be added in penninge the statut:

But he affirmed the second to be needeles for saied he the Statut that giveth releife, appointeth the occupiers of the lands to paie it, and the King will not keepe such lands in his handes and so the occupiers remaine chargeable:

Sir Tho[mas] Beamont moved that another course should be taken viz. that order might be taken that popish Recusants should not kepe howse for then could not preists resort to them, neither could they have opportunity to practise and their waunt of meanes would drive away followers from them.

f. 8. b] 2. The Church wardeins and Constables of every parishe or some of them to present monthly the names of all Recusants within their precinct, the names of their servants and children.

3. Every Recusant conformed to receave the Communion once within the first yeare of his conformity, and in the yeere following once every halfe yeere:[3] It was by the most parte thought fit that such conformed Recusant should more then one yeere after the first yeere receave the Communion and I thinke it was thereuppon enlarged unto two yeeres. And it was moved that such as do come to church and bene Recusants shall receave in such sort as shalbe thought fitt.

4. A new forme of an oath sett downe to be taken by Recusants conformed: about this oath was much debate, and in the ende the same was referred to the subcommittees. And the howse would proceede to the next article.

The Lords sent Sir John Crooke one of the Kings Serieants at Lawe, Sir Mathew Carew and Sir Edw[ard] Stanhope masters of the chauncery unto the howse, whose coming being by the Serieant

---

[1] 29 Eliz. c. 6. *Statutes of the Realm*, IV, 771.

[2] 23 Eliz. c. 1. *Statutes of the Realm*, IV, 657.

[3] Later in a conference "the Lords stood very stiff, not to be tied to receive the communion twice-a-year, the archbishop leaning on their side." *C. & T.* I, 61.

of the howse made knowen to Mr. Speaker, he acquaint the howse therwithall, wheruppon they weare called in: and coming upp the howse with 3 severall Salutacions and standing before the clerks deske, and directing their speach to Mr. Speaker the[y] declared[1] that the Lords having a speciall care that the busines against Recusants the greate enemies of the church and state should proceede with all speed do desier a conference with the Lower howse thereabouts and that the Lords would be forty which being doon they weare desiered a while to forbeare the roome which they did: Then Mr. Speaker, declared the Lords message to the howse who generalely entertained that mocion and determined that 80 of this howse should be appointed to confere with the 40 Lords: for it was alleaged and agreed, that the nomber of the commons ought to doble the Lords: Then weare the said messingers called in, to whom was notified the resolucion of the howse, and they shewed that the Lords desiered the place to be the painted chamber and the tyme on thursday next at two of the clocke which was yelded:

Note that Mr. Speaker stoode upp unto the Lords' messingers at their first coming in, with his hatt on: and when they came in the second tyme he sate still with his hat on his hed: in the meane tyme such lawyers as should be appointed to confere with the Lords weare requier[ed] to enforme them selves in the statuts against Recusants:

5. The law to be explaned the husband to aunswere for his wives Recusancy. Uppon this Article was much debate and speaches on both sides in conclusion it was referred backe to the Committees. And 80 persons weare named [2] and agreed on to Confere, with the Lords *ut Supra*. *Quorum* the committees that had labored in theis Articles to be first who in nomber weare 27 and among others R[obert] B[owyer] was one to make upp the nomber of 80.

A member of the howse delivered a petition[3] to Mr. Speaker which was directed to Mr. Speaker and the howse:

f. 9. a]   4 FEBR. 1605.

SIR H[ENRY] HUBBERT[4] Atturny of the wardes being one of the

---

[1] See the Lords' message in *L.J.* II, 367.
[2] See the committee list in *C.J.* I, 263.
[3] The petition of Roger Brereton for privilege. *C.J.* I, 262.
[4] Cf. report and debate in *C.J.* I, 263. "The 4th of February and the

Committees for the bill of Recusants declared that yesterday only the 4 and the 5 articles was referred to the Consideracion of the Committees.

The 4th is touching the oath, wherein are fower things to be considered: viz:

1. who shall minister the oath.
2. To whome the oath shalbe ministred.
3. In what place the oath shalbe ministred.
4. What penaltie shalbe inflicted on the refusers to take the oathes:

The 5th article, requiereth that it be explained that the husband shall aunsweare for his wifes recusancie:

Which 5th Article groweth uppon the statut of 35 Elizabeth[1] and concerning this fift article the Committees thought good that it should be declared that where the husbande was chargeable before this act for his wives Recusancy there he to be chargeable: but not in such other case as by this act is made or provided to be Recusancy:

Touching the 4th Article the Committees have left it to the howse whether anie woman Covert or sole or which shall take the oath: and under what penaltie: In conclusion it was passed over and not putt to the question.

SIR FRA[NCIS] BACON moved touchinge the Conference to be had on Thursday with the Lords That the Committees maie first meete and conferre, Allso for asmuch as in his opinion the conference is not to rest meerely upon proposicions of the Lords but the Committees appointed to conferre do likewise propose to their Lordships: their[fore] he wished that some might be sent to their Lordships to signifie so much and to desier that their Committees maie come authorised accordinglie: and that this howse would be pleased to authorise the Committees for the conference to propose as well as to heare, and to direct them what and how to propose, for said he otherwise if they shall only heare what the Lords will saie this is no conference:

Mr. Speaker remembered the effect of the Lords message, and that the howse did yesterdaie requier the subcommittees to advise

<hr>

5th, time was spent in debating of certain heads for drawing of a bill against the recusants." *C. & T.* I, 50.

[1] 35 Eliz. c. 1. *Statutes of the Realm*, IV, 842.

and enforme them selves concerning all statutes now in force touching recusants[1] and what is defective, what unnecessarie and what fit to be continued, which saied he is the effect of the Lords' message and of the entended conference: And as the gentleman hath well moved (saied Mr. Speaker) it will not be amisse that unto certaine selected persons be appointed what they every one handle and speake unto, not restraining anie other of the Committees:

SIR EDW[ARD] MONTAGUE thought that wee ought not to shew our proceedings but to heare only what the Lords will propose:

DOCTOR PERKINS thought that wee ought allso to propound otherwise it weare no conference but a reference:

f. 9. b] SIR FRA[NCIS] HASTINGS: thought that wee ought not to propound untell wee had[?] a conference in the meane tyme wee are only to talke with the Lords of that which was yesterday referred to the subcommittees viz. touching the Lawes now in force against Recusants, but not to declare our articles now in hande and treatie heare in this howse:

In conclusion it was ordered that the subcommittees shall meete this after noone and all Committees for Conference to meete to morrow in the after noone heare:

5: FEBR: 1605.

SIR RO[BERT] JOHNSON, one of the Committees of the watermens bill[2] brought it in and setting in his place desiered that it might be reached to the clerke, to which Mr. Speaker aunsweared that he that bringeth in a bill must by the orders of the howse be delivered with his owne hand to the clerke and shew the amendements: which he did:

Note the Serieant was sent into the hall to requier the lawyers which are members of the howse to come up and give ther attendance and he tooke his mace.

The 6. 7. 8. 9. 10: 11: 12 and 13 article of the bill for recusants

---

[1] The Lords' committee was ordered to do the same. *L.J.* II, 367.

[2] This bill was to amend one clause of a statute of 1 Jac. I. c. 16 (*Statutes of the Realm*, IV, 1034), which provided that watermen should not have apprentices until they had rowed for five years. This was to be lengthened to fifteen years. Petition of Thames Watermen to Salisbury, March, 1606. Salisbury MSS.

weare read and allowed to be put into the first bill: after much dispute uppon some of them:

6 Febr:

An act for the better execucion of the offices of petit constables *primo lecta.*

Then weare readde Five articles[1] to be enserted into a second bill for Recusants: Viz.

1. That the Children of convicted Recusants being of abilitie be taken from them a[t] 9 yeares of age and brought upp by the direccion of the Justices of peace at the chargs of their parents.

2. No Recusant to be gardein in Socage, in Chivalry, nor in Nurture to anie the kings subiects but the next of kynne to whome the land cannot discend to have the wardship or gardinship to the use of the heir.

3. Any child sent over without his Majesties licence or licence of sixe of the counceill wherof the Principall Secretarie to be one to be disabled to enherite. etc.

4. Whereas many neither being merchants nor their factors soldiers nor Marriners have hertofore gon over sea without licence such persons to returne within 12 monethes after this cession and within one moneth after his or their returne to take the oath *ut supra:*

5. To be explained that if anie be reconciled without the Kings dominions etc. the same to be treason and the triall to be in any county as in the Article.

6. Moved by Mr. Ove[r]b[u]ry and allowed by the howse that a sixthe Article should likewise be enserted, to this effect, viz: No popish Recusant indicted or to be endicted shalbe admitted to bring anie writt of Error, or otherwise to reverse anie such endictment or outlawry against him or them untell he or she shall conforme them selves and shall have receaved the oath.

f. 10. a]   7 Febr.

A man may speake to a bill at the first readinge:

After a bill committed no man may speake: with this observacion: that if uppon the question of committing, some say yea some no, and that the yea be the greater there it holdeth that no man

---

[1] Cf. *C.J.* I, 264 and *C. & T.* I, 50.

after such committing maie speake to it: but if the same be committed uppon the question and no Nay, there any man maie speake to it:

Day was given unto the Clerks of all severall Courts to bring their counceill to speeke in their defence to the bill of fees, And allso to Mr. Nicholson touching the bill exhibited by Mr. Ognell: viz. thursday next:

Sir Tho[mas] Lakes bill brought in by the Committees with this amendement only viz. 3000 made 2600 which amendements being readde the bill was putt to engrossing:

Agreed that our Articles should be faire wrightten and delivered to My Lord Chauncellor¹ on satterday: and the Lords' articles to be receaved by Mr. Speaker:²

MR. FULLER declared that the Articles of the gardeinship en chivalry appertaning to recusants shalbe given to the disposicion of the court of wards was so readde to the Lords which was contrary to the iudgement of the howse who reiected that article and thought it fit that the next of kynne to whom the enherittance cannot come shold be gardein.

---

¹ Thomas Egerton, Baron Ellesmere.

² The conference concerning anti-Catholic laws had been held on Feb. 6, at which time an exchange of articles was determined upon. See reports of the conference in *C.J.* I, 265; *C. & T.* I, 51. Salisbury described the conference for James in a letter to Dirleton, the King's secretary. Salisbury MSS. The same letter is found in Stowe MSS 4160, ff. 260–261: "Being newly come from a long and late session in Parliament, and being close by my chimney's end, a place proper for Beagles, I was in dispute whether I should trouble his Majesty with this day's journal, having heard a report of his purpose to return tomorrow. Nevertheless conceiving it will not be unpleasing to his Majesty to hear as well the truth from my pen as from others' report, I have thought good to entreat you to acquaint him as follows. This afternoon 40 of my Lords met with 4 score of the Lower House, to whom that was delivered in general, as the cause of our meeting, wherewith his Majesty was acquainted by me before his going. The first part whereof was concerning the priests and Papists, wherein they came prepared with divers articles. So did we, and by that means it appeared that both Houses had one end, and wanted only the assurance to attain it by one and the same way: a matter though rather formal than essential, yet of such necessity in passing of bills as, being left unreconciled, much time would be expended. Of which point I will say no more at this time, but that we are very like to concur: having in a manner sympathized in all things, as well appeared to both our content-

He also moved and the howse ordered that an article should be added touching soldiers passing over:

An article to be added that persons passing over the sea to serve forraine princes shall take this new oath and enter into bond of 20£. etc.

f. 10. b]　　　　　　　8 FEBR. 1605.

SIR CHRISTOPHER PERKYNS, in an eloquent speach not long

ments, when the articles of each side were compared. After which dispute *in pleno Concilio*, I took out a writing, and used this speech (as near as I can remember), that as that people was happy which either lived under philosophers, or had kings that were philosophers, so might I speak of our felicity, whose Sovereign was not only rich in wisdom, but in zeal, without which wisdom were folly. That for proof of the zeal, and the wisdom thereof, I was able to shew them fair and clear records, wherein because I daily discerned how great an advantage we had that lived at the feet of Gamaliel in respect of others more removed; and found so good cause to wish them part of our contentments, I would encroach upon his Majesty's future interpretation, rather than to deprive them of that joy and consolation which I conceived they would gather from the excellent composition of his Majesty's private meditations: not doubting but they would join with a Secretary so far as to free him by their suit *a poena*, though not *a culpa*, if I had strained too far upon the liberty to make use of his Majesty's Papers: adding thereunto that I had suffered all men to use the liberty of their own sense before I would produce this, lest any man might have conceived I had sought thereby to lead or bind up any man's judgment by the weight and authority of Princes' propositions. And so, after an earnest calling for it to be read, and general attention, it was read, and received with infinite applause and acclamation, being, I protest unto you, different in nothing from their projects, but in that which is only the attribute of a king, that is full of mercy. Much more passed of him than I will write: for I love not to praise him, where his eyes shall look upon me, or upon my words. . . . . For the rest which we intended should be only accidental, and rather remembrances that such things must have their turn, than as now intending to propound them, they were pertinently touched and sufficiently conceived, being two things in general: the one to supply the necessities of the Crown for the good of the same: the other to remember that the work of our commission, by which the differences in laws and customs were reconciled, and all things duly and carefully ordered, which were necessary for the common good of both kingdoms, must not longer lie asleep than mere necessity required. To conclude, all this will be reported, and we intend tomorrow some of us to consult, who shall now amongst them set those things awork, without attending further circumstance. Thus have you in effect the true state of Parliament causes. . . . ."

declared that as the Pope had founded seminaryes of schollers to perswade our nation from faith to allmightie God and obedience to the King so had he with the helpe of his frends provided a seminary of marshall men to invade and assault us when occasion might serve, he shewed that the English serving under the Archduke[1] did not ayme at the low countries but entended all their purposes against Englande and that their commen speach and talke is of our countrie: and therefore advised that wee should devise and set a course of prevencion. SIR EDWYN SANDES second that speach with a veary well and comely speach, wherin he affirmed that the oath by us by our articles ordained though with greate wisdome, yet serveth to litle purpose to restraine them, for saied he, they will sweare, and then resort to their confessors and be absolved and then are they as honest men as the best. He declared that it is affirmed by divers gentlemen that are come over that the English serving under the archduke have no other speach so frequent as the state of Englande to be altered by their endeavors and with divers other wise and well delivered arguments moved a deepe consideration of some course to be taken for them:[2]

Then Mr. Speaker declared that he had receaved the Lords' articles and moved that ours might by the committees be perfected according to that which the howse had agreed, and so it was ordered: then he redde the Lords' articles to the ende every man might observe and consider of them and moved that the Committees for this bill might have a coppie therof so as they might prepare them selves against the conference:

The Lords' articles concerning Recusants.

Proiects touchinge Recusants committed to farder consideracion:

---

[1] Archduke Albert, Regent of Flanders.

[2] Cf. *Cal. St. P. Venetian, 1603–1607*, 322. Later in February James forbade any further levies of English troops to be made for service with the Archduke. Salisbury wrote to Sir Thomas Edmondes that the excuse offered to Spain must be "that the Lower House had conceived such a deep impression that those soldiers which served the Archduke would have been made the sword for England's destruction, as they were now about to make laws for the general restraint of any that should offer to go." Salisbury added that there must be no opposition in the House at this time since "all other his Majesty's desires that are to be affected by the Parliament might receive interruption." Feb. 27. Salisbury MSS.

1. The first concerned paiment of 12d. for absence.

2. The second for takinge the children of Recusants from them to be brought upp at the discrecion of the Justices of peace at the charge of their parents that are of abilitie and others to be bond apprentices by like discrecion.

3. Sendinge of any unto Semynaryes or Releavinge of any there, to be *Premunire*.

4. Englishmen serving beyond the seas to returne within [*blank*] monthes under paine of [*blank*].

5. No recusant convict to send any person.

6. [*blank*.]

7. Refusers to take the oath treasonyes.

8. [*blank*.]

9. Recusants to be disarmed etc.

10. The King to chose to have 20£ the moneth or 2 parts of Recusants lands. Nothing to descend to any recusant.

11. The Law.

f. 11. a] 12. Refusing [*blank*].

13. [*blank*.]

14. Bishops Chauncellors to certifie the names of all Recusants to the Justices of Assize:

15. Every recusants to cause his child to be baptised in the parish church chappell or other lawful place of common prayer within one moneth etc.

10 FEBR. 1605.

An act to enable all the Kings subiects of England and wales freely to trade into spayne, portugale and fraunce: 2do. *lecta* and committed: to meete on Wednesday next:

An act for the better establishinge of trew religion *primo lecta* preferred as I thinke by SIR EDWYN SANDYS:

DOCTOR PERKINS[1] one of the committees touching Articles to be added to the former concerning recusants declared that 3 points weare referred to them viz:

A remedy against soldiers servinge princes of an other religion: nothing therein doon but left to the howse and by the howse left to the conference with the Lords at the meeting for the other articles:

---

[1] Cf. the debate in *C.J.* I, 265–266.

A course to limitt Recusants to their owne dwelling howses:

To anull conveiances made by Recusants to the King's preiudice.

That in the two latter nothing was doon:

SIR THOMAS RIDGEWAY moved a graunt[1] to the King and the same to be referred to a committee.

SIR MAURICE BERKLEY seconded him.

SIR EDW[ARD] MONTAGUE moved a grant to be presently agreed on: without committment: and because one subsidy and 2 fifteenes weare perhaps to litle for supply of the King's occasions and 3 subsidyes and 6 fifteenes to greate for the country to beare therefore his opinion was that 2 Subsidies and 4 Fifteenes weare fit to be yelded voluntarily: the first Subsidy to be paied in Easter terme next the tow first Fifteenes in Michaelmas terme next, the second Subsidy in Easter terme twelve moneth and the last fifteenes in Michaelmas terme following: and this matter to be handled in open court not by committment:

After manie speaches, (divers to small purpose) it was agreed that it should be referred to a Committee to draw a bill for graunt of 2 subsidies and 4 fifteenes:

f. 11. b]   11 FEBR. 1605.

This day Mr. Speaker came into the howse about 10 of the clocke

---

[1] For this debate on supply, which showed a fairly cordial attitude towards the Crown and which resulted in the grant of two subsidies and four fifteenths, see *C.J.* I, 266; Spedding, V, 178. See also *C. & T.* I, 52. For the expectation of considerable opposition to any grant, see *Cal. St. P. Venetian, 1603–1607*, 280, 281, 285. Salisbury was behind the motion for supply. Lord Dirleton wrote him on Feb. 10: "Quhen his Majeste vent to supper he commonde me to remember you (althoe he kneu perfytlye your Lordship vas bothe careful & myndful of his besines in the louer houss) that you vold imploye your self bothe to the Committie and the holle houss that he may rother hove a subsidye then onye motter by the yeir quhiche he knoing wilbe no great motter nor fitt releif for his extraordinorye debts. . . . ." St. P. Dom. XVIII, 77.

The King and Council were not content with the amount of the grant and hoped to draw the Commons to a higher figure. Winwood, II, 198; M. de la Fontaine to M. de Villeroy, Feb. 16/26, 1606. Paris Transcripts. Sir Edward Hoby wrote on March 7, "It seemed the former day's work [Feb. 10] propounded by Sir Thomas Ridgeway, and seconded by such like (for I must tell you, that I think the State scorneth to have any privy counsellors of any understanding in the House) came short to expectation and necessity." *C. & T.* I, 60.

before whose coming praiers weare readde by the Clerke of the howse and ended.

The Speaker excused his absence or slackenesse, and declared[1] that the same happened by reason that his Majestie sent for him. He farder declared that his Majestie commaunded him to relate and shew unto the howse that he understoode of their forwarde and willing consent to offer unto him such subsidy as yesterdaie was spoken of and agreed with one accord in the howse: That the King taketh it and doth accept it most ioifully as a token of their loves and doth take more comfort in being King over such a people so well affected towards him then in anie thing in the woorlde: for that this willing forwardnes to shew their affection will not only be a great incoragement to his good subiects and fre[n]ds abroode but a discomfort and discoragement to persons evelly affected towards him and the state: and for the King's owne particuler this graunt so voluntarily agreed on doth yeld him more ioy and contentment then if 1000 tymes so much had fallen unto him by anie other occasion or accident:

Secondlie the King taketh this guift thanckfullie in signe wherof he will not spare to spend both the same and what else he hath in the woorld and to adventure his owne person in defence and mantenance of religion and this howse and the whole realme. That his highnes doth yeld unto their desier for removing the oppressions by purveiors, which kind of people his Majestie doth so much detest that he wishes both the corruption and name of them to be utterly taken away and abolished. Lastlie his Majesties commaundement was I should move you to appoint a Committee to conferre with the Lords and from the Lords both to understande the Kings occasions, [and] to declare to their Lordships the greavances of the people.

Which speach being ended MR. JOHN HARE stoode upp and after he had in a soberly fashion opened the ioy which himselfe in particuler from his hart tooke and had conceaved by that which Mr. Speaker delivered from his Majestie, he desiered to know the pleasure and resolucion of the howse whether [the] bill of Purveiors which he then had in his hande perfected by the Committees shoulde be proceeded in or to sleepe and the matter referred wholly to conference with the Lords as Mr. Speaker had declared the

---

[1] Cf. his speech in *C.J.* I, 266–267; *C. & T.* I, 59–60.

King's mocion, wheruppon it was aunswered and resolved that both courses should be prosecuted viz. the matter to be opened to the Lords with the humble Suyt of this howse unto his Majestie in that behalfe and allso the bill to be proceeded in. And the Committees for the bill of Purveiors appointed to attend the Lords according to his Majesties gracious proposicion.

SIR ROWLAND LITTON moved that the said Committees should consider of the abuses in taking Post horses.

SIR ROB[ER]T WINGFIELD and some others moved that a colleccion of all greavances wherwith the country is greaved might be made and delivered to the Committees[1] and the Committees to acquaint the Lords therwithall to thentent their Lordships may f. 12. a] make the same knowen to his Majestie:

This mocion was well liked of by the howse but it was thought fit the same should be referred to an other severall bill or articles and not encluded with the busines of the Purveiors. So as to my conceipt and understanding it was ordered that the treaty touching Purveiors should not be intricated with anie other matter:

Sir Tho[mas] Lakes bill brought in engrossed and readde, and allowed to passe:

12 FEBR. 1605.

An acte for the trew makinge of woollen cloaths: *primo lecta:*

Then was readde the Lords' articles touching to be drawen against Recusants.

After was readde an other bill intituled [*blank*].

An act for the trew makinge and dressinge of woollen cloathes. *primo lecta:*

MR. FULLER of Grayes Inne, a prime man in the Counceill of London, stoode upp and having spoken somewhat in commendacion of the first bill, saied that in the second bill is nothing but what is conteined in the former, and forasmuch as both the said bills are vearie long and much time wilbe readde[2] when the same shalbe read againe, therefore he wished that the second bill only should have a second reading and the[n] that being committed he advised that the second should be committed to the consideracion of those committees, for that it is tedious to be read and nothing

---

[1] For the subsidy.

[2] *Lost* is meant.

in it materiall not contained in the first. Then Mr. Speaker moved the howse to allow of Mr. Fullers mocion, declaring farder that the first bill was read the last cession,[1] but wanted time to be proceeded in, and this bill saieth he was commended by my Lord Chief Justice: and quoth he the cittie of London put in the latter bill which Mr. Fuller speaketh against. Yea Sir quoth MR. GORE governor of the merchants adventurers that is his error whereat Mr. Fuller started: as acknowledging his fault, and desierous to have recalled his speeche:

13 FEBR: 1605.

MR. HARE reported[2] to the howse the proceedings of the Committees for the cause of purviors at their conference yesterday to this effect: viz: that they had altered the bill in some few woords and so he delivered the same to the clerke: Next that the Committees did thincke fit that the said bill shall rest with the Clerke and the course of proceeding in the busines to be by conference with the Lords and proponding to them the desier of the howse touching reformacion and to understand what course their Lordships will propose:

f. 12. b] The bill for observacion of the Sabboth daie was brought into the howse by SIR FRA[NCIS] EVERS[3] one of the Committees with some amendements which weare twise readde, and when it should have ben put to the question for engrossinge, An old man[4] being Burgesse for Yarmouth moved consideracion to be had for that in his towne the[y] have a faire once every yeare begininge att Michaelmas daie: and continuing 40 daies in which time are sixe Sabboth daies: this faire consisteth not on horses or anie other cattell but is meerely for sale of Herings and such like fish taken on that coast, and into that port comes in some time 300 sale of fishers in one day during that faire which is their only season: and if the fisher man be compelled to keepe his hearing but one daie it falleth out manie tymes he may throw the same away next daie for they will be good for nothing unlesse the[y] be presentlie handled as appurtaineth: wherefore he desiered that some proviso may be added to the bill for prevencion of this inconvenience:

---

[1] See *C.J.* I, 237, 241, 252.
[2] Cf. the report in *C.J.* I, 267.
[3] Sir Francis Eure. *C.J.* I, 267.
[4] Thomas Damett, who first served for Great Yarmouth in 1586.

SIR THO[MAS] HOLCRAFT then moved that the penalty of this statut for breach of the Sabboth might not be given to the parish where the offence is committed but to the towne where it shalbe committed: for quoth he in the North where I dwell One parish manie times containeth 10, 20 30 and sometyme 40 twones or villages: and some Justice of peace being Lord of some one out twone or villiage having reduced his tenants eaven to beggary by extreame racking of them will and often doth releife such poore so by him empoverished uppon the forfeitures and penalties of the inhabitants of an other towne within that parishe, who living under a more conscionable landlord are of more abilitie and live well:

SIR [HENRY?] SAVILE desiered that consideracion might be had of an other parte of the bill viz: wheras it is by this bill provided that every offendor faulting by breach of the Sabboth daie contrary to the act, shall forfeite 10s. or set in the stocks, and for that many times mens children and their servants do offend this way who have not 10s. to paie and the father or master not being willing to paie for them if now the partie should be sett in the stocks the father or master will theruppon cast such partie off as a person publiquely defamed, wherby it happeneth that wee shall in this case prepare and make the said parties ready for the gallowse being not fit for honest company: And uppon theis mocions the bill was recommitted to the same parties.

An act for the grauntinge and confirminge of certein allowances to the merchantes of Yorke Newcastell uppon Tyne and Kingeston uppon Hull: touchinge the custome of their cloathes: *primo lecta:* ^{Recommittment}

An act for the better establishinge of trew religion 2do. *lecta* and committed to the former committees for churche causes: this bill was brought in by Sir Edw[in] Sandys.

Brewertons priviledge was moved: viz. that the Committees founde he ought to have priviledge and uppon the question it was ordered that he should not be sett at libertie by a Serieant at Mace, bicause he was imprisoned by order of a iudiciall court viz. the Kings bench: but that therefore he shoulde be discharged by a writt.

f. 13. a] MR. BROOKE of Yorke complained that he was arrested veary dispitefully in westminster hall in the last Michaelmas terme within 3 daies after the adiornement of the parliament by the meanes of Andrew Mallory and his servaunt Holborne knowing him to be of the howse: wheruppon it was ordered that the Serieant should be sent for them both: Mr. Speaker moved to know whether the howse had intention to punish Mallory, to which was aunsweared yea: hereuppon he put them in mynde that the Committees had report[ed] 16 daies to be a reasonable tyme of priviledge and freedome before and after every cession: and quoth he if you remember Martyns case in [*blank*][1] Elizabeth it was thought he should have 20 daies priviledge and being arrested within that time he was sett at libertie by the howse but the other party not punished: Whereunto SIR JOHN HIGHAM aunsweared that Martyns adversarie was spared in respect he did not know that 20 daies or so long time would be thought reasonable for priviledge but this man could not be ignorant that 3 daies is within the time of priviledge: and therefore he is to be punished which reasons being well understoode by the howse they enclined to punish Mallory, if he cannot satisfie them at his come[ing] to the barre:

The greate Committee for the Articles touching Recusants to meete heare after noone to advise what course shall be held with the Lords on monday: An Article was offered by SIR ROB[ER]T DRURY to be added to the articles for recusants the effect wherof is: To prevent the ordinary recourse of Recusants to and neere the citty of London: which was well penned and referred to the former committees:

14 FEBR: 1605.

An act for some addicions to a statut made in the last cession[2] for explanacion of a statut made 5 Elizabeth[3] intituled an act for wages of spinsters and weavers: *primo lecta:*

Mr. Mallory was brought to the barre to aunsweare the arresting of Mr. Brooke of Yorke, the effect of his defence was that he knew him not to be a member of the howse and that as soone as he understoode it he lett fall his accion, then Mallory being withdrawen MR. BROOKE seemed satisfied and the howse in favor spared punishing of Mallory:

---

[1] 29 Elizabeth. 27 February, 1586–87. D'Ewes, 410, 412, 414. Hatsell, *Precedents* (ed. of 1818), I, 99–100.

[2] 1 Jac. I. c. 6. *Statutes of the Realm*, IV, 1022. This is the act entitled "An Act for Spinsters and Weavers."

[3] 5 Eliz. c. 4. *Statutes of the Realm*, IV, 414.

Mr. Warrein was brought to the barre for serving proces out of the starre chamber uppon Mr. Skepwith[1] a member of this howse 7 daies before this cession of parliament viz. 16 January in Wales nine score miles from hence: It appeared and was not denied that Mr. Warrein knew Mr. Skepweth to be of the howse, but thought that Mr. Skepweth would not have given attendance heare, to which conceipt he was lead for that the last cession Mr. Skepweth excused him selfe and did not attende in regard he was the sheriffe of the shire: and he was at the time of the arrest discharged, which Warrein pretended together with a speach which he had herd to that effect and the shorttnes of the time for him to come upp in, made him believe he entended not to come upp and so to presume to arrest him: Skepweth alleaged that Warrein did this terme prosecute him and enforced him to aunswere in the starre chamber and there to aunswere also interogatories: Warrein affirmed that there was an other suyt by him brought and depending in the starre chamber against Skepweth which is auncient f. 13. b] and before this proces or arrest now complained on. And that therein allso he did nothing this terme against Mr. Skepweth saving that Mr. Skepweths attorny urged his attorny to call for an aunswere to enterrogatories which if he had not accordinglie theruppon called for then by the course of that court Mr. Skepweth should have ben admitted to aunswere by attorny and freed of aunswereing interogatories: this matter was referred to the consideracion of the Committees for the privilegs of the howse, which on satterday the XVth of February reported the state of matter to be as Warrein had confessed and declared: so as the howse was not so much offended with Warrein as before, howbeit for that the howse held the arresting of Skepweth to be a contempt and contrary to the priviledges of the howse, and Mr. Warreins aunswere not sufficient being only that (he thought Skepweth would not have attended) therefore the howse held him in iustice punishable thought not by sending him to the Tower in regard he did not afterwards prosecute the suit, yet that for his offence he should be committed and remaine three daies in custody of the Serieant of this howse:

---

[1] Alban Stepneth was member for Pembrokeshire. He was also sheriff of the shire. *Bulletin of the Institute of Historical Research*, V, 105; *Lists and Indexes No. IX. List of Sheriffs for England and Wales . . . . to 1831.* Cf. account in *C.J.* I, 268-269.

The bill for mittigacion of Clerks fees, was this 14th of February readde the second time: and Mr. Crew being of counceill with the sixe Clerks and Mr. Kiddermester one of the sixe clerks weare admitted to speake att the barre against the bill: The effect of a long speach delivered by Mr. Crew was that tyme out of mynde they had used to take these fees which now the[y] demaunde and receave, and proved a lawfull title in them by prescription, wherof if the[y] weare disseised they might have an assise as of their freholde:[1] as well as in Waife stray etc. but he spake nothing of the smallness of the pag nor of the few lines on a side nor few woords in the lines: which being ended they went foorth and uppon dispute in the howse the stronger opinion seemed to weigh that the Clerks had title in such fees as auncientlie they had taken and now prescribe in but the most held it fit that by a bill reformacion should be had of the smallness of the pages the widenes of the lines and the fewe woords contrary to the opinion of others who would that the reformacion might be referred to the cheife Judges of the Courts where anie clerke so offending should serve: and to them that woulde have had the bill throwen out of the howse: And so was the bill committed.

Purveiors   In the afternoone of the same daie Certaine of the Lords as committees and a nomber of the Commens in proporcion aun-swearable did meete in the painted chamber:[2] to the ende that the Commens might according to his Majesties most gracious invitacion acquaint the Lords and by them the King with their greavances wherof they might have redresse and from their Lordships understande the Kings occasions, At which tyme Mr. John Hare, Clerke of the court of wardes according to the appointment and order of this howse spake unto the Lords be-ginning to this effect,[3] My Lords it hath pleased the lower howse

---

[1] "Officers, as well as Freeholders, may have their Writt of Assise, if they be disturbed." *C.J.* I, 268. Cf. debate *ibid*.

[2] See the report of this conference in *C.J.* I, 269. See also *C. & T.* I, 60; Spedding, III, 267.

[3] Hare in this speech attacked purveyors in a rather violent manner, which offended the Lords. The Speaker wrote Salisbury later in the day: "According to your honorable directions (my most honored good Lord) I will bend my endevors to add execution to your Lordship's directions at this instance receaved and having receaved understanding of the most undescreete behavior of an unconsiderat fyerbrand of this

of parliament to commaunde my service this daie unto your Lordships in performance wherof I shall open nor deliver nothing
unto you but sorrow and greafe: he proceeded with a long narracion of the abuses wrongs and oppressions endured by the people,
from and by purveiors: herein he shewed that this is [no] new
f. 14. a] matter nor unknowen to their Lordships who well may
and do remember that the same complaint was offered unto their
Lordships and to his Majestie:[1] at which tyme it was affirmed to
the King that the people had no such cause of greife but that the
complaint was meere untrew, and his highnes officers of his honorable howshold therby wrongfullie slaundered: but my Lords
quoth he this it hath not ben in former tymes for the good Kings
of this lande (and heare he made an enumeracion of them) did all
make lawes against theis wicked people the purveiors and commandement the dew execucion therof. So as one among the rest
ordained that all Archbishops and Bishopps should once every
[*blank*][2] cause these statuts to be proclaimed and to denounce the

afternoones work, I presumed to endevoure to prevente anie sodayne
question to be stirred in the howse untill it were better mollifyed and to
that end did send to have conference with as manie as the shortnesse of
the tyme would permitt and whoe although they much desire reformacion
of the abuses of purveyors yet doe utterlie condempne his insolency and
therefore doe beseach your Lordship that the howse may not be taxed
with the fyery spiritt of his humor, for his warrant was only firste to desire
your Lordships to comend the humble thanks of the Lower howse to his
Majestie for his graciouse message by me delivered them, secondlie to
make knowne the abuses and curruptions of the purveyors and lastly to
petition your Lordships to be pleased to propounde some meane of
remedie, and if your Lordships propounded a Composition, that then they
should forbeare to conclude untill the howse were thereof made acquainted. This was the summe of that he was warrented to doe and
whatsoever elles he did was beyond his Shuritie, for I protest unto your
Lordship, never Howse of Parliament did more dutifullie entertayne his
graciouse pleasure then nowe & in this, and therefore doe moste humblie
beseach your Lordship to prevent anie distaste of his Majestie for this
grosse error to the howse whereof I dare presume to assure your Lordship
thaie are innocent. . . . ." St. P. Dom. XVIII, 89.

[1] In 1604. *C.J.* I, 190, 200, 204.

[2] I can find no proclamation of purveyance statutes by bishops. They
were to be proclaimed by the sheriffs in 1422 (*Statutes of the Realm*, II,
213) and in 1442 (*ibid.* II, 321) and by the justices of the peace in 1445
(*ibid.* II, 328).

violaters of the same to be [*blank*]. The matter which now wee complaine of is the oppression by theis purveiors: which is three-fold: viz. in Cartakinge: secondly in Purveing for victualles woods etc. and lastlie in takings for the stable: The thing which wee desier is only execucion of such good lawes as now stande in force in that behalfe. Wee are not ignorant that his Majestie is swoorne to Magna Charta, which saieth *Nulli negabimus, nulli vendemus Justiciam aut rectum:* and wee know and are assured by his gracious message which it pleased his highness to send and was delivered unto us by the mouth of Mr. Speaker[1] that his gracious disposicion and mynde is wee should have redresse, yet wee finde that if anie man gaine saie theis ungodlie people the purveiors in their uniust commaundes, such person is straight waie sent for and punished by imprisonment and otherwise by the officers of the Greenecloath contrary to Law, and Justice so as no good subiect though never so well and dutifullie affected knoweth not how to yelde his obedience in this case of purveiance: heare he shewed the abuses generally: in cartaking: viz. in compounding with some hundreds within a county and fetcheing twice so manie as the Kings service requiereth in other hundreds farder of[f] from the Kings place of remove, and such like: also in purveance of victualls and woode, in that the purveiors commissions do not containe the quantities requisite for the Kings service nor have any blanks or schedules annexed in which the quantities which the purveiors have taken with the time, place, price etc. maie be wrightten according to lawe: and the like for the Stable: and generallie for that Cartaking is used for others then the King Queen and Prince: and manie like abuses. And my Lords quoth he lest I seeme to complaint of generallities I will be a suiter to your Lordships if you thincke it fit that forasmuch as manie of your Lordships were not present the last cession when wee presented and red to the Kings Majestie a noate of the particuler abuses of purveiors that I maie now againe reade them: Heare the Lords advised privately and softly as the[y] sate at the table and then willed him to reade them. f. 14. b] He concluded that he most hartely thancked god that the people had so good and gracious a King as woulde redresse their greavaunces if the same weare made known unto him and that the

---

[1] On February 11.

King had so dutifull and obedient subiects that being thus oppressed no man did so much as hold upp his hand or cast upp his
foote against it: and so he opened unto their Lordships that the
neither howse had prepared [a] bill for redresse of theis heavie
oppressions, but had thought good before anie persecution therof
humbly to desier their Lordships favorable aides for the reformacion of the said wronge and rooting out of theis wicked seed of the
divells which like the froggs in Pharoes tyme skippe in every mans
dishe:

Which speach was long and well composed and being ended one
of the Lords requiered to have from him the said articles which he
redde against the Purveiors wherunto he aunswered that his
Majestie receaved the like the last cession, wherwith he doubted
not but some of their Lordships weare well acquainted, Theis which
he now had are but his blotted coppie, which albeit he doubt not
but the howse would be contented he should deliver to their Lordships yet for that he had no direccions so to do he humbly desiered
to be in that behalfe forbourne untell he might acquaint the howse
with their Lordships demaunde therin which he promised to do
with all speede:

The Earl of Salisbury his Majesties principall Secretary declared
that the Lords had commaunded him to declare their myndes:
And began thus, Wee brought hether myndes not to have begon
with sorrow and greife,[1] and at our last conference[2] wee parted
thincking wee had left you without discontent, wee tolde you wee
had other matters to disburden our selves of and to imparte unto
you, wee knoweing more then you, as being by fortune and favor
neerer to the headde. And this occasion now ministred by your
speach doth not discharge us of our promyse. The subject of this
Conference should have followed the other and not to have begunne
with sorrow and greife. This kinde of opening grevaunces with
such circumstances as hath ben used shewed diffidence and mistrust. The Kings message was to let you know how graciously he
taketh your free and hartie offers of guift unto him: and to let you
know how strong he holdeth himselfe bycause both [in] forraine
states and at home it maie be seen how strong he is in possessing
the harts of such loving subiects: He accompteth himselfe but

---

[1] The opening words of Hare's speech.
[2] On Feb. 6 concerning laws against the Catholics.

your stewerd of whatsoever you give him: and he will be *fidus depositorius:* I must also tell you that *Beneficium dando accipit qui dat* etc. In his princely love and favor he willed you to shewe your greavaunces, yet he is not ignorant how dangerous a thing it is to sommon subiects to complaine but thinking that there was none among you that woulde take on them to be Tribunes of the people: and the King namely spake of the abuse of Purveiors. Now herin you have surprised us by speaking of the Lawe which wee know not how it standeth and whereas you tell us of examples of tymes in which weare disobedience I had rather you had given examples of times of Love and obedience: For the substance of your complaint wee[?] will deliver it to the King, if you will deliver us the noate of the particulers which you red but I must saie that the manner of your complaint is mixed with vineger.

Mr. Hare breifely replied: with an humble desier that the speaches which he had delivered might not be imputed unto himselfe aloane. And my Lords quoth he your Lordships have already the Articles,[1] and this which I redde is but a blotted coppy which notwithstanding I must crave pardon though I deliver not for that I have no warrant from the howse so to do, howbeit I will therin move the howse who I doubt not will be pleased that your Lordships have them.

f. 15. a] Then the Lord Chauncellor used a short speach to this effect viz. Wee are sorry that in steede of gratulacion wee should begin with sorrow and ende with misery for (a miserable cas) was the last woorde. Our coming cheifely that the King now knowing your loves and voluntary offers to helpe him, you maie on the other side understande his highnes occasions, which by an officer that better doth know the same then myselfe, shalbe declared unto you.

The Lord Treasurer[2] then spake to this effect: viz.

I will begin in a course contrary to Mr. Hare: namely with ioy and comfort which comfort cometh of your selves that did so freely offer aide unto the King's Majestie. And to the ende you may understande his highnes occasions, their Lordships have commaunded mee to declare the same unto you. Nexte he excused his

---

[1] From the last session.

[2] Thomas Sackville, Earl of Dorset. "My Lord Treasurer confessed that they had examined the Officers, and had found the Articles all true." *C.J.* I, 269.

owne disabilitie, namely that his memory was neaver good and that now time had impaired both that and his understanding for I come saied he within sixe monthes of those yeeres after which David pronounceth that nothing remaineth but sorrow and labour: wherefore I desier that you will give mee leave to use the benefit of my noates which I have set downe to be able to give you satisfaccion in this matter: And I will devide my speach[1] into three partes: namely:

1. A declaracion of the King's present estate.
2. The meanes of the Kings necessityes.
3. An aunsweare to Certaine obiections whereby is pretended that his Majestie hath no such occasions and waunts as is alleaged.

His Majestie present estate is waunt which groweth by a doble necessitie the first in that the Kings ordinary resceipts are not able to supplie the ordinary expence:[2] Then his Majesties greate debtes which growe severall wayes:

First Queene Elisabeth left the crowne in debt.... 4006000£.[3]
The Kings debts by himselfe
The Charge of the King's Cominge hether...........10000£.
The buriall of the late Queene.....................20000£.
The coronacion of the King's majestie..............20000£:
The augmentacion of the Kinges yeerely charge more then the late Queenes was First in the charge of his howse which is more then the late Queene spent *per annum*..............55000£:
His yeere revennew is lessened *per Annum*............[blank] cheifely by guifts since his coming and those either to persons which long before had doon him good and dutifull service or

---

[1] A brief note of this speech is in *Roger Wilbraham* (*Camden Misc.* X), 75–76. Dorset practically repeated his speech at a second conference on Feb. 19. His second speech, contained in Additional MSS 34324, ff. 37–41, is printed in Appendix A.

For the financial situation in 1606, see Gardiner, *History of England from the Accession of James I to the Outbreak of the Civil War* (ed. of 1900), I, 293–298; *Parliamentary Debates in 1610* (*Camden Society*), Introduction; W. R. Scott, *The Constitution and Finance of English, Scottish, and Irish Joint Stock Companies to 1720*, I, 133–139; III, 509.

[2] Cf. Appendix A.

[3] £400,000 roughly. See Scott, III, 509. Cf. the following items in Appendix A.

elles to such as have since his coming by their acceptable service deserved his favour: And somme out of his good and princely disposicion apt and inclinable to give eaven where small desert is uppon meere instance: This is not strange at the first coming of a Prince to a Kingdome for Queene Mary within (and named a small time which then I could not take and I have since forgotten) by giving diminished the revennew of the crown 50000£. *per Annum.*[1]

The Kings debt in all as his Lordship delivered it is now 734000£.[2]

f. 15. b] 1. It maie [be] obiected that the Kings occasions cannot be such as I have declared in regard he hath peace.

2. Secondly for that Queene Elisabeth left paiable unto the King twoo whole subsidies and 4 fifteens.

I would have you know that of one subsidy and 2 fifteens there cometh no more cleere to the King then............130000£: which was soone spent, for albeit wee enioy. peace, and by that meanes have the benefit of generall trade and had this peace at and by the Kings coming, yet the King had only the name of peace, for the whole charge of Irelande being at the death of Queene Elisabeth [*blank*] horse and [*blank*] Foote continued [*blank*] monethes then was it less[en]ed unto [*blank*] horse and [*blank*] foote and yet continued at [*blank*] horse and Foote:[3] Allso the charge of the Low countryes at the death of Queene Elisabeth was *per annum* [*blank*][4] and then drawen and continueth at [*blank*][5] *per annum.*

---

[1] Mary sacrificed certain revenues because of her loyalty to the old church. But generally speaking she was extremely economical. See F. C. Dietz, "English Government Finance, 1485–1558," *University of Illinois Studies in the Social Sciences*, IX, No. 3, 202–214.

[2] The official amount is in St. P. Dom. XIX, 45, as £735,280.

[3] See *Cal. St. P. Irish, 1601–1603,* 550; *1603–1606,* 90, 186, 200, 436. In Jan., 1603 there were 1,000 horse and 12,370 foot in Ireland. In March, 1606, 374 horse and 1,150 foot.

[4] See figures in F. C. Dietz, "The Exchequer in Elizabeth's Reign," *Smith College Studies in History,* VIII, 98–104. The last figure is £21,651 for 1602. See also tables in Scott, III, 520–527.

[5] Lansd. MSS 156, f. 396 (Treasury Papers of Sir Julius Caesar), states that James spent £16,145 3s. 4d. yearly to keep 1,150 men in the Cautionary Towns.

Yet is not the governement of the state in Queen Elisabeth's tyme to be blamed for that shee died in debt for it was by hir and hir counceill found necessary that shee should mainteine the Low countries which ought hir [*blank*].[1] Allso that shee assist the now French King on whose head shee maie well be saied to have set that crowne, and he ought hir [*blank*][2] at hir death. And lastlie the charge of Irelande in hir latter time:[3] And saied his Lordship having shewed the Kings state and necessity I will not discourse of the meane to releave and supplie it: but do leave it to your selves. Only I will promise as the King often hath saied and signified his mynde, that the first fruites of your benevolence be it whatsoever shalbe imploied for paiment of the Loanes:

15 Febr: 1605.

Warrein who served Mr. Skepweth with a subpena in the country 3 daies before the beginning of this cession to appeare in the starre chamber, was brought by the Serieant to the barre, and there kneeling at the barre confessed that he indeed did know Mr. Skepweth to be a member of this howse at such time as he served the said subpena on him but for his excuse protested that he then thought Mr. Skepweth would not have attended this cession which he partly believed by reason he had so herd and partly bycause the last cession. Mr. Skepweth being high sheriffe made that an occasion to staie in the country and insomuch as he continued sheriffe at the serving of the saied subpena and long since and the parliament being so nere at hand he thought that now he would likewise have forborne to attend in this howse: farder wheras Mr. Skepweth enformed this howse that Mr. Warrein did presente that suit against him this terme and enforced him to aunswere in the starre [chamber] and there also to aunswere interrogatories it appeared uppon examinacion that Mr. Warrein did not this terme f. 16. a] last past in anie sort prosecute that suit for which the subpena was served on Mr. Skepweth, but whereas there was a former

---

[1] £800,000 in 1598. The debt is given as £818,408 in 1605. Lansd. MSS 156, f. 396.

[2] Elizabeth loaned a total of £297,480 to the French King. *Cal. St. P. Dom. 1601–1603,* 304.

[3] See Dietz, "The Exchequer in Elizabeth's Reign," *Smith College Studies in History,* VIII, 96–104. See also Scott, III, 520–527.

suit brought in the same court by him against Skepweth: the said Mr. Skepweth and his attorny so called on the matter that he provoked Mr. Warrein to put in Interrogatories otherwise (according to the course of that court) he had ben dismissed and admitted to aunswere by attorney whereuppon he did put in Interrogatories wheron Mr. Skepweth was examined. All which premises dewly weighed, it was thought that Mr. Warrein was to be punished then the question was how and in what degrea he was to be punished, in the ende it was resolved that he shoulde remaine 3 daies with the Serieant of the howse, and so with an admonision to be dismissed: and theruppon Mr. Warrein was called to the barre and to him Mr. Speaker delivered the censure of this howse.

Then MR. HARE[1] reported to the House what had passed betweene the Lords and the Committees of this howse at the last conference wherin he did faithfullie relate what him selfe had spoken to the Lords and their Lordships' speaches omitting few woords either materiall or woorth repetition saving those of the Earl of Salisbury, to this effect viz. that the Lords did not expect anie to speake as the Tribunes of the people:

16 WAS SONDAY.

18 FEBR: 1605.

26 *Aprilis*[2] 1604 this howse exhibited a petition to the King's majestie wherunto was annexed a noate of divers particuler unlawfull oppressions by the Cartakers towards the people:

f. 16. b] The Committees for the priviledges of the howse have authoritie to examine all wrongs offered to the priviledges and to report the same to the howse, but not to send for anie man.

Sir John Herbert Knight his Majesties 2d. Secretary accompanied with divers others was sent to the Lords to lett their Lordships know that to morrow this howse would deliver them the Articles against purveiors and be ready to attende their Lordships in the cause: Her uppon their Lordships sent Mr. Serieant Crooke and Dr. Swale to signifie their readinesse to ioine with us in reforming those grevaunces: and that their Lordships do desier to have the Articles in the forenoone and to meete at 2 of the clocke

---

[1] See *C.J.* I, 269; *C.& T.* I, 60.

[2] *C.J.* I, 190 (note at bottom of page), would indicate that the petition was presented on April 27.

after dynner in the painted chamber which this howse liked of and accordinglie returned aunsweare.

In consideracion of the Articles against Purveiors it was by one moved that wee should go prepared to the Lords as well to aunsweare what might be obiected in defence of Purveiance as to obiect or complaine of Purveiors: and it was farder wished that among other obiections it should be thought how to aunswere this: viz:

In the statut of 18. E. 1.[1] there is savinge unto the King his right of auncient prises of wynes and other things: wher unto was aunswered that (Auncient prises) i: *recta prisa* viz. prisage.

An other obiection may be that in the statut of 28. H. 6.[2] of taking horses and carriags are theis woords viz. (savinge to the Kinge his prerogative of and to the premisses): which was thus aunswered The prerogative: i: the preemption: namely first to be served for his money:

19 Febr: 1605.

An act for toleracion of shootinge in gunnes by the Inhabitants dwellinge within five myles of the Sea Coastes for the better defence of their howses and country: *primo lecta:* .

An act for the trew makinge and searchinge of linnen cloathes 2do. *lecta* which was brought in by Mr. Fuller for London:

An act for the trew makinge of woollen cloathes 2do. *lecta:* commended by the Lord Chief Justice:

Unto the former Articles against Purveiors there was now added 4 more entituled Greavances suffered by the merchants of London thorowgh the purveiors:

f. 17. a]   20 Febr. 1605.

Heare one[3] of the speciall members appointed a committee to conferre with the Lords delivered the effect of that conference, Beginning first with relacion of the Earle of Salisburyes speach who[se] speach began with allusion to the woords used at the last

---

[1] A mistake for 28 Ed. I. c. 2. *Statutes of the Realm*, I, 138.

[2] *Statutes of the Realm*, II, 355.

[3] Sir Henry Montague. See *C.J.* I, 271–272. He is reporting a second conference on purveyors held on Feb. 19. The Lords were quite conciliatory. Dorset's speech is in Appendix A.

"Rien ne s'est resolu en Parlement. Le Roi a fort loué et remercié aux de la Chambre Inferirure et de leur soin a sa conservation et de leur

conference by one of the members of this howse (inuendo Mr. Hare) to this effect that their Lordships conceaved that somewhat spoken by some of them was miscarried by the other and speaking of that gentleman his carriage, his Lordship used theis woords *Modestus et iustus dolor linguam non dentes habet:* But he said no more bycause he wished it might be no more remembered, they knew the party whom this howse sent is honest and wise and cleered him of all saving of miscarriage. Touching the articles sent, of such as weare not newe, wee should aunsweare. Next spake the learned Earle[1] to the Lords Knights and Burgesses then present, that he hoped the matter [*blank*].

f. 17. b]   21 FEBR. 1605.

An act for revivinge of one branche of a statut made 23. H. 8.[2] for bringinge in of wynes in seasonable tymes with provision against false wynes. *primo lecta.*

Sir Rob[er]t Leigh was brought with his counceill[3] to the barre to aunswere his contempt in committing two of the servants of Sir Edwyne Sandys without baile *ut supra*, and bicause he alleaged that he had present witnesses which could depose farder and other matter for his excuse then was before delivered to the Committees therefore the howse directed that the same Committees shoulde againe go upp presentlie into the Committee chamber and examine such new matter: Sir Rob[er]t Leigh at his departure from the barre, veary simply and foolishly endeavored to excuse himselfe by saieing that if he had offended in anie thing it was for desier to be acquainted with Sir Edwyne Sandys, which he desiered having readde some of his booke:[4] whereat the howse greatly laughed: afterwards the Committees returned but by cause the tyme was

contribution accordeé. Si ne laisse il pas d'y avoir du mescontentement contre eux pour le refus qu'ilz ont faiet de plusieurs grand subsides, et d'ailheurs de leur part pour des paroles qu'ilz n'ont pas accoustumé d'ovir et qui ne conviennent gueres aux privileges et à l'authorite de leurs chambres. D'autre part, il n'y a pas trop d'accord en la Chambre des Seigneurs, mais non que cela puisse entr'eux venir à consequense." M. de la Fontaine to M. de Villeroy, Feb. 26/March 8, 1606. Paris Transcripts.

[1] The Earl of Northampton.

[2] 23 Hen. VIII. c. 7. *Statutes of the Realm*, III, 374. See p. 96 note.

[3] Mr. Finch. For case of privilege, see *C.J.* I, 270, 272–273.

[4] No doubt his *Europae Speculum* published in 1605 under the title *A Relation of the State of Religion.*

passed therefore the howse referred to heare their report or to give
direccion in the cause untell the next daie: and so the prisoner
departed.

An act for the better explanacion of an act made 34 and 35. H.
8.[1] concerninge ordinances made for Wales and establishinge the
authority of the Lord president and councell there 2do. *lecta* and
committed:[2]

At the first the howse cried away with it, but SIR HERBERT
CROFT[3] stoode up [and] in a veary long speache declared the importance of the bill, he shewed that the fower shires viz. Hereford
Gloucester Woorcester and Salop weare neaver in the marches:
Then he declared how by encrochment those shires weare drawen
in: and lastly how much they are hurt and oppressed with that
gouvernement: in which he shewed manie wrongs and oppression:
to the number of 100: and about all which he said himselfe and
certaine other gentlemen had putt under their hand and would
Justifie:

After him MR. HOSKYNS spake to second him: and among other
things he affirmed that they which labored to free those 4 shires
from that arbitrable or commissionary governement do not impeach the Kings prerogative, but quoth he they which will against
Law imprison the Kings subiects and not deliver them uppon a
Habeas Corpus they stand against the prerogative, for they will
not suffer the King to free the person of a subiect whome they have
uniustlie imprisoned. And with this argument the day was spent
and the bill Committed.

f. 18. a]   23 FEBR:[4]

The act for transferring of bonds made for assurance of lands
unto the assignees of the lands brought backe by the committees
with some alteracions which weare twice redde, and the bill uppon
the question of engrossing thrown out of the howse:

---

[1] *Statutes of the Realm*, III, 926.

[2] St. P. Dom. XIX, 33, is a copy of the act. Cott. MSS, Vitellius C I,
f. 142 contains arguments for and against the bill. Sir Richard Lewknor
wrote to Lord Zouche opposing the bill Jan. 20. Salisbury MSS.

[3] Cf. *C.J.* I, 272. "Many indignities uttered against that council
[of Wales]." *C. & T.* I, 61.

[4] The correct date is Saturday, 22 February.

Sir Ro[bert] Leigh was brought to the barre, to whome it was declared by the Speaker that the howse having herd him and Counceill and dewly considered the Report of the Committees to whome at the first the consideracion of the matter was referred, and who since by speciall direccion had examined such farder proofes as he alleaged he could produce for his cleering, have iudged him guiltie of endeavoring to enfrenge and breake the priviledges of the howse: howbeit out of their grace not out of Justice, the rather seeing his humilitie and somwhat in regard he had satisfied the partie greaved whereby it seemed his proceeding was rather of ignorance the[n] malice to the party or want. of respect to the howse, and seeing he had ben some tyme already under the Serieants custody are pleased to shewe him favor and to discharge him, he confessing his fault, Who aunsweared that him-selfe serveth the King according to his witt and understanding not to his will: which is good and dutifull and desierus to do right. And if quoth he I have offended this honorable howse I crave favor: hereuppon he was withdrawen: and then it grew to a question whether this condicionall acknowledgement weare sufficient, And it was remembred that the last cession, the Wardein of the Fleete for making his submission in the like woords viz. if I have offended etc. was sent to litle ease: So after some debate the question was thus made; As many as are satisfied with the Submission which Sir Ro[bert] Leigh hath made say yea: and then on the contrary: the voices in sound being somwhat indifferent, it was for avoiding devision of the howse agreed that the Knight should be called to the barre to declare whether his submission weare absolute or condicionell, if absolute then to be dismissed if otherwise then to be farder punished: and being so at the barre he acknowledged that such punishment as the howse should inflict on him was iust: and theruppon he was discharged:

It was agreed that by the order of the howse, After the question is agreed on and once asked it must be determined before any thinge else be begoon.

Sir Morice Berckley in a veary good speache moved[1] that before the howse did proceede to anie busines they shoulde cleere Mr. Hare whome they had used to the Lords in the cause of Purve-

---

[1] Cf. debate in *C.J.* I, 273.

iors, and that to be doon not only heare wheare he was neaver accused but to the Lords so as their Lordships may know that wee have cleered the gentleman, and that wee desier all reprehension at Conferences to be forborne, for quoth he if we meete uppon such disadvantage I could wish our conferences should not be so frequent as they have ben this cession:

Mr. RECORDER and some others moved that the howse should not send to the Lords in generall but mildly to use some such speach to the Lords' Committees at the next Conference (who also weare the Committees from whome this greavance grew) as shalbe thought meete.

Mr. MARTYN contra: For quoth he the Lords' Committees are not bounde to take notice nor to report [to] the other Lords our message in this behalfe.

Mr. FULLER with Mr. Recorder for this point: And farder wished that concerning our articles which the howse having formerly delivered the same to the Lords should now requier aunswere therof from their Lordships.

f. 18. b] Mr. HYDE wee ought to send this message that hath ben spoken of to the Lords' howse in generall, and that presently: The Lords ought not to taxe us nor wee them. The last cession the Lords sent one to us, who wronged us,[1] wee sent their Lordships woorde of it, their Lordships honorably examined it and punished the fault: and in like sort they ought to deale with us: Let us send to the Lords mildly to signifie to them where our greife is and to desier them if any thing from us do offend them they wilbe pleased to signifie it to us and not to censure us and that wee with all reverence will respect their Lordships as becometh us. At the last it was agreed that a selected committee of 10 or 12 persons[2] should

---

[1] This may possibly refer to a speech of the Bishop of London in a conference. *L.J.* II, 325, 332.

[2] The *C.J.* I, 273, names twelve members. The Speaker wrote Salisbury: "So uppon Saturday [Feb. 22] (my moste honored good Lord) in the heate of the howse it was resolved then instantlie to send unto your Lordships a message of Complaynt concerning the proceeding with Hare, which then I prevented under Cullor to move them to a Comittee, to advise of the manner thereof, where by the same in theire Cowld bloud is well caulmed, for uppon the reporte thereof to the howse this laste day monday [Feb. 24], they then grewe in hott resulucion to proceed with theire Bill [concerning purveyors]." St. P. Dom. XVIII, 115.

be chosen to meete this afternoone in the exchequer chamber and to consider of a forme of delivery of the pleasure of this howse touching the premisses and to declare the same to this howse on monday next in the morninge.

24 FEBR. 1605:[1]

An act for makinge the river of Aven passable to and from Evesham to the river of Severne with boates barges: etc:

An act for the more sure establishinge and assurance of trew religion: brought in by the Committees with amendements. The Matter most stoode on was for that the bill requiered that no alteracions should be of anie substanciall point of religion but by parliament with the advise and assent of the clergy in convocacion: Some misliked that the power of the parliament should depend on the Bishops and clergy: Others (and namely SIR EDWYNE SANDYS who brought in the bill) alleaged that every man ought to be advised withall and to direct in his owne profession:[2] and that the Papists would saie, not without shew, that wee professed only a statut religion:[3] Divers not of least noate wished that all that Clause, viz. (That no alteracion should be of any Substanciall poynt of Religion etc.) should be left owt of the bill for that the same did include or make shew of a doubt of alteracion which for divers reasons they thought not fit: to which mocion as I understoode the most did incline and direccion given accordingly.

MR. YELVERTON,[4] reported that the Committees thought fit that Mr. Hares iustificacion shoulde be delivered unto the same Lords' Committees that did reprehend him and not to the Lords in generall: Secondly that it should be doon at the next conference for the matter of Purveiors: Thirdly that the Lords should mildly be requested to forbeare from hence forwarde to taxe any member

---

[1] "The same day Sir John Fortescue appeared in the Parliament House." *C. & T.* I, 61.

[2] It was probably in the debates on this bill that Sir Robert Cotton made a speech (date uncertain) in which he showed by a list of precedents drawn from the history of the Roman Emperors, the Saxon Kings, and the English Parliament, that ecclesiastical laws should not be made by temporal men. The speech was "delivered to his Majesty after it was spoken in Parliament." Harl. MSS 6849, ff. 268–272v; 3142, ff. 64–67.

[3] The *C.J.* attributes these words to Yelverton.

[4] See the report and debate in *C.J.* I, 273.

whome this howse shoulde send or use unto them, and that if their Lordships shall finde anie fault with anie such messenger sent from this howse, that they woulde be pleased to send woord thereof hither that thereuppon this howse may examine it. Lastlie if their Lordships shall requier to know what reason wee taking the matter f. 19. a] on us all have to take their reprehension in evell parte, wee shall then aunswere them with silence, for wee are a counceill of state and therefore *quod scripsimus, scripsimus* but if they presse an aunsweare in reason from us, then that to every particuler which their Lordships shall stand on, an aunsweare to be given in mild-nesse. Sir Fra[ncis] Bacon thought fit that this course reported to be convenient by the Committees should be doon with this Pre-amble That wee do not do it by reason of expostulacion of things past but to avoide inconveniences to come: Also quoth he I would have reasons given of our doings: viz. That if reprehension shoulde be used it woulde hinder the service of this howse; next it will make the howse unwillinge to crave or admitt conference, which woulde be to the hinderance of the service of both howses: and this was by the howse admitted to be added to the opinion of the Committees:

25 Febr. 1605.

An act for better Security of owners and purchasers of lands and for preventinge of forgery periury and other secret and fraudulent conveyances. *primo lecta:* which being the first tyme redde manie cried (away with it) then Mr. Trever of the Inner Temple, being a follower of the Lord Admyrall,[1] spake in favor of the bill, only this farre that it might be voutsafed a second reading and to be considered of by a Committee: but the howse without farder question threw out the bill, Fearing least it would breade a new office which they thought some greate man aymed at:

Much debate[2] was whether the howse in the case of Purveiance, should proceed with the bill which had ben twise redde and com-mitted and now with some amendements was to be delivered in: or by way of Composicion: herin much argumente was used and tyme spent in the ende it was putt to the Question: this viz: Such as thinck it fit and convenient the bill to be proceeded in say yea: to which all say yea, and to the contrary question only

---

[1] Charles Howard, Earl of Nottingham.
[2] See *C.J.* I, 273–274.

Sir Lewes Lewckner saied no: then would not the howse go to any other question touching the composicion as some desiered, but it was requiered that the amendements should be readde but by cause Mr. Hare being demaunded by the Speaker whether the saide amendements weare long aunsweared yea therefore the tyme being spent the reading therof was deferred untell the next day:[1]

26 Febr.

The Speaker wrote unto the clerke being in the howse that he shoulde excuse him to the companie for that having taken pills over night which did not woorke as was expected he had not ben well all night, but woulde attend betweene 9 and 10: at which tyme he came accordingly: in the meane time the opinion of the howse and the ordinary speache was that he had taken a pill from the purveiors.

[1] The Speaker wrote to Salisbury on February 25: "This laste day monday [Feb. 24], they grewe in hott resulucion to proceed with theire Bill [about purveyors], but being by me remembred that the first motion of conference grewe from his gracious message to the howse, and secondlie from the honorable offer of you my Lord [to] the Comittees, I drewe them to a Comittee to advise what was fitt in theire next conference to your Lordships to be propounded, and till then the Bill to staie. Which the Comittees this day [Feb. 25] reporting what they had concluded of, the howse in the end were enflamed to call for theire proceeding in the Bill, and much pressed me also to make a question whether they would compounde or noe. To satisfie theire ymportunitie which I could not avoyd, I made the question whether they would proceed with the Bill, but tooke occasion to forbeare the second question concerning the Composition, for that I fownd as the state of the howse then stood, it would be reiected. They then would have pressed me to have made a question upon the engrosing of the Bill, which by some meanes I delayed to doe, not withoute the distaste of some as I understand. Which theire humor in putting it to the question to engrose the Bill noe doubte they will egerlie to-morrow pursue, and therefore all message or honorable offers made before wilbe to them distastefull (as I feare). Notwithstanding I will followe the direction I receaved, except otherwise I shalbe by your Lordship comaunded. We have this afternoone loste one of our seedemen of this sedicion and I heere within twoe dayes we shall loose another, of whome if we were delivered, I then doubte not the good successe of proceeding in this and other things of this nature, for experience teacheth me that twoe such fiery spirits will enflame more than manie discreete mynds will coole or temperate againe. Pardon me my good Lord I humblie beseach you in this my presumption to acquainte you with the estate of the howse as I conceave it, leaving the rest to your honorable wisdome." St. P. Dom. XVIII, 115.

f. 19. b] When the Speaker was sett, Sir Fra[ncis] Hastings delivered in a bill touching restoring of ministers,[1] And then the howse called for the bill against Purveiors whereuppon Mr. Hare declared what the Committees had putt out and what they had amended and so delivered the bill to the Clerke who redd the amendements twise.

Sir John Crooke one of his Majesties Serieants at Lawe and Sir Geo[rge] Coppin clerke of the Crowne in Chauncery came from the Lords whose message was in effect that their Lordships since the last conference touching the purveiors have expected a seconde meeting, concerning that busines and that now they are desiorous of a conference to consider what course may be taken not only to reforme abuses but to abolishe the veary name of purveiors: and how in lieu therof to yelde the King some amends in regard of his greate charge, and the Iudges to be called to be present to advise of a course for our securitie to enioy what shalbe thought fitt: this conference was interteined and the Iudges presence allowed and the next day after dinner in the painted chamber, the Conference appointed.

It was agreed that if anie woorde be to be added after a bill hath ben committed and brought in, the same must be doon by one of the Committees.

The bill prohibiting reseince of married men with their wives and children in cathedrall churches, Colleges etc. was brought into the howse engrossed: Where it is to be noated that thorough the body of the bill it was wrightten: (Oxōn and Cambridge) and on the outside the indorcement was (Cambridge and Oxō⁻) whereuppon it was much insisted whether University should be first named, for which purpose divers statuts weare produced in which Oxōn was first named and one wherein Cambridge was first mencioned: Mr. Camdines booke[2] was vouched Pro et Con: One viz. Sir Fra[ncis] Vane affirmed that the iunior Master of Arte of Cambridge had precedency before the senior Master of Oxōn being both of one yeere, who afterward declared the mystery of his meaning viz. for that the Act or Commencement in Cambridge is before that in Oxō⁻: An other viz. R[obert] B[owyer] alleaged

---

[1] Deprived of their churches by the strict Canons of 1604. See W. H. Frere, *The English Church in the Reigns of Elizabeth and James I*, 313–323.

[2] The *Britannia*.

that in Oxo   two Kings had found[ed] two severall Colleges whereas only one had found[ed] a college in Cambridge: Also that Oxōn
was dignified with a Cathedrall church and the See of a Bishop,
which Cambridge had not: afterwards it appeared that when the
bill was readde in the howse and when the Clerke delivered it to
his servant to be engrossed, the same was endorced Oxōn and Cambridge and that two ministers cambridge men being without by
him caused him to endorce it Cambridge and Oxōn: how beit it
was agreed to put it to the question, which being doon Oxōn prevailed[1] and the endorced was [to] be amended and made Oxōn
and Cambridge:

27 Febr:

The Counceill of Le Grice and of Cottrell weare herd at the
barre. Le Grice desired a bill to passe for sale of Cotteralls lands
goods and enquiery of debts dew to him and for disseisinge therof
and of all lands which Cotterall had since a day past for satisfaccion
f. 20. a] of a decrea in the Chauncery, wherby Cotterell was
ordered to pay 807£ to Le Grice, Counceill of both sides being herd
the howse putt over the cause without order to be given at this
time for that direccion was presently to be considered of and given
unto such as shold in the after noone be imploied to the Lords
touching the cause of purveiors. Which busines held all the morning:[2]

ULTIMO Febr: 1605:

An act for restoringe of deprived ministers *primo lecta:* brought
in by Sir Fra[ncis] Hastings:

An act for confirmacion of orders made by the Masters wardeins
and assistants of the company of Joyners Cealers and Carvers of
London *primo lecta:*

An act for the assurance of the office of Clerke of the treasury
and warrantes in the Kings bench unto Will[ia]m Davison Esquire
and Christopher Davison his Soon: *primo lecta:*

The reading and discussing of some few of the Articles for the
bill of Recusants spent all the morninge:[3]

---

[1] "By many voices." *C. & T.* I, 62.
[2] See short debate in *C.J.* I, 275.
[3] See *C.J.* I, 275–276.

1 Martii 1605.

Some moved that wee shoulde ioine with the Lords in appointing a committee to draw a bill wherein the articles conceaved by both houses touching recusants might be inserted: but after sondry mocions both wayes the rule of the howse was that wee shoulde not ioine with the Lords in appointing any committees *ut supra:* but that wee shoulde of our selves draw our bill: and their Lordships one other if they shall thincke fit and convenient. For it was affirmed to be contrary to the custome and usage of this howse to ioine in drawing anie bill but that every bill ought to be drawen and passed in one of the howses and sent to the other. Only it was saied that the last cession a committee[1] was appointed by both howses to draw a bill for the Union, which being the most extraordinary case that ever was ought to be no president to direct anie other:

The 2 Houses not to joyne in drawinge a bill

Sir Fra[ncis] Bacon reported the last conference[2] and declared that the Lords did conclude with a mocion [that] this howse would appoint Lawyers to consider, and prepare them selves to dispute the right of the King's Majestie to purveiance, viz. whether any other the[n] preemption, or whether anie thing in prise: and the Kings counceill not beinge of the howse to study the like, and the Iudges to be assistants and afterwards to proceede to the other questions of Assurance, Conveniency and Proporcion: the tyme to be on monday next, the place, the painted chamber. Divers in this howse did thincke that wee shoulde dispute the question of right uppon greate disadvantage, first for that our warning is veary short: and the matter requiereth greate study, and no doubt but their Lordships have had good advise. And perhaps they understand the opinion of the Iudges already, which saied one for my parte I had rather rely on when they give it setting in court then otherwise at conferences. In the ende it was concluded that f. 20. b] certein committees shall prepare them selves for the conference against monday next: then to meete with the Lords

---

[1] There was such a joint committee. This becomes evident, however, only by a study of the committee through several weeks. See *C.J.* I, 172-211; *L.J.* II, 290-308.

[2] Held on Feb. 27. See *C.J.* I, 276, for this report and the debate that followed. See also *Roger Wilbraham* (*Camden Misc.* X), 76.

and to argue the point of the Kings Right of prerogative to the matter of price in purveiance:

MONDAY 3 MARTII:

An act for prohibitinge residence of married men with their wyves and familyes in colleges, cathedrall churches, Halles etc. in the Universityes of Oxon and Cambridge:[1] Many favored this bill and divers spake against it to long to set downe in particuler but of that which was spoken this I observed viz. SIR JOHN BENNET Doctor of the Lawes made a long and learned speache against the bill: Touching the making of Lawes he proposed this Rule or guide that every Law maker should observe touchinge his Law

> *Ut Religioni congruat:*
> *Ut disciplinae conveniat:*
> *Ut saluti prospiciat:*

MR. HOSKYNS spake for the bill and his speache went uppon theis groundes:

> Virginity a virtue:
> Marriage not of necessity:

Voluntas donatoris observetur: and the founders would that the heads of their howses shoulde be single and unmaried:

R[OBERT] B[OWYER] from MR. HACKWELL and MR. HOSKYNS, and first all the reasons which Mr. Hackwell used for the bill was: Who knoweth not how the manners of younge men are corrupted and drawen from their studyes by the ordinary sight and conversacion with women: who knoweth not how covetous hedds of howses are to maintaine preferre and provide for their wyves and children: Who knoweth not how much women prevaile with their husbands to the overthrowe of learninge discipline yea and of the colleges: this argument said R[obert] B[owyer] is called in Oxon *peticio principii* it is a simple fallacy the opponant craveth a ground to be given him which he is not able to prove, and this is a bare yea a begging or a beggerly argument: it requiereth no aunswere but a simple denyall I thincke no man heare knoweth it to be as the question deserveth to be graunted: And whereas Mr. Hoskyns goeth uppon this ground *Voluntas donatoris* etc: Wee

---

[1] Lansd. MSS 487, ff. 28–29 is a copy either of this bill or of a similar one introduced in 1604.

are to know that the will of the founder either is direct that the head of his colledge shall not be married and in that case there needeth no act of parliament or ells it is implied which for the most parte is in theis woords *esto presbiter:* and a preist he coulde not be if he weare married so then if he be a preist or minister it suffiseth to satisfie the founders will, if you will enferre there fore he must be unmarried I must conclude *ergo* preist may not marrie and yet this ientleman saieth he is not popish:

MR. WISEMAN uppon occasion of a proviso offered, did affirme that he that will offer a Proviso to be added to a bill engrossed ought to bring and put it ingrossed in parchement.

f. 21. a] Mr. Speaker declared, There [were] 3 questions to every bill viz.

Whether it shalbe committed:

Whether it shalbe engrossed:

Whether it shall passe:

And therefore the proviso ought to have the same questions: and therefore to come in paper. But SIR EDW[ARD] MONTAGUE and others thought otherwise and that the proviso ought to come in like the bill in parchement and so said SIR JOHN BOYS and the reason is when a bill hath had his 3 readings it may not deferre it untell the proviso be prepared: The order of the howse was granted to be so but it was alleaged and agreed to be to late for that the howse had before given order the said proviso should be engrossed.

Md. that uppon the question of passing the bill against resiance of married men with their wyves etc. in colleges etc. the howse was devided[1] and by the greater voice the bill passed:

4 MARTII: 1605.

Md. it was saied that *tempore* H. 2.[2] no Law was reported for of those tymes it was saied *Ad Libitum Regis Sonuit Sententia Legis:*

5 MARTII: 1605.

Then the howse entered into dispute[3] whether a composicion for Purveiance should be yelded unto: and MR. FRA[NCIS] MORE

---

[1] The first division of the session. *C. & T.* I, 63.

[2] Richard II. *C.J.* I, 277. This point was made in a report of a conference with the Lords concerning purveyance.

[3] Cf. debate in *C.J.* I, 277–278.

for Composicion: he shewed that wee should purchase a thing valueable, and he only ment to speake to that point, for as touching the Assurance and the proporcion of Composicion he would not deale but would leave the Assurance to the opinion of the Judges and the proporcion to men of experience. But saied he if wee redeeme a matter valueable then is it a proofe of the conveniencie of Compounding which is the first of the three points proposed and considerable: touching which saied he I must breifely tell you that the King is to have a reasonable price, which reasonable price is not the trew valew as hath ben supposed nor to be rated at the highest although it be doon uppon oath for on the contrary parte wee see that though extents of lands be uppon oath f. 21. b] yet are they neaver to the veary valew: Likewise prising of goods uppon any extents or execucions are not to the veary valew though the same be on oath. Allso he that sueth livery of lands woorth 20£. *per Annum* sueth it as 40s. *per annum*, and albeit uppon every licence of Alienacion or pardon the King be to have a yeeres profit, yet that yeeres profitt is rated under the veary valew and as well as in theis cases the King doth departe with his right under the valew so is he to purveiance under the valew albeit in all theis cases the veary valew is appointed to be paied:

Sir Hen[ry] Poole against the composicion but no great matter in his speach.

Sir Edw[ard] Grevill for composicion: but no great reason:

Mr. Gawyn against composicion with good conceipts him selfe being a plaine man:

Mr. Fuller against composicion as yet for saied he I was for composicion but I am now of an other mynde for I lately herd the cheife not in place only but in iudgement[1] say that the statuts for Purveiors doe not bind the King, and it is not my opinion nor any one of yours but the iudgement is theirs in whose mouthes Judgement is putt. Therefore untell wee may be satisfied that wee may have assurance and that the iudges do directly affirme wee may have security lett us not talke of Composicion. Againe saied he if greavances may be removed the King may have 60000£. yeerely which now others take, wherefore untell wee have meete on thurs-

---

[1] Probably Sir John Popham, Chief Justice of the King's Bench, whose knowledge and judgement were highly esteemed.

day touching greavances, and be satisfied of security let the speach of composicion rest:

SIR RO[BERT] HITCHAM was for composicion and used a long senselesse declaracion:

MR. HOSKYNS contra: *Inter alia* to prove the King had no such valuable right in purveiance as might be woorth much he disproved that which the Lord Archbishop did speake att the last conference, uppon this text *Hoc est ius regis:* for quoth he in the booke of Samuell[1] from whence this text is drawen God spake of an evell King whom he would sett over the people who should oppresse them as there appeareth, but quoth he in the 17 of Deutronomy[2] wheare a good King is described there is not such power saied to be in the King as that he could take the goods of the subiects: He concluded merily: viz. that if wee proceeded in a composicion he feared wee should do like unthrifts who begin with a Rent charge, then proceede to a Mortgage, and in conclusion departe with the lande itselfe:

6: MARTII: 1605.

An act for the sale of certein lands of Sir Edw[ard] Downes Esquire for paiment of his debts, brought in by the Committees with amendements.

An act for reformacion of certain abuses and disorders in the court of Marshalsey and in the officers and ministers of the same: *primo lecta:*

An act for the assurance of certaine lands of Sir John Skynners unto Sir W[illiam] Smyth and Sir Michael Hixt knights, redde ingrossed and passed:

An act for reedifieinge of a bridge over the river of Severne neere Upton uppon Severne, red ingrossed and passed:

An act for confirmacion of leases and estates made by the Right Honorable Rob[er]t Lord Spencer his father deceased, and Mother now lyvinge, red ingrossed and passed:

f. 22. a] When a bill is once passed, the howse cannot amende anie thinge in it:

Then the howse fell into the question, whether any composicion shalbe agreed unto, in lieu of purveiance.

---

[1] I Sam. 8:11.
[2] Verses 16–20.

Mr. Hare[1] spake first and was against Composicion but thought fit that in liew of purveiance some other requitall might be offered to his Majestie.

Sir Tho[mas] Ridgeway for Composicion *totis viribus:* but not with much reason.

Sir Will[ia]m Morrice against composicion in a long discourse to litle effect.

Mr. Bond against composicion but moved that in the graunt of Subsidyes wee should encrease our guift: viz. to give 3 Subsidyes and 6 Fifteenes.

Sir Maurice Barkley:[2] against composicion for wee may as lawfully though not so possibly be drawen to compounde for our lives and lands as for the Matter of purveiance: allso the prerogative cannot nor ought not to be bought or compounded for: neither anie encrease of subsidy for when that money shalbe spent the Kings wants will remaine: I wish such course may be taken for supply of the Kings occasions as may serve for perpetuity without charge to the people, whereunto I shall yeld most willingly if anie such way may be devised:

Mr. Willson for composicion, and the same to be temporall and to continue only for a tyme, and with condicion:

Mr. Dyet[3] contra composicion: in a long learned speach: and *inter alia* he aunswered some things spoken by Mr. Fra[ncis]

---

[1] Cf. the debate in *C.J.* I, 278–279.

"Mr. Hare against the composition, he would never hear the name of it more. That if we return without affecting our will the country's griefs will be doubled and the purveyors' abuses ten times trebled. Instead of composition he would give the King a donation.

"Sir Tho. Ridgeway; not to spurn with our feet at the ball which was cast amongst us by your Lo[rdships] at our last conference.

"Sir Willm. Maurice; to give the King 4 subsidies and 6 fifteenths." Proceedings in Parliament, March 6, 1606. Salisbury MSS.

[2] "Sir Maurice Berkly to let the bill [for purveyors] have his course." Salisbury MSS.

[3] "Mr. Diet ript up again the point of prerogative saying that in buying and matter of that kind it was nothing but preemption, which word though we found not in the law yet the substance was there.

"Sir William Stroude to make the question either for another conference with the lords, or whether we shall yield to a composition or no." Salisbury MSS.

More the daie before concerning primer seissin and licences of alienacion *et huius[mo]di:*

MR. LAWRENCE HYDE[1] contra composicion or increase of Subsidy, for to encrease the subsidyes weare to yeld the thancks to the Lords which our selves have receaved from the Kings Majestie greate favor: he perswaded to proceede in our bill: for saied he if wee do our best though wee prevaile not yet wee are excused, and quoth he if you shall do otherwise and let it sleepe wee should as it weare kill our selves and *felo de se* is the woorst of all others or wee should kill our owne child which weare monstrous: And by following our bill wee shall offer no wounde to the Kings honor for if it be thought good that it passe not as a lawe the Lords will quashe it and so kepe the wounde from the King: I wish the King should be aided in an other sort viz. such able men as have lent on privie seales let them yeld up their privie seales and quitt their debt and others also which are sufficient and have not lent let them give proporcionably to such of their abilitie as have lent: furder I coulde wish that a statut of Resumption weare made to resume where his Majestie without speciall service or desert hath uppon importunity given anie thing: and to whom his Highnes would not give if it weare againe to be doon, or for my owne parte I shalbe willing to yeld to anie other good course to releive the Kings wants but not by composicion nor by encrease of subsidy: for that I thincke if they weare heare for whome wee come they would not do it:

MR. MARTYN[2] neither pro nor contra: but advised that wee

---

[1] "Mr. Hide, that he heard not yet reason enough to make him consent to composition though we could have security. To have the bill go on. For the King's relief subsidy already granted but not to be augmented; releasing of the King's debt on privy seals; resumption of gifts given to unworthy persons." *Ibid.*

[2] "Mr. Martin, that the composition was reprieved yesterday, strangled now, and he would not give it new life. Moved that we might hear the Judges before the Lords, and that if prerogative could be proved and security could be made he saw no reason not to yield to composition." Salisbury MSS.

"Mr. Marten speche after Mr. Hids repeating his division wich was 5 part. 1. wither composition thought uppon securyty. 2. wither by increasing of our gift to the King we should not loss the glory of our first wiche was merly out of our owne motion and now may by an increas seem to be wrought from us. 3. wither to crose the bill and proceed to an other shoulde not growe to the question: but holde correspondency with the Lords before wee conclude.

SIR JOHN FORTESCUE, delivered a speach touching purveiors but for that he spake with a low voice I coulde not heare him: he spoke also concerning the Kings estate and therin *inter alia:* he saied that the King at his first coming to the crowne did pardon fowre score thousand pounds forfeited unto him for want of licence of alienacion and for licences:

f. 22. b]   7 MARTII 1605.

The bill against clerks fees brought in by MR. BROCKE one of the committees who reported that the Committees thought good it should sleepe for divers imperfeccions and that two of the Committees weare entreated to drawe a new bill such as might be more fit, This was put the question and so slept by order of the howse:

The bill exhibited by Mr. Ognall against Mr. Nicholson was brought in by one[1] of the committees and by order of the howse after report made by him that brought in, it was laied to sleepe.

An act for revivinge of one branch of a statute made 23. H. 8. for bringinge in of wyne in seasonable tymes with provision against falsifieinge of wines 2do. *lecta:* It was moved that all *non obstantes*

course wiche wer not fitt although the lords have protested to stop it. Better lett them do it then we to kile our own child or in our own sight. 4. was to move for supply of the kinge That the privy sealls lent might be forgiven and thos that have not lent to lent in resonable proportion. 5. was to have an act of resumption to resume suche lands and anuites and pencions as the king hathe geven to unworthy person. Mr. Marten begun with the last and forgave the king all the detts he ought him and did regrant all the lands and pencions he had of the kings gift and forgave all the good and bad woods he had bestowed uppon him as most willing to begine the score anew. And wyshed that other men would doe the lyk wiche som murmuring against he sayd I cry you mercy I will not persuinge so for then I should do the king honor wrong who hath providet for repayment of the loanes. Then sayd he would speek in ernest for yf ther may be securyty I never hard as yett any one against the Question and therfor the Gentleman that spake last hathe much changed the statt of the Question. The lords moved wither we would treat by lawe of Justice of affection. Now if ther be no security ther needeth no disput and the lords ar nether suche Sirens nor we such ill mariners that we need fear to be drawen out. Therfor wisheth a conference agayn." Harl. MSS 6850, f. 57. The hand is that of Sir Robert Harley.

[1] Sir Edward Greville. *C.J.* I, 279.

and other dispensacions or licence contrary to the purvey[?] of this act shalbe voide and this mocion well liked:

Then the howse fell into the question whether wee should compound for taking away purveiors and purveiance:[1] and first

Sir Fra[ncis] Bacon in a long well framed speach perswaded composicion: the Course of whose argument was first to aunsweare some obiections viz:

1. It is obiected that hereby wee shall bring a perpetuall taxe on the Realme. To which it is aunswered, that it is not desiered it should be perpetuall nor other then a probation for a tyme so as Doomes day (herin he glaunced at Mr. Hoskyns who two dayes before had used that woorde) is not to be expected before the Inconvenience hereof be founde, except the next parliament be saied to be the day of doome, if for anie inconvenience it take away and censure this composicion: if it weare perpetuall, I must put you in mynde that your selves have heretofore offered to compounde in perpetuity with a continuall charge for wardes[2] etc.

2. [*blank.*]

3. [*blank.*]

4. It standeth not with the Kings honor to departe with anie parte of his prerogative. This is trew where anie parte of his prerogative is evicted but not when he doth therof dismisse him selfe:

5. It is impossible for the Kinge to dismisse himselfe of any parte of his prerogative. I aunswere it is impossible where the thing is essentiall and inseparable as to iudge or do Iustice, but for the King to breake up his howse or the like is not impossible, for this being doon he neaverthelesse remaineth a King as before:

6. Tonnage and Pondage was given at the first for Wastage, now continued of right so will this be in tyme a right and the consideracion faile. I say Tonnage and Pondage did not begin *ut supra:* but hath ben ever in the King by Proscription.

7. Prisage and Butlerage cannot be departed with all *ergo:* f. 23. a] 8. Composicion already made is found heavy albeit voluntary.

As some say that the countryes where they serve do finde it

---

[1] Cf. the debate in *C.J.* I, 279–280. See also *Roger Wilbraham (Camden Misc.* X), 76–78.

[2] In 1604 for the abolition of the Court of Wards.

heavy so I heare some others say that the place where they serve do find it easy and do desier it.

9. To compounde for abolishinge purveiors and purveiance is to buy Justice: *ergo:*

I say it is not a buyeing of Justice but agreeing or buying if you will of Interest of ease of quiet for say the King have nothing but as some call it preemption and power to buy and take carrages for the veary valew against the owners will (wherof is no doubt) yet may this be doon at such tymes and in such place as may be exceeding inconvenient:

Nota: a man might have replied on Sir Fra[ncis] Bacon, viz. that such takeing is against lawe which appointeth purveing to be in convenable sorte and easy, without villany: And saied Sir Fra[ncis] Bacon it may be compared to a way over my ground which is litle woorth to be bought by mee if it weare neaver used but orderly, but for that it cannot nor is not so used, I would give more for it then it is woorth:

10. 36 Lawes against Purveiors have not bounde *ergo* one more though wee compound will not helpe:

SIR RICH[ARD] SPENCER was against composicion for that no security can be given from the King. For as saied he as love is only betweene equalls in some degrea or measure so contracts and if such a contract be broken on the Kings side there is no remedy [but] to sue by peticion. And if a law passe on that behalfe no man can forbid the King to dispence with it.[1] In conclusion he perswaded some course to be taken to replenish the Kings treasure:

SIR GEORGE MORE offered and stoode up to speake who the day before had spoken much for composicion: hereuppon grew a question viz. Whether a Man that had spoken one day may another day speake to the same matter:

To this SIR MAURICE BERKLEY vouched 2 presidents[2] the last cession of this parliament the one in the case of Sir Fra[ncis] Goodwyn, the other in the case of free trade: Then it was saied by divers and Mr. Speaker seemed to encline to it viz. that to a bill a man can speake but once and not againe in anie other day: but

---

[1] "Fit to desist from this Course, and proceed with a Bill." *C.J.* I, 280.

[2] The editor cannot locate these precedents.

to a proposition a man maie speake once every day so long as the dispute continueth unlesse in case where the howse perceaving the matter likely to prove long doth give order that no man shall speake more then once: The reason was yelded by one to be for that a bill sheweth all that is in question so as every man at the first is entendeth to speake all he knoweth to it but proposicions yeld new matter as occasions requier: In conclusion the Clerke was ordered to seeke up the presidents against the morrow.

Sir Will[ia]m Paddy spoke against composicion: And *inter alia*, If wee shall compounde for removinge this greavance, it will be occasion to draw us to compounde for all other greavaunces: he councelled that wee should proceede with our bill, he saied, it much greaved him to heare it spoken that the King hath Neede, yet because he maie have neede hereafter Lett us provide to furnish his treasure before hand, and albeit I will not take uppon mee f. 23. b] to direct the course neither would I wish the howse to appoint it, but let us move the Lords whether they will go hand in hand with us and according to every mans severall degrea place and office to give freely to his Majestie and in the meane tyme to proceede in our bill and not to resolve on composicion nor the contrary:

Mr. Wynche pro composicion if wee maie have good securitie:

Mr. Secretary Herbert, As the King tooke your kind and dutifull offer of gratuity graciously so you having since understoode his necessities if now you shall augment your guift to satisfie his occasions I doubt not but he will yeld you such redresse for your greavances as you shall hold your selves bound unto him, and well satisfied in that you seeke:

Mr. James *inter alia* if wee compounde for the avoiding of purveiance and purveiors, wee shall binde our posteritie, and when our greavances shall notwithstandinge continue, if we be greaved for breach, and that we are notwithstanding trobled with purveiors wee shall have but a story of the Romanes and the Sabines, and for south wee have tied the King to condicions which he cannot keepe and so shall wee be urged to new composicion:

Saturday 8. Martii 1605.

The bill for sale of certein lands of Sir Edw[ard] Downes for paiment of his debts, which formerly had ben committed, was

brought in by one of the said committees who declared that the
committees had considered of the bill and allowed therof with a
proviso or rather an addicion without which the bill was insensible
and that the said proviso or addicion was in a severall paper fixed
to the bill and is lost: The bill was put to the question for engrossing. Sir John Higham moved that if it stande with the order of
the howse the bill may be recommitted, but it was agreed negatively, and ordered that the bill shalbe new wrightten and the
same with the addicion twise redde in one day:

Where a bill is exhibited of grace and not of right, it ought to
conclude And he shall dayly pray for your highnes, this opinion
was given in a bill exhibited for naturalizinge Danyell Godfrey:

This morning Mr. Speaker attende[d] the Kings Majestie uppon
his highnes pleasure signified in that behalfe: so as it was past
nyne of the clocke when he came to the howse: At his coming
(which was long after prayers) he declared the Cause of his staie:
he then shewed[1] that the King was acquainted both with the mat-

---

[1] Harl. MSS 6846, ff. 197–197*v*, contains this message and a speech
of Sandys in reply. The manuscript is in the hand of Sir Robert Harley.
"The kings speche. 3. parts: Matter of Form: 2 and .3. matter of substance. Forms whither a member of the howse may speak twise in one
cause the same day. The king desirethe that all Questions may be removed
concerning him. And hathe no purpose to break any privilege of the howse
in his cause.

"2. Matter ether of 1 Composition or 2 of releiving the kings wants.
Concerning the first it [*in* in MS] proceded from his Maiestyes own [*one*
in MS] motion first and that for .2. causes. 1. Intollerable charges by
purveors: 2. Agrevance of the Subiect. His motion was to prevent the
one and to ease the other therfore thought fitt to root them out protesting
he had no meaning ether to greve his subiect or benifit himself. His
Maiestie in conference withe the lords proposed .3. things. 1. Right.
2. Security. 3. Conveniency. For the 1 and 2 he desired resolution of the
Jugges. For the third if it be inconvenient he desireth ther be no more
proceeding in it since he never intended it but to the good of the subiects.
For Purveors he hathe commanded me to say, that he hath had ever a
great care to prevent ther bad courses and hath had a care to punishe the
offenders Not afore the Grenecloth but at the Starchamber. And the[y]
shall either be left to law or if left to him he will tak suche order as the
Jugges shall thinke fitt and that afore the next parlament that ther shalbe
no caus to complaine. And this is his gracious message. For the .3. his
Maiesty received your exceding love to him without motion for matter
of relief to supply the wants of his coffers withe greater ioy then any thinge

ter and manner of the busines now in hande among us, and first for the manner or forme, that he understoode the question lately moved and depending, viz. Whether a member of this howse having spoken one day in a matter maie afterwarde on an other daie speake to the same.[1] Touching the matter of substance consisting of the dispute both heare and with the Lords concerning Purveiance. And this the Kings Majestie saieth grew originally from him selfe and was occasioned from his highnes desier to reform the abuse of purveiors and to reliefe the greavances of his people endured by theis meanes: and which he conceaved could no way be so well remedied as by rooting out of Purveiors, and this he entended for the subiects good not for his owne gaine. Three things his Majestie thinketh herin fit to be considered, viz.

1. His owne right.
2. Security of his subiects.
3. Conveniency:

f. 24. a] If question be of this right he wisheth the same may be decided by the Judges: and likewise touching securitie. But if it be thought inconvenient then his Majestie desiereth it maie proceede no farder. For the matter of Purveiors his Majestie hath as greate care to redresse the harmes of his people as for anie good to himselfe: And he saieth that he will hereafter leave the reformacion to the Justice of the Lawe: or if complaint be made to himselfe he will take order for reformacion by Lawe:[2] Farther the Kings Majestie taketh notice of your forwardnes to releife his waunts and accepteth it as a firme token of your loves. And albeit it be inconvenient for a Prince to open his wauntes yet being assured of your Loves he hath opened him selfe, and he will propose no course, but leave it to your Loves and wisedome:

since his reigne. His Maiesty did then require that ther myght be a conference with the Lords about matters of Purveors and from them to receave then the statt of his Needs wich althoughe he thoughte it unfitt in regard of forayn Ears yett he hathe revealed the secrett of his statt. Nott meaning to increse his coffers but releav his wants as being desirous to leav him self to your love he will propound nothing but restethe uppon whatt you shall thinke fitt." Cf. *C.J.* I, 280.

[1] Sir George More, who had wished to speak again, was a supporter of the Crown.

[2] Rather than leave the matter to the Court of the Green Cloth or to the Star Chamber. *C.J.* I, 280.

Heruppon the howse fell into the former question whether Composicion or not:

SIR EDWYN SANDYS[1] spake against Composicion and in his speach was veary long, yea above an hower and half: wherein he used manie arguments *inter alia:* viz:

1. Wee cannot give a supply or satisfaccion to the Kinge aunswerable to the thinge.

2. If 36 Lawes hath not helped us, one more will not ease or availe us, or at the least not [our] successors.

3. It may be dangerous to compounde, First in president for if wee should compound for it accordinge to the woorth that would be

---

[1] "Sir Edwin Sands. You have mad a right ioyfull report of a most gracious message from the king. We may be glad of suche a princ as sendethe suche reports. I pray god as good success in reports to him. Means of easing the Country and suppliing his Maiesty the one cravethe duty to our Country the other to the king. He layethe perticuler grounds comparatively of both and desirethe to mix them with some other formerly spoken. He hathe bin a hearer and no speaker. And offerethe his Witt to the tresure of ther councell. It is [*it* in MS] well to fly from extremity. Extremity of Flatery to the princ popularity to the statt for the[y] that ar so to the princes desires have no assurance and the other to repose in popularity is dangerous and of the two I hold the latter the greater. What Flatery dothe gett the[y] know, what it hathe gotten storyes do tell, what it should gett Soloman sayethe, the[y] spread a nett for ther owne feett. Popularity is wone with a trifell and lost in an instant. Great men can only be populers for from hence we returne to our privat. For my popularity I protest I come hether though withe a weake understanding yett with a tarfull hart. For thos Consultations that tend not to the good of bothe ar good for nether the head and body. The report of the lords is grevous (as being a desease of so hard cuer the king great debt and that his *exitus* dothe of necescyty exced his *introitus*). Nott out of popularity but out of thos words fear god and honor the king: His entranc hath brought us many blessings peac and tranquility. But divine wisdom hathe layd worwood uppon our peac on sending to peac a plage that hathe wasted more then an hundred years of war. For herby the poer man cannot vent his corne nor the grasiur his cattell. More rents behind then formerly. Gentell men before hand not .3. in a shire. 30. behind. I speak not to hinder liberallity because speches have gone all one way. But to lay thes in a contrary ballance. Now to purveors from his Maiestyes leave to give leave to confere. Of this I may make thre heads: 1. wither a Bill; 2 wither courses from thelords. 3 a New device or proiect. In the first is concerned the wisdom of the house. In the next our duty to the King in the last our care to the Country." Harl. MSS 6846, ff. 197–197*v*. Cf. *C.J.* I, 280–281.

litle, and not sufficient to serve the Kings occasions: If we should compound for the incomberance and oppression we might by the same reason also be drawen to compounde for removing anie other greavance. Allso it maie be dangerous in that it will make all the Lande tributary: And it is not like the case of composicion which was desiered for wardships, for it should only have ben imposed on Lands holden: The third danger of composicion is, for that it wilbe like a rent charge, for which distresse may be taken for the King on all the parties lands.

Touching our bill against Purveiors I thincke wee ought not to let it sleepe for as well and by the like course uppon like message anie other bill which wee shall have heare maie be kept from his Majesties heares: Againe it was a fault the last cession that in our owne default this bill slept wherin wee did not do our dutyes: therefore I would have our bill made ready, but not in hast to be sent up, for I doubt not but before the parliament breake upp wee shall give his Majestie satisfaccion.

There hath ben fowre proiects to supplie the Kings occasions and to give him satisfaccion: I will adde a fift: And first to diminish his howse to maintaine his demeanes, And if his *Introitus* be lesse then his ordinary *Exitus* I could wish that whereas divers woorthy personages have undertaken the drayning of the Fennes about the Isle of Ely and those parts at their charge, for which they are to have a greate share of the Lands which shalbe recovered[1] I could wish this woorke weare doon by the commen charge of the Realme and the King to have the benefit which wilbe woorth more then forty thowsand pounds *per annum:*[2] The obiections are:

---

[1] See *Cal. St. P. Dom. 1603-1610*, 290.

[2] This proposal was renewed in May at which time the agreement was to be that the King would give up purveyance when his income from this source amounted to £30,000 per annum. St. P. Dom. XXI, 13, contains the project and the names of eleven men who backed it. The scheme came to nothing. It was, however, taken seriously. Sir Thomas Lake, the King's secretary, wrote to Salisbury: "With your packet, there came a letter directed on the outside by Sir Anthony Ashley, but the letter within was from Mr. Speaker to his Majesty, which his Highness commanded me to send back to you, and made but light reckoning of it. But I thought it not amiss to let you know that he read it so hastily as I doubt whether he did receive the particularities into his mind: He said you might speak with him of it at his return, and so went to his horse. It is about the

first whether feisible: 2. Not presently to be doon: 3. Iniurious to the undertakers: 4. Greavous to the people. First it is feasible for the ground lieth higher [than] the sea and hath his easie currant thether: 2. In seaven yeeres no doubt but it wilbe performed and for the present wee may devise some waye to supply the Kings occasions which I leave to others: 3. I doubt not of the cheife undertakers [those] with whome I have spoken are willing to receave their money disbursed and to yeld the advantage to the King. 4. It will be more acceptable to the people that the King receave the profit then any other:

It was agreed that Sir George More should speake, though he had spoken the day before.

f. 24. b]   10 Martii 1605.

Mr. Speaker declared to the howse that he was yesterday with his Majestie in the afternoone about fowre of the Clocke: and that his Majestie requiered an aunsweare of the message which before I had delivered unto the howse from his highnes: I shewed unto his Majestie your thanckfull acceptance, then his Majestie enquiered what use made of it: I aunsweared that the howse before the message had then spent three daies in discussing the matter and uppon the message had proceeded therin, but not resolved anie thing: Then his Majestie desiered expedicion and what consideracion you should thincke good, And if you shall doubt of the securitie in this case, his Majestie will referre you for satisfaccion in that behalfe unto the opinion of the Judges, howbeit if that point shalbe cleered, yet if it shall be held inconvenient his Majestie is well pleased that you forbeare to compounde:[1] Then

renewing of the offer for draining the fens for his Majesty's use, wherein I think the Speaker would not have written to his Majesty but with your privity." Newmarket, May 8. Salisbury MSS.

[1] The Speaker continued: "His Majesty moved principally out of two considerations: first if you should yield to the composition upon the conditional offer to be safe from any future burden arising from the abuse of purveyance, all the time that is spent in it would prove lost time if in that case should appear impossibility to make you such an assurance as should not extinguish one as long as the other continueth; secondly, because so many abroad are possessed with that conceit, besides those that speak in a Parliament and have dispute of the doubt and danger thereof all this while, as it may be conceived until it be cleared that his

touching the proposicion for supplieing the Kings wantes I aunsweared his highnes that in the howse had ben manie and divers
proiects but none as yet resolved on: Now quoth Mr. Speaker for
that the tyme is somewhat spent I would desier to understand your
pleasure whether you will now proceede in theis businesses at this
tyme or referre it untell to morrow: whereuppon the generall
clamor being to morrow; Mr. Speaker desiered them to meete in
the same place by eight of the clocke in the morninge: and so it
was agreed:

11 Martii 1605.

An act for the better preservacion of his Majesties Subjects in
their dew obedience. *primo lecta.*

This bill is one of the bills in to which the matter touching
Recusants was contrived: and in this bill are contained 3 principall
matters or pointes viz. 1. That such person as shall reforme himselfe shall receave the Communion once within the yeare next
after such reformacion: 2: the oath which is to be taken by persons
compellable by that law to take the same: 3. The Kings elecion
to take 20£ *per mensem* or 2 partes of such recusants lands.

When a bill cometh from the Lords and hath ben twise redde if
the howse do amende anie thing it must be putt to the question
whether it shalbe red a third tyme and sent upp to the Lords with
the Amendements in paper annexed, and so ordered in a bill for
Corpus Christi colledge in Oxon.

f. 25. a] The matter of compounding for this matter of purveiance
spent all this daie[1] and first Mr. Bond moved 4 things to be considered viz:

Majesty did not forethink himself of that point in any sort when he
propounded the motion because his eye was only upon his own profit and
meant to leave the rest to adventure if the cares and doubts had not
moved from themselves." Salisbury MSS.

Salisbury wrote the real policy of the Government in a letter to the
Earl of Mar. March 9, 1606. "We had two whole Subsidies given us but
there is such a heate, because his Majesty will not put downe Purveyors
and Purveyance, by which he should loose 50,000£ a yeare, as we are now
onely seeking to temper that particular grievance by making a law to
punishe the abuse, but in no case to put downe the use; and if it be possible
to gett somewhat more then two Subsidies, whereof if we had made a good
dispatche, then have on to our Union." St. P. Dom. XIX, 27.

[1] Cf. *C.J.* I, 282–283.

1. Whether the composicion shall sleepe.
2. Whether we shall signifie to the Lords that the composicion doth sleepe.
3. Whether we shall proceede with the bill of purveiors now in the howse or frame a newe:[1]
4. Whether we shall appoint committees to treate of this matter of subsidy, and him selfe did wish that whereas wee have with all alacritie given 2 subsidyes and 4 fifteenes now for as much as the Kings occasions do requier more, and for that fifteenes do fall on the poorer Sort he wished wee might graunt 2 subsidies more:

Sir Ja[mes] Perrot concluded his speech with desier that the course for drayning the marshes in and neere the Isle of Ely might be holden, and the same given to the King according to the tenor of Sir Edwyne Sandys his mocion the last day:

Mr. Middleton of the [*word illegible*] howse shewed the inconvenience of compounding by the experience in London:

Sir Jo[hn] Boys spake for the composicion, whose speech was grounded uppon three points viz:

$$\left.\begin{array}{l} \text{Security} \\ \text{Conveniency} \\ \text{proporcion} \end{array}\right\} \text{ of composicion.}$$

As touching securitie he thought veary good might be made, and herin he observed that divers thinges belonginge to the crowne the King cannot grant, as to pardon felony, to take my Lande to build castles or forts on etc. but sondry other prerogatives the King may grant and departe with all, as a warde before it fall may be granted by his Majestie. The King hath Justice, by which wee may pray removing the authoritie of the Greenecloth in the case of Purveiance, for the Greenecloth is no court of Justice, and that being removed wee shall do well enough with purveiors by using our accions when they take against Lawe: or do not pay ready money: The King may graunt to any man yea to a whole county to be free of Purveiance, and such priviledge or immunity Kent had uppon the first winninge of Calaice and the same had continued if Callaice had not ben lost: And there is no doubt but all charters of immunity had remayned good if the statut of 27. H. 8.[2] had not

---

[1] "The Country expects, we should proceed by Bill." *C.J.* I, 282.
[2] *Statutes of the Realm*, III, 556.

ben made wherby purveiance is given in places exempt as well as in others: he wished that if uppon conference with the Lords assurance sufficient shalbe devised by the Judges and the proporcion sett downe by the Lords may be easie: that then wee should proceede but not so as if the King had anie right to take under the valew or without ready money:

MR. RECORDER OF LONDON, declared that the charter of London was granted 21 E 3[1] and that the cittie doth enioy the same, except it be in cases where certaine companies have voluntarily yelded to composicion: therefore their not enioyeing their charter to be no argument or motive to keepe us backe from compounding:

MR. YELVERTON: howsoever the securitie be, howsoever the proporcion be easie, it is inconvenient to compounde: For this composicion must be chargeable and lye either on the Lands, the person, or the goods: Uppon the Lands it cannot before a generall survey and I must tell you it is the develles walke to treade over England and Wales, and full it is of danger to have it knowen what land the realme containeth: and how much every man hath in possession: againe you must in this case erect new offices and officers for the collecting of this money so rated on the landes, and new fees appointed to the officers of the Eschequer for doing their duityes in enterances, giving Tallyes *et huius*[mo]*di:* Also for this duity the Kings officers may distreine in all a mans lands and in every or anie acre for the whole due by the partie, and no replevyn lieth, so as hereby the Fermers are or may be undoon: If you should laie this composicion on the goods, then do you give a great authoritie to Justices of peace who no doubt will spare them selves: Lastlie if you impose it on the persons of men then will it be necessary to build new prisons for the old already knowen will not suffice: But no doubt the Kings counceill will advise it to be imposed on the lands being the best for the King, though inconvenient and mischievous as hath ben saied. And I would not have it f. 25. b] a probationer for then after that tyme the Purveiors having ben restrained wilbe woorse then ever before: To conclude he wished the composicion should sleepe and not be put [to] the question.

SIR HEN[RY] HUBBERT attorney of the wardes, for composicion:

---

[1] Probably 1 Ed. III. (thus in *C.J.*), in which year London was given a very liberal charter. *Rolls Series, Liber Albus*, I, 144–148.

He affirmed that besides the matter of Purveiance the King hath more then a power to take at the right valew in an other matter equall in greavance to this of Purveiance, which matter he veary modestly seemed unwilling to mencion and yet for south in much wisdome moved the howse to urge him to declare his meaning, which in conclusion he opened to be, this viz: For Carriage the Kinge is not bound to give the best price but hath a certaine price by the statut of Magna carta[1] which alone he saied is woorth the compounding for: And quoth he the statut of 28 H 8[2] giveth to shew of this matter of Carriages. And saied he the statut of 2. E. 6.[3] alloweth the King carriags for 2d.[4] the mile: and heare is also a president of compounding in this kinde: for there it appeareth that theis carriags did cease for 3 yeeres[5] during which tyme the King had (as Sir Hen[ry] Hubbert saied) a certaine some of every etc. but the statut doth mencion no such composicion or paiment to the King: And saied he after the 3 yeeres the matter was at large. He farder affirmed that the statut of 14 E 3.[6] doth discharge all the clergy generally of purveiance and why may not the King dischar[ge] purveiance altogether:[7]

In the ende the howse ordered that the former committees appointed to consider of greavances should consider farder therof, and likewise what is fit to be doon for supplie of the Kings occa-

[1] *Statutes of the Realm*, I, 24.

[2] Mistake for 28 Hen. VI. c. 2. *Statutes of the Realm*, II, 355.

[3] *Statutes of the Realm*, IV, 41–42.

[4] 4d. *Ibid.*

[5] *Ibid.*

[6] *Statutes of the Realm*, I, 293.

[7] The attitude of the House was so clear that the Speaker said, "Composition not to be put to Question, but to be left dormant:—Not to be disgraced." *C.J.* I, 283. The House was therefore to proceed by bill. The Speaker wrote Salisbury on March 17: "I was pressed to putt the Bill of purveyors to the question. But I put the same over as not beinge whollie ingrossed. But I think the violence of that humor will againe call for it to marrowe and excepte your Lordships comaund me the contrarie I yet think fitt to give waie to the same before I propound his Majesties gracious pleasure in those thinges that I shall receave in commandment to deliver." St. P. Dom. XIX, 51.

The bill passed on March 20 but was thrown out by the Lords. *L.J.* II, 412. See provisions in *Roger Wilbraham (Camden Misc. X)*, 79–80.

sions,[1] and at this Committee anie of the howse to be present and every man present to have a voice as a Committee, the tyme to be to morrow being wensday 12 *Martii* in the afternoone, the place, the parliament chamber:

12 MARTII 1605.

An act for sale of certain lands of Edw[ard] Downes for payment of his debts 2do. *lecta* this act having ben before committed and by the committees agreed to be engrossed.[2]

An act for explanacion of a statute made 19. H. 7.[3] concerninge ordinaunces made by Guylds and corporacions, ingrossed 3: *lecta* and dashed uppon the question:

The Bill against purveiors was brought in by MR. HARE one of the Committees with amendements, which weare twise redde, and the bill uppon the question put to engrossing:

In the after noone in the parliament howse the greate Committee did meete for greavances and to advise of meanes for supply of the Kings occasions at which tyme, I came late of the greavances, and found them treating of supply to the King: to which matter divers spoke and *inter alios:* Mr. Gawyn a plaine fellowe who remembered that the Kings debts weare delivered by an honorable personage to be seaven hundred seaventy thowsand pounds[4] but quoth he heare is no mencion of any deduccion in respecte of 2 subsidies and a halfe and 4 Fifteenes graunted to the late Queene and since her death paied to his Majestie: wherby the debt ought to be so much the lesse: And saied he whereas it is moved wee should fill the Kings Cofers, it would be likewise understood whether they wilbe filled for if the bottomes be out then can they not be filled.

f. 26. a] Mr. Hoskyns: Greavances weare aunciently sent upp to the King: but to treate of them att Conference or Committees doth butt disclose our harts and make our selves to be singled out: And as touching the matter, I must say that betweene theis proposi-

---

[1] "Mr. Fuller:—Grievances to be reported first, and then a Question [on subsidy]." *C.J.* I, 283.

[2] See *C.J.* I, 272, 278, 281.

[3] 19 Hen. VII. c. 7. *Statutes of the Realm,* II, 652.

[4] The Lord Treasurer had given the amount as £734,000 on February 14.

cions: 1: A Kinge may not waunt: 2. Subiects ought not to examine how it is spent: A supply may easily be spent so may a resupply, and so the Fortunes of the crowne may runne a circle and whatsoever wee give, wee cannot give that [which] may suffice.

Sir Will[ia]m Stroude, advised according to our former purpose, Tow subsidies and 4 Fifteenes: And One subsidy and two fifteenes more to be now granted, the later subsidy and fifteenes to be paiable within 40 dayes after the King shall proclaime warre either with Spaine or Fraunce:

Heare the busines of supplieing the Kings waunts was put of untell the next morning to be dealt in, in the howse:

13 Martii: 1605.

An act for grantinge and establishinge of certaine former allowances unto the merchants of Newcastle, Yorke, and Hull: in the custome of their cloathes accordinge to a privie seale A? 33 Elizabeth:[1] 2do. *lecta* and passed:

Mr. Wiseman moved that the Lord Danvers bill of restitucion may be staied and not to passe, in regarde of graunt[2] which he hath, being so much to the greavance of the Kings subiects. Notwithstanding it passed:[3]

Eight bills weare sent up to the Lords and it was moved by a gentleman being a member of the howse that the bill of free trade being among the said bills, should be placed foremost and specially commended to the Lords and it was ordered accordingly:

An act for better conforming of Recusants their wyves children and servants to trew religion, established heare in Englande: This bill having ben proceeded in with greate deliberacion and brought in but this morning and so not breviated the howse was pleased to forbeare the Speakers repeticion.

14 Martii 1605.

An act for inablinge deprived Ministers to sue and prosecute their Appeales brought in by the committees with this new title for it first was put in with this title viz. An act for restoring

---

[1] See *Cal. St. P. Dom. 1591–1594*, 62.
[2] See *Cal. St. P. Dom. 1603–1610*, 311.
[3] It passed its second reading. *C.J.* I, 283

deprived Ministers: The amendements weare twise redde and uppon a mocion of Mr. Yelverton putt to the question.[1]

Mr. Holt[2] against any farder grant of subsidy, in which speach he termed it the bottomelesse gulfe of the Exchequer.

Sir Will[ia]m Paddy in the course of his speach tolde us that one of Alex[ander's] soldiers told his generall that he escaped punishment for that he was the greatest thefe.

f. 26. b] Mr. Noe, disswaded anie farder graunt of subsidy then already wee had given, for quoth he 28 H 6:[3] there was a grant of 6d. in every 20s. which anie man had either free or coppy hold land Annuity or office, and above 20s. untell 20£. yeerely, 12d. in the pound, and from 20£. unto 200£. and from 200£. upwarde to pay 2s. for every 20s. as well of the layty as clergy guardeins of wards men having Fees and all corporacions: But saied he what followed, the King was constrained to accept an estate for his life in the crowne and though he had a soon, yet an other was declared gover-

---

[1] In *C.J.* I, 284, Yelverton declared "that there was some Course taken for Helping of the Intention of the Bill; and so the Bill stayed, by Order, from Question."

St. P. Dom. XIX, 37, contains the abstract of a speech by Sir Robert Cotton probably given at the meeting of the committee for this bill.

[2] There had been some question as to the order of business. In the C.J. MS, Jac. I, II, f. 72v (March 13), there is this item, "The grievances and the Kings Supply to be handled tomorrow at eight a clock." This is changed to "The Kings Supply first & then the grievances to be handled tomorrow at eight a clock."

Cf. debate in *C.J.* I, 284–285, especially speeches of Sir Henry Hobart and the Recorder of London who were working for increased supply. Hobart wrote a letter to Salisbury, which the present editor has dated March 13. "I was at the Parliament House yesterday, and on Tuesday before the Recorder, and pressed the proceeding, and the House refused to proceed till the term done, that they might have the attendance of the lawyers. Thereupon they put it off till tomorrow morning [March 14]; and I have instructed Mr. Recorder as well with my part, which is not great, as he is instructed in his own. But rather than the least offence should be taken, I will be there tomorrow morning and despatch my part, and then come to the Star Chamber, wherewith I must acquaint my Lord Chancellor this afternoon. But it is hard if the backwardness of the House should be turned upon my blame, that was most desirous to discharge it. Direct what you please and I will follow it presently. I hold it best that I do it myself as I said, and then come to the Star Chamber, if you think so good." Salisbury MSS.

[3] *Rotuli Parliamentorum*, V, 172–173.

nor of the realme and heir apparent: and this saied he I have seene
in the recorde, Againe in the tyme of Queene Elisabeth it was by
the adversaryes wrightten in disgrace of religion that in that
Queenes tymes weare more subsidyes and taxacions then in one
hundred yeares before, and what will they now saie: but sure as
much if not much more:

Then saied R[OBERT] B[OWYER] Keeper of the Records in the
Tower, Sir it is not my desier to heare my self speake nor to offende anie other man that hath caused mee now to arrise, but
I am in some sort tied by speciall duity to declare somewhat
touching the last gentleman's speach, he might have farder shewed
you, that it was not the greate graunt in 28 H 6 that turned the
King to that greate preiudice, but it was the strength of the Duke
of Yorks credit that prevailed for in the parliament of 31 H 6, he
was made protector of the Kingdome,[1] and in 39 he exhibited his
claime to the crowne,[2] wherunto the Kings counceill refused to
answere: And he might have tolde you of a farre greater guift in
the tyme of R 2:[3] such as I thincke his Majestie woulde not in
his princely disposicion have spoken nor anie of you thanke mee to
remember, but I will remember you of 13 E 3[4] when the King
being 300000£. in Debt the Parliament for want of money granted
to him the tenth sheafe of their corne:

Mr. SOLLICITOR arrose and over bitterly spoke to that which Mr.
Noe had formerly saied for saied he perhaps he that spake belowe
(for so Mr. Noe did sett) who spake of [a] captaine of Ireland who
for waunt of woorke requiered releife heare the last cession, I saie
he was perhaps a procter or maker of peticion from some particuler
person: And he that imputeth the taxes to religion I doubt of his
loialtie, whereat the howse called Mr. Sollicitor to the barre, the
rather for that before in the same speach he had used bitter woords
towards Mr. Noe, to this effect, Have you not learned this: have
you forgott this? *et huius*[mo]*di:* Then Mr. Speaker offered to excuse what Mr. Sollicitor had saied but the howse called out Lett
him excuse himselfe, and thereuppon Mr. Sollicitor saied that he
ment that he that so wrightt had no loiall mynde, and saied he I

---

[1] 32 Hen. VI. *Rot. Parl.* V, 242.

[2] *Rot. Parl.* V, 375.

[3] The largest grant was the Poll Tax of 1380. *Rot. Parl.* III, 90.

[4] *Rot. Parl.* II, 104, 112.

have spoken out of a good conscience and I care not where or when I aunsweare it:

Sir Edwyne Sandys in a short eloquent speach moved that the 2 subsidyes and 4 fifteenes which wee had willingly given should go aloane and not to be tainted with anie heavy or unpleaseing guift: and that then wee should bethincke of some other proiects to supply the Kings occasions:

f. 27. a] Some would have had the question; Whether the howse would give any more then formerly had ben graunted viz. 2 subsidyes and 4 fifteenes. Others proposed the Question thus viz. Whether the house by way of subsidy would give any more then before, in conclusion the matter was deferred untell the next morning:

15 Martii 1605.

The Speaker came to the howse a little before Tenne of the clock having (as was saied) before waited on the Kings Majestie but to the howse he gave no excuse of his absence or late cominge:

Mr. Fuller one of the Committees for greavances delivered in the same in wrightinge: wherof some concerned the churche and others the commenwelth:[1] viz: [*blank*].

Monday. 17. Martii.

An act for explanacion of a statut made *Anno* 8 Elisabeth[2] 2do. *lecta: md.* this bill tendeth to sett the trade to Moscovie free and at large to all men and to dissolve the moscovie companie: Sir Roger Owen spake much for the bill declaring him selfe to be one of the Companie: he declared that his parte of the stocke is 300£. and that in 2 or 3 yeeres it was dobled unto him: he alleaged that this trade or companie is not like others for this whole trade doth not vent above thirty or forty thowsand pounds *per Annum*, And if every particuler person maie trade how he please then one or two men may send more then the whole country of Moscovy will vent: therefore the trading with one ioint stocke and governement by Consulls and assistantes doth keepe order and mainteineth the trade and so perswaded that the bill should be cast out: On the

---

[1] See the debate in *C.J.* I, 285.

[2] An Act for the Incorporation of Merchant Adventurers for the Discovering of New Trades. *Statutes of the Realm*, IV, 482. See Scott, II, 41-42.

other side SIR Ro[BERT] MAUNSELL Treasurer of the Navy did confidentlie affirme that the King and the Realme do pay one penny in three more for the commodityes of that countrye by reason of this corporacion or companie then otherwise they shoulde: The bill was committed viz. on Thursday in the Eschequer chamber:

An act for trew makinge of broade woollen clothes in Kent and Sussex: 2do. *lecta* and reiected:

The day beinge farre spent the howse entered a litle into the Greavances and after some dispute referred them all to a Recommittment.[1]

f. 27. b]   TUESDAY 18 MARTII:

The bill for trading butter and cheese, which was first only for London, was by the Committees made generall, and now so brought in and put to the question was reiected.

Mr. Speaker declared that on Satturday last he was sent for by the King, which was the cause of his late coming that day to attende the service of the howse: he shewed that his Majestie Commaunded him to do a message[2] to the howse which consisted on two points. viz.

1. Concerning aide so much heare disputed besides the 2 subsidyes and fowre fifteenes voluntarily offered by the howse:

2. Concerning the question of greavances which hath ben heare proceeded in by committees.

---

[1] Cf. *C.J.* I, 286. The Speaker wrote Salisbury, "But nowe may it please your Lordship to knowe that the grievances pretended were this daie soe carried that the propounders themselves were driven to desire a Recommittment for that upon my openinge of the severall parts of them they held them cleane owte of proportion and fashion." St. P. Dom. XIX, 51.

[2] Before the Speaker delivered the message, the bill concerning purveyors passed the House. The Speaker had written Salisbury the day before, suggesting that this be allowed "before I propound his Majesties gracious pleasure in those thinges that I shall receave in commandment to deliver; I have prepared my poore strengthe, unto to morrowes work, and doe much hope of the good success thereof, and if it may not offend his Majesties gracious pleasure and your Lordships direction I shall humblie desire, as the presente occasion shall require, leave in matter of circumstance to use my poor descretion, not varying from the matter whereunto I shalbe prescribed but therein and in all thinges else I subiect myself unto Direction." St. P. Dom. XIX, 51.

And said Mr. Speaker I desiered his Majestie that before I shoulde deliver it unto you, he would be pleased to give mee leave to set it downe in wrightinge, wherewith he was well pleased and accordingly I committed it to wrighting[1] and on Sonday night I brought it to his highnes which he then perused and therein altered what he thought good. I then desiered I might reade it to you which his Majestie allowed: and when you have digested the matters of greavances you be admitted to his presence and so personally to deliver the same: wherein he wisheth you should use moderacion and iudgement for that uppon publique notice of this purpose if a man will give eare to every complaintes it is dangerous lest his eares be filled with untruthes.[2] His Majestie in your resolucions requiereth expedicion aswell for that there is danger in keepe[ing] companie together [at] this tyme, and also for that it is chargeable and inconvenient for the countrie that such companie should heare be so long staied especially in a tyme when your presence is so necessary in your countryes for prevencion of inconveniences and practises. Againe his Majesty remembereth that by this common discourse of his waunts strangers become privie of *Arcana Imperii,* He is now resolved to understand of you whether he shall expect anie farder addicion to that which you have already graunted to him, and would have you know that, *Bis dat qui cito dat:*[3]

Touching the second he understandeth that you are entered into a course to take notice and herken to complaintes of all

---

[1] St. P. Dom. XIX, 57, which contains this message, is in the hand of Salisbury. Perhaps the Speaker made a copy of Salisbury's draft. Or he may be giving the Commons a plausible explanation for the written message.

The latter half of St. P. Dom. XIX, 57, is printed in Spedding, III, 279–280.

[2] James complained that his message of Feb. 11 "hath laytlie produced no other effect but the multiplicity of Arguments, ... rising from your course you have fallen into, in making yourselves so liberall Collectors of all sorts of grievances." St. P. Dom. XIX, 57.

[3] The King "knoweth, yow are so wise, as to conceyve, that if the noyse of more doubts, debates and contradictions should now contynue but a fewe dayes longer, not onely the value of that addition which is desired, would be lessend by that forme of giving, but much of the estimacion would be impaired of those subsidies, whereof, by your honest gratuites yow have alreadye putt his Majestie in possession." St. P. Dom. XIX, 57.

natures contrary to his expectacion: howbeit he is pleased in case where the lawes do come short or are defective, to adde his authority by parliament where neede shalbe: or otherwise by himselfe with advise of his counceill, wherein he will not be behind but before any of his predecessors: and he hopeth you will containe your selves within such greavances, as be either 1. Monopolyes, 2. Hinderances to Justice. 3. Oppressions, 4. or Corruptions as do tende to the hurt of the people.

f. 28. a] To all which he will give you speedy aunswere and releife by advise of his counceill, or otherwise committ it over to the course of commen Justice and therin will commende it over to his Justices. And this was the effect of the Kings Majesties message so sett downe in wrighting and readde unto the howse by Mr. Speaker. Which being doon Mr. Speaker would have propounded the question which on Satterday he moved: But SIR HEN[RY] SAVILE moved that it might be deferred and first considered of: Notwithstanding Mr. Speaker moved the question thus: Whether according to the Kings desier the howse woulde grow to the question: which question prevaled in the affirmative: but after much speache it was thought by the most that the question should be as neere the Kings request as might be wherof the woords be Whether he shall expecte any farder addicion to that which already hath ben given: But the howse differed what should be the question. Mr. Speaker declared that there is two questions one generall namely, Whether you will give any more, etc. the other particuler viz. Whether by way of subsidy and fifteenes: Uppon much speach it coulde not be agreed whether the generall question or the particuler should be first proposed: They which studied to please etc. requiering the generall question and such as continued according to their first opinion moved only out of conscience calling for the particuler question: In conclusion it was made a question, whether question should be first proposed viz: As many as thinck it fit and convenient to give any more to his Majestie then hath ben already given say yea: and then *econverso:* and uppon division of the howse, the Yea, was 140, and the Nay 139.[1]

---

[1] Cf. *C.J.* I, 286. The Government forced the vote but secured a majority of only one. Nevertheless Salisbury wrote Sir Henry Wotton on March 19: "They have . . . . carryed themselves very lovingly and

Then the next question was As many as thinck it fit and convenient to adde a farder helpe to his Majesties occasions by way of
Subsidy and Fifteenes say yea: and hereuppon also the howse
was devided, and the Yea exceeded the No, more then 26:

Then said Mr. Speaker The next matter is touching the quan-
titie. The first question last aunswered quoth Sɪʀ W[ɪʟʟɪᴀᴍ]
Sᴋɪᴘᴡɪᴛʜ hath ended all for it was (by way of Subsidy and Fifteenes) which expresseth it to be but one subsidy and such fyf-
teene[s] as doth accompanie it which is two: And Mr. Speaker
concluded to the same purpose: then he passed it thus:

As many as thincke it fit and convenient to grant to his Majestie
one subsidy and 2 fifteenes more then hath ben already granted say
yea: and the affirmative prevailed: for few as he proposed it
econverso, saied No:

19 Mᴀʀᴛɪɪ:

An act for *Capias Utligatum* to be awarded by Justices of peace
uppon indictmentes before them selves. *primo lecta:*
f. 28. b] Mr. Speaker declared to the howse that yesterday in the
afternoone his Majestie sent for him and accordinglie he waited
on his highnes: At which tyme it pleased his Majestie to com-

dutifully to his Majesty, haveing given him three Subsidyes, & six Fifteens,
which is no other Precident in times of Peace." St. P. Dom. XIX, 59.

For the opposition of the Commons, see *Cal. St. P. Venetian, 1603–
1607*, 329. Also a letter from M. de la Fontaine to M. de Villeroy, March
23/April 2: "Au Parlement de ce pais, après beaucoup de courroux de la
part du Roy contre la Maison Basse et force harengues d'aultre part en
grande liberté contré le gouvernement present sans y espargner personne,
finalement y avient esté mis en deliberation d'accorder ou refuger à plein
au Roy contribution plus grande que les deux subsides et quinziesmes des-
ja afferts, une seule voix faisant la pluralité, on a accordé de plus un troisiesme subside et ensemble resolu un acte contre les exactions de la maison
roiale: restera au Roi de l'approuver avec faveur ou rejectter avec mescontentement. Et, combien que ceste contribution, moins liberale que
la demande et peu franchement accordée n'eut pas du tout contenté,
on prend toutesfois cela sur et tant moins en esperance de plus par les
deputez mieux choises au Parlement suivant." Paris Transcripts.

Sir Robert Drury refers to this vote in a letter to Salisbury: " . . . . it·
being by good hap, by my coming at the instant wheñ the House was
debating the question, to sway our part by a single voice; wherein if I
had been contrary, as wrong reports had delivered, every man knows it
had then been contrarily contraried." April 1, 1606. Salisbury MSS.

maund mee (saied Mr. Speaker) to let you know[1] that he taketh notice of your proceeding yesterday in the forenoone, And first to declare unto you his gracious and kind acceptance of your first voluntary graunt of Tow subsidies and 4 Fifteenes which he acknowledgeth to have come only out of the wales of this howse without anie mocion on his behalfe or understanding on your parte of his waunts or occasions, and is a certaine token unto his Majestie of your exceeding love and duity towards him. And whereas uppon knowledge and notice of his Majesties wants from him selfe you have farder extended your bounty (for that was his Majesties woorde which otherwise I would not use betweene the soveraigne and the subiect) he also taketh it in veary thanckfull sort, and the more for that he observeth your forwardnes therin to give him content in that you proceeded therunto foorthwith laieing aside all other businesse and grew in this matter to a present resolucion, And in this guyft he allso observeth that albeit difference was among you in the manner sort or fashion of supplieing him, yet you did all veary willingly concurre in the willing resolucion to aide his highnes which was the ende. His Majestie farder commaunded mee to signifie unto you that not only that which now you have given him but whatsoever ells is his either by nature or otherwise shalbe imploied for defence of religion and of you his subiects. And touching your priviledges he is and allwaies wilbe as willing to maintaine them as your selves and he will rather adde therunto then in anie point to preiudice you.

Lastlie he letteth you know that you have enabled him to keepe his woorde which is and ever shalbe to him most deare, namely you have given him meanes to repay such greate sommes as uppon his Missives (for so he termed it) he was constrained to borrow and for this he giveth you harty thankes.

Nota when a bill at the first reading is to be retained or reiected the question must be this: viz: Whether the bill shalbe reiected and not this whether it shalbe retayned: viz. it must be this As many as will have the bill reiected may it please you to say Yea: and afterwards As many as thinck it fit and convenient this bill be not reiected may it please you to say No:

---

[1] This message is in St. P. Dom. XIX, 58; Salisbury MSS. The latter is corrected by Salisbury.

20 MARTII: 1605.

An act for confirmacion of Letters patent made to the Governors of the free grammar schole of St. Bees in county Cumberland of the foundation of [*blank*][1] Greindall late Archbishop of Yorke brought in by one[2] of the committees with amendements, readde ingrossed and uppon the question passed:

f. 29. a] An act to enable Marmion Haselwood to sell certaine lands for payment of his debts and preferrement of his younger children. Uppon both the questions viz. first of the committement and after of the engrossement it was reiected.

An act to reforme the multitude of unnecessary buildings in and about London etc. brought in by one[3] of the Committees with amendements which weare twise redde: MR. WYNCH moved that the whole bill shoulde be readde againe in the howse that men might the better conceave of it by reason the Amendements and alteracions are manie. But Mr. Speaker and the howse ruled that it is against the orders of the howse, but yet it might be recommitted and so it was:

An act for the better execucion of a statute made 31 Elizabeth[4] entituled an act against erecting of Cottages etc. 3.° *lecta* engrossed, and reiected uppon division of the howse: The drift of the bill was to avoide a proviso of the statute of Elizabeth aforesaid whereby Corporate townes weare exempt, and by that meanes no Cottage should be erected in anie such towne except certein acres of lande weare laied thereunto in like case as in the cuntry:

An act for explanacion of a statute made 43 Elizabeth[5] entituled an act for the trew makinge and woorkinge of woollen cloath: *primo lecta.*

Memorandum that whereas there weare 6 or 7 bills passed the Commens howse and entended to be this day sent upp to the Lords it was moved by MR. YELVERTON that the bill against Purveiors being one of the nomber of the saied passed bills shold be first sent up aloane with speciall recommendacion to their Lordships from this howse: which mocion was allowed and SIR FRA[NCIS] BACON

---

[1] Edmund Grindal, who died in 1583.
[2] Mr. Brooke. *C.J.* I, 287.
[3] Sir Henry Montague, Recorder of London. *C.J.* I, 258, 287.
[4] 31 Eliz. c. 7. *Statutes of the Realm*, IV, 804.
[5] 43 Eliz. c. 10. *Statutes of the Realm*, IV, 975.

appointed to carrie up the same who accordingly with some modest excuse undertooke the charge: and the rest of the said bills weare by order of the howse retained to be sent upp to the Lords the next day: Many of the howse did accompanie Sir Fra[ncis] Bacon in the carrieing upp of the bill, Att which time of delivery he used only theis woords in effect, viz. that the howse had sent upp this bill for execucion of divers statutes against purveiors wherof they had speciall care howbeit he shold not neede to use anie speciall recommendacion other then may appeare to their Lordships by the number of them that doth accompanie this bill using the two verses [blank] *irritant animas dimissa par aures quam quas sunt oculis commissa fidelibus.*[1] [blank] and secondly having divers bills ready yet have they sent up only this, as that wherof they have speciall care.

f. 29. b]   21 Martii 1605.

An act for choosinge Knights and Burgesses to serve in Parliament of such as are or shalbe resiant or dwellinge within the saide countyes or Borrowes. *primo lecta:*

22 Martii 1605.

An act for better discovery and [blank] of symony and other corrupt procuringe of ecclesiasticall lyvings: *primo lecta:*

This bill Mr. Speaker repeated with a heavy voice, and countenance discomforted: whereof the reason presentlie appeared for Sir Geo[rge] Moore, openly declared the speach or newes abroad to be that the Kings Majestie was this morning murdered or dangerously hurt in his bed:[2] this newes was soddaine, for my Lord Treasurer knew it not neither had herd anie such thing when his Lordship this morninge went into the parliament howse: on whome I waited and leaving his Lordship entering into the parliament howse I repaired to the Commens howse and found them

---

[1] "Segnius irritant animos demissa per aures quam quae sunt oculis subiecta fidelibus." Horace, *Ars Poetica,* 180.

[2] For the origin and rapid spread of this rumor, see *Cal. St. P. Venetian, 1603–1607,* 332–333; Lodge, *Illustrations of British History,* III, 178–179. See also A. Wilson, *History of Great Britain* (1653), 32; Winwood, *Memorials,* II, 204–205; Steele, *Tudor and Stuart Proclamations,* I, 119.

there at the ordinary praiers: after Sir Geo[rge] Moore had ended
his speach which was short, the howse resolved to deale no farder
in anie busines, and likewise resolved not to departe out of the
howse, and the mocion of certaine being that wee should take
present order that for our security in the place a guard shold be
set at the neither doore and in the palace was reiected: and two
or three sent from the howse to the Lords to understande how the
state of things stoode, in the meane tyme SIR RO[BERT] HITCHAM
the Queene[s] attorney declared that coming over the feilds from
Greys Inne he saw 2 men pursueing 2 Jesuites, that the pursuors
saied to him You are the Queenes attorney, and wee are in Pursuyt
of 2 Jesuyts wee pray you assist us, but he hasted to the Court
and went upp into the Gallory at Whitehall, whether (as he saied)
Browne the messenger whom the Lords had sent to the King returned and reported to their Lordships that the King is yet living
at which saied he (the said Sir Ro[bert] Iitcham) their Lordships
for ioy gave a great whoote, within a while the messengers returned
whom the howse had sent to the Lords (*quorum* as I remember
Sir W[illiam] Stroude was one) and brought woord that the Lords
had not yet herd anie thing from the King nor of him but assoone
as they should heare any thing wee should know it. By which
Sir Ro[bert] Itchams credit, in the opinion of divers was much
impaired:

SIR EDWYNE SANDYS saied to the howse that heretofore he had
declared to the now Lord Archbishop a proiect to remove all
papists from London and 20 miles compas, and wished that some
such course might now be thought of: which mocion was entertained with applause but nothing doon nor farder spoken in it.

About 10 of the clocke SIR RO[BERT] NEDHAM (for that he saied
he had a running horse ready) Sir Maurice Berckly and another
Knight[1] weare by the howse sent to the King to understand
how he did and to signify their humble duityes. Halfe an hower
after SIR ED[WARD] MOUNTAGUE was sent by the howse to see what

---

[1] Sir Robert Oxenbridge. *C.J.* I, 288. "Sir Rob. Oxenbridge moveth
that some (*d.* two) select Gentlemen might goe from the House to understand of the Kings health. (*d.* But they never wer sent because answeare
was expected from the messenger which was already gone.)" C. J. MS,
Jac. I, II, f. 82. The messengers were sent. Cf. Winwood, II, 204.

was doon in the upper howse who after some staie returned aunswere that the Lord Chancellor Lord Treasurer and some few of other Lords with the Bishops weare at his coming at the ordinary praiers, which by reason of this bruite were before omitted: and that at his coming away the Lord Chancellor was reading of a bill: But the Commens howse continued untell 11 of the clocke only expecting to heare from the Lords and the[n] arose and departed every man his waie.

f. 30. a]   24 MARTII BEING MONDAY:

At the setting of the courte one[1] of the Knights which on satturday the 22th of this month were sent by the howse to do the Commens duity unto his Majestie declared their successe thus: viz: One mile beyond Kingeston wee mette with his Majestie, and [by] meanes of some good friendes wee weare presently brought unto him: The King asked of us whether the howse did sett at our coming away, to which wee aunsweared affirmatively and that it was sett before the bruite of his Majesties danger, he saied he marveiled how so greate a noise could growe of so small a cause, but being so, he could (as he said) make this use, viz. he understoode the good affeccions of his people.

Mr. Speaker declared that yesterday the King sent for him to signifie to the howse that this is the day that he is to give thanckes for the generall receaving of him this day three yeeres, Againe it is the day that he is to thancke you for the love and care of him, as appeared to his highnes by your messengers for which it pleased his Majestie to saie that he is to give you thanckes againe for that since your messengers came from you to him, he hath also understoode by the Lords of your greate affeccion love and care towards him, in so often sending unto their Lordships during the tyme of the rumors of his being hurt, to learne and understand of his health:

END OF BOOK I

---

[1] Sir Maurice Berkeley. *C.J.* I, 288.

BOOK II
[HARLEIAN MS]
f. 139]   25 MARTII. 1606.[1]

No clause can be committed before it hath bene reade, so ruled upon a ridiculous Proviso offered by SIR HENRY POOLE to be added to the Bill of Recusants,[2] to this Purpose, viz. That a man conformable shall not be answerable for his Wives Recusancy, reiected for that it was thought fit after long debate that the Bill should not include them, but to leave it to the Construction of Lawe.

Mr. Speaker prayed leave of the House to speake, and then declared, That yesterday his Majesty sent for him, and commanded him to deliver a Message to this House to this effect, viz: His Majesty could not but remember and remember againe, the assured Testimony given this Session of Parliament of your Love, First by your cleere and voluntary Grant of 2. Subsidies and fower Fifteenes. 2dly. That having long disputed upon his Occasions signified unto you, and whether thereupon it might be fitt to enlarge your former voluntary Grant, you did upon his Majestyes Motion grow to a present Resolution. 3ly. That thereupon you did give him such further Supportation as you then thought good, he then moving only your Resolution. Lastly, Your Generall great Griefe upon the false Rumour of his death violently wrought, which was first signified to him from yourselves, and then declared to him by the Lords. His Majesty taketh Notice that the late Queene did often borrowe and was never driven to breake her word, but in the last only, and therein she was aided to make Payment by the helpe of her Subiects; Now he desireth you to consider That his Word and Honor is ingaged for Payment of the Loane which he made late from his good subiects, therefore

---

[1] "The Bill touching Fees for Copies (*d.* reiected because yt differed from the agreement with the Committee).

"Agreed to receive a second Reading." C.J. MS, Jac. I, II, f. 83. The Clerk expected the bill would be rejected and so made his entry.

[2] (*d.* "Sir Henry Hubbard delivereth in the Bill against Recusants the first that was drawne with amendments which being twyse read was ordered to be ingrossed).

"Bill for the Preservation of his Majestys Subjects in their due Obedience brought in from the Committee by Sir H. Hubbard with Amendments, Alterations, Additions etc., which were twice read." C.J. MS, Jac. I, II, f. 83. The Clerk at first had not known the exact title of the bill.

f. 140] he desireth you to dispose of that which you have given him, or of so much thereof as may save his Word and Honor, which now lieth engaged, which he shall take as thankfully as the Gift.

Hereupon the House entered into Consultation how the 3. Subsidies and 6 Fifteenes which they had granted, should be paid, and after much Argument[1] and long dispute, it was resolved, That the 1st. payment of the 1st. Subsidy, viz. two Parts thereof, and one Fifteene should be paid on the first of August next, and the latter Payment viz. the other third Parte of the first Subsidy, and one other Fifteene on the 1st. day of may following. The Payment of the residue I referre to the Act. It is to be noted, That the greatest Argument against the speedy Payment was used by Mr. Yelverton, and was this, viz. That heretofore the 3£—and 5£—man of whom consisteth the strength and greatest parte of the Payments were wont to gaine 10s. for every 5s. which they payed to the King upon Subsidies and Fifteenes, for the Generall Pardon did forgive unto them Issues for not Appearance upon Juries, Intrusions, Alienations etc. All which are now in grant to Subiects by Letters Pattents, so as the same cannot be forgiven by the Pardon.

Sir Hugh Beeston affirmed That he serveth for a Towne as poore and poorer then any in the Realme, yet he would undertake That they would pay in August the 1st. Payment of the first Subsidy, and said he, if they shall be unwilling, I will lay it out for them. Next to him spake Mr. Dyett of the Temple, who concurred with him in Opinion for the tyme of Payment, but said he I will offer as the last Gentleman did to pay for the Towne for which I serve as he hath done, for perhaps he serveth for One of the Cinq Ports, who pay nothing.

The House was devided concerning the first Payment, but the Yea, which would have it, 1° August was 13. more then the No.

26. Martii. 1606.

After the Question of Committing, and not Committing, if the No be greater, then must a 2d. question be asked, viz: as many as

---

[1] See debate in *C.J.* I, 289. Bacon reported from the Committee for the Subsidy. He had expected to make the report on Monday (March 24) but it was put off as Monday was the anniversary of the King's accession and many of the "King's servants" would be at Court. See letter to

think it fitt and convenient That this Bill shall be ingrossed, may it please you to say Yea, and then *E contra.*

MR. FRANCIS MORE moved the House for Exposition of a Case of Priviledge viz. Mr. Brewerton a Member of this House being in Execution, was by this House this Session discharged upon his Praier to be allowed his Priviledge, and being in that sort enlarged is since departed and gone into the Country about his Private Affaires without leave. Upon the 1st. Apprehension it was generally conceived, That for as much as his Priviledge was granted as in all like Cases to the end the Party may attend and doe his Service in the House, therefore that in absenting himself he had committed a great contempt, and should be sent for to answere f. 141] the same: The truth of the Case did appeare to be that Brewerton was adiudged in the Kings Bench to account, and Auditors assigned to him, and for that he willfully refused to account accordingly, therefore by Judgement he was awarded to Prison without Baile or Mainprise *Quousque* he should account and this was generally holden, as if he had bene in Execution. It was moved by some that seemed to favour him, as SIR JOHN SAVILL and others, that this Gentleman should not be singled out alone, but all to be sent for that were departed without Lycence of the House; and every one to answere for himselfe. Mr. Speaker wished That the House would advise of a Course to be herein holden (viz) not to send generally, but the House to be called, and thereupon they that should appeare to be absent without leave to be sent for. But diverse were against the calling of the House viz. MR. MARTYN and others, for that (as they alledged) upon the calling no Member can be punished for absence, but he be first therefore indicted in the Kings Bench and in such Case the Party delinquent is to be put to Fyne and Ransome at the Kings Pleasure, which said they, will be hard. An other moved That the Speaker should write to all the Sheriffs in England to make Proclamation every One in his County, That all such Members of this House soe departed without Lycence, should returne by a day about some fortnight after: This was not liked as being

Salisbury in Spedding, III, 275. Bacon later drew up the Preamble to the Act of Subsidy. See letters to Salisbury in Spedding, III, 277, and to King James, *ibid.* III, 294.

without Example of the Like.   Mr. Fuller moved That the Committees for the Priviledges should have Power from the House to write to every such Member so departed to returne by a day; which Motion for the like Cause was reiected.   Sir Oliver St. John moved, That every one of the House now present should write to his friend so departed to returne by a day, and that at that day the House should be called; He also affirmed that 13. Elizabeth the House was called every 14. dayes,[1] for said he it is not Fyne and Ransome to the Party absent without leave, but in such Case the Burrough is to be amerced.   In the end it was resolved That the Committees for Priviledges should consider of some Course to be taken in the Case, and to reporte their Opinions to the House, and diverse were added to the former Committees, and the Meeting appointed to be the next day.

27. Martii. 1606.

An Act for releiving Poore Prisoners in Execution and of their Creditors in some indifferent manner 2.° *Lecta* and was reiected from Committment upon diverse Arguments on both sides, *inter Alios*, Gawyn began with these words, I am sure the wise men of this House marvaile That I speake at this tyme, but thus it is, if this Bill passe many will as hath bene said, lye in Prison, and live f. 142] one yeare on the Almes baskett: And afterwards when they are confined to abide within 5. miles, they will remaine in London, and their worke shall be to stirr up Suits and to solicitt against them at whose Suit they were imprisoned: Myself have bene so used, therefore I pray you either passe not the Bill or confine the Parties 5. miles from London.

A Bill was brought from the Lords for the Settling of the Estate in Sudley Castle etc. and with this Bill was the Message to this effect, viz. That the House of the Lord Shandois was in great danger by Suits in Lawe and Troubles to be rent in sunder, but that the Lords in their wisedomes and honorable Care of the˙ Continuance of the same had appeased Matters betweene the Parties, so as by this Act quietnesse is to be settled.   And whereas Giles Lord Shandois had disposed certaine Lands for the Prefer-

---

[1] Probably a mistake for 23 Elizabeth in which year the House was called a number of times. There is but one calling recorded in 13 Elizabeth. D'Ewes, *Journal of all the Parliaments during . . . . Elizabeth*, 156.

ment of Katherine his youngest daughter, their Lordships had
setled those Lands upon the Lord Shandois,[1] and taken Order
That his Lordship shall pay in Consideration thereof the Summe
of 7000£. the said money to be paid unto the Lady Shandois[2]
mother of the said Katherine, their Lordships presuming That
her Ladiship would assure and secure the same Summe to be
paid unto her daughter Katherine at her Marriage or within
6. Monthes after, or at her full age of 21. yeares or within 6.
Monthes after, which should first happen; But for as much as
this Act being thus passed the Lordes House, and the said Lady
Shandois being sent for by their Lordships,[3] doth refuse to give
Bond or Security for Payment of the said Summe of 7000£. unto
her said Daughter, therefore their Lordships doe desire That this
House will take order either by adding of a Provisoe, or by altering the Payment from the said Lady Shandois to be made by the
Lord Shandois to some other Person with sufficient Caution, as
to their Wisedomes shall seeme good, so as the Summe of 7000£.
aforesaid may be payed to the yong Gentlewoman as aforesaid.

Nota That in the Journall or Diary of the Clerke of this House,
viz: *De Sessione 3a. and 4a. Parliamenti Reginae Elizabeth* N?
1580.[4] An Order in the House, That every Knight departing
without Lycence or good excuse shall pay as a Fyne to the Queenes
use—[*blank*].[5] And every Baron and Burgesse 10£.—And this
made an Ordinance to continue, viz: where any such Party shall
so departe without licence of the House, or of the Speaker, besides Forfeiture of his Fees to be subiect to such Fyne and amerce-
ment as the House upon Examination of the Cause shall thinke
good.[6]

31. Martii. 1606.

An Act for the reviving of a branch of a Statute made 28. H.
f. 143] 8.[7] for bringing in of Wynes, with Provision against

---

[1] Grey Brydges, fifth Lord Chandos.

[2] Lady Frances Clinton. See *D.N.B.* under Giles Bridges.

[3] *L.J.* II, 393, 395, 402.

[4] The third session of the fourth Parliament of Elizabeth.

[5] £20. D'Ewes, 309.

[6] Bowyer inserts this precedent here though it is not part of the
day's debate. He uses it in the House on March 31. See below.

[7] A mistake for 23 Hen. VIII. c. 7 (*Statutes of the Realm*, III, 374).
The bill was to prohibit the importation of French wines between Michael-

falsifying of of Wines: *tertio lecta.* being ingrossed, and so passed.

In the handling of this Bill, it was by the House agreed and ruled, That, if any thing shall be amended after that the Bill is ingrossed, and hath bene thrice reade, such Amendements must be made in the open House, presently, and neither by the Clerkes man without, nor above in the Committee Chamber by the Committees.

SIR FRANCIS HASTYNGS One of the Committees with the Generall Committees of Priviledge, and diverse others added to consider what Course should be taken for the speedy calling back of such Members of this House as were departed without Licence, reported to the House That the Committees had agreed That a Letter should be written from the Speaker to the Sheriffs of every County to give Notice to the Knights of their Shires and to the Burrough townes, That they should returne forthwith for that their Service is most necessary, and further that it is resolved the House shall be called within a convenient tyme: And said he to this Purpose a Letter is drawn by One of the Committees, which Letter I have if it shall please the House to heare it reade; Whereupon the House called for the Letter, which being reade, the Effect was this, Whereas very many Members of this House were departed since the beginning of the Session without Licence for as much as diverse great busines, and Affaires are to be treated of and handled, for the better Proceeding wherein their Presence is thought most necessary, therefore the Sheriffe to give notice to the Knights of that County, and to the Burrough Townes, that the said Knights and burgesses for the said Townes doe with all Expedition resort up and attend the Servise; And further to require the Sheriffe to certify unto the Speaker at what tyme these Letters came to their hands, and their Proceedings therein. This Letter many approved, onely Mr. Speaker wished the House would advise whether it were fitt to require the Sheriffes etc. or rather to pray them etc. diverse liked notwithstanding the Letter, only SIR THOMAS HOLCROFT misliked the Course, for he wished

mas and Christmas. St. P. Dom. XIX, 19, 20, and Cott. MSS, Titus F IV, ff. 289–290v contain arguments in favor of the bill. See also *Roger Wilbraham (Camden Misc.* X), 78–79.

no Writing to be.[1] Sir Edwyn Sandys stood up and declared
That he was of the Committee, that the Committees generally
allowed of that Course, and that the words Require, was no more
than to desire, and so used in all the North Partes where he had
lived, and so observed.

Lastly Robert Bowyer informed the House, That himselfe
was also one of the Committees but not present at the Meeting,
touching the matter he durst say confidently, That anciently,
absence of the Lords was punished in that House without any
Letters of like Nature as now namely by Fynes imposed on the
absent,[2] and of any Presidents to the contrary in this House,
there is anciently none found; And touching the Experience of
this House, the Clerk can shew a President of the 3. Session of
the 4th. Parliament of Queen Elizabeth when this House without
further Ceremony of Letters or otherwise did likewise lay Fynes
f. 144] of such as were departed without Licence: And said he I
could wish the Company full in regard of the busines which is
expected, yet will I not soe narrowly impound the Discretion and
Sufficiency of those that remaine, as to think them unable to proceed in such matters as they shall have in hand, and for that
which remaineth, it will suffice that all that are absent, Yea all
the Realme is intended present, and many tymes *Presumptio
Juris potior est Veritate;* For my owne parte said he, I wish every
man here should writte to his absent Friend to returne speedily:
Notwithstanding if the House shall be pleased that a Letter be
sent as hath bene moved, then could I wish that some other
word more apt then Require be used to the Sheriff being the
Kings Officer; For *Loquendum cum Vulgo* and howsoever Require
may Signify in some speciall place, yet with us it is a Kinde of
Commande not used but by a man to such over whom he hath
Power or Jurisdiction.

In conclusion, the House resolved not to writte, but that
every Member present should write to his friend absent to wish
him to returne speedily, and that the House shall be called on
Wednesday Sennight, viz. 9? *Aprilis.*

---

[1] "That it will be a Scandal, to shew, what we have done is done
with so small Number." *C.J.* I, 291.

[2] 5 Rich. II. Stat. II. *Statutes of the Realm,* II, 25.

1° Aprilis. 1606.

An Act concerning Sale of Wares in market Townes 2° *Lecta:* upon the Question of Committing, No, was the greater, and then upon the second Question, viz. of Engrossing, it was reiected.

2° Aprilis. 1606.

An Act for the Assurance of certaine Lands late Sir John Skinners etc sent back from the Lords with some Additions which were twice reade and passed.

It was upon occasion of this Bill ruled, That a Provisoe added by the Lords to a Bill formerly sent from this House ought to come in Parchment; also to be put to the Question upon 2d. reading, viz: of Engrossing, and of Passing upon the third reading.

When no man speaketh for a Bill upon the 2d. reading, the Question must be for the engrossing, not for the Committing.

This day the Question was againe moved touching recalling of such Members as without Licence were departed:[1] Some would have that the House should be called to morrow, and Letters sent thereupon to all the Burroughs whose Burgesses were departed, that they would send them back: And it was agreed That this calling would not turne the Parties to Fyne and Ransome, nor any other Preiudice, and likewise that it would not crosse, but stood well with the former Order of this House for calling the House on this day Sennight.

f. 145] In conclusion upon the Question, it was agreed, That the Speaker shall write as from the House to the sherriffe of Every County to give notice to every Knight of the County to returne and to every Burrough Towne to Send back their Burgesses forthwith, without any calling of the House, before this said day Sennight: and the Letters which before were drawn by some of the Committees was recommitted to the same Committees to be considered of: And they also to consider of a Course how the said Letters should be sent, and at whose charge: Which committee mett after dynner, and having done little in the Matter did adiourne the further Consultation untill to Morrow Morning.

Nota, Sir John Boys moved to Know how Fynes imposed by this House on any member should be levyed; For said he A°

---

[1] Cf. *C.J.* I, 292.

1580. Arthur Hall was here amercied, and because the House could not levie it, they caused An Act to be drawen for levying of it, which this House passed, but before it passed the Upper House, the Parliament brake up, therefore it was never levyed.[1] *Ad quod non fuit Responsum.*

3.º APRILIS. 1606.

SIR FRANCIS HASTINGS offered to the House a Letter as considered of by the Gentlemen, which should be written from Mr. Speaker unto the Sheriff of every County, to the effect that he should send word to all Burrough Townes to send back their Burgesses which were departed from hence, and likewise to the Knights of their severall Shires to returne: these Letters he reported are by the Opinion of the said Committees to be sent to the Sheriffs by the Knights of every Shire which are here abiding; The matter of charge in Sending these Letters he said is by the said Committees left to the direction and wisedome of the House.

Mr. Speaker declared to the House, That the King taketh Notice of the care this House hath that the House be full when any great busines shall be sent downe; And that his Majesty doth wish the Same; Also said he, his Majesty taketh notice of the purpose to write unto every Sheriffe for the sending notice to absent Knights of Countyes to returne, and Burrough Townes to send back such Members of this House whom they have chosen to serve for them: And must tell you that hereof he liketh not, namely that you should send to his Officers over whom you have no Power, but of the other Proiect to write to the Burrough townes to send back such as they chose, and returned to serve for them and who are departed, this his Majesty alloweth: And he would have you Know that he is carefull you should have a full House when any busines of weight is sent you: Therefore for the recalling of your Members, if you shall desire his Majestyes Assistance he will ioyne and add his Authority to aide you. But the House generally thought not good to be Suitors[2] to his Majesty for aide in this Cause, the raison thereof SIR JOHN SAVILL did expressely in good termes and with all good duty deliver to be, for that

---

[1] There is no record of this. In 1580 Hall was fined 500 marks by the House. See *Miscellanea Antiqua Anglicana,* ix–xiv.

[2] See a short debate in *C.J.* I, 293.

f. 146] would be Preiudiciall to the Priviledges of the House, that themselves could not deale with the Members of the Same. This matter of sueing to his Majesty to aide the House by way of Proclamation (for so it was generally understood) or to send of our selves, or what Course might be most convenient, was againe referred to the Consideration of the former Committees, who are there upon to advise and report unto the House their opinions to Morrow. Mr. Speaker said to the House, That no matters of great moment would be sent unto them, before the House was full, and if any such should be sent, they might advise and forbeare to proceed untill the House were full.

An Act concerning the Election of the Members of the Commons House of Parliament, 2.° *Lecta* and committed.

The Purport of this Bill is, That none being Householde Servant or retayner to any Noble man, or to any of this House shall be returned a Member of this House, nor any to be chosen upon any Letters Mandatory or of Request, nor for Money or other Gift: This Bill was preferred by Mr. Brooke of Yorke.

If a Bill after it be engrossed, be recommitted, and brought in againe with a Provisoe, which is also twice reade, the same Proviso must likewise be put in Parchment, and then reade againe, and so sent up to the Lords.

From the Lords House was sent by the Lord Chief Baron[1] etc. a Bill intituled, An Act for the attainder of diverse Offendors in the late most Barbarous, most monstrous, detestable and damnable Treasons: And this Bill was specially recommended by the Lord Chief Baron from the Lords unto the House with declaration that it was Matter of great moment, in which it was desired That Expedition Might be used.

Mr. Speaker moved the House That this being a Matter of much consequence, they would advise what Course is to be holden therein; And for that diverse Offendors named in the Bill are absent, he wished the House to consider if it be not fitt to heare Counsell at the Barr to prove the Parties guilty: The House seemed to incline to that Motion, and the rather for that Mr. Alford affirmed That the same Course was herein held by the Lords.[2] In Conclusion it was ordered and directed, That the

---

[1] Sir Thomas Fleming.
[2] *L.J.* II, 404.

Clerke should seeke and search what Presidents had bene in like Case.

4. APRILL. 1606.

SIR FRANCIS HASTINGS[1] declared, That the Committees appointed by this House to consider touching the sending for the Members of this House, and Matters thereon depending, had resolved, That in their Opinion, it were good to attend and expect the calling of the House on Wednesday, which perhaps might present a House full in good Measure, and in the Meane while f. 147] not to trouble his Majesty to aide us (as he gratiously offered) with his Authority for recalling of them, nor in any other sort to proceede or doe any thing therein; which Opinion by the generall consent of the House was allowed. Mr. Speaker said, That untill the House be full, no matter of great moment shall be offerd us; or if any such doe come, That we may forbeare to deale therein, untill the Company be full.

The Bill of Attainder of Catesdy, Percy, and Others Traytors, Actors, and Conspirators in the Action of blowing up the Parliament House was offered to be reade, but many of the House required That it should be deferred untill Thursday, That the House might be first called: And first MR. HOLT spake to that Effect; Then SIR Ro[BERT] WINGFIELD for the present reading of it; MR. YELVERTON was against the present reading; MR. RECORDER of London that it should be reade; SIR THOMAS HOLCROFT *ad idem*, with some words of Imputation to him which last save one spake against the present reading; Then SIR EDWYN SANDYS in defence of Mr. Yelverton, and reproving the last Man for casting any Aspersion of Disloyalty on him for moving the deferring, shewing That he was no doubt as forward to passe the Act (for so his words declared) as any man, but it was desired That this Act of Attainder might passe without Cause to the Adversaries to obiect the hast and slender Course holden therein. SIR GEORGE MOORE was for the present reading of the Bill: In Conclusion, whether out of humour of desire to heare Novelties, or how else I Knowe not, but upon the Question the greatest voice prevailed to have it presently reade, which was done accordingly, the Tytle being thus, viz. An Act for the Attainder of

---

[1] Sir Francis Goodwin, according to *C.J.*

diverse Offendors in the late most Barbarous, most Monstrous, Detestable and Damnable Treason. *primo Lecta.*

An Act for Sale of certaine Lands of Edw[ard] Downes for Payment of his debts, 3°. *lecta.* engrossed. *Nota,* That before the Question of passing was made, it was enformed to the Speaker and the House by SIR JOHN HIGHAM, who most and principally followed the passing of this Act; That a Proviso was left out which was agreed on, and therefore the Bill was staied from the Question of passing, diverse affirming That the Provisoe might be added in the House, and so the Bill and the Provisoe to passe: But some, viz. Sir John Boys to me in private denyed That any Provisoe can be added to a Bill after the third reading: But this latter matter moved was not openly, but without any thing further moved the Clerke proceeded to reade an other Bill.

5. APRILL. 1606.

After the third reading, a Provisoe was added to the Bill of Transportation of Beere, and the Bill with the same Provisoe passed.

MR. FULLER, one of the Committees appointed to take Conf. 148] sideration of such Grievances as should be exhibited, did now deliver into the House, a note of the Grievances touching Ecclesiasticall Matters,[1] upon which Conference by former appointment is to be had with the Lords before the same be exhibited to his Majesty, Which were openly reade in the House, being in Number 4. whereof the 1st. was in Effect To restore Ministers deprived, Suspended, or Silenced by force of the Cannon in the last Synode for want of Subscription to their Appeale.[2] The 2d. To give remedy, and redresse to the Multitude of Spirituall Commissions, Commonly called High Commissions, whereby diverse Bishops have, and all may have more Authority then appertayneth to the ArchBishop in his ordinary Iurisdiction; Therefore it is desired, That there may be only two such Commissions, *vid.* The one to be executed and set on in London, or within 10. miles

---

[1] Fuller had reported these grievances on March 15, but they had been recommitted on March 17.

[2] And not to expect that ministers will do more than is demanded of them by the statute of 13 Elizabeth. Harl. MSS 6846, f. 116. This manuscript is a brief note of the four points.

thereof for the Precinct of Canterbury: The other at Yorke or within 10. Miles thereof for the Province of Yorke; The third requiring That in the Summons against any Person should be contained the matter to be obiected against him.[1] Fourthly, That Excommunication be not used for triffling Causes.[2] This done the House ordered That a Message should be sent to the Lords, generally to pray a Conference, concerning certaine Ecclesiasticall Causes; For this Purpose, Mr. Sollicitor was sent to the Lords by directions of the House and upon occasion of his dispatch, it was agreed that when this House doth pray Conference, we must leave the tyme, place, and Number of Committees to the Lords appointment.

Nota a Provisoe which yesterday was omitted, and should have bene annexed to Downes his Bill, was now brought in, and thrice reade, and then the Bill and Proviso put together to the Question of passing and passed.

An Act for the better and more due Execution of Speciall Lawes, 2° *lecta*. Comitted; And Because the whole drift of this Bill is to restraine abuses in Promoters, Sir JOHN SAVILL declared That about him certaine troublesome fellowes of that Trade, will not be called Promoters, But Relators, wherefore he moved that Relators may also be comprehended, and expressely named in the Bill, which motion was generally embraced.

MR. SOLLICITOR brought answere from the Lords, That their Lordships are not yet resolved of tyme, place, and Number for Conference, but said he, because their Lordships would not long stay us whom you sent, they doe let you Knowe, That as soone as they are resolved, this House shall heare from them.

An Act for assurance of the Clerkeship of the Treasury and Warrants unto W[illia]m Davison Esquire and Francis, Sonne of the said W[illia]m 3° *lecta*. being ingrossed. When this Bill had bene the 3d. tyme reade, and should have bene put to the Question, MR. BROOK of Yorke moved That it might be reiected, in respect that considered Mr. Davisons former State,[3] *Rebus Sic Stantibus*, as now, its to be thought that passing this Bill f. 149] will offend his Majesty. SIR ROBERT WINGFIELD affirmed

---

[1] And also the name of the accuser. Harl. MSS 6846, f. 116.
[2] See a message of the King on this point in *L.J.* II, 405.
[3] See *D.N.B.* under William Davison.

directly, That the King is pleased it should proceed; SIR MAURICE BERKLEY with the 1st. Man, saying further, That the King is not pleased with the Proceeding of this Bill, and further, That a Member of this House is interested in the Reversion of this office, who shall be preiudiced if the Bill proceed, therefore that it be thought fitt to continue this Bill, yet he desired that Councell may be heard on the other Partie. SIR FRANCIS HASTINGS was for the passing of the Bill, and affirmed That My Lord Chief Justice told him that My Lord of Kinlosse delivered unto his Lordship, That the King is well pleased the Bill shall passe,[1] and that if it passe the two Houses, it shall not staie at his Majesty. He further opened the Right of the Lord Chief Justice to give the place and the Benefitt now by this Bill arising to the puisne Judge of the Kings Bench. Lastly, That Sir John Leigh (whom Sir Maurice Berckley at the Commandement of the House named to be the Partie concerned for whom he spake) hath no Right, nor Tytle, nor is allowed by the Lord Chief Justice, he concluded That he well liked notwithstanding that Councell might be heard on his behalfe, if it so please the House: Whereupon, and upon MR. FRANCIS MOORE his Speech, to that Effect, Thursday next is appointed for Sir John Leigh his Councell to be heard.

From the Lords came Mr. Attorney Generall and Sir Edw[ard] Stanhope, with a Message to this Effect, viz. That the Lords doe desire to understand more Particulers touching those Matters for which Conference is desired, and thereupon their Lordships will give further answere; These Messengers being withdrawne, It was agreed by the House, That the Generall Effect of the said 4. Articles should be sent to the Lords, and the same to be sent by Messengers of our owne; And Mr. Attorney and Sir Ed[ward] Stanhope being called in againe, were sent back with that Answere.

Then was the Effect of the said 4. Articles briefly written in a Paper, not to be given to the Lords, but to serve only for direction to the Messenger of this House, who is to deliver the Matter by word. MR. SOLLICITOR was againe nominated by the House to carry this 2d. Message, who excused himselfe, desiring for diverse Causes Known to himself to be hereof excused; Saying further, That the Lords might conceive this House to be slenderly fur-

---

[1] A roundabout way of hearing the opinion of the King.

nished, if they shall send one man twice together. It pleased the House to accept of this excuse, and to Sir Henry Nevill of Berks the busines or Message was committed. Then Mr. MARTYN with a Protestation of his Affection to Mr. Sollicitor, did put the House in minde, That it is against the Order and Custome that any Member shall refuse any Service committed to him upon any Excuse, and desired that this may be no President: For said he, the Lords in their Wisedomes Know that a Messenger sent from hence, saith nothing of himself, but meerely by direction, f. 150] which cannot be any way laied to the Parties charge: This Motion was generally allowed and approved.

Sir Henry Nevill having delivered his Errand to the Lords, he and his Associates were withdrawne into the painted Chamber; And after a small tyme, was called in againe to the Lords, to whom the Lord Chief Justice who by Commission supplyed the Lord Chancellor's turne, as the Mouth of that House, delivered for Answer, That their Lordships had considered of the 4. points sent by himself from the Commons, and found the same to be of great Moment; Wherefore, and for that the tyme is now spent, their Lordships can give no present Answer, but as soone as the Lords shall have had Opportunity to advise thereof, the Commons shall heare from them; And with this Answer SIR HENRY NEVILL returned, and reported the same to this House.

7. APRILL. 1606.

MR. FULLER offered to the Consideration of the House, Seaven Grievances agreed on by the Committees, and referred to the House, and diverse others exhibited to the Committees but not by them agreed on: The Tytle was thus, Grievances to be exhibited to the Kings Majesty by way of Petition, the 1st., Imposition upon Currants and other Merchandise after long Journies.

Herein he affirmed That it was declared to the Committees, and will be iustified, That whereas heretofore there was yearly diverse great Ships built by Our Marchants, now of late this Imposition being raised from 18d. unto 5s. 6d. is soe heavy, that men have given over to build Ships, Yea the best Marchant of London is determined to sell foure great Shipps, and doth offer in them to lose diverse thousand Pounds.

Mr. Speaker moved That the Grievances might be devided into

two sorts, viz: Grievances against the Lawe and Grievances though Warrantable by Law, yet fitt to be redressed.

Here this busines was interrupted by SIR HENRY HUBBERT Attorney of the Wards, who being One of the Committees for one of the Bills of Recusants, delivered in the same Bill with Amendements and some Additions: And first that the Tytle might more aptly and fully declare or referr to the body of the Act, the said Committees had altered the Tytle, and brought it in with this Title. viz. An Act for the better discovery and repressing of Popish Recusants, and for the Education of their Children in true Religion. The Amendements and Additions were twice reade, and then the Bill with the same Amendments and Additions, upon the Question was put to Engrossing.

In the afternoone, after that I had attended My Lord Burkhurst in the Exchequer Chamber, at a Committee of a Bill touching fishing or Preservation of the Spawne, or yong Fry of fish, we went both into the House, where the Committees were hand-f. 151] ling the Matter of Grievances; And *Inter Alia*, Mr. Hoskyns spake of a Grievance by a Commission,[1] by rolle, whereof one now is easily perspicuous, for that he rideth on horseback, doth prevent the Kings Subiects of the Benefitt of his Majesty Grace, whereby they may establish, and have their Estates amended upon Composition with Certaine Commissionors. And his Course is, First he sendeth for the Party by a Letter from the Commissionors, when such Partie cometh to him, he telleth him to this Effect, You hold such Lands, That Tytle is defective, This is the Case, and then he delivereth him such Cases he thinketh good, and with all he requireth to see the Parties Evidence and upon Sight thereof, and notes taken out of it, or having such Evidence left with him, he then seeketh how a Quirke may be found in the Tytle, and for this Purpose he hath obtayned Warrants for Sight of the Kings Records in diverse Offices, as namely in the Augmentation Records which he hath soe handled, That a man may tracke him easily where he hath bene (and note here, Mr. Hoskyns used plaine words signifying that this Fellowe hath blotted and falsified many Records there) yea said he, he hath

---

[1] A commission to treat with persons to whom Crown lands had been given and who were willing to compound for having defects in their titles rectified. See *Cal. St. P. Dom. 1598–1601*, 470.

gotten a lease of 40. or 41. Mannors and when the Tenants or Owners of them come up to compound, they come too late: And all this he doth upon Promise to bring one hundred thousand Pounds to the King in fyve yeares; And for reward, he and an other have the fourth Part of all they shall soe bring in: But hitherto he hath not brought to the King, I thinck one thousand Pounds. In Conclusion his name is Tipper.[1] This My Lord Burkhurst among many others did heare, and myselfe afterwards the same day in the Evening Meeting Mr. Tipper did tell him in Generall That he was named this afternoone where I was, yea said he in the Parliament House, and albeit he pressed to understand the Effect of the Speech, yet did I forbeare to tell the Same, saving uncertainly of a Lease which he had gotten. Oh! said he I Know *Unde hoc*, why quoth I? Marry said Mr. Tipper, he meant That by Mr. Pelham.[2]

8. APRILL. 1606

The 2d. Bill against Recusants was delivered in by SIR JOHN BOYS with Additions and Amendements, of which the first was of the Tytle now made thus, An Act to prevent and avoid dangers which may growe by Popish Recusants.

This busines was a while interrupted by a Message from the Lords brought by Mr. Attorney Generall, Sir Ed[ward] Stanhope, and Doctor Hone to this Effect, viz: That the Lords doe willingly assent to the Conference which wee before moved concerning fower heads of Ecclesiasticall Causes, and to shew their Allacrity, have appointed the tyme for this Conference to be presently if it be not too late, or otherwise in the afternoone in the painted chamber, and their Lordships will be the Number of 30ty. The said Messengers being withdrawne, were after short Speech called f. 152] in againe and returned with this Answer, viz. That this House will fortwith send Answer to their Lordships by Messengers of their owne. They being departed SIR ROBERT WINGFIELD used a short Speech to this Effect, That this Appointment of so Sud-

---

[1] William Typper, who had had a commission for concealed lands in 1600 (*Cal. St. P. Dom. 1598–1601*, 470), had been accused before. *Cal. St. P. Dom. 1603–1610*, 43; *C.J.* I, 199, 200, 206, 212. But he was rewarded by the Crown. *Cal. St. P. Dom. 1598–1601*, 537; *1603–1610*, 331, 424.
[2] Thomas Pelham of Sussex. See *Cal. St. P. Dom. 1603–1610*, 160.

daine a tyme by the Lords did, he feared, not proceed from their
Allacrity to conferr, but it is rather to surprise us of a Suddaine,
whereof as their Lordships have had three dayes of Deliberation
since our sending (said he) to pray a Conference, so I wish we may
have the like tyme to advise in what Course to conferr, before
we meete with their Lordships. Then was Mr. Secretary Herbert
sent to the Lords to deliver to them thankes from the House for
their honorable Acceptance of the Conference, and to declare
That the House desireth to be forborne this day for that the
forenoone is already passed, and this afternoone the Committees
for framing the Preface to the Act of Subsidy are to bring in the
same, And on Wednesday in the afternoone by Appointment
long since this House is to be called, after which day the House will
appoint certaine to attend their Lordships with double the Number
that their Lordships have appointed to be viz. 60.

During the tyme that Mr. Secretary was absent thus imployed
to the Lords Sir MAURICE BERKELEY moved That whereas the
House had appointed to heare Counsell in Mr. Davisons Bill on
Thursday, that for as much as both Parties doe in contrary sort
relie on the Kings Pleasure, the One to give Passage and Approbation to the Bill, the other *E converso:* Therefore that the day be
putt of, and no Proceeding to be had in that Cause untill his
Majestyes Pleasure be further understood. Mr. Speaker directing his Speech to Sir Maurice Berkeley said, That he had understood so much that except he were much pressed, he would doe
nothing in that busines, untill he should heare more; And hereupon
Order was given that neither Partie should provide or being[1]
Counsell to be heard in this House untill further direction in
that behalfe.

MR. SECRETARY HERBERT returned with an Answer from the
Lords touching the Conference to this effect. viz. That on Thursday the Lords are to meete about the great Bill the Exemption
of the 4. Shires out of the Marches of Wales; That Friday is Convocation day, and on Saturday the Lords of the Counsell are to
meete about Important busines of his Majesty: Therefore with
the soonest that they can, which is on Monday in the afternoone

---

[1] *Bring* is meant.

at two of the clocke in the painted Chamber their Lordships will conferr with this House.

9. APRILL. 1606.

MR. FULLER delivered into the House the Grievances to be f. 153] read,[1] to the end That the same having already bene examined by the Committees and thought in their Iudgements to be Grievances fitt by way of Petition to be offered to his Majesty to be redressed, shall so be also allowed by the House, then the same to be afterwards Marshalled by the Committees, or as the House shall direct. The said Grievances were reade, but not in Order as they stood in the Booke given in by Mr. Fuller, but according as was thought fitt and agreed by Mr. Speaker and Mr. Fuller.

First was reade the 14. Article or Grievance *in haec verba*, viz.

Amongst many Grievances, there is none more hurtfull and dangerous to the State of the Realme, then the much Transportation of Iron Ordinance,[2] and of cast Shott, or Bullet of Iron, which hath so furnished and strengthened the Townes, Castles, and Shipps of Forrein Princes, as that hereby this Realme of England, which in that Kinde of force exceeded all the Nations of the World, and our Navie which heretofore was of greate force and command at the Sea, is now of small account, and will be lesse and lesse if it be not speedily prevented by restraining such Transportation. This Article was by the House allowed for a Grievance.

Secondly was placed the Imposition upon Currants, which is also the 2d. of the Grievances, *in haec verba*.

The late Imposition upon Currants of 5s—6d—[3] for every hundred over and besides the ancient Custume of 18d; A charge to the Marchants Eight or Ten Thousand Pounds the yeare; and other late Impositions upon Marchandise after their long Voyages,

---

[1] Cf. *C.J.* I, 295.

[2] The King at times granted licenses to export fixed amounts. Lansd. MSS 169, ff. 49–51*v*, is a list of such grants between 1592 and 1605, with the amount paid for each.

[3] Imposed in 1603. *Cal. St. P. Dom. 1603–1610*, 51. See discussion in Gardiner, II, 1–7. See also *Cal. St. P. Dom. 1603–1610*, 136, 161, 165, 168, 169, 211, 228, 311.

and great adventures, be grievous to the Marchants, and to other Subiects, by inhancing the prices of such things which are of good use, and hath bene, and will be the decay of great Shipps, to the Damage of the Realme. Because it was affirmed, That the Fermers[1] of this Imposition desired to be heard; Therefore it was ordered that Counsell shall be heard as well for them as on the part of the Marchants grieved, on Friday.

Next in the third place was reade the Lycence for Selling of Wines, which in the Grievances is set first, *in haec verba.*

Whereas in the last Session of Parliament (amongst other things) there were repealed two Branches of the Statute of 7. E. 6.[2] whereof one was concerning Selling of Wines at certaine Prices, by means whereof the Commons then assembled conceived that there should have bene no further dispensation or Monopolies of Taverns, or for retayling of wines; That notwithstanding certaine Persons[3] by force of some Statuts out of use, which are Impossible to be observed, and by Color of some Grant or Warrant from his Majesty have increased the Number of Taverns, and inhaunced the Prices of Wines, disanulled all the Grants under the Great Seale made to the same Purpose in the tyme of the late Queen Elizabeth. And have obtained from his Majestyes Subiects very great Summes of money for Fynes, besides that they doe receive of the said Subiects great yearly Rents, to the great f. 154] Grief and Charge of the said Subiect: And of late yeares some Licences[4] have bene granted to sell wines in diverse Villages and small Townes where no Wynes were usually sold in such sort before, and to some unruly Alehouse Keepers, who for their disorder have bene suppressed by Iustices of Peace to the great increase of Drunkennesse, and other disorders amongst the Subiects. Allowed by the House as a Grievance.

Fourthly the Preemption of Tynne which among the Articles is the third, was reade *in haec verba.*

---

[1] Sir Roger Dallison and Richard Wright.

[2] 7 Ed. VI. c. 5. *Statutes of the Realm,* IV, 168. Sections 1 and 2 repealed by 1 Jac. I. c. 25. *Statutes of the Realm,* IV, 1052.

[3] The Earl of Nottingham and his son Lord Effingham. *Cal. St. P. Dom. 1603–1610,* 174.

[4] See *Cal. St. P. Dom. 1603–1610,* 219, 220, 391, 429.

The Preemption of Tynne,[1] which is abused and made a sole Emption or Monopolie of Tynne (notwithstanding the Kings Majestyes Proclamation lately made to set it at Liberty, is of late made very grievous to the Subiects who are forced to pay for every Pound weight of Tynn 1d. $\frac{1}{2}$d, which is more then 13s. upon every hundred more then they lately paied, whereby the Proclamation for Tynn was set at Liberty, and besides the excessive Price of Tynn, the poore Pewterers[2] can buy no Tynn unlesse they pay present money for it, and take One fift Part of drosse Tynn to the undoeing of many of them; And notwithstanding the Pewterers many tymes want Tynn, yet a very great quantity of Tynn remaineth in his Majesty hands unsould, amounting to the Valewe of Threescore thousand Pounds. The Substance of this Article is allowed by the House for a Grievance, but recommitted to the former Committees for the forme and Order of setting it downe more fitt to be offered to the King.

Next the Patent of Logwood alias Blockwood, which among the Articles is in the fourth Place, was reade *in haec verba*.

Logwood alias Blockwood being a thing prohibited by three severall Statuts[3] for that it is used to make false Collors, and hath wrought deceipt and discredit to the English Cloth vented beyond Seas, and doth hinder the Kings Majesty neere Ten Thousand Pounds every yeare in his Custome, which would grow due for Woode, Cochenello, Indico, Argall, Gales, Shumack, and other Commodities for the use of Dyeing, if Blockwood were not brought into the Realme, and depriveth many poore men of their Labor and fruite of their labour, yet neverthelesse a Patent of Tolleration or use of it is lately granted to Sir Arthur Asheton[4] and others, who raise excessive gaines to themselves by selling that after 45s. the hundreth, which is bought for 15s. the hundreth, amounting to ten thousand Pounds the yeare, and doe very

---

[1] The right to buy tin from the tinners to sell or export. See *Cal. St. P. Dom. 1599–1601*, 274; *1603–1610*, 14, 84. See also Unwin, *Industrial Organization in the 16th and 17th Centuries*, 153–154.

[2] See *Cal. St. P. Dom. 1603–1610*, 157, 334, 335, for complaints of the Pewterers' Company.

[3] 24 Hen. VIII. c. 2 (*Statutes of the Realm*, III, 419); 23 Eliz. c. 9 (*ibid.* IV, 671); 39 Eliz. c. 11 (*ibid.* IV, 911).

[4] *Cal. St. P. Dom. 1603–1610*, 146. See Scott, I, 137.

much vex and grieve the Subiects by their violent Courses, and by Cullor of their Patent raising uniustly out of an other wood called Martyna wood about two thousand Pounds by the yeare, to the great hurt and Grief of the People. This Grievance was allowed of. And here Sir Rob[ert] Wingfield moved That in these Grievances no man should be named, but the Matter sett downe in such sort as the Committees shall think fitt, and therein no man to be named; Which motion the House approved, and gave direction accordingly.

f. 155] Sixthly, the Searching and Sealing of the new Drapery was dealt in, which is the fift Grievance, *in haec verba*.

The Letters Patents lately granted to the Duke of Lennox for Searching and Sealing of new Draperyes[1] and other things, whereof many are not meete to be Searched, or Sealed, exacting of the subiects Excessive Fees in nature of Sudsidies heretofore granted by Parliament upon woollen Clothes, and other Penalties and Forfeitures together with the great abuse of the Fermers and Deputies of the same Pattents, who doe many tymes take foure tymes more then is limitted by the Letters Patents, and doe Search, Seise, and take the Subiects goods violently from them in the High waies as forfeited, where there is no Color of Forfeiture, which is very grievous and burdensome to the subiects. Sir Ed[ward] Greveill moved that the Duke of Lennox Councell may be heard, which Motion was yielded to, and a day therefore given.

The Seaventh Article reade was that which among the Grievances is the 6th. viz. The Patent granted to the Lord Danvers, and Sir John Gilbert, touching Issues, *in haec verba*.

The Letter Patents granted of late to the Lord Danvers and Sir John Gilbert Knight[2] of 3. Parts in 4. Parts to be divided of the Overplus over and above 2800£. which the Kings Majesty usually before tyme received yearly of all Issues, Amerciaments,

---

[1] A patent to set the Government seal on certain cloths before they could be sold. It was secured by the Duke of Lenox in 1605. *Cal. St. P. Dom. 1603–1610*, 233. See also Price, *The English Patents of Monopoly*, 27–28, note.

[2] In 1604. St. P. Dom. XX, 23. The patent was a grant of the fines and forfeitures on penal statutes coming to the Crown above the annual sum of £2,800.

Fynes *Pro Licentia Concordandi*, and other Fynes, Forfeitures, and Recognizances, and for the Peace, good behaviour, Appearance for Felony, Murder, or Manslaughter or Suspicion of them, or to answer what shall be obiected, or for, or concerning Alehouse Keepers, or Victuallers, and other things incident to the Crowne, rysing and growing in England and Wales, and never soe before granted to any whereby One Principall Dignity of the King to use Mercy and favour where it is meete, is in some sort taken from the King, and from the Judges of the Land, and Power to dispence with faultes is given to them who are not meete to have it, whereby the Subiects shall be in greater Bondage and danger then before tymes, to their great Griefe. This was allowed for a Grievance.[1]

The Ninth Grievance was reade *In haec verba.*

The Merchants of Yorke having alwayes heretofore used to put their Merchandize at Yorke into little Vessells upon the River of Owse, and soe carried the same to Hull, there to be customed before the same be put into greater Vessells, and transported beyond the Seas, without any Forfeiture or losse, now of late since the last Parliament, their goods have bene seised as forfeit by the Farmers of the Customes for so doeing, to their greate hinderance.[2] And this was allowed as a Grievance.

f.156] Then was spoken of the Green Wax within the Dutchy of Lancaster mentioned as the tenth Grievance, *in haec verba.*

The like Letters Patents[3] of All Fynes, Amerciaments, and other Penalties and Forfeitures Knowne under the Name of The Green-Wax, rysing within the County Palatine of Lancaster, which is or may be of very great yearly value, is granted to Sir

---

[1] In the margin of St. P. Dom. XX, 23, is written: "One of the committyes did demaunde counsell for the patentees, but it was denyed, though afterwards to others (doubtinge to be taxed of injustice) they never denyed counsell, and so the patentees only were barred of that lawfull Iustificacion. And therefore the pretence in the preamble to the grevances to this point is untrue." A letter begging for help, dated July 17, 1606, from Lord Danvers to Salisbury is in the Salisbury MSS.

[2] *C. J.* I, 295, makes this a broader complaint against the farmers of the customs in several places.

[3] A patent like that of Danvers and Gilbert. *Cal. St. P. Dom. 1603–1610*, 158, 174, 175.

Roger Aston for many yeares under a small Rent of 48£.—by the yeare, which preventeth those subiects of the Dutchy from such Mercy and favour as alwayes heretofore hath bene used to good and loving Subiects, and giveth Power to Private men to dispence with great faults, which is hurtfull to the Commonwealth, and may be the undoeing of many. This was much argued Pro and Contra, but SIR ROGER ASTON himself did best defend this Grant, by shewing That the thing was in grant long before the Kings Letters Patents thereof made to him; That his Grant is yet but in Reversion, and the former Grant hath continuance; for which present Grant he gave a great Summe of money and offered upon termes which seemed very reasonable, to yeild the same up to the King. He further demanded how it is more grievous, or offensive then the same would be if now there were a Duke of Lancaster, who then being a Subject were to dispose thereof, and not the King. Diverse spake against it, *Inter quos*, MR. HOSKYNS merrily said of this *et huiusmodi*, that *Misericordia*, in latine is by this meanes come unto Amerciaments. MR. FANSHAW Auditor of the Dutchy beyond Trent Northward informed the House, That this Green-wax to Sir Roger Aston beyond Trent is in Possession, and on this side Trent in Reversion, and that Sir Roger hath only Issues, Fynes, Amerciaments, and Fynes *Pro Licentia Concordandi*, and not Licences for Alehouses, Recognisances *et huiusmodi*, for that the Duke of Lennox hath, except only the County Palatine which latter thing is excepted to Sir Roger Aston.

In Conclusion it was referred to the Committees to frame such an Article in this Point as shall be fitt: wherein they are to insert Sir Henr[y] Bronchards Patent,[1] and the like, but no man to be particularly named: the Residue was referred unto to Morrow.

This afternoone the House was called, and then appeared present 367[2] Persons, Knights and Burgesses; The House accepted the Excuse almost of all men that were affirmed to be Sick, and forebore to impose any Fyne on any person upon opinion that they had no Power after to release, or discharge, or mittigate their Punishments of that Kinde.

[1] Upon the motion of Sir Robert Hitcham. *C. J.* I, 295. See p. 127.

[2] "There were found in the House 299, and in the House and Town 367." *Ibid.*

10. APRILL. 1606.

Upon SIR GEORGE MOORE his Motion to the House, he was dis-charged of being Receivor and Distributor for the Poore, viz. of f.157] such Monies as shall be collected for that Purpose in the House.

MR. SOLLICITOR brought and delivered in the Bill of the Sub-sidy; The reading whereof was put of untill Saturday morning at Seaven of the clocke; For the Order is to reade it first in a fore-noone, and then 2dly. in an afternoone.

SIR HERBERT CROFT moved That the House by a Message would recommend unto the Lords the care of correcting an Error in the Bill sent from them to their Lordships for severing the 4. Shires of Hereford, Wigorn, Salop, and Glocester out of the Com-mission of the Marches of Wales; which Error as he affirmed doth consist in words of aboundance to be stricken out by the Committees of the Lords House, which he shewed was no other then this Session their Lordships did, who when they sent to us the Bill for settling the Possessions of the Lord Shandois, did by their Messengers recomend to this House Provision for Payment of money to the late Lord shandois Daughter by her mother the Widdow Lady, for that she now contrary to their Lordships Expectation refused to pay the same as was conceived and hoped by their Lordhsips: After some dispute is was ruled, That with a Bill a Message may be sent, but after a Bill hath passed here, and remaineth with the Lords, we cannot send any Message of Re-formation.

vid: 7. H. 4. n. 11.[1] the Commons send for their Bill to amend it.

SIR ROBERT MANSELL moved, That whereas he found diverse set downe in the Clerks note for Committees in the Bill for free Trade, whom he heard not named in the House, and some of them such as are interested in the Corporations by the Bill desired to be dissolved; And the same Persons interlined, he desired further Consideration to be thereof had by the House. To this Mr. Speaker answered, That the Order of the House is, when any mans speciall Case is in question, he is to have no Voice, but he is to withdrawe himselfe out of the Place, but if the Bill be Generall in that Case

---

[1] *Rot. Parl.* III, 568. "A Precedent procured by Sir Rob. Cotton." *C. J.* I, 296. The House then appointed a committee to examine this prece-dent. Bowyer was to attend the committee.

a Party specially interested hath a Voice, and is fitt and able to be a Committee: Also he that speaketh against the body of a Bill cannot be of a Committee.

In handling the Bill of Attainders, in which Case Councill was to deliver Evidence at the Barr, it was ruled, That the Kings Councell being Members of this House (viz) Mr. Sollicitor and Sir Francis Bacon) cannot, nor may not at the Barr for the King deliver Evidence to prove the Treasons, and so in all other Cases, for every Member is a Judge and cannot therefore give Evidence as Counsell at the Barr; Neverthelesse in such Case, the Kings Counsell as any other Member may deliver what he thinketh good, as well to informe the House in the Matter of Fact, as by way of advise, Keeping his Place but not at Barr.

Sir John Crooke One of the Kings Serieants at Law, and Sir Ed[ward] Stanhope One of the Masters of the Chancery brought 2.[1] Bills from the Lords, with a Message that the Lords are now in Conference of matter of great Importance, and forthwith f. 158] upon their Conclusion they will send to the House: Hereupon the House being then purposed to rise, determined to set and expect their Lordships Message.

Mr. Speaker moved, That according to the ancient order, it might be allowed, and ordered That any Matter of what Consequence soever, may be put to the question as soone as it shall be Eight of the clocke; Which was condescended, and ordered accordingly.

An Act for the cutting of infinite Suits brought against many his Majesty Subiects by Informers, I° *lecta*. The effect whereof is only to make playing at Bowles a Lawfull game.

Mr. Attorney Generall, Sir Edward Stanhope one of the Masters of the Chancery, and Dr. Sone, from the Lords brought a Message which Mr. Attorney delivered to this effect, viz: That the Lords doe desire a Conference with this House touching three Matters 1. The Bill of Purveyors; which was sent up to them from this House. 2. The Bill of free Trade,[2] sent likewise up to the Lords from hence. 3. The Union. That in these three Points the Lords desire a Con-

---

[1] Three bills according to *C. J.*
[2] An act to enable all his Majesty's loving subjects of England and Wales to trade freely into the dominions of Spain, Portugal, and France.

ference with a selected Committee of this House; The Matter of
the Union now to be dealt in, will be, Whether to proceede therein
this Session, or to deferr it further: And albeit Friday being to
Morrow is a Convocation day, yet to further this busines, their
Lordships will request their Lordships the Bishops to forbeare the
Convocation; And the tyme to be to Morrow in the afternoone in
the painted Chamber the Number of the Lords to be 40. and then
the great Cause to be ended, or at least adiurned untill the next
Session.

IITH. APRIL. 1606.

Mr. WISEMAN informed the House, That the Bill for Chepstow
bridge now returned into the House by the Committees is by them
wholy made new, and twice so long as before, only the face of the
old Bill remaineth, and upon Examination, it appeared That the
Bill was much enlarged; But upon the question, the Bill soe altered,
and enlarged stood, and was allowed; For it was ruled That a Committee may alter, add, and diminish what, and as much as they
thinke good, so as they bring backe the same Bill in Substance.

SIR ED[WARD] HOBBY to the House That himself and 3. other
of the 4. thereunto appointed by the House were yesterday at the
Office of the Records in the Tower, and there also (said he) would
the 4th. have bene if he had understood he had bene one of Committee, for our busines it was so prepared by the Care and Dil-
ligence of the Officer[1] that we were speedily and fully satisfied in
the Matter; wee required a Coppye of so much as we thought upon
f. 159] reading of the Record to be materiall, and having received
and examined the same, because it was in old French, I have turned
it into English as well as I could; And so he delivered the Writing
unto the Speaker being translated.

The Grievance of Currants[2] was called for, which being the
2d. that was reade 9? *die Aprilis*, day was given untill this day
to heare Counsell; For declaration and proofe of which Grievance,
Counsell attended without, according to former Order. But 1st.

---

[1] Robert Bowyer. The committee was to examine a precedent (see
p. 115) in which the Commons recalled a bill sent to the Lords in order
to amend it.

[2] Cf. *C.J.* I, 297.

SIR FRA[NCIS] BACON standing in his place as a Member of the House, not at the Barr, nor in Presence of the adverse Counsell, spake in defence of the Imposition, viz, as a Judge to informe his Fellowes; for as of Counsell with the King, he could not by the Order of the House speake at the Barr. Then SIR JOHN FORTESCUE declared, That in the tyme of Queen Elizabeth at what tyme he was Undertreasurer, the Turky Marchants did themselves impose 4000£. per Annum Taxe upon this Commodity, under Color that they could not otherwise beare and discharge the Taxes on them beyond the Seas, and the Necessary charges of their said Trade; Thereupon Queene Elizabeth imposed a Taxe on that Commodity, as Lawfully she might; Then the Turky Company became Suitors to farme this last mentioned Imposition of the said late Queenes; And when they had therein prevailed, they accounted themselves much Bound to her;[1] And as well as you may take from the King this Imposition under Color of a Grievance, by the same reason, you may take from him the 6s. 8d. upon a Cloth, which amounteth unto 30000£.—per Annum; And likewise the Imposition on Allome, and the like; and then must we be driven to seeke new wayes to aide the King for maintenance of the State. MR. FULLER moved That Counsell on the Merchants behalfe may be heard, otherwise he would say on his owne Knowledge more for the Marchants. Then was Mr. Hitchcocke being of Counsell with the Marchants called in to the Barr; And his Clyents that came with him into the House were Mr. Cordall, Mr. Eldred, Mr. Ofeild, and Others.   The Effect of Mr. Hitchcocks speech was, That Currants is a Commodity so necessary for the life of Man, as that an Imposition can be put on it by Law, no more then upon corne brought into this Realme, *vid.* I: Elizabeth in My Lord Dyer[2] there was an Imposition upon Clothes; And said he, by reason of this Imposition, there is raised upon the Subiects at the least 10000£.—per Annum, Whether it goeth I Know not, It was then affirmed by One of the Masters of the Trinity house That a great many of bigg Shipps doe now lie idle betweene London Bridge and Woolwich, because the Merchants are not able to set them on

---

[1] This was in 1600. See Gardiner, II, 2–3.

[2] Sir James Dyer, *Reports of Cases in the Reigns of Henry VIII, Edward VI, Mary, and Elizabeth* (ed. of 1794), II, 165–166.

Worke; when Mr. Hitchcock went from the Barr he[1] moved for Consideration to be had of Mr. Bate a Marchand committed to close Prison for this Cause, of not paying the Imposition on f. 160] Currants, which seemed to be by meanes of One MR. WRIGHT a Member of this house, who was not suffered to answere before the others were withdrawen, and then made no other defence, nor gave any other Satisfaction to the House, But only that Mr. Bate was committed by the Lords of the Councell, for the refusing to pay the Imposition aforesaid.

MR. MIDDLETON, as well the like Imposition may be imposed on all other Commodities, and then Marchandize must fall, and the great Grief is, That the Profitt of these Impositions goeth not to the King immediately, but to meane men like myself, and by this meanes for their Sakes, the younger Sonnes of Gentlemen which might and have heretofore risen by the Course of Marchandize, must be unprovided of this good meanes of defence and Trafficke.

SIR JOHN SAVILL observed out of Sir Fran[cis] Bacons Speech, That the King may forbid the bringing in of Forraine Commodities, and therefore he may set a Taxe or Imposition on such Commodities if he thinkes good to suffer them to come in: Hereupon said the Knight is to be observed, the reason why the King may forbid the bringing in of Forraine Commodities, and that reason is to be observed in such Impositions as are to be laied: And first said he it is against Policy to bring in more Store of Forraine Commodities then we vent of home, for we must provide that at the least the home Commodities transported may contervaile the Forraine brought in, otherwise the Treasure of the Realme must be carried forth to pay for the Overplus: And because if unnecessary and needlesse Commodities should be brought in then of necessity must a requisite Proportion and quantity of needfull things be besides brought in, therefore, the King as head of the Common Wealth hath the Moderation and guide of these things, and Power to forbid what in his Royall and Princely Wisedome he shall think unfitt and in a Convenient sort to set Impositions;

---

[1] In *C.J.* I, 297, Mr. Cordell, a merchant, petitions the House concerning Bate. Bate's case was not decided till November.

See *Cal. St. P. Venetian, 1603–1607*, 338, for the hopeful attitude of the merchants.

But on the other side, if these Impositions shall exceede, then will the same by necessary Consequence fall upon our owne home growen Commodities, to the Preiudice of all the Subiects, as he shewed by Evident and necessary Consequence, which said he is worthy Consideration: For my owne Parte said he, I was by the Speech of the learned Gentleman that first spake (meaning Sir Francis Bacon) almost transported to the other opinion untill I now upon hearing more have further considered on the Matter: Then he concluded with a merrie conceite; I remember said he, when I was a Boy I heard them say Mercury was a Thiefe, at which I marvailed in regard they also said he was a God, but since I came to better Judgement I perceive it is meant that Eloquence whereof Mercury was esteemed God, is the Thiefe. In conclusion, the Substance of this Article touching Currants was by the House f. 161] ordered should be inserted among the Grievances to be presented to his Majesty, but the Order of setting downe the same is referred to the Committee.

12. Aprill. 1606.

An Act for 3. Subsidies and 6. Fifteenes granted to his Majesty 1°. *Lecta*. Note, That the Speaker doth of this Bill repeate no more but the Title, and dayes of Payment.

Mr. Hare delivered the Effect of so much of the Conference[1] Yesterday with the Lords as concerned the Bill of Purveyors to which he shewed that there was 19. Exceptions taken, viz. in the Tytle, the Preamble, and the Body of the Bill; of which he shewed many in particular among which one was, That in the Bill there was no forme of Commission set downe, also that Mr. Attorney said, no forme could otherwise be devised, to answer all the Statuts in force, but it would be so long that 40. Scriveners must be assigned to every Purveyor. That if the King should pay ready money, and according to the value, then the King must send a guard with his money, up and downe the Countrey. That the Bill giveth Power to all men to resist Purveyors if they hold not the Course of Law in their taking, which is a way to raise Tumults etc. And in such Case we would make the King stay many tymes for his dinner. And said he, My Lord Chief Justice said, That the King hath a Prerogative Price of some things, but shewed not in

[1] See *C.J.* I, 297; *Roger Wilbraham* (*Camden Misc.* X), 79–81.

what; and that he had seene a Record[1] that doth mention an hereditary Price. Much more he repeated at that Conference, which I noted not.

MR. FULLER One of the Committees in this Conference affirmed That this is a weighty Matter, and said he, I find it very weighty to me; and I did offend some in this, That I moved we might have tyme to answer such Matters as were obiected against the Bill: And a great One told me, I had spoken that which had bene better unspoken. And when their Lordships required the opinion of the Judges t' ching the Bill, I did acknowledge that the Judges are indeed Assistants in the upper House to aide and assist the Lords when Matter of Law falleth in debate among them, but I desired that their Opinions might be at that tyme forborne, for I did think, and still shall think a great difference betweene the words of a Judge sitting Judicially in a Court of Judgement, and speaking in that Kinde, and his speech in any other place, for in Judgement I Know he speaketh Sworne, and the best Subiect is to stand before him uncovered, but elsewhere he is an other Kinde of man, and in Judgement I doe desire, and never will refuse to be bound by the Opinion of the Judges, for they heare both sides before they speake, but elsewhere it is not so; Therefore if their Lordships would heare the Judges, I Know it was no more then before that Conference they had heard, soe as to their Satisfaction it tended not; And I saw no reason, that should bind us to what they should f. 162] then and there have spoken: Wherefore I moved, That if their Lordships would heare the Iudges Opinions, we might be licensed in the mean tyme to withdrawe our selves, for I saw no reason the Judges Opinions in that place should bind us; And againe Our Commission from this House was to conferr with their Lordships, and not to heare any other Opinions. And now said he, I desire Wittnesse, and that it be remembred, That I have spoken nothing offensively: And all the House with a Generall Acclamation and Approbation of his speech, did cleere him of all fault, and allowe his speech to the Lords.

SIR JOHN SAVILL reported some parte of the said late Conference touching the Bill of Purveyors, as omitted by them that before had spoken. There was 4. Exceptions said he, 1. That we had by

---

[1] "The old Grene Clothe bookes." *Roger Wilbraham* (*Camden Misc.* X), 80.

this Bill made a Law to hang an Innocent Man, for we make that Felony in the Purveyor to take contrary to Law, when he Knoweth not the Law, being in that Point manifold, and not expressed in his Commission, so as the fault is in him that makes the Commission, and we will hang the Innocent Purveyor. 2. we endanger his Soule, by the Oath we appoint for him to take. 3. we have made a Bill of Sedition, in giving Power to resist if the Purveyor take without ready money, or contrary to Lawe. 4. we have made a Law to famish the King.

MR. YELVERTON declared That the Bill notwithstanding any thing which at the said Conference was obiected, is iust, reasonable, and fitt to passe, and no other in almost all Points then the present Law now requireth: It seemeth by him the first and third Obiection remembred by Sir John Savill are by the Law now in force at this tyme required, then this is not to famish the King, but his Provision will be alltogether as ready as now it is: But said he the Purveyors bring profitt to the Greene Cloth, Great is Diana of Ephesus, why? marry they got money by her Temple, so doth the Greene Cloth by the Purveyors; I protest I meane not the great Lords of the Greene Cloth, but the Inferior Officers. Here he shewed the Course holden at the Green Cloth, viz. In sending for men upon the Purveyors Complaint, and committing them, which is directly against the Law, for no man is to be restrained of his Liberty, but by Course of Law; nor to be impeached of his Goods, but by Course of Law; The Green Cloth is no Court; neither can they imprison the Kings Subiects, but if any offend in Case of Purveyance, he is to answer it by Law, and not before them, and the Kings Prerogative is to maintaine Law, and by this Course, it is not the Kings Prerogative, but the Authority and Profitt of the Green Cloth that is sought.

The Price by Law ought to be upon Oath, therefore no Prerogative or certaine Price. And whereas they obiect, That the Bill appointeth Purveyarie to be where there is greatest and best f. 163] Plenty, which is said is impossible for the Purveyor to understand, for it may be some little more plentifull in an other place, not farr of, with an other man; I say this obiection is nothing, for it is the word of other Lawes, and the phrase of other Law, and is meant and taken to avoide Partiality, and Oppression apparent, not to tye men precisely to the Letter. I think it fitt as hath bene moved, that we should pray a 2d. Conference with the Lords touching this matter, not that I hope that Resolution to uphold the Greatnesse of the Green Cloth, can by Arguments or Answers given to Obiections be altered; But if our Childe must needs dye let it appeare to the World that it dieth not of any naturall Corruption within it, but that it is crushed.[1]

Hereupon the House upon advise did send presently to the Lords to crave a 2d. Conference touching the Bill of Purveyors. But MR. WENTWORTH his Motion though to my understanding the House agreed it should be Parcell of the Message, yet was by Mr. Speaker omitted in the direction to the Messenger; The motion was that requiring a 2d. Conference, we should further pray a Coppy of the Exceptions which were taken against the Bill at the last Conference: And by an other it was moved that the Messenger also pray a note of such Records as were at the said Conference vouched against the Points of the Bill, and which are not printed; And likewise of the Bookes which were then said to mention hereditary Prices; But this last motion it was not greatly urged or applauded though well liked of many, so was it also omitted in the directing of the Message.[2]

When a Bill cometh from the Lords, and after the 2d. reading is here committed if the Committees doe add any Provisoe, they must bring in such Provisoe in Parchment, and if they bring in any Amendments to such Bill, the Same must be in Paper, and

---

[1] Carleton wrote Chamberlain on April 17: "The Parlement hath bin more busied in committees and conferences these few dayes past then since the first sitting. . . . . The bill of Purvayors was the maine matter which bred trouble on all sides. For first it was araigned by the Atturney at a conference, and 10 charges layde to it as impossibilities to have it pass; which was reported to the lower house, and Sir John Saville made a collection owt of the 10 obiections reducing them to 4. hanging the innocent, damning the ignorant, raysing rebellion and starving the king. Wherupon Yelverton, the old Tribune of the house, tooke uppon him the answearing of the Atturney, as desirous to nurce and foster a babe which had bin bred with so much payne and travell. . . . ." St. P. Dom. XX, 36.

[2] The Commons also considered asking that "the Bill may not proceed to Question." *C.J.* I, 297. The committee of the Lords reported from the conference that they held "the Bill unfit to be any further proceeded in." *L.J.* II, 412. This ended the matter in spite of a second conference. See p. 134.

The Bill of Purveyors "was not so well listened unto of the higher house, because of the manner of seeking relief." *Diary of Walter Yonge* (*Camden Society*), 4.

so the Provisoe sent up to the Lords in Parchment and the Amendements in Paper.

Mr. Recorder of London returned from the Lords with Answer
to this Effect: That their Lordships were now in hand with a
weightye Bill, and the Matter of our Message is of Importance,
and the tyme spent, but at their Lordships next setting, when
their House should be more full, this House shall receive Answer
by a Messenger of their owne.

Then Mr. Recorder reported the other two Points of Yerster-
daies Conference, and said he the Lords did first treate of the last
of the said Points, viz: Whether the Matter of the Union shall
now be dealt in, or deferred: wherein the Lords desired Our advise
and wee (quoth he) referred it over to their Lordships as having
had better and longer Consideration of it then Our selves; They
declared that they wished it to be deferred; Whereunto we assented: Then grew the Question, How, and by what Course the
f. 164] Same should be deferred,[1] viz: Whether by Consent
mutuall or by a Bill; And their Lordships wished it to be done by
Bill; Whereunto likewise we agreed.

The next Point of the Conference was touching free Trade: And
to this Exceptions was taken, viz. Exceptions in Law, and Exceptions of Inconveniencie; Exceptions in Law in this, That it is too
Generall to suffer all men to trade: And 2dly. Inconvenient for
it is too Speciall in this that the Bill saith, notwithstanding any
thing done, or to be done to the contrary: For it would set all
men free, and able to trade, so as the King shall have no Power to
restraine any; In Conclusion, the Lords desired tyme to Consider
further of it, and that we shall heare more of them.

Touching the Union, it was now resolved in the House to be by
Bill, as at the Conference had bene agreed, and further that this
Bill shall come from the Lords. Note, That it seemed the Reporters
of this last Conference had no other directions then themselves
in the place could take, and not the help of any notes delivered to

---

[1] The Venetian ambassador wrote that James allowed the Union
to be deferred because he was convinced that nothing could be accomplished for the present. *Cal. St. P. Venetian, 1603–1607*, 280, 329. "La
brouillerie de 'Escosse est tousjours en mesme estat. Je croi que le Roi
sera conseillé de ne paster oultre." Feb. 16/26, 1606, M. de la Fontaine
to M. de Villeroy. Paris Transcripts.

them by any of the Lords that spake, as in former Conferences I
Know was done; when it was thought good That the Kings
necessities, and other unknown Matters of State, and Arguments
thought fitt to be fully Known were delivered.

14. APRILL. 1606.

An Act for Relief of John Rogers against Ro[bert] Taylor, Paul
Taylor etc. for defrauding of a Trust etc. sent from the Lords.
1°. *Lecta.*

An Act to reduce to the Crowne, the Inheritance of Lands given
by his Majesty for want of Issue Male of the Donees, exhibited
by SIR JOHN SAVILL, 1°. *Lecta.*

Mr. Serieant Crooke, and Sir Edw[ard] Stanhop brought a
Message from the Lords to this Effect, viz. That the Lords have
considered of the request of this House for a 2d. Conference touching the Bill of Purveyors, sent from hence to them, and albeit a
2d. Conference is not usuall, yet such is the Lords desire to receive
Satisfaction in this matter, if it be possible, that they willingly
condescend to such a 2d. Conference as is desired; And therefore
for that Purpose will the same Committees come againe to the
former Place the Painted Chamber to Morrow in the afternoone
at 3. of the clock attended as before with the Judges and the
Kings Councell who may give their Lordships Satisfaction in
matter of Law, as neede shall require.

Upon the reading of One of the Bills against Recusants,[1]
MR. BOND moved as formerly he had done, That the Clause
whereby the Recusants convict are enacted to stand as outlawed
Persons disabled, might be striken out, for said he, if a man beate
such a Person, he can bring no Action, and soe wanteth the aide
of Law, for defence of his Person, which is against Nature, and
f. 165] Cruell. To him DR. JAMES answered, That this Parte of the
Law is not uniust nor unmercifull; as Mr. Bond termed it, but is
most iust, fitt, and convenient: For said he, this Law doth not
as the Law now and anciently in force doth provide, for by the
Cannon Lawe the Ordinary ought actually to excommunicate
every such Recusant, and in such Case the Party standeth excommunicate untill Absolution. But he which by this Law is, or

---

[1] "The Bill to Avoid Dangers by Popish Recusants."

standeth in Case excommunicate, No *Capias ut legatum* lieth; againe he is cleered and standeth upright as before, whensoever he will conforme himself without Absolution or further Circumstance of Law. Againe *Lex Talionis* is the most iust Law, and this Law doth not returne the like in no Measure to them, that their Law inflicteth on us: For their Lawe doth excommunicate us (reckoning us Hereticks) from the Communion of Saints, from holy things etc. Yea it doth excommunicate *Amicos, Defensores, Sub Poena Anathematis*: Yea more, it delivereth them over to the Secular Power to be burnt with fire: And much the Doctor spake to that Effect and upon the Question the Bill passed.

15TH. APRILL. 1606.

Here the House proceeded to consider of the Grievances. The 7th. Article among the Grievances was read, which concerneth the Grant of the Green Wax within the Dutchy of Lancaster which before at the last reading was named to be granted to Sir Ro[ger] Aston.

Mr. Serieant Crooke and Dr. Hone brought two Bills from the Lords the One for establishing in the Crowne, the Lands of Henry late Lord Cobham, and George Brooke Esquire attainted of High Treason, with Confirmation of Letters Patents made of diverse parts thereof, The other An Act for Naturalizing of Sir David Fowles Knight with Confirmation of Certaine Grants made to him by his Majesty.

The words of the Grievance concerning Sir Roger Astons Patent was thus. The like Letters Patents (*vid.* to the Grant made to the Lord Danvers) of all the Fynes, Amerciaments, and of other Penalties and Forfeitures Knowen under the Name of the Green Wax, rysing within the Dutchy of Lancaster, which is or may be of very great yearely value, is granted to Sir Roger Aston for many yeares, under a small Rent of 48£—by the yeare, which preventeth those Subiects of the Dutchy from such Mercy and favour as alwaies heretofore hath bene used to good and loving Subiects, and giveth to private men to dispence with great faults, which is hurtfull to the Common Wealth, and may be the undoeing of many. This being put to the Question,[1] and the House devided,

---

[1] For the debate see *C.J.* I, 298.

was agreed for a Grievance to be presented with the others unto his Majesty. And note that upon the Division of the House, the Yea were 109 and No. were 104.

f. 166] Sir Henry Bronchards Patent[1] was defended by MR. FANSHAWE Auditor of the Dutchy, briefely to this Effect (viz) That his Patent is altogether unlike to those Letters Patents made either to the Lord Danvers, or to Sir Roger Aston, for he affirmed these words, to Sir Henry Bronchard, to be a Grant of all Issues at Sessions, and Assizes, or in any of the Kings Courts which shall come into the Exchequer above such a Summ; and for the bringing in of such Issues Sir Henry is made Surveyer of the Issues, so as he serveth to punish such as make defaultes whereby men are urged to appeare for Service of the Country: And this Patent, said he, is assigned to a Gentleman for satisfaction of a great Debt, who is undone if this grant be revoked: Againe, Sir Henry Bronchard is now in Ireland, and no man present to defend his Cause. In conclusion, upon this Motion day was given for Sir Henries Counsell to be heard untill the next Meeting of this House after the Now rising.

SIR HENRY HOBART made Report of the Conference Yesterday with the Lords. viz. That the Committee from this House had mett with the Lords touching the 4. Points of Ecclesiasticall Causes:[2] And (said he) after the first parte was by us delivered, we made a little Pause, expecting an Answer from the Lords.

---

[1] Bruncard, Lord President of Munster, had a patent of the money coming to the Crown above a certain sum from the amercements of jurors for non-appearance at trials. Probably granted in 1603. *Cal. St. P. Dom. 1603–1610*, 59. Arguments in favor of the patent are contained in St. P. Dom. XXII, 27, 28.

[2] "For Church matters theyr were fower points very curiously and learnedly handled by fower Apostles of the lower house, deprivation, citation, excommunication, and the authority of the high commissions, by Sir Francis Bacon, the Atturney of the wards, the Recorder and Sollicitor, in which the Lords tooke time till this day for answeare. And as there was then a general fast and prayers amongst the bretheren in this towne for goode success in theyr affaires so doe they now hasten goode friday a day sooner and are all at theyr devotions." Carleton to Chamberlain, April 17. St. P. Dom. XX, 36. See account in *Roger Wilbraham* (*Camden Misc.* X), 81–82.

"Ceux de la Maison Basse y voudroient bien donner quelque atteinte à l'aucthorité des evesques, et le feroient si le Roy s'y monstroit encliné

Whereupon they required to heare all that we would say touching all the Points, and then they would answere accordingly. Then we proceeded to the other 3. Points; which ended, the Great Prelate[1] answered in name of the Lords, That these Matters are great and Weighty requiring mature Deliberation: That their Lordships would report to the Lords in the House what had passed, and then would us answere; Afterwards the same Prelate spake some thing of himself, which said Sir Henry Hobart I think not good to report, for we had no Authority to treate with any One man, but with their Lordships. It was moved, it might be knowne what day the House should be adiourned, and to meete againe; and agreed to be adiourned on Thursday Morning.

Mr. Serieant Crooke, and Dr. Hone brought a Message from the Lords to this effect, viz. That their Lordships had entred into Consideration of the greate, learned, well performed Conference handled with such Gravity, Wisedome, Modesty, Temper, and Conscience, with such Duty to his Majesty and good Respect to all men, and for Answer in that Matter their Lordships would give meeting to this House on Thursday next in the afternoone at 2. of the clocke in the painted Chamber with the same Committees. After the Messengers had bene withdrawne, and being called in againe, Mr. Speaker delivered, That this House had entertained the Lords Message with great Comfort, doe returne answer with many humble Thankes that the House will accordingly appointe Committees to attend on Thursday next at the Place by their Lordships appointed. The Messengers being dispatched it was considered that the House by reason of this Conference to be on f. 167] Thursday cannot adiourne their Setting untill Friday, Wherefore it was ordered That the House will set, and that day adiourne their further Setting untill that day Sennight then following.

16TH. APRIL. 1606.

An Act for Naturalizing Sir David Fowles Knight, and for

---

tant soit peu. Les autres au contraire pour se confermer ès bounes graces du Roy se sont volontairement chargez d'un subside par dessus ceux que la communalté a, mais peu franchement, accordez." M. de la Fontaine to M. de Villeroy, April 6/16, 1606. Paris Transcripts.

[1] Archbishop Bancroft.

Confirmation of certaine Letters Patents made to him by his Majesty. 1°. *Lecta.*

An Act for cleering the Passage by Water from London to Oxford, 1°. *Lecta.*

The Duke of Lennox Counsell[1] was heard to defend certaine Letters Patents made to the Duke for Searching and Sealing of new Draperies, and other things, whereof many are not meete to be Searched, or Sealed, being the 6th. Article amongst the Grievances; And on the other side Mr. Hitchcocks was heard also at the Barr to maintaine the Grievance against the Patent; Who declared that the Grievance consisteth in matter against Lawe, and in the Manner of Execution. Touching Matter of Lawe this Patent containeth Authority given to the Alneager to measure etc. things not Alnegeable, for *Alnagium* is from *Ulna*, and from thence the Alneager who is with the yard to measure etc., But the Dukes Patent extendeth to Stockings, Night capps, and *Similia*: Likewise thereby is a Fee granted payable by the Kings Subiects which was never payable before: Also Subsidy granted to be paid by Subiects to a Subiect, which no man never Knew, nor reade of before; For Subsidy is *Subsidium*, or Aide from the Subiect to the King. Next there is a Forfeiture of 20s—granted or imposed by these Letters Patents upon every Subiect which shall refuse to pay the Fees and Subsidy aforesaid. And with all, Authority is granted to the Patentee and his officers, to take away Mens Goods which deny to pay the Fees aforesaid, and which is more Power, and Authority, to committ such as shall refuse to pay *ut Supra.*

The other Exceptions are to the undue Order of executing this Patent, for it is to be proved, That the Deputies of the Patentee doe take Mens Goods on the High waies, and open their Packs even such wherein there is money, and detaine their Goods so opened.

The Dukes Counsell made a short, weake defence, and desired That Right be ordered, the Validity of the Patent to be tryed in any Court of his Majesty in Westminster hall, to which Tryall the Duke (as he said) will submit himselfe.

In the Eleaventh Place was reade the 9th. Article or Grief *in haec verba.*

The Marchants of Yorke having alwayes heretofore used to put

---

[1] Mr. Hadsor. See *C.J.* I, 299.

their Merchandize at Yorke into little Vessels upon the River of Owse, and so carried the same to Hull there to be Customed before the same be put into greater Vessells, and transported beyond the Seas without any Forfeiture, or Losse; Now of late, since the last f. 168] Parliament, their Goods have bene seised as forfeit by the Farmers of the Custome for so doeing, to their great hinderance; Upon the Question this was reiected.

In the 12th. Place was reade the 10th. Article *in haec verba*, viz.

The Compulsory Taxe laid upon the Subiects in diverse Countryes by Lieutenants and their Deputies to maintaine Muster Masters, and such like things at the Charge of the Subiects against their willes in this tyme of Peace, and the Imprisonment of the Subiects for not Payment thereof is grievous and uniust. Sir Henry Poole declared to the House That the Lord Lieutenant of the County of Wilts (Innuendo the Earl of Hertford) imposeth a Taxe of 6d.—for every footeman, and 12d. for every horseman upon the County, to be paid to a Muster Master, to which place he appointeth his Secretary:[1] He threatneth and imprisoneth such as refuse to pay the same, yea and besides other disgracefull words which he giveth (said the Knight) unto us; his Lordship said that if he had not bene perswaded otherwise and entreated by a speciall friend, he would in his hott blood have hanged some of us for refusing to pay the said Taxe: Much the Knight spake to this effect, and required Mr. Speakers Knowledge whether in Somerset-Shire[2] the County be not in like sort oppressed.

Mr. Chocke affirmed That upon Consideration of this Grievance, and other hard measure offered by Lieutenants of Counties to the Countryes, he not long since being with two great Judges asked of them Whether the Sheriffe be not Lieutenant of his County, whereunto the Judges answered Affirmatively, then (quoth I) what use of the Lord Lieutenants, to which the Iudges replied, That the latter Commission doth always countermande the former; In which Case Mr. Chocke conceived That the Sheriffe is many times at great Inconveniencie, and in hard takeing; which conceit had good reason. Diverse afterwards seconding Sir Henry Poole, this was allowed for a Grievance to be presented.

---

[1] Josias Kirton. See p. 154.
[2] The Earl of Hertford was lieutenant of both Wilts and Somerset.

In the 13th. Place was reade the 11th. Article *in haec verba.*

The Clothiers of the Realme, and many other good Subiects receive great Losses and Damages by force of a Licence to buy and sell Woolls contrary to the Lawes, and Statuts[1] of the Realme, granted by Letters Patents to Sir Edw[ard] Hobby Knight for many yeares,[2] Whereby the Prices of Wooll is increased, and much deceit used in the Sale thereof, to the hurt of the Common wealth.

Here SIR HENRY HOBBY desired to be heard by his Councell which was yeilded, and a day given for that Purpose, viz. this day Sennight: And because one rose up to speake Sir Ed[ward] Hobby offered to withdrawe himself out of the House according to the Order when any mans Particular is treated of, but the House f. 169] willed him to stay, having lately given that favour to Sir Roger Aston; So the Knight staied a While, and of himselfe went forth, contrary to Expectation. The Obiections were, That such as had Lycence or Warrant from Sir Ed[ward] Hobby doe at the end of the yeare buy up all the Wooll, and so inforce the Clothiers to buy of them at High Rates, and doe mingle Water and Sand with the Woll to make it weigh; which is a greate fraude; So the matter was putt off untill the day before appointed for Councell to be heard.

In the 14th. Place was reade the 12th. Article among the Grievances *in haec verba.*

The Abuse of such as have Commission to make Salt Peeter[3] is exceeding great to the Subiect in digging up their Dove houses at unseasonable tymes, and other Houses at their Pleasure; And in takeing their Carts, and their wood up and other things in more violent and unlawfull sort now, then in tyme of warr; And albeit they have made great quantity of Salt-peeter by force of their Commission, to the great Charge of the Subiects, no parte thereof is come to the Possession and use of his Majesty.

---

[1] 5 & 6 Ed. VI. c. 7. *Statutes of the Realm,* IV, 141.

[2] Granted by Elizabeth in 1594 and confirmed by James in 1604. *Cal. St. P. Dom. 1603–1610,* 134.

[3] A patent to dig for saltpetre granted to Mr. Harding John and Robert Evelyn in 1604 for twenty-one years. *Cal. St. P. Dom. 1603–1610,* 156.

Hereupon SIR ROBERT JOHNSON[1] being an Officer of the Ordinance, declared that since the Kings coming, neither Peter nor Powder hath come into the store for the said Office; And said he, I would we might be Suitors to the King, that neither Salt-peeter, Gunpowder nor any other Abiliment of Warr, may be transported without his Majestyes owne direct Privity. This spoken, the said Article was agreed to be presented as a Grievance, and direction that it should be drawne in particular, viz. the Abuse dayly committed in unorderly digging of Houses, for it was agreed, that to digg Houses for the Service aforesaid is necessary.

In the 15th. place was reade the 13th. Article of the Grievances *in haec verba.* viz. The Monopoly Patent granted of late[2] to Abraham Le Basser Stranger borne, for the sole makeing and selling of Smare alias Blew Starch,* or to bring any from beyond the Seas for the terme of 21 yeares, with a beggerly Kinde of Sale thereof from Doore to Doore in the Streets by them used, to the hinderance of such as kept Shops and houses for that purpose, is very grievous and unlawfull in such Manner as that is used. Here MR. TWYNHOR stood up and professed himself to be the Patentee and desired his Councell may be heard, which was granted, and Monday come Sennight appointed for that purpose.

*and prohibiting all others to make any Starch.

The 14th. Article of the Grievances is formerly ordered in the first place. MR. FULLER moved that as a Grievance, might be delivered, the Oppression of the Green Cloth, with humble suit, that no man may be committed or impeached by the Officers of the Green Cloth for doeing that which by Lawe he may iustify. f. 170] Mr. Hoskyns delivered to Mr. Fuller a Grievance in writing against Tipper, which Mr. Fuller delivered to the Speaker, which was reade *in haec verba.*

Many Cathedrall Churches, Colledges, Hospitalls, Corporations and Foundations erected to charitable uses, infinite Numbers of the Kings Tenants are grieved with the uniust vexation and subtill Practices of Tipper,[3] he pretendeth himselfe to be an Officer

---

[1] Sir Robert Johnson wrote Salisbury on Oct. 31, 1606: "As a Parliament man, I was not the second that excepted against the use made of that Commission [for digging saltpetre], being wholly directed to private ends against his Majesty's purpose therein." Salisbury MSS.

[2] Granted in June, 1605. Price, 29. See also *Cal. St. P. Dom. 1603-1610,* 323, 501.

[3] See p. 106.

authorized to deale with all such as have defective Tytles and
Estates derived out of the Crowne, and by Color thereof carrieth a
great Port and Countenance Keepeth an Office without Warrant,
and he and his Clerk takes unlawfull Fees, and Extorts of the Kings
Subiects great Summes of Money; He hath accesse to the Kings
Records, perswadeth the Clerks of the Court of Augmentations
and the Exchequer that they suffer not the Subiect to have sight
of the Records for strengthning their Tytles; And since his Accesse,
the Records are misplaced, unperfect, and imbezelled: He hath
procured to himselfe Grants of the whole Estates of Cathedrall
Churches, and other Corporations, and of particular Persons, and
vexed them without Cause: He hath now a Grant of 41. Mannors,
with diverse other Granges and Fermes to his use, for the Consider-
tion of 20£—only paid by Clerck and Clerk: And when the Kings
Tenants and others called up to compound for defective Tytles
by his Majesty honorable Commissioners authorized to make them
good Estates, doe offer Composition, after such tyme as the said
Tipper hath by long Molestation discovered their Tytles, then he
interposeth his said lease betwixt them, and his Majesty favour
intended by the said Commission, in fraud of his Majestyes Grace,
and dishonour of the Commission, he first giveth false Coppies to
such as come to Compound, then searcheth their Evidences, and
either taketh bribes, or multiplieth Endlesse Suites. He and his
Partaker[1] hath covenanted to bring into his Majesty 100000£—
in few yeares by discovery of Tytles, and is to have together with
his Partaker either a fourth part of the same 100000£—and what
ever else he shall bring in in money, or a fourth part of the Lands
so evicted in lease for 90 yeares at his Election. And hath undertaken debts due to the King, but little or nothing is brought in
by this Course to the King, infinite Number of Subiects troubled
and Scandall raysed by this Course, which in Common Persons
is Barretry and Maintenance. It is humbly desired that his
Majesty Service be supplied by a man of honnor, Reputation, and
by the direction of his Majesty Judges or learned Counsell, and
that they be not referred over to such a person to worke upon them
by undirect Sleights to their great Charge and Grievance.

Upon some Motion it was ordered That Mr. Tipper shall on

---

[1] Sir Edward Dyer. *Cal. St. P. Dom. 1598–1601*, 537.

Monday come Sennight be heard in the House with his Councell.

MR. RECORDER reported the Effect of the Conference[1] had yesterday with the Lords concerning our Bill of Purveyors: wherein after he had declared diverse Exceptions taken to the f. 171] Bill by Mr. Attorney, and how the same were answered by the Committees of this House; He shewed That My Lord Chief Justice declared, That upon the Statute of 36. E. 3.[2] he could make no other Exposition, but that the King hath Prerogative; Also that the King is not bound to make present Payment, but yet must make Payment to the Subiect in the place where the taking was: Also that Acts of Parliament may expound, and limitt

---

[1] See *Roger Wilbraham* (*Camden Misc.* X), 82–86; *C.J.* I, 299. "Yelverton, the old Tribune of the house, tooke uppon him the answearing of the Atturney [April 12], as desirous to nurce and foster a babe which had bin bred with so much payne and travell and as he used this metaphor in the house so was it his florish at the second conference; which he stoode somewhat too much uppon, and the Lords looking for it, were well provided of an answeare, saying that his love to a babe of so small hope was rather fondnes then true affection; and that it were better be crusht in the cradle then nurced up and prove a monster. Whereuppon Ned Wimarke who sealdome speakes at a conference could not containe himself from expressing his sorrow in an audible voice to see theyr babe betrayed in so goode company. For materiall points they were handled well and substantially. But the Judges overruled all on Prerogative side and gave it owt for law that the king had both prising and preemption, and that he was not bownd to payment but uppon these terms, *quand bonnement il peut*, and delivered one Iudgment in all mens opinions of dangerous consequence, that the prerogative was not subiect to law, but that it was a transcendent above the reach of parlement. In the end the Lords closed up the matter with the kings favorable intention, that in kindnes he would doe much, but uppon constraint nothing and that of him self he would see that reformation in this disorder which Parlement could not provide for. It was then onely observed how Nick Fuller not well marking what was sayde but conceaving that the Lords did promise a passage of the Bill, desired to be heard, and prayed theyr Lordships there might be a proviso putt in for the city of London: which made a merry end of a sharp bickering." Chamberlain to Carleton. St. P. Dom. XX, 36.

This conference was useless. The King issued on April 23 a proclamation against the worst evils of purveyance. Steele, *Tudor and Stuart Proclamations*, I, 120; Spedding, III, 272. The House later passed a new bill against purveyors but the Lords refused to consider it. *L.J.* II, 435.

[2] Mistake for 27 Ed. III. Stat. II (*Statutes of the Realm*, I, 334–335). See *Roger Wilbraham* (*Camden Misc.* X), 83. The Statute of 36 Ed. III. c. 2–6 (*Statutes of the Realm*, I, 371–373) was cited by the Commons.

the Prerogative, but not take it away absolutely without Recompence. Then he declared, that the Lord Chancellor moved That by this Bill the King is tied so, as with an *Non obstante* he shall be able to doe nothing, which said his Lordship is voide, for the Statute of [*blank*][1] is, that no man shall be Sheriffe longer then one yeare, no not with a *Non obstante* and yet the King with a *Non Obstante* of that *Non obstante* may continue Sheriffe longer then one yeare.

17. APRILL. 1606.

An Act for the better Preservation of Sea fish 3°. *Lecta.* being ingrossed, recommitted to the Same and some other Committees. *Nota*, it was agreed, That a Bill once committed and brought back, and engrossed, and put to the question, may not be recommitted out of the House, but either at the Cubbard, or in the Committee Chamber it may be recommitted, and considered of by the Committees.

18TH. APRILL. 1606.

Mr. Speaker moved That some Members of the House may be appointed to put forme unto the Grievances against the next meeting of the House, which was done accordingly, because it would be too much labour for one man to doe; And further to the Entent this might more conveniently be done by the Severall Persons named therefore, it was agreed upon motion made by MR. BROOKE, That these Committees should meete as soone as might be, and devide the Articles so as no Man to be burthened with more then one Article.

24TH.[2] APRILL. 1606.

An Act to cutt off infinite Suites commenced and brought against many his Majesty Subiects by Informers: 2°. *Lecta.* And upon the Question of committing, the House was divided, whereupon it fell out that they which went forth with Yea, were 25. and they which did sitt still with Noe, were also 25. so as the Speaker was to give a voice, which in such Case is the binding voice, and this voice Mr. Speaker gave against the Committement. Then before the Bill was put to the 2d. question of engrossing, diverse

---

[1] 23 Hen. VI. c. 7 (*Statutes of the Realm*, II, 333).
[2] The House adjourned between April 18 and April 24.

Members came into the House, which were not present before, and upon this 2d. question, the House was againe devided, and then the Number of those that went forth with Yea, were 35. and f. 172] of them which staid with No, 26. so the Bill was to be engrossed without any Committment. This Bill cometh short of the Title for the whole body of the Bill being not on[e] Sheete of Paper on one side, is only to ordaine that Bowling shall be a Law-full Game.

The Committees for the Matter of Grievances or so many of them as were present, and such as offered and arose voluntarily to accompany them; went up into the Committee Chamber to Marshall these Grievances, during which tyme being a full hower the House did sitt idle without doeing anything; after which long pawsing, the Committees sent word that they would come downe into the House (if so it pleased the House) and conferr with the Company, not as in the House, but by way of Committee: This the Speaker having received from them by the Sergeant, did deliver to the House, and the House alloweing thereof; The Speaker added, that himself in this Case was to departe the place, which with allowance he did, and the most of the Company departed with him; a few staid untill after eleeven of the clock expecting the coming downe of the Committees, and then likewise departed; and after them the Committees followed.[1]

25. APRILL. 1606.

An Act as well for Relief of Prisoners in Execution, as also for Creditors to have Satisfaction of their debts 1º. *Lecta.*

For want of other worke, by Motion of Mr. Speaker, and con-sent of those few which were present, the Proclamation newly set out against Purveyors was reade; Which done and halfe an hower spent afterwards in Idle looking one upon an other, Mr. Speaker arose, and the House departed.

26TH. APRILL. 1606.

An Act against unlawfull hunting and Stealing of Deare and Conneys, 2º. *Lecta.* The House was devided upon the question of Committment,[2] and the Number that said Yea, was 39. and the

---

[1] This procedure foreshadows the Committee of the Whole House.
[2] "(*d.* Committed. Sir Wm. Stroud, Sir Wm. Skipwith, Sir Nath.

Number that said Noe was 41. Then the question of engrossing being demanded; It was said that a Bill begun here in this house, after denyall of Committment, must before any other or third reading, be put to the question of engrossing, but this Bill came from the Lords, and is already ingrossed and therefore must be reade againe before the question of passing.

An Act for repeale of a Branch of a Statute made 33. H. 8.[1] intituled An Act for Maintenance of Artillary and debarring of unlawfull Games, 1° *Lecta*. And afterwards within one hower, for want of other busines 2° *Lecta*. and committed. It was this day ordered, that the Committees formerly by the House appointed f. 173] to take Consideration for marshalling the Grievances shall presently[2] goe up into the Committee Chamber, and for the better expediting of the busines, to devide the said Grievances among themselves, and each Person to penn and make perfect such of the said Grievances as shall be to him or them assigned, and then to conferr together for disposing of the Same; And afterwards to present their Labor to the House.

An Act for the rating and levying the Charges of conveying Malefactors and offenders to the Gaole, 3° *Lecta*. The Clerke moved Mr. Speaker, and the House, that whereas at a former reading of the Bill last specified, it was agreed that a clause should be thereunto added to this effect, viz. This Act to continue untill the first Session of the next Parliament, that now the said Clause may be added to the End of the Bill, and presently to be engrossed under the Same Bill, which was ordered accordingly.

An Act to repayre the High way from Nonsuch to Kingston[3] etc. It was moved by SIR NICHOLAS SAUNDERS That whereas in default of the Justices of Peace of the County of Surrey, the Lord Chancellor hath Power by this Act to appoint Commissioners to execute the ordinance of this Statute, there may be added to the words, Commissioners, these words (of the said County). Hereupon it was agreed that these words required may be added

---

Bacon, Mr. [*blank*].)" C.J. MS, Jac. I, II, f. 108*v*. The Clerk, expecting the bill would be committed, began writing down the names of the speakers.

[1] *Statutes of the Realm*, III, 837.

[2] "Greivances (*d*. this afternoon) presently, Court of Wards." C.J. MS, Jac. I, II, f. 109. The time was changed from afternoon to morning.

[3] Nonsuch to Talworth. *C.J.* I, 301.

by the Clerke, and thought fitt in this Case so to be, but Mr. Speaker wished it not to be stood on, for that the Lord Chancellor will never appoint any Commissioners to supply the defect of the Justices of Peace of Surrey, but Persons of the same County.

28TH. APRILL. 1606.

An Act for Naturalizing Sir David Fowles Knight and for Confirmation of certaine Letters Patents[1] made by his most Excellent Majesty unto him.

This Bill was now brought in by the Committees[2] without Alteration and 3°. *Lecta.* For it came from the Lords and passed. It was moved that only such of his Children as should be borne in England might by this Act be naturalized, but the desert of the Gentleman was declared to be so good, heretofore by good offices towards this Nation, and now in the Education of the Prince, as that it was not thought good to begin this Course with him; Which notwithstanding was thought and agreed to be fitt and good course hereafter to be held with others in like Case: And touching the Lands conteyned in the said Letters Patents, it was declared what the valew was, which appeared small, and also that the same are parcells of the late Countesse of Lennox,[3] and so descended to the King, and by Grant thereof the Possessions of the Crowne are not diminished.

f. 174] An Act for restraint of Arrests on the Sabbath day, 3°. *Lecta.* by Order recommitted, and brought in againe amended, and ordered, that a new bill shall be framed.

Sir John Crooke and Dr. Hone brought from the Lords two Bills, with a Message, that the Lords doe desire a Meeting on Wednesday in the afternoone at 2. of the Clocke in the painted Chamber with the same Committees that before were for the Conference in the Bill of Free Trade, and the Merchants[4] on both sides to be warned to attend the same tyme.

---

[1] See *Cal. St. P. Dom. 1603–1610*, 7, 72, 155.

[2] Reported by Sir Robert Hitcham. "Mr. Fuller offereth a Proviso, to exclude him from Parliament." *C.J.* I, 301.

[3] Margaret, Countess of Lenox.

[4] This act (3 Jac. I. c. 6. *Statutes of the Realm*, IV, 1083) threw open the trade to Spain, Portugal, and France. See Gardiner, I, 347–348; Unwin, *Industrial Organization in the 16th and 17th Centuries*, 174. As the act

The Bills which the said Messengers brought were viz.

An Act for prohibiting Such from brewing of Beere and Ale as sell the Same againe by retayle, and to compell brewers to Keepe the Lawfull Assize of Beere and Ale.

An Act to relieve such as professe the handycraft and Trade of Skynners.

The House yeilded to the Conference or meeting on Wednesday with the same Committees of this House as were last, and the calling of the House is putt off untill Thursday.

29TH. APRILL. 1606.

MR. FRANCIS MOORE moved Whether Mr. Attorney Generall coming to informe the House touching the Bill of Attainders[1] shall stand at the doore, or come within the Barr. It was remembred that My Lord Dyer came into the House to iustify an Error supposed to be committed by him in a Verdict, and stood at the Barr, whereto was answered, that My Lord Dyer came as accused, and in Conclusion it was ruled that Mr. Attorney in the Case as he now cometh is to stand without the Barr, and so he did; whom the House used with great respect at his Entrance, and when he had proceeded a little in his Speech, a Stoole was brought and placed behind him, which he used not untill after one hower, and then sparingly for his Ease.

The Bill said Mr. Attorney doth consist of,
1. A Preamble.
2. The body.
   In the Preamble two things, viz.
      1. What the Spanish Treason is.
      2. What the reason is that the Spanish Treason being in the Preamble, is left out of the Body.
The Body of the Bill hath 4. things, viz.
   1. The Persons to be attainted.
   2. The offence whereof.
   3. The Clause and Forfeiture.
   4. The Saving.

dissolved the charter of the Spanish merchants, they protested against it. St. P. Dom. XXI, 2, contains their arguments.

[1] Against the gunpowder conspirators. Coke is counsel for the Crown. For his speech, see *C.J.* I, 301–302; St. P. Dom. XX, 52. For Bacon's part in this matter, see Spedding, III, 294.

In the Offence three things are Considerable.
f. 175] 1. The Tyme.   2. The Matter.   3. The Manner.

30TH. APRILL. 1606.

An Act to reforme the Abuses touching writing of Coppyes in
Paper in English words in many Courts of Record or Offices
belonging to those Courts in or about Westminster hall to reduce
the great Charges which the Subiect often payeth for one Coppy,
to a more reasonable rate. 1°. *Lecta*.[1]

An Act to reduce to the Crowne the Inheritance of the Lands
given by his Majesty for default of Issue Male of the Donees
2°. *Lecta*. and reiected. Now came in Councell[2] for Sir Lewis
Tresham brother of Fran[cis] Tresham, and for the Lady Digby
Widdow of Sir Edw[ard] Digby, and for Thom[as] Winters Wife,
and her Sonn John, who desired Provision for their Tytles and
Rights, to be inserted into the Bill of Attaindor of certaine Persons
attainted in the late Barbarous Treason, and being heard, departed; And the Bill committed,[3] the Committees to meete on
Friday in the Exchequer Chamber.

An Act to enable Sir Christopher Hatton Knight to dispose of
certaine Lands etc. notwithstanding etc.[4] was brought back by

---

[1] Harl. MSS 6808, ff. 90–98, contains an undated request to the
House of Commons for redress in this matter. This paper states that
clerks usually received 8*d*. a page which was much more than in the time
of Elizabeth. An officer to supervise copying is suggested.

[2] Serjeant Harris and Mr. Crewe. See *C.J.* I, 303.

[3] Sir Thomas Lake wrote to Salisbury on May 4: "The King upon
perusal of your letter seemed to find some contrariety in that which you
wrote in this letter about Tresham, and that which you had written before
to my Lord of Dirleton, the first being, as his Majesty said, that it was
a thing resolved in the house: this letter that you had it in hope. I told
him that you might have written the one as your judgment of the success,
because we were so persuaded in the Lower House, for ought I could discern, that it would proceed as touching his blood, considering the great
reason was in it why it should be so. And the other according to the ob-
servations you made of men's dispositions after the disputation of it; which
at my coming away had not been spoken of in the House, but only the
evidence heard. It seems this conceit of his is somewhat grounded upon
a letter of Sir Roger Ashton's written to my Lord of Dirleton, wherein
he advertises his conceits, and the means made by Tresham's brothers
for saving of his blood. . . . ." Salisbury MSS.

[4] "Notwithstanding a Limitation or Clause of Perpetuitie annexed

Mr. Attorney of the Wards, with some Alterations, especially in two Points viz. 2000 Marks per Annum to be Kept in the same State by this Act that formerly it was. Secondly a Provisoe for the Lady Francis, wife of Sir Robert Rich. When the Provisoe was reade, Mr. Speaker moved the House, that if they thought fitt the word (Lady Francis) might be made (Dame Francis) which was accordingly ordered to be so amended presently by the Clerke in the Court 3° *Lecta.* and passed.

An Act to disable Margarett Whittell alias Mildemay for having Dower or Jointure of the Possessions of Sir Thomas Mildmay Knight. 1° *Lecta.* Reiected.

An Act for the better Execution of a Statute made A° 31. Eliz.[1] intituted an Act against the erecting and Maintayning of Cottages 3° *Lecta.* Reiected.

PRIMO MAII. 1606.

An Act to restraine Purveyors that they exceede not the limitts of their Commissions. 1° *Lecta.*

The Bill for 8£—in the hundred[2] exhibited by Sir Edw[ard] Grevill was 2° *Lecta.*

Sir Edw[ard] Hobby brought his Councell to the Barr to shew Cause why certaine Letters Patents made unto him for Wooll jobbing and brogging, should be no Grievance; And first the Grievance was reade, and urged by Serieant Altom to be a Grievance, and shewed that Queen Elizabeth A° 44.[3] granted a dispensation to Sir Edw[ard] Hobby and his Assignes for 10. yeares for 20£.—rent to buy Wooll in certaine Counties, viz. 500 Sarplers, which is 20. thousand Todd per Annum notwithstanding the Statute of 5. E. 6. and said he, this Lycence is diverse way hurtfull, for,

f. 176] 1. It maketh great Scarcity of Wooll to the Clothiers.

2. It is the Cause that Clothiers cannot have the Wooll pure, and cleane in his Nature, but mixt to the great deceipt of Clothiers, and of all that weare Cloth.

3. It maintaineth many idle fellowes.

to the Estate." *Statutes of the Realm*, IV, 1066. For persons concerned, see *D.N.B.* under Sir Christopher Hatton.

[1] *Statutes of the Realm*, IV, 804.
[2] A bill against usury.
[3] The grant was made in 1594.

4. The Broggers beate downe the Price of Wooll to the Sellers, and enhaunceth it to the Clothiers.

5. They have 16. Shires in England and all wales to buy Wooll, no man Knoweth when they have bought their Proportion.

6. These Idle deputies of Sir Edw[ard] Hobby leave their trades and by this Course must raise the Kings rent which is 20£ per Annum: And Sir Edw[ard] Hobbyes Rent which is 500£ per Annum and maintaine their Wives and Charge.

7. They mixe it with Sande and Water etc.

Mr. Crewe of Councell for the Patent; And said he Mr. Bowyer[1] had the like Grant before; And said he, before this Patent to Sir Edw[ard] Hobby passed, it was disputed at the Councell table, and allowed: Afterwards when the King came Sir Edw[ard] Hobby desired a Confirmation of this Patent, the King referred it to the Lord Chancellor and Lord Treasurer, who hearing Councell on both sides, reported That it was no Inconveniencie, but that it was fitt and necessary:[2] Sir Edw[ard] Hobby is to buy in Countryes where no Clothing is. It hath bene said, That the Patentees Deputies buy Wooll on the Sheepes back, and prevent the Clothiers, if this Kinde of buying be gainfull, the Clothier is at Liberty to buy in like Sorte, for the Patent containeth no restraint. Also this Statute of E. 6. is determinable by the Kings Proclamation at his Majesty Pleasure, and this Patent doth set the full Power of buying, at Liberty only in Parte. This Matter was ruled to be no Grievance.

A Message was brought from the Lords by Sir John Crooke One of his Majesty Serieants, and Sir Edw[ard] Stanhope, and Dr. Swale, masters of the Chancery, they brought a Bill[3] intituled, An Act declaratory explaining An Act made in the 1st. Session of this Parliament, intituled An Act authorizing certaine Commissioners of England to treate with certaine Commissioners of Scotland for the Weale of both Kingdomes.

---

[1] Mr. Simon Bowyer had the grant in 1576. Lansd. MSS 22, f. 35; *Cal. St. P. Dom. 1595–1597*, 150. No relation of Robert Bowyer.

[2] For the importance of middlemen in this industry, see Unwin, 188–189; 234–236.

[3] James was much concerned over this act. Lake wrote Salisbury on May 4 that the King "longed to hear of the bill concerning the continuation of the treaty of Union, whereof you made no mention. I told

Mr. Secretary Herbert was sent to the Lords to request a Conference for a replie touching the 4. Points concerning the Ecclesiasticall Grievances.

An Act for establishing in the Crowne the Lands and Possessions of the late Lord Cobham,[1] and George Brooke Esquire attainted of Treason, with Confirmation of Grants made by his Majesty 2? *Lecta.* sent by the Lords.

Then came to the Barr the Counsell of Sir John Brooke, viz. Serieant Harris for Duke Brooke, and the Bill, and Mr. Stephens f. 177] for Sir John Brooke, and against the Bill. Mr. Stephens urged a Privisoe to the Bill for Preservation of certaine remainders limitted by Sir W[illia]m Brooke Grandfather to the late Lord Cobham attainted, and also of Duke Brooke and Sir John Brooke, and afterwards the Bill was committed.

Mr. Secretary Herbert brought back word that the Lords would returne answer by Messengers of their owne; which accordingly Sir John Crooke and Dr. Swale did bring, that their Lordships would give meeting and Conference as was desired this afternoone at 3. of the Clocke in the painted Chamber.

2? Maii. 1606.

An Act prohibiting such from brewing of Beere and Ale, as sell the same againe by retayle, and that all Common Brewers doe

---

him because that was a thing already agreed on by the consent of both Houses, it was like to be the last that would come in, being but short, and quickly to be dispatched." Salisbury MSS.

Salisbury wrote Lake on May 7: "Having understood by the Erle of Arrundell that his Majesty is desirous to understand what is become of the Bill of Union, I think it good to let you know, that it hath ben twice read in the Lower Howse [on May 2 and May 3], & though there be no question of the passing (for men are free from phrensy) yet it is held such a wisdome to be formall, as it hath received a committment, & from thence is to returne to be passt. In the same estate is the Bill of Attaynders, & yet both of them like to be concluded before his Majestys returne, but this is true, & so wee find it, that their opinion in the Lower Howse is such of the purpose to conclude the Parliament as soone as these two are done, as they doe rather spinn out things in formalitie, wherof ther will be no question, because they will gaine therby a time for presentment of their greevances, and for those three Bill which they have passed concerning Recusants." St. P. Dom. XXI, 15.

[1] Henry Brooke, Lord Cobham. George Brooke was his younger brother.

Keepe the Lawfull Assize of Beere and Ale, 2° *Lecta*. sent from the Lords, upon the question it was denied to be committed, and ordered that all bills denied Committment for fault Generall in the Body of the Bill, shall be putt presently to the third Question of Reiecting: And this Bill being accordingly put that question, was reiected and throwen out: Upon this doubt chiefely, that upon this Bill a Patent of Dispensation would be procured by some Courtier.

Sir Edwyn Sandys made a Report[1] of the Conference with the Lords touching the Bill of Free Trade, wherein he declared that the Lords did yeild to the reason alledged by Our Committees, and he hoped the Bill sent up by this House will passe the Lords House.

3° Maii. 1606.

An Act restraining Purveyors that they exceede not the Limitts of their Commissions, preferred by Sir Rob[ert] Johnson 2° *Lecta*. Committed;[2] And ruled That a Bill having bene twice reade must be Committed presently or denied Committment, for it was moved that this Bill should be forborne committment untill a Bill of like nature exhibited by Mr. Laurence Hyde, might be twice reade and committed together, which for the reason of the said Rule was denied: Thereupon Mr. Hydes Bill was called for and delivered Viz. An Act for better executing of Statutes concerning Purveyors and Carttakers. 1° *Lecta*.

Mr. Yelverton reported the Effect[3] of the Conference with the Lords on Thursday last touching the first Ecclesiasticall

---

[1] See *C.J.* I, 304.

[2] Sir Thomas Lake wrote Salisbury on May 4: "Sir Roger's letter [to the King] contains also somewhat about a new bill of purveyors, whereat his Majesty was much moved." Salisbury MSS.

[3] Cf. *C.J.* I, 304. James complained that Salisbury had not reported this conference to him in sufficient detail. Sir Thomas Lake wrote to Salisbury on May 4: "In the same letter [a letter from Sir Roger Ashton to the King] is also somewhat written about the causes ecclesiastical, and of words between my Lord of Canterbury and Mr. Yelverton, whereof his Majesty marvelled that there was no particularity in your letter. To which I answered that if there had been ought meet for his knowledge, it would not have been omitted, but that you thought it needless to advertise every interlocutory speech, but rather having your eye upon the issue, and the appearance that was of the success thereof, gave your judg-

Grievance, wherein this House heretofore required Conference viz. concerning deprived and silenced Ministers. And his Speech for these Ministers, he first reported, and therein the Chief Point was, that the Statute in the first Session of the King[1] doth repeale the Statute of Queen Mary[2] which did repeale the Statute f. 178] of E. 6.[3] the Effect of which Statute of E. 6. is, That all Bishops and Archbishops shall make their Processe in the name of the King, and themselves, viz. the Bishop is to be but *Testis*; And said Mr. Yelverton, your Lordships my Lords of the Bishops

ment in general, that it was like to be to his contentment. If anything fell out otherwise he was like to hear of it as soon as there was cause it should come to his knowledge." Salisbury MSS.

This letter induced Salisbury to write again about the conference, for Lake wrote him on May 6: "I am commanded expressly by his Majesty to signify to you how much he is pleased with the discourse you have written of the Conference: which though he acknowledge to have been very painful to you, after so many laborious sittings and other despatches of his affairs, yet when you shall hear that it has brought him more contentment than all the sports he has had here, he assures himself you will account the pains well bestowed. His Majesty seems to hope by the success of that day's work that all the controversies about these Church causes will either die, or be weakly pursued. Upon that point of your advertisement which reports the quirks of the repeal of Queen Mary's statutes, his Highness discovered the ground of a suit made to him by a letter from the Lady Arbella, brought hither this day, which was (as much as I can gather by his speech) that she might have the benefit of the seals of *non obstantes* for causes ecclesiastical; which suit his Majesty could not conceive how it was grounded till he read your letter. But upon sight thereof, and knowing withal that Mr. Yelverton has access to her, he both conceived the scope of the suit and from what invention it proceeded. Upon that point he willed me to say to you that he liked very well of your conceit of a new short law, for the explaining of the law in that point touching the statute of King Edward; and that if you thought it fit to be propounded at this Session and likely to be passed, he would wish it taken in hand, and thought the House would rather like to have it so to be done than that either his Majesty should grant in every diocese a commission to rectify for the Bishops' actions judicial by *non obstantes.* Also he wished that the bill about the Union might be hastened, and that of the subsidy, to the end he might be able to discern at his return how long the Parliament shall be needful to be held together." Salisbury MSS.

[1] 1 Jac. I. c. 25. *Statutes of the Realm*, IV, 1052.
[2] 1 Mar. Stat. II. c. 2. *Statutes of the Realm*, IV, 202.
[3] 1 Ed. VI. c. 2. *Statutes of the Realm*, IV, 4.

having continued Proces in your owne names, the Proceedings
are *Coram non Iudice*, and voide.

The Lords touching this Point required the Opinion of the Kings
learned Counsell: Then Mr. Attorney in a long learned discourse
shewed that the Bishops Courts are, and ever were the Kings
Courts, and never belonged to the Pope; And vouched a discourse
or Case by him before published in English, and likewise in Latin.[1]
Then he shewed that the Statute of the first Session of the King
doth indeed repeale Queen Maries Statute which did repeale the
Statute of E. 6. so as now the Statute of E. 6. is on foote, and in
force againe; But said he, the Statute of E. 6. is only in the Affirmative, viz. That the Proces in Bishops Courts shall be in the Kings
Name, and if any Bishop doe otherwise, he shall be in the Kings
mercie. So as the said Statute appointing the Proces to be in the
Kings name, doth not saye, And no otherwise; so as if it be otherwise, the only Punishment is that the Bishop is in the Kings mercy,
but the Proceedings is good.[2]

Then the Lords required the Opinion of the Lord Chief Justice,
who concurred with Mr. Attorney, and added this, viz. That the
Statute of E. 6. is onely concerning Party and Party, but the
Ministers for whom the Commons speake were not convented by
Processe in any matter or suite betweene Party and Party, and
the High Commissioners by which these men were censured, is
out of that Statute.

This being in the Kings Mercy did much dismay the Bishops
and My Lord Chiefe Justice wished that this matter had not bene
minded, but said he, the 1st. Session of Parliament did also by
repealing of sundry Statuts together, set also an other Inconveni-

---

[1] See *D.N.B.* under Sir Edward Coke.

[2] "Mr. Attorney, in his Argument, confessed that the Bishops were
all in the King's Mercy." *C.J.* I, 304. But see Coke, *Reports* (ed. of 1826),
VI, 199–202. If the Bishops could not issue writs in their own names,
many cases would go into the King's courts and swell his revenue. Harl.
MSS 4807, No. 20, ff. 35–36 contains a list of such cases. See also St.
P. Dom. XIX, 86; XXI, 18.

See account in *Cal. St. P. Venetian, 1603–1607*, 353. M. de la Fontaine
wrote on April 26/May 6: "Nostre Parlement a faiet les festes. Auquel
la Chambre et Maison Basse avec partie de la Haulte est en contestation
contre les évesques. Mais le Roi porte pour ceux-cy à la balance." Paris
Transcripts.

ence on foote, no lesse then this against the Bishops: And there
with all spake softly to the Earle of Salisbury, which I heard not,
but I suppose, and did a Gentleman of great worth say unto me,
That Sanctuary is revived by the said Statute of Repeale.

The Marshall of the Marshalsey having received a Writt of
Habeas Corpus from this House to bring into the Court the body
of Valentine Sire, servant to the Clerke of this House, and returned
his Writt whereby it appeared that he was delivered to the
Marshall out of the King's Bench upon a *Capias ad Satisfaciendum*
for debt and Damages [*blank*][1] dayes before the beginning of
this Session, which is within the 16. daies agreed and ordered
to be a reasonable tyme before, and after every Session, for coming
and returning to the Parliament; And the Prisoner was discharged,
and agreed that by the Statute of the last Session[2] the Execution
is saved to the Party.

After dinner Councell came to the Barr to shew Cause, and
f. 179] satisfy the House, why the Article and matter exhibited
into the House should not be exhibited to the King as a Grievance.
Tipper desired to be discharged in particular, and he would answer
thereto particularly; Generally he said, That 50. E. 3. untill the
tyme of H. 4. there went forth almost yearely Commissions to
enquire of Concealements, and that in the late Queens tyme diverse
Bookes of Concealement were granted: All which by this Commission of amendement of defective Titles, wherein he is imploied,
are avoided; Then he shewed the Course holden in this Commission.

To this after he was withdrawnen, it was answered That the
Commission proceeded from a gratious minde in the King, and
was performed most honorably by the Lord Commissioners after
that the Parties came to them, but Tipper being employed in the
Execution hereof, doth grieve the People, as in the Articles is
set downe. And therefore out of the Tower was vouched a Record
mentioning a Petition of the Commons to the King, that he would
please to use Serieants at Law and other Persons of good fame,
in searching out and enquiring his concealed Titles: And shewed
That Tipper is a Person Notorious for his Evill Courses; for he

---

[1] Syre was arrested on Nov. 20, 1605, eleven days after Parliament
was prorogued. See Hatsell, *Precedents* (edition of 1796), I, 195.

[2] 1 Jac. I. c. 13. *Statutes of the Realm*, IV, 1029.

was sued from two Colledges, and 40. Churches in Wales, whereof he tooke a lease for 40s. per Annum of Queen Elizabeth: And in that Suite it appeareth that the Queen had 100 Marks yearely out of the Premises for tenthes etc. and in that Suite a decree passed against Tipper and Dawes defendants it is mentioned thus, viz. In detestation of the Wicked, Odious, and Ungodly Practises of the Defendants and these words were reade out of the Exemplification of the decree.

Then came a Message from the Lords by Sir John Crooke and Dr. Hone, viz. that the Lords desired a Conference with the Commons, touching the other 3. points of Ecceliasticall Grievances left the last meeting unhandled; This Conference now required to be in the painted Chamber on Monday next in the afternoone, also they brought 2. Bills[1] from the Lords The One An Act for assuring certaine small parcells of Land to Robert Earl of Sarum, for the enlarging of his House in the Strand by Ivy Bridge etc. with a Recompence to the Bishop of Duresme. This Bill was also reade this day.

Against Tipper it was *inter alia* alledged, that he did threaten some that heretofore kept the Records in the Tower, for shewing them to Suitors. Tipper said he never had but 3. Suites, viz. One with Mr. Dutton, an other with Mr. Pelham of Sussex; The third with Mr. Tirwitt of Lynconshire.

5.° Maii. 1606.

An Act for naturalizing James Demetrius[2] of the Parish of St. Botolph without Algate and Mary his Wife, 3.° *Lecta.* upon the Question, and division of the House. Reiected.

f. 180] Where this House sendeth a Bill up to the Lords and they returne it with some Amendements, the same must be accordingly amended in the House, and it must be sent up againe presently, and may not be retained in this House untill the End of the Session: So ruled in the Bill of Free Trade.

An Act against Scandalous and unworthy Ministers 3.° *Lecta.* passed, and sent up with other Bills to the Lords.

Sir Thom[as] Holcroft moved the House to be satisfied, Whether the word Minister, be an apt and fitt word to be used in

---

[1] Three bills in *C.J.*
[2] James Desmaistres. *Ibid.*

the Bill last mentioned, and who are meant by the word Minister; For said he, the old and usuall word is, Clerke and they are either Deane, Arch-deacons etc. And agreed by the House that the word minister both in this Session and diverse other Parliaments hath bene used, and is now usuall and well understood, and an apt and good Terme.

An Act to restraine the Utterance of Ale and Beere to Ale house Keepers and Tiplers not licensed, 3? *Lecta.* And upon the question, and division of the House, reiected.

When this House sendeth up Bills to the Lords, such Bills as came from the Lords formerly to us, are to be placed and delivered first.

Sir John Crooke and Dr. Swale from the Lords brought back a Bill from hence to them formerly sent, for repayring and maintaining of Chepstow Bridge, with some small amendements. In this Bill, where the words were (Chancery) the Lords required among their Amendements, that it should be (or any Court of Equity) hereupon SIR ROGER OWEN moved it should be added thus (at Westminster) which seemed to be, for that he would exclude the Iurisdiction of the Counsell of the Marches of Wales; But it was agreed and ruled by the House that to an Amendement sent from the Lords to one of Our Bills this House can add nothing: But we must either accept of it, as their Lordships send it, or dash the Bill if we like it not so reformed.

6? MAII. 1606.

The Preamble to be used, or written before the Petition to the King for Reformation of Grievances was reade.

Then came to the Barr Counsell for and against the Bill for drayning of the Fenns in the Isle of Ely etc. viz. Mr. Thom[as] Stephens for the Bill; and a Counsellor[1] whose name I knew not on the other side: And he against the Bill by direction of Mr. Speaker began, who spake not against the bill, but delivered reasons for some things to be inserted, viz. the Worke not to be done only by discretion of the Commissioners, but by Iury. Then matter of Exception, namely in the Countyes of Cambridge and Suffolke, much of the Lands are worth 6s. 8d. an Acre; And as the Lords are provided for, whose Lands are of that worth, so

---

[1] Mr. Shurdie. *Ibid.*

f. 181] it is prayed that the Commoners may have their Common excepted of that worth. Thirdly, matter of Exception; That whereas it is provided that if any man be damnified, he shall have any Action of debt against the Undertakers, or out of the Lands recovered, touching the Noble undertakers said he, we desire not to sue them; Touching the Lands to be recovered, we know not yet where it is, or whether it will be recovered. Lastly, we desire That the Noble undertakers will accept from us in Cambridgeshire, whose Lands are already worth 5s. the Acre; And where the Lands within the Severall Parishes are scant, or not sufficient to maintaine the People, a Recompence in money, and not in Land. Mr. Stephen for the Bill, vouched many Cases, where for a Common Good a mans freehold may be hurt and dealt with all out of Common Course. Touching Exceptions of the Countyes of Cambridge and Suffolke, he thereunto opposed the Report of an honorable undertaker and others made to the King upon Survey of the Premises, whereby they certify that except the whole Levell be dealt with all, the worke cannot proceede: Againe if any such Lands be now worth 1s. the Acre, it will after drayning be worth 10s. and no Lands are by this Act to be set out to the undertakers but proportionably to the Benefitt the Owners have by it.

Touching Recompense which is desired to be given in Money, and not in Land, that is Impossible, in respect, first of the Doers, then of the Commoners of the Land, and lastly of the worke. First the Doers are men of great Quallity, and such as come not to offer their Labour for money, and if this be offered them, they will be discouraged.

In respect of the Owners, for that they are for the most part Poore, and after the Lands are drayned, it will be hard to get money from them, and to make Money they must be enforced to sell part of that which shall be drayned: In which Case it were better they departed with such reasonable parte unto the Undertakers in respect of their Charges and Paines. Lastly the Keeping and continuying the Land firme after the drayning, will be a continuall Charge, wherein if the Undertakers faile, the Owners are to have their Land againe, whereas if the Undertakers receive Money from the owners, and then faile to performe their Contract, for Counting the Land firme, the Money given is utterly gone and lost.

An Act to enlarge the Statuts now in force against Usury, 3? *Lecta.*

Sir Francis Bacon for the Bill, shewed how much Usury is against the Common and Ancient Lawes of England: To this Purpose he vouched the Statute intituled *De Iudaismo:*[1] Also the Statute of Merton ca. 5. 15. E. 3.[2] The Punishment of an Usurer dead belongeth to the King, and against an Usurer living, to the Bishop. Then he vouched the Statute of H. 8.[3] Lastly of f. 182] Queen Elizabeth[4] all this while all Interest is forbidden.[5] Then he shewed that Usury is against Morality, namely, that money should begett money.

Also it is against Policy, for the great Marchants will not venter at Sea, Winde etc. neither will the Witt of man labor upon drayning of Marshes, or in any other good or ingenious devise, but imploy their Money to more certaine Profitt at use: And so this sluggish Trade of usury taketh away all Invention, and Trade; Whereas other waies where money is, there would be devises to imploy it. Lastly it maketh Land cheape; for if money were not thus imployed to an Excessive gaine, Rich men would give good Prices for Lande, rather then Keepe Money.

The Councell of Nice, which was the most excellent Councell that ever was, condemneth Usury. And the Councell of Lateran affirmeth it not to be Lawfull to lend to Usury, no not to redeem a Christian out of the hands of a Turke.[6]

Agreed That after a Bill hath bene ingrossed, and the third tyme reade, it may be recommitted, but not out of the House, or

---

[1] *Statutes of the Realm,* I, 221. This forbids usury to the Jews.

[2] *Statutes of the Realm,* I, 296.

[3] 37 Hen. VIII. c. 9. *Statutes of the Realm,* III, 996.

[4] 13 Eliz. c. 8. *Statutes of the Realm,* IV, 542.

[5] This was not strictly true. The statute of Henry VIII, while condemning all usury, allowed interest not exceeding 10 per cent. An act of Edward (5 and 6 Ed. VI. c. 20. *Statutes of the Realm,* IV, 155) forbade all usury. But the act of Elizabeth returned in practice to the settlement of Henry VIII, though it provided that interest under 10 per cent should be forfeited. Presumably this provision was not strictly enforced. The act of Elizabeth was continued and finally made perpetual. *Statutes of the Realm,* IV, 718, 770, 808, 854, 917.

[6] Council of Nice, Canon XVII. Third Lateran Council. 1179, Canon XXV.

the Committee Chamber, and accordingly this Bill of Usury was recommitted.[1]

7? Maii. 1606.

If a Bill passe this House, and be sent up, when it cometh back om the Lords with Amendements, no Member of this House may spake against the body of the Bill, but against the Amendements and Provisoes added, and if then upon the Question the Amendements doe not passe, the Bill is to be wholy reiected.

Agreed That after a Bill is put to the Question, and the first Branch of the Question, viz. the Affirmative Parte answered any member of the House may speake untill the Negative be answered.

In the passing of the Bill against Regrators,[2] it was agreed, that when a Bill hath bene the third tyme reade, the thing misliked shall be amended, and the next question must be of the Passage.

8? Maii. 1606.

Mr. Hoskyns as One of the Committees, brought in the Bill of Clerks Fees, and reported the same viz. That more then 20. Committees appeared; That it was resolved by them, that it was not fitt for them to deale with the Matter of Fees; nor to alter the Rates now and heretofore taken, but to leave that Point as it is, for if they be iust Fees, the Committees thought no reason to diminish them, and if encroched, it is Extortion, and remedy lyeth in that Case by Lawe. Also such as prosecuted this Bill, thought not good further at this tyme to deale in it: Whereupon it was agreed among them that the Bill shall sleepe.

f. 183] Sir John Crooke, Sir Nich[olas] Swale, and Sir John Tyndall brought from the Lords the Bill of Subsidy granted by the Clergy with a Message, viz. That whereas diverse Conferences have bene betweene the Lords and Committees nominated by this House touching Grievances Ecclesiasticall, their Lordships will with the same Committees give a meeting to this House, and answere the Premises on Saturday at 2. of the Clocke. After the Messengers were withdrawen, they were againe called in, to deliver Whether the Lords will only give their Answer, or conferr also touching the

report concerning the Clarkes fees of the House of Commons.

---

[1] In *C.J.* I, 306, the bill was rejected.
[2] "The bill against Forestallers and Regrators of Victual." *Ibid.*

said Matters; Whereunto was answered by the Messengers, that the Lords would only give meeting, and Answer; To which meeting the House agreed, and thought not good to give any Instructions to the Committees for Conference, or Disputation.

Agreed, That the Act for Subsidy of the Clergy is but once to be reade in this House, for this House can mende nothing, upon which reason it is never by this House committed, neither is it sent hether for any other Cause, but that it be here confirmed.

Subsidy of the Clergy reade but once in the House of Commons.

9? Maii. 1606.

An Act for the 3. Subsidies, and 6. fifteenes granted by the Laity. 3? *Lecta*. passed.[1]

Sir Edwyn Sandys declared, that himselfe heretofore had moved that the fower Northern Shires viz. The Bishoprick of Durham, Cumberland, Northumberland, Westmerland, which heretofore were usually excepted from payment of Subsidies, in respect of their continuall Service on the Borders, might not be excepted in this Act that Cause now ceasing, but for as much as it was shewed how great charge these Partes were necessarily put unto at his Majestyes first coming to the Crowne of this Realme, by the Outrages of the Borderers of both Kingdomes, he changed his Opinion, but only did so alter for this tyme; Howbeit hereafter when and as often as like Subsidies shall be granted he holdeth it iust and reasonable that those Countyes Contribute as farr forth, and in like sort as other parts of the Realme, and therefore moved that the Saving or Exception of them in this Act or Grant of Subsidy, should be expressed to be only *hac vice*; Which was agreed; to which Purpose he ten'dered a Provisoe which was reade, and put to the Question, and so added to the Bill.

10? Maii. 1606.

An Act for the better Execution of sundry Statuts against Purveyors 3tio. *lecta*. Passed.

The Grievances delivered in by Mr. Fuller, and reade by the Clerke, in effect thus.

1? Letting out of Penalties to Subiects.

---

[1] See dispute in *C.J.* I, 307, as to whether the Subsidy should be read before the Grievances.

f. 184] 2. Letters Patents to the Lord Danvers, and Sir John Gilbert etc. Letters Patents of the Green wax of the Dutchy granted to Sir Roger Aston, and Master Grimsditch.

Sir Henry Bronchards Patents of Issues, etc.

The Lord Admiralls Patent of dispensation for selling Wines.

3. The Patent for Logwood and Blockword, etc.

4. Raising the Rates of Marchandise since the Kings coming; To satisfy the House, Mr. Woolstenholme, and an other of the Custome House, being also One or both of them fermors were heard at the Barr, notwithstanding whose excuse, the House continued this Article as a Grievance.

5. Imposition upon Currance.[1]

6. Imposition of 6s. 8d. upon the Pound of Tobacco.[2]

7. The Patent of the new Drapery, granted to the Duke of Lennox.

8. Charge in Passing Sheriffes accompts in the Exchequer, which in same Shires cometh to 60£—100£—170£.

9. Taxes sett in tyme of Warr and still continued, namely the Charge of Muster Masters.

Earl of Hertfords Defence. Here Sir John Hollis spake a little in defence of Mylord of Hertfords Honor which the other daye at the Examination of this Grievance was in some plaine Manner impeached to his Lordships great Grief: And in his Lordship Behalfe the Knight endeavored to answere certaine Obiections beside made, viz. 1. His Lordship made his Secretary Muster Master. 2. That his Lordship reviled such Iustices of Peace as came to complaine of this Iniury, and unlawfull Exaction. 3. His Lordship committed such as refused to pay the said Taxation. And said the Knight at the first exhibiting of the Grievances, I did forbeare to speake, not being then informed, since which tyme I have received a Letter[3] from Mylord of Hertford, which I desire may be reade, whereunto was generally agreed, and by those Letters My Lord declared his Griefe in that his Honor should in this House be questioned, where he greatly

---

[1] The Venetian ambassador wrote that the merchants were not as hopeful as they had been at first. "The private interests of several great personages, who draw no small profit from this duty, are a serious obsticle." *Cal. St. P. Venetian, 1603–1607*, 343.

[2] Rymer, *Foedera*, XVI, 601–602.

[3] *Hist. MSS Com. 1st Report*, App. (John Harvey MSS), 63.

desireth to be well thought of; In which respect he had thought
good to write unto the Knight (terming him his Cosen) and desiring
him to declare the effect unto the House: And in this Letter mylord
denied all three Points; touching the first, That Kirton was Muster
Master before his Lordship was Lieutenant,[1] when he had no
Dependency on his Lordship. The Second, he denyeth upon his
Honor. To the third, That his Lordship hath bene five yeares
Lieutenant, in all which tyme, he only hath in both the Counties
of Wilts and Somersett committed only two Persons, The one for
raising a Mutiny with 800. men, the other for appearing upon his
Lordships Warrant accompanied with 33. of his Companions.
f. 185] Then SR HENRY POOLE stood up to iustify what he had
formerly spoken in this House, touching Mylord of Hertford, and
to add (as he spake) somewhat which he might have spoken in that
Matter, and did before forbeare: And for proofe, he desired the
Clerk might reade the Coppy of a Letter which he offered, and
was written from many Iustices of Peace at the Sessions unto the
Lords of the Counsell, of the truth of which Coppy, he offered good
Proofe, the Testimony of some now in the House: And said he,
the Order of leavying this Taxation, is this: His Lordship sendeth
his Warrants to the Constables etc. to leavy it, and if any refuse
so to doe, he threateneth to hang him, and diverse he imprisoneth
for that Cause, namely One Trist, a Servant of Sir Edw[ard]
Hungerford, and the Queenes Tenant, who being ordered to pay,
and desiring, that in regard he is the Queenes Tenant he might
be forborne untill he may send unto My Lord of Sarum High
Steward to the Queenes Majesty, but in respect of displeasure
which his Lordship bare to Sir Edward Hungerford, he committed
this man upon Cullor of not paying this Taxe: And said he, this
man Kirton is one who within these ten yeares stood in the Pillory.
My Lord (said Sir Henry Poole) affirmed that in Somerset Shire
he threatned to have hanged one, for not paying, and that in his
hott blood he would have done it, if others had not intreated the
contrary: So as (said the Knight) as a great Bishop spake in an
other Case was there ever Bishop thus handled by a House of
Parliament, so may I say, was there ever poore Gentlemen thus

---

[1] This was not true. See *Cal. St. P. Dom. 1603–1610*, 126; *D.N.B.*
under Edward Seymour, Earl of Hertford.

handled; Where at the House laughed greatly, as likeing and being well pleased with his pleasent Conclusion.

Then Mr. KIRTON,[1] One of Mylord of Hertfords followers, delivered a sober Speach in defence of My Lords Honor, to this Effect, That the Gentleman for whose maintenance this Taxe was said to be raised, was Muster Master before My Lords tyme of Lieutenantship: That My Lord never imprisoned more then 2. Persons, viz: in five Yeares, The one in Somersetshire, the other in Wilts Shire, and those for the Causes before expressed. That indeed Kirton the Muster Master did ten yeares since stand in the Pillory, but he desired the House to consider that the Cause was not for any Criminall offence committed by him, but only for that he reported the Proceedings in the Starr chamber formerly had against one Booth,[2] to have bene uniust; And these words and his Punishment was ten yeares since, when he was very young. Lastly he craved that this matter might be referred to the Consideration of Committees who might report to the House the Order of My Lords Proceeding in the Premises, and the truth or State of the Allegacion against his Lordship, which motion was denied. f. 186] Sir John Crooke and Dr. Hone brought from the Lords 3. Bills, and a Message to this Effect, viz: That their Lordships desire a Conference touching the 2. Bills of Recusants on Tuesday next in the afternoone at 2. of the Clocke in the painted Chamber, where their Lordships would be 40. Committees. Which Conference was granted, and that this House will send 80. Committees.

The 10th. Grievance was the abused Preemption of Tynn.

11th. The Patent of Smalt alias Blew Starch.

12th. The Green Cloth Warrants to the Maintenance of Purveyors and lessning the Price of mens goods by second Prisalls, and generally against the usurped Authority of the Green cloth, in Committing the Kings Subiects against Lawe.

13th. Transporting of Iron Ordinances, and cast Bullets.

14th. Abusing the Patent of Salt peeter, both in digging mens Houses unorderly etc. and by transportation of Salt peeter and Gunpowder.

Then Mr. SOLLICITOR reported the Conference with the Lords

---

[1] Mr. James Kirton. *C.J.* I, 307. Not the Muster Master, whose name was Josias Kirton.

[2] Roger Booth. See *Cal. St. P. Dom. 1595-1597*, 137.

touching the Bills of Attaindors; some Exceptions he remembred taken by the Committees of this House in the painted Chamber, which I noted not: Others to some parte of the body of the Bill; Namely, That the Papists were termed Romish Catholicks, which word Catholicks, hath heretofore given them occasion out of our owne Writings to vaunt they are proved Catholicks, whereas they never acknowledged us other than Hereticks, Whereupon said he their Lordships agreed to amende these words and assented to alter, and to call them Papists.

Next whereas the words be (heretofore attainted etc.) their Lordships assented to amend it and to make it (during this Session attainted.)[1]

Then whereas the Words be (which they shall claime by any Conveyance) it is now made (by any Lawfull Conveyance.)

Touching the Provisoe for the goods etc. their Lordships did consider the Provisoe of 1? Mary.[2]

After which Report, upon SIR W[ILLIA]M SKIPWITHS Motion it was agreed that Digbyes Councell shall be heard here in the House on Monday.

12TH. MAII. 1606.

The Bill for drayning the Fenns in and neere the Isle of Ely. 3? *Lecta*; and upon the Question dashed.

Agreed in dispute of the Grievances, That the Speaker is to speake as the House shall appoint him unto the King, but not to deliver any Writing.

Sir John Crooke and Dr. Hone Came from the Lords with a Message to this Effect, viz. That the Lords received a Bill from this House intituled An Act for Transportation of Beere, and touching that Bill doe require a Conference on Wednesday next f. 187] at 2. of the Clock in the afternoone in the painted Chamber; in which place 20. Committees of the Lords House will be present. This Conference was granted, and according to the usuall Order 40. of this House there to attend that Service.

---

[1] The statute reads "by this Acte attainted." Other changes are in the statute.

[2] 1 and 2 Phil. and Mar. c. 10 (*Statutes of the Realm*, IV, 257). This was a general saving for those not involved in the crime. For its application here, see *Statutes of the Realm*, IV, 1070.

SIR ANTHONY COPE declared that contrary to the order of this House, at the last Conference we staied with the Lords longer then to receive their Lordships answere; To which only Our Commission and directions did extend, and now said he, Conferences growe so long and wearisome, and therefore it were good that we should require Seates, for we staie long before their Lordships come; And if we departe before the Conference be ended, we offend, and many of us that are old, cannot stand so long but we shall fall downe.

13TH. MAII. 1606.

After a Bill is here passed and sent to the Lords, and from them returned with Amendements, no man can speake against the Bill, but to the Amendements only: Agreed in the Bill exhibited by Le Grice, and sent back from the Lords.

The Grievances engrossed were reade by the Clerke.

Agreed that Sir Francis Bacon shall reade the Grievances to his Majesty.

MR. FULLER delivered some Notes touching Conferences with the Lords, which he desired might be considered, viz. 1. We stand long. 2. The Lords both conferr, and set as Moderators, for when they please, the Kings Counsell and Iudges over-rule us with their Censure, and when we desire the Opinion of the Iudges it is denied: He here shewed in what Point the Iudges did at the last Conference over-rule us in point of Law, viz. the Statute of 35. H. 8.[1] for the Proceeding of the Bishops in their owne Names, whereas that Statute said he, is repealed, and so the Law not as the Iudges did Peremptorily rule it: And said he, I reverence their Opinions, but at Conferences, they sitt as Assistants, not as Iudges.

MR. SOLLICITOR reported the effect of the last Conference, viz. That My Lord Chancellor by the direction of the Lords House delivered, that their Lordships had considered of the 4. Eccesiasticall Grievances,[2] wherein this House had formerly desired they

Notes touching conferences with the Lords.

---

[1] A mistake for 25 Hen. VIII. c. 20 (*Statutes of the Realm*, III, 464). The renewal of this act in 1 Elizabeth was said to nullify the act of 1 Edward VI concerning the jurisdiction of the Bishops. St. P. Dom. XXI, 20. See p. 145.

[2] These were (1) silenced ministers; (2) multiplicity of ecclesiastical commissions; (3) the form of citations; (4) excommunication for slight causes.

should ioyne with us in a Petition to his Majesty. Concerning the first said his Lordship, if Obedience had bene used, that Article had not needed, *Et* for as much as the same concerneth the King in his Power Eccesiasticall, it might be some Aspersion if it should be conceived he hath not care to doe these men right for whom we speake, without our Suite: Therefore not convenient their Lordships should ioyne with us, in any Petition of that Kinde.

Touching the Second, their Lordships likewise thought it not f. 188] fitt nor convenient to ioyne with us, but to leave it to such as have Authority in that behalfe.

Touching the third viz. of Proces *Quorum Nomina*, it will be redressed otherwise in what there is abuse; And as touching Oathes Ex Officio, the same hath bene anciently used in this realme, and not thought convenient by their Lordships for them to ioyne now with us in Petition for Alteration. Lastly Excommunication *Pro Levioribus*, is by Order already taken to be redressed and therefore needelesse for their Lordships to ioyne with us in Petition for reformation thereof.

It was remembred, That 28. Elizabeth a Petition in writing was to be delivered to the Queene, and it was sent by such of the Privie Councell as were of this House. And 43. Elizabeth a Petition touching Monopolies was likewise sent by such Privie Councellors as then were of the House.[1]

SIR GEORGE MOORE said it was fitt the Grievances to be reade by a Member of this House, accompanied with diverse of the House, as the last Session, that of the Purveyors was reade by Mr. Hare,[2] at which tyme diverse did associate him: Hereupon it was concluded, That Sir Francis Bacon (with such Preface as he should thinck good) should reade these Grievances to his Majesty, and be accompanied with such number of this House as his Majesty should be pleased to admitt. Hereupon it was ordered, That presently Mr. Secretary Herbert accompanied with Sir Roger Aston, should waite on the King, and from this House to beseech His Highnesse to give Audiance to our Speaker, and also to be pleased to admitt Sir Francis Bacon from this House to offer to his Majesty Our Grievance, he to be accompanied with such

Sir Fran[cis] Bacon the Grievances to the King.

---

[1] Neither of these cases is to be found in D'Ewes, but other examples might have been cited.

[2] April 30, 1604. *C.J.* I, 190.

Number of this House, as his Majesty shall please to admitt;
Who accordingly went to the Court, and returned with this
Answer, That his Majesty did gratiously yeild our Suite; And for
as much as his Highnesse understandeth that this afternoone, the
Lords and we doe meete upon Conference, and for that to morrow
in the afternoone the Ambassadors of France and Spaine are to
have Audience, and on Thursday his majesty removeth, therefore
his Majesty appointeth and is pleased to morrow at 10. of the
Clocke to heare Sir Franc[is] Bacon reade the Grievances, and to
be accompanied with such Number of modest Gentlemen of this
House, as the House shall thinck good, and presently after his
Majesty will give Audience to Mr. Speaker. And diverse Members
are by the House appointed to repaire to Mr. Speaker at his House
this afternoone there to agree what Course, and upon what points
Mr. Speaker shall to morrow speake to his Majesty: The generall
Effect being, that the Jesuits and Priests may be executed; And
then for deprived Ministers and touching our other Ecclesiasticall
Grievances.

f. 189]   14.º Maii. 1606.

Mr. Speaker came late to the House, and then signified from
the King, That by reason certaine Ambassadors are to come to his
Majesty presence, he cannot give Audience this forenoone at 10.
of the Clocke unto such of this House as he had formerly appointed
at that tyme to attend him: And therefore is pleased to give us
accesse at three of the clock this afternoone; And accordingly the
House named 40. of the House to accompany Sir Francis Bacon
in this Service.

The Con-   Mr. Sollicitor reported the Conference yesterday had with
ference re-   the Lords touching the 2. Bills of Recusants, wherein first he
ported   repeated the Preface used by the great Earle (as he termed him,
touching   meaning the Earl of Salisbury) and said he, there were two
the Bills of principall things noted as difference in those Bills, betweene the
Recusants.   Lords and us,[1] viz. the receiving the Communion, and takeing the

---

[1] Salisbury wrote Lake that the Commons exaggerated these differences " . . . . because they will gaine therby a time for presentment of
their greevances, and for those three Bills which they have passed concerning Recusants, the length wherof is such & the intricacy with some
absurd escapes which they have made in their Bill, as they assure them-

Children of Recusants from them. In the first Mr. Sollicitor conceived the difference to rest only in this, that the Lords in their Clemency doe encline to allow a longer tyme, and this House in their Iustice doe enioyne a shorter tyme unto them to receive the Communion:[1] In the matter of taking the Children from Recusants, the difference consisteth in diverse difficulties.[2]

Then that Great Earle aymed at diverse other Inconveniencies and faults in those Bills, whereupon we desired to understand all such points whereunto their Lordships would except, that therewith all wee might acquaint the House, and give answer to all such Matters together. Then said the Lord Arch Bishop That we had in the End of one of our Bills reserved unto the Bishops all such Power to deale and proceede with Recusants as formerly they had; But said he, you have, 1. By the same Bill confined

---

selves that it will cost us ten dayes before wee can reconcile them, wherin because wee are as desirous as they to perfect that good worke, & have a Bill in our Howse, for rectifying some things in the Bishops proceeding, which by the late accident I wrote of wanted some formalitie, we sit both forenoone & afternoone in the Parliament Howse. Wherof I pray you informe his Majesty, as a circumstance of our diligence & care, which shall be sufficient to be represented at this time." May 7, 1606. St. P. Dom. XXI, 15.

[1] Before they be declared recusants. Salisbury wrote the Earl of Mar on March 9: "Concerning the busynese of parlement the lower house beganne with sharpe lawes against Papysts, wherein wee in the higher house have been forwerd; onely in one point, concerning receyving of the communion, some in the lower house would have had that punished with the same sharpe paines that are [*was appointed to be* crossed out] due to an obstinate and convicted recusant, wherin wee on the contrarie made some difficultie because heerby men should be barred from comminge to the place where they might learne to come further: seeing faith comes by hearing, and *quicquid ex fide non est, precatum est*: neither did wee stand in this as thinking any man truly of our Church, that refuseth our Sacrements, but onely because the Ecclesiasticall Lawe is in force to excommunicate them, wee thought it impertinent to lay our further loade at this tyme. Nevertheless because the bill had many other excellent parts, which wee were loath to overthrowe, wee consented in the end to appoint a punishment upon the non Communicant, though he doth come to Church, after 2. yeares tryall." St. P. Dom. XIX, 27.

[2] The objections of the Lords were referred to a committee of the Commons that reported on May 17. See that date (p. 170) for further discussion.

all Recusants,[1] and none can send for any such Person so confined, except only Councellors, and then cannot we Bishops send
for them, in which Case we cannot conforme, or wynn them.

2. Next said the Earle before named, by your Bill you require
of Noble men as of other Inferior Persons to take the Oath when
they passe over,[2] whereas by the Statute of [*blank*][3] Elizabeth
and [*blank*] Elizabeth they are not bound to take the Oath of
Supremacy.

3. Then it is directed (said the Earle of Northampton being
Guardian of the Cinq Ports, that such Persons as passe over shall
take the Oath before the Maior of the Towne, and such Officers
of the Porte: Whereas said he, the Warden of the Ports hath
heretofore alwaies bene trusted to looke to such as have passed
or come into the Realme by the five Ports, he declared that his
Lieutenant[4] is a Worthy Gentleman as ever served in that
f. 190] Place: And albeit he acknowledged himself in many respects inferior to many to whom the Wardenship hath heretofore
bene committed, yet he shewed that his Care in that Service hath
bene Equall with the best, and offered to shew a Paper of
Instructions and Orders by him given for Execution of that
Place.

4. Then it was declared by that Earle that spake first, that
where any Childe goeth over etc. we give his Land to his next
of Kynn, where we should in that Case appointe it to the next
Heire.

5. Also we appointe that if the Committee of the Warde doe
grant the Warde to a Recusant, this grant shall be voide, in which
Case perhaps, and no doubt but the first Committee hath received money to the Valewe, and now by this Law he is againe
to have the Wardship, whereas it were more fitt that it should
returne to be againe granted by the Court of Wards, or in some
other Course.

---

[1] To within five miles of their abodes.

[2] All persons going abroad to serve a foreign prince should take an
Oath of Allegiance contained in the act.

[3] 1 Eliz. c. 1 (*Statutes of the Realm*, IV, 352); 5 Eliz. c. 1 (*Statutes of the
Realm*, IV, 405).

[4] Sir Thomas Waller, lieutenant of Dover Castle. *Cal. St. P. Dom.
1603–1610*, 374.

6. Then said the Great Iudge[1] having Charge of the Great Seale; In this Bill you make the Non-communicant unable to sue any Action; So as if a Man kill the husband of a Woman Non-communicant, or the father of a man non-communicant, they are without remedy by Appeale; So in Case of Battery of a Recusant.

7. Then spake the Great Earl that first did speake in this matter: In this also said he, is a defect; That by one of these Bills, it is to be enacted, That soever passeth out of the Realme, is to be bound with two Suerties remayning in the Realme etc. So as if one of these two Suerties doe afterwards at any tyme departe out of the Kingdome, the first party so passing over is a Felon.

8. Next, we tye the father being a Recusant, That he cannot alien any more then the One half of his Lands from his Eldest Sonne, who shall be taken from him, and disposed of according to this Act; Whereas perhaps the father may have iust Cause wholy to disherite such Sonne: And so you make the Sonne many tymes Carelesse of his father.

Hereunto said Mr. Sollicitor we answered that their Lordships did at the tyme they required a Conference of us, only signify the Generall matter, Whereupon the Conference was to be had, namely, touching the two Bills of Recusants, did not make Knowne the severall Points, so as we that then did attend their Lordships, had no direction what to speake, but we would faithfully report to the House, what their Lordships had bene pleased to say, and with all possible Speede that may be, we would signify to their Lordships what the House shall determine. All this being spoken, the House gave Order that the Committees before imployed in these Bills of Recusants, shall consider of the matter, and report to the House what they shall think fitt to f. 191] be done; And for this Purpose the one Bill was delivered to Mr. Sollicitor, and the other to Mr. Winch: Sir John Boys this afternoone to conferr with Mr. Sollicitor, and Mr. Winch to carrie the other Bill to Sir Henry Hobart Attorney of the Wards, and they foure respectively to conferr this afternoone, and to morrow in this place, the whole Committees to meete and conferr of the busines.

---

[1] Lord Chancellor Ellesmere.

15. Maii. 1606.

The Bill of Subsidy sent up to the Lords with the whole House.

An Act for Confirmation of 4. Subsidies granted by the Clergy, 3° *Lecta.* passed. And then first[1] the Subsidy granted in this House was sent up to the Lords by Mr. Secretary Herbert, who by speciall motion of the Speaker, was accompanied with this whole House.

Then was the Subsidy of the Clergy sent up by the same Mr. Secretary, accompanied with a Competent Number, viz. about 20. Persons.

The Bill for Exemption of the foure Shires out of the Commission of the Marches of Wales, was delivered in by the Committees, and upon a Motion of Sir Herbert Croft, it was suffered to sleepe; which Motion was grounded upon assured hope which he conceived out of the Kings Speech yesterday, that Reformation shall be had in that behalfe.

An excuse from the Lords to this Effect; That whereas yesterday 20. Committees should have conferred with a proportionable Number of this House in the painted Chamber about the Bill sent from hence touching Transportation of Beere, which conference could not hold by reason of their Lordships Attendance on the King: And whereas their Lordships had given direction that so much should have bene made Knowne beforehand to this House, wherein the Persons trusted have failed to doe their Message: Their Lordships are thereof sorry: And conceiving well of the Bill, doe desire a conference of the like number in the same place, for that service, to morrow at 3. of the clock in the afternoone, which was yielded to.

The Bill of Fees of the Marshalsey was returned by the Committees and thereunto certaine Idle Exceptions taken; And the Speaker (as it seemed) willing to hinder the Bill, declared That of 6. Sheetes delivered to the Committees, there now was returned but 6. lines of the same: But it was enough, and upon the Question the Bill put to engrossing.[2]

In Argument touching the Bill of Transportation of Beere, it was agreed, that Committees for Conference touching a Bill sent from hence to the Lords, have Authority to dispute, but not to conclude any Alteration.

---

[1] That is, after the Grievances had been presented the day before.

[2] For points of this bill, see *Hist. MSS Com. 4th Report*, App. 118.

SIR FRANCIS BACON reported[1] the Order of presenting the Grievances yesterday unto his Majesty, with his Majesty acceptance and Answer.   The Accesse was regular, and according to Order, and the Committees admitted, and they called in by f. 192] name; Others even of the Privie Chamber and Bed chamber, and the Nobility who were not of the Councell, excluded, and so none present but the Committees of this House, and the Lords of the Councell.   I did after Reverence make my Proposition and then shewed that though the Instrument were bigg, yet was not the Writing much, but the Volume great in respect and by reason of the fairenesse of the Letter.   I shewed That according to the Nature of the things we marshalled them in Order; That we had prefixed a Preamble[2] in such dutifull sort as we hoped became us; So as my Speech would be but a Preamble to a Preamble; Neverthelesse thus much I would presume to trouble his Highnesse with all, namely, to say That though these were Grievances, yet were they not any Aspersions or Imputations meant any way to be laid to his Majestyes Gouvernment, but the diseases of tyme, and things which were heretofore growen and cut downe partly by his Royall Majesty, and yet sprung up againe in tyme; And where of we nothing doubted of his Majestyes Princely Regard etc.   And so repeated his owne Speech used to the King before he did reade the Grievance, which was an Eloquent Speech, which was not long, yet impossible for me, or any man to take in such sorte as he delivered the Same.

Then his Majesty answered, That diverse of them might be iust yet could he not on the Suddaine iudge of them, but such matters as should be presented by a House of Parliament in so good sort he would never deny to heare reade.   And so I reade them; Then his Majestyes Answer had two maine Points.   One a Prudent Challenge to some Circumstances of our Proceedings in these Grievances; The other a gratious Answer.   The Challenge consisted of 4. parts.   First that we had as well matter of Gratulation to have wrought on, as Grievances: For our change by his Majestyes coming, is changed from a Prince of a Weake Sex, unto a King; from an old Prince, to a King replenished with Children;

The Order of presenting the Grievances to the King was reported.

---

[1] Cf. *C.J.* I, 309.

[2] This preamble, which is a petition for redress, is contained in Harl. MSS 6846, ff. 201–207; Cott. MSS, Titus F IV, ff. 25–34*v*.

from Religion begun, unto Religion Established; from factions
to unity; from a State rent from her Bowells in respect of Ireland,
to a State conioyned in respect of Scotland.

The next challenge was by way of question, namely, whether
these Grievances were not Grievances of former tymes, and yet
then we found no fault, but commended the Gouvernment: An
other question whether the Countryes from whence we came did
possesse us with these Grievances, or that the Same were suggested here in London.

Next his Majesty said that we had digressed from the first
f. 193] Purpose and offer unto us, which was onely concerning
Purveyors, and now by us extended to all Grievances: And here
his Majesty stood long upon the matter of Purveyors: And herein
among other things, his Majesty said, That touching the Officers
of the Green Cloth, as we flattered them not, so he would flatter
them lesse if he findes them in fault; He said the Booke which
we presented was too long, and himself no Angell; And therefore
could give no present Answer: But these Grievances should be
reade and reade againe, both to himselfe, and with his Councell;
That he would put them in their proper forge: And touching
Matter of Lawe, he would advise with the Iudges: In Matters
of State with his Councell: In Matters of Trafficke, with men
skillfull that way: His Majesty admonished, That where the
Grievance is small, and the Alteration great and weighty to the
Crowne, we should not urge it; as himself on the other Side would
not preferr his owne small Profitt before a Common Grievance of
great Moment. He protested, That not 40. alluding as I conceived to our Number then before him; nor 400. referring to the
whole Company of this House, nor all the People of Britaine
should make him doe any thing uniust; againe, no man, in, or
out of Parliament should iustly seeke redresse of any thing, but
he would yeild it.[1] And here said Sir Franc[is] Bacon, you Mr.
Speaker presented your Selfe, according to the direction of the
House, whereof you may please to make report. Then Mr. Speaker
standing up said, That he supposed and expected that the Gentleman that last spake would have reported the whole daies Attendance yesterday on the King, upon which Opinion he had

[1] James's reply occasioned general discontent. See *Cal. St. P. Venetian, 1603–1607, 353.*

not provided to make reporte of that which was by the House committed to his Charge; But said he, if you will command me presently to report it, I must obey, otherwise I shall be glad of some tyme to call things to memory, Whereupon the House gave him his Choice to make Relation either presently, or to morrow; so with hearty thankes, he chose to report to morrow.

16? Maii. 1606.

An Act for naturalizing Sir David Murray Knight Gentleman of the Prince his Bedchamber, and Thomas Murray Esquire Schoole master to the Duke of Yorke. 3? *Lecta* passed.

It was here moved by diverse, That in all Bills of this Kinde there should be inserted a clause that the Party naturalized shall have no voice in Parliament, which was generally liked, and assented unto; But agreed as before at the first reading of this Bill that the first inserting of this Clause or Provisoe shall not begin with these two Gentlemen, but the rule f. 194] to begin, and hold hereafter without Exception: Howbeit Sir Edwyn Sandys, moved that in respect of this Session *Sera Parcimonia in fundo*, but wished that all this matter may be moved at the beginning of the next Session; Which was thought good accordingly, and yet agreed contrary to his Opinion, viz: Agreed that the House may not make an Order to hold the next Session.

Mr. Speaker reported[1] the order by him observed on Wednesday in delivery of the two Petitions from this House to his Majesty, and the Successe: The Petitions he sayd were two.

The One for Execution of the Statutes against Iesuits and Priests.

The Second for favour and Grace to be extended towards Ministers deprived, suspended, and silenced: And likewise for Reformation of the Multiplicity of high Commissions; The abuse in Citations; And the frequent using of Excommunication *pro Levioribus*.

For delivery of the first matter which concerned the Iesuits, and Priests (said Mr. Speaker) you left the manner thereof unto my Selfe: For ordering and disposing the 2d. parte, you appointed speciall Committees to consider thereof, and to direct me a Course,

---

[1] Cf. *C.J.* I, 309–310.

which they did; And I to the best of my Skill have performed accordingly.

Touching the first matter (said he) left to my discretion, I devided it into 3. partes. 1. An Information. 2. A Complaint. 3. A Petition. In the first I remembred, That from the first yeare of the late Queen, unto the 11th. yeare of her Raigne, this Kingdome had few, or no Recusants; And untill that tyme, here was no Treason, no Rebellion, or Disquiet that way in the State, and then the Cause of the Alteration was not out of Religion, for then they would have practised sooner; Nor for any Alteration of the Gouvernment, for Queen Elizabeth raigned 34. yeares after; But originally from the Bull[1] of the Pope Pius Quintus, which was published in the same 11th. yeare of Queen Elizabeth: which I proved, said he, 1st. out of matter of Practise, and then out of matter of Doctrine: Here he discoursed all the Treasons from 11th. Elizabeth unto the Treason of Dr. Parrey, and so to this last damnable Treason: All which severall Treasons he shewed to have been plotted and practised by Iesuits and Priests. Touching the Positions and Doctrine; The Papists hold we have no Religion etc. That no Faith is to be kept with us, etc. That a Protestant Prince is not to be suffered to succeede. Then he shewed the danger of their doctrine of Equivocation[2] even in *Articulo Mortis*. I presumed said he, to answere one Obiection, viz. That the Papists doe say, that these Points or Positions of doctrine are but the Opinions of some few and not any generall doctrine, but that they doe love and honor the King, and will dye for him: But said I, myselfe have heard, when it hath bene asked of some of them, which so said, what they would doe if the King were deprived by the Pope, whether then they would obey him, to which all being 8. in number answered, That if it were so, they f. 195] must doe as the church commanded them. Then said he, I spake of the 2d. matter, which concerneth deprived Ministers Multiplicity of high Commissions, Inconveniencies in the forme of Citations and over much abuse of Excommunication *Pro minimis*; Of the three last, I spake as directed me: In the first, I handled 2. Points, the Matter and the Persons; In the Persons, I excluded some of those deprived, and shewed that Our suit was

---

[1] The Bull *Regnans in Excelsis*, published Feb. 25, 1570.
[2] Garnet, *Treatise on Equivocation*. See Gardiner, I, 280–282.

not for all, nor for any that repugne his Majesty Supreame
Gouvernment, nor for any that seeke Parity, but for such as honor
his Majesty Proceedings, and yet in some tendernesse of Conscience doe forbeare to use Ceremonies, or to Subscribe as is required in respect of some few small matters. The matter I declared
to be that men of this latter quality may be restored to the
Ministry, so long as their Labours may be for the good of the
Church, and not to disturbe the quiett thereof. Now I am (said
Mr. Speaker) perplexed to deliver his Majesty Answer, for I cannot doe it with that life as he spake it. To the first which concerned the Iesuits and Priests, he said, he should forgett whose
Messenger he is, if he should not regard what we desire, the
same Proceeding out of Religion, and from care for him; for
which he rendred Princely thancks: He remembred his owne
conceite of those Persons at his first coming into this Kingdome;
for he alwaies thought a Fox will be a Fox; but he purposed not
to drawe his Sword of Iustice against them, unlesse first they
practised against him; he said, I should not neede to have remembred the Examples of Practises in the tyme of Queen Elizabeth. This late horrible Treason had bene enough to put him
in minde, that they are Enemies to God, him, and this Kingdome, and therefore that he would commande his Ministers to
execute Iustice on them.

He concluded That there are Lawes very good against them,
full of Iustice, and sufficient to restraine them; with a Caution,
That we in making Lawes, should be advised, that we make
none but such as may be iust and indifferent, and without too
much Severity; for which Purpose he willed us to conferr with
the Lords.

Touching the deprived and silenced Ministers from whom we
said, his Majesty returned one Argument, which I used both
myselfe, viz. That if the Matters be small in themselves, then said
he, their fault of disobedience is the more, and obedience is better
then Sacrifice, and said he, you Mr. Speaker said, there ought
to be but one Faith, one God, one Gouvernment, one King;
speaking of the Iesuits and Priests, so say I of these men: And
said he, I pray you remember, that at my first coming, these men
had a Conference, then an admonition, and lastly Proceeding
against them. Now you sue for mercy and favour on their be-

halfe, and yet have they not submitted, and conformed themselves: whereas first Repentance should precede, and mercy f. 196] follow; And said his Majesty if these men will reforme themselves, every of them shall be either restored to the same living, from which he was deprived, or be preferred to an other of my guift, better then that was; Wherefore said his Majesty, I pray you Good Gentlemen, (for that was his word) let me turne your Petition into an Admonition, which is, That you will wish them to conforme themselves, and to returne, that there may be One Gouvernment, and I will shew them what favour you can desire for them. Of the other 3. Points of Ecclesiasticall matters, I observed nothing to be reported by Mr. Speaker.

17.° Maii. 1606.

An Act for naturalizing James demetrius and Mary his Wife of the Parish of Saint Botolph without Algate London, 1.° *Lecta.* and reiected.

An Act for reformation of abuses in the Officers and Ministers of the Marshalsey, and for declaration of the Iurisdiction of the said Court, 3.° *Lecta* passed.

Upon the third reading of this Bill, it was agreed, That after the Affirmative Question, any man may speake unto the Bill before the Negative Question is asked.

An Act for the true making of Woollen Cloth, 3.° *Lecta.* disputed, and the Question reserved untill Monday.

Sir Henry Hobbart reported the Proceedings of the Committees for the first of the two Bills concerning Recusants,[1] thus, The Committees stand resolute that Non-communicants by the Space named in the Bill, viz. One yeare and halfe, shall be deemed Recusants.

The Committees have resolved to maintaine with reason what this House hath done, and reserve to our selves the further Power to conferr of what their Lordships shall alter, and such is their Opinion for the Generallity.

Then to proceede in the particulers; The Second Exception is, In that an Oath by this Statute is to be ministred to all Persons: For their Lordships desire that themselves may be excepted ac-

---

[1] For the points in this report, cf. pp. 160-163 and *Statutes of the Realm*, IV, 1071-82.

cording as in the Statute of 1.° Elizabeth for the Supremacy,
Lords were excepted from taking that Oath of Supremacy. In this
Likewise the Committees are resolute, upon this reason, viz:
The Oath by this Act appointed, and whereof the Lords desire
to be exempted, is but an Oath of Obedience, namely, That the
Pope hath no Power to depose the King: which is meerly matter
of Obedience, and not any way of Conscience, for it saith not
that the Pope cannot Excommunicate the King, although that
also in the Negative is true, albeit not so cleere to Some. Againe
the King himself at his Coronation Sweareth to doe Right to his
People, why then should not all Subiects, even the best, sweare
obedience to the King: The Oath of Supremacy appointed by
f. 197] 1.° Elizabeth differeth from this Oath here appointed by
reason of the time, and in nature: For Queen Elizabeth came to
the State not setled in Religion, yea bent to Popery, when safely
she could not urge the greatest to this Oath of Supremacy: And
the Nature of that Oath was somewhat upon Conscience, but
now the tymes are setled and this Oath meerly of Obedience.
And further this Exemption of the Lords from this Oath may be
a President to exempt them of all Oathes of Obedience hereafter.

The third Exception was, that by this Act, it is appointed that
Bonds shall be taken of such as passe over by the Officers of the
Ports, which was said to be much in Derogation of the Warden
of the Cinq Ports, who only from tyme to tyme have ever heretofore bene trusted with the oversight of Passengers by the Ports;
of this the Committees though they thought not good to give Allowance, yet they thought fitt to leave it to the Consideration
of this House, when the Lords shall send it back in any sort
altered with the Bill.

The 4th. Exception was taken by the Lords in this Point also
of the Bonds, namely, That the Bill as it is sent up, doth appoint
that Persons passing over shall enter Bond with two Suerties,
remayning in the Realme: Now said the Lords, if either of these
two Suerties doe afterwards passe over out of the Realme, the
first Person incurreth danger of the Penalty, which is Felony;
because both his Suerties doe not remaine here. To this the
Committees thought good a double Answer should be made, the
first, That this Point is agreable to the Article agreed on betweene
the Lords and us at out first Conference touching this Matter.

Secondly this word (remaining) doth not limitt how long the Suerties shall remayne in the Realme, but it sufficeth if at the passing
over of the Person his Suerties be here remaining.[1]

The fift Exception is the taking away of Recusants Children,
and the Order of providing for them, and disposing of them. The
Lords conceive this to be unnaturall, dangerous, exceeding difficult, and scandalous. To this the Committees thought fitt it
should be answered, That it is not unnaturall; for though the
Parent have much in the Childe, yet the Common-Wealth hath
more Interest in every mans Person then himselfe; Therefore in
every mans Childe, and this Point of takeing away, and placing
the Children of Recusants, was approved by the King in his Instructions to this House; It was approved also by the Lords, for
their Lordships had an Article to this Purpose in their Proiect,
as well, as we: Neither is it without President, for the Statute of
[*blank*][2] doth give Power to the Church Wardens to take the
Children of Poore men, and to put them Apprentices: The State
of France tooke away the Prince of Condé his Childe, because
the father was a Protestant;[3] And the King of Spaine tooke away
the Prince of Orenge his Sonne;[4] But on this last Example, I
will not stand, for that the Prince of Orenge in his Apologie, pre-
f. 198] tendeth this as a wrong, whereby among others he was
stirred up. Againe, this Law which we have passed, doth not
saie, you shall take away the Children of Recusants, but giveth
Power that you may take them etc. Also the Parents have one
yeare and a halfe to place their owne Children in Places of sound
Religion: And in their default, the Power of placing such Children,
is not given to any meaner Persons, then unto Iustices of the
Peace, nor to fewer then two: And they must call the Parents
and examine their Ability, and what Exhibition they doe presently
make, of what charge they are presently at with the Children,
that are to be removed, and accordingly to take Order for Allowance to be made after such Children are removed, which doth
answer one other Obiection made by the Lords viz. That the Recu-

---

[1] See two letters in Winwood, *Memorials*, II, 216–217, 219.

[2] 43 Eliz. c. 2. *Statutes of the Realm*, IV, 963.

[3] See R. B. Borthwick, *Duc d'Aumale's History of the Princes de Condé*,
II, 181.

[4] See Ruth Putnam, *William the Silent*, I, 287–288.

sants living being divided among his Children will not leave perhaps enough for himselfe.

He concluded, That the Committees had directed that by the foresaid reasons, and such others as might be thought fitt, we should at out meeting with the Lords defend the former Points of our first Bill, and neither to pronounce, That we are resolute to alter nothing therein, nor to affirme that the House is purposed to yeild to all or any of these Exceptions to be altered by the Lords; But to leave it to their Lordships Wisedome to deale with the Bill as they think good by Alteration, or otherwise, and to reserve our Power to doe as Cause shall require when the Lords shall send it back to us.

Then MR. SOLICITOR reported the Proceedings of the Committees touching the second Bill of Recusants. And said he, the first Exception taken by the Lords to this Bill, is, That in confining Recusants we have straightned by our Bill the Ecclesiasticall Iurisdiction, for the Bishops cannot now send for any Recusant to conferr with them: To which the Committees have thought fitt we should answer, That we doe by this Act which we have now passed make no new Lawe, for the Statute of 35. Elizabeth made it, only we have repealed one Provisoe in that Statute, and added another:[1] Wee have only ordered That all Persons except the King and his Councell, warranted to send for any Recusants shall in his Lycence expresse the Cause of such Lycence, or sending for such Recusant, and the tyme of their aboade: We have saved to the Bishops if not sufficiently we must leave it to the Lords to alter and amende as in their Wisedomes shall be fitt, retayning our Power, when the Bill shall be sent and returned back.

The 2d. Exception the Lords tooke, was, That we have in this Bill given Power unto 2. Iustices of Peace to search the House of any Person, which by the Space of one yeare hath bene a Non-Communicant. This it is thought good we should iustify as done advisedly, and Iustly. For first it agreeth with the Lawe f. 199] of God etc. And by the Ecclesiasticall Law, every man

---

[1] 35 Eliz. c. 2 (*Statutes of the Realm*, IV, 843) confined recusants to within five miles of their homes. The Commons wished to make it more difficult to travel further. *Statutes of the Realm*, IV, 1078, 1079, 1082.

ought to receive three tymes in every yeare. Againe, it was among us observed by some of this House, That Iesuits and Priests doe not harbor in the House of convicted Recusants, but of Non-Communicants coming to Church, who are lesse suspected Whilest the eyes of all men are cast on a Recusant convict: And so these Non-Communicants are more dangerous and iustly to be suspected. Againe the Person whose House is searched, is thereby put to no losse. Againe, a Petty Constable for petit larceny, may search the House of any man suspected; And this Non-Communicants House is to be searched by 2. Iustices of Peace, and they may by the Statute give a Possession.

The third Exception taken by the Lords was, That we have ordained, That when an Infant is sent over etc. he shall take no benifitt etc. but the next of Kynn shall receive the Profitt[1] etc. So these 2. Exceptions were taken by the Lords, first, that we say the next of Kynn, and not the next Heire; To this we answer, That for the most parte, the next Heire is the next of Kynn, and because it is not alwaies soe, therefore it can be no otherwise set downe then here it is by words (next of Kinn) for if we should say next Heire, if the next Heire be also a Recusant, he must notwithstanding have the Profitts of the Lands; For none can be next Heire, but one, but we may say the (next of Kinn being a Protestant) and in that Case, if one, or more neerest of Kynn be Recusants, the next that is a Protestant shall take it.

An other Obiection is, That if the Childe die beyond Sea, this Act doth not say how long the next of Kynn shall take the Profitts of the Lands. This is answered thus, That the next of Kynn doth by this Lawe take the Profitts, but as a Guardian in Soccage, who is to accompt, and it is easily knowen how long he shall by Law receive the Profitts: And this Answer likewise will serve to the former Obiection: For being in Nature of a Gardeinship in Soccage, it is fitter to goe to the next of Kynn, then to the next Heire.

An other Exception was, That our Bill doth ordaine every Grant or Assignement of a Warde to a Recusant to be voide; Whereupon it will follow That the first granted having received

---

[1] Children sent abroad should not inherit property in England until they took the Oath of Allegiance. Till then the next of kin who was not Catholic should enjoy the property.

Money for the Warde, and assigned him over to a Recusant, shall now have againe the Warde and so retaine both ward and Money. It is answered, That the Recusant Knowing himself unable to take, is unworthy to enioy, if notwithstanding he will buy.

The last Obiection was, That we make a Non-Communicant by the Space of certaine tyme after his Coming to Church to be disabled as a Person Excommunicate. This is iustified also as reasonable; For the Ecclesiaticall Court for contumacy may ex-
f. 200] communicate, *Ergo*. Againe such Person is not disabled to all intents to sue, for he may by this Act sue for any Cause which concerneth such livelyhood as hereby is limitted unto him: And in no Case is his Action abated but only he is disabled for the tyme, and upon his Conformity may proceede: and upon his Conformity, he needeth no Absolution.

19º. Maii. 1606.

A Sub Poena out of the Chancery was served by a serving man[1] upon Sir Richard Buckley, and the Party upon Complaint thereof was brought to the Barr, and confessed That his Master directed him so to doe; and ordered that the Party shall remaine with the Serieant of this House untill his Master come into the House. It was moved by Mr. Speaker, as a thing to be considered: Whether any difference be betweene A Sub Poena to answer, and a Sub Poena to reioyne, for in the former, the Defendant is to appeare personally, and putt in his Answer, whereby he is drawen from attendance in this House: But he may reioyne by directions to his Attorney without his owne Personall Presence. To this was replied by a Member of this House, That he heard this Session the Opinion of the House, that no Processe is to be served on any of this House, for though his Person be not drawen from his Corporall Attendance; yet his minde is withdrawne, whereby the House hath no use of his Presence. In Conclusion, the Matter was referred to the Consideration of the Committees for the Priviledges.

Touching the Conference with the Lords, concerning the 2. Bills of Recusants, it was agreed, That when the Committees of this House have delivered the reasons agreed on for Maintenance

---

[1] Owen ap Rice, servant of Mr. Lloyd. See Hatsell, *Precedents*, I, 168.

of the Bills, and for satisfaction of the Exceptions taken thereunto by the Lords, they shall leave the Lords to their Wisedomes.
Which in the Afternoone was done accordingly; and that being
done, the Earle of Salisbury concluded the Conference to this
Effect, That the Lords having heard the reasons as the same have
bene delivered, would consider thereof, and he doubted not but
their Lordships would either passe our Bills in sort as we have
passed them, or else so amende them as we shall not reiect them.
All Committees which are appointed for this day, are put over
untill to Morrow, because of the Conference.

20.º Maii. 1606.

An Act concerning Sanctuary, 2.º *Lecta*, committed, to morrow
in the Middle Temple Hall.

An Act for the bringing of a fresh Spring or running Water to
the North Parte of the Citty of London, 3.º *Lecta*. passed.

This Bill was much withstood, upon diverse reasons. Sir
W[illia]m Stroude thought That it would hurt the Citty: Which
Opinion he grounded upon his Experience in the river brought
f. 201] to Plymouth into which the Cittizens doe so cast all the
soyle and filth of the Citty, and sweepe the Streats into it after
raine, that the same running into the Haven, doth make great
Obstructions there; And so would this Streame offend the River
of Thames: But this reason moved not. Next a Patent granted
to Captain Colhurst by Queen Elizabeth[1] by allowance of the
Lord Maior and Aldermen, whereby Colhurst had diverse yeares,
of which 7. are yet to come, was opposed, and urged that he
hath bestowed 1000. Marks in the Worke, and brought it 3. or
4. Miles onward, that the Invention was his: When as the Citty
having in 13.º Elizabeth an Act[2] to enable them to doe this worke,
and 10. yeares Space thereby appointed for doeing of it, the
Citty gave it over as not feasible. Whereupon it was moved,
That Mr. Colhurst might enioy his Patent, or have his Costs,
and Consideration for his Invention from the Citty, and that to
be answerable unto the gaine which he might make if he should
performe the Worke, and declared that in that Case he should
have turned the third part into the Commonsewer, and have had

---

[1] This grant was made in 1604. *Cal. St. P. Dom. 1603–1610*, 93.
[2] 13 Eliz. c. 18. *Statutes of the Realm*, IV, 553.

the Benefitt of the other 2. third Parts of the Water to his owne use, by bringing it to mens Houses that would Compound therefore with him. Hereupon it was moved, That some short Provisoe should be added for Consideration to be made by the Citty to Mr. Colhurst etc. But Mr. Speaker diverted that Course by urging an offer of Sir Henry Mountague Recorder of London, to this Purpose, viz, Sir Henry Mountague promised that the Lord Maior etc. shall make such Satisfaction to Captain Colhurst as the Lord Chancellor shall direct; Howbeit the House notwithstanding was devided upon the Question of passing the Bill, and it passed; and Sir Henry Mountagues Promise entred in the Clerks Booke of this House: But it was moved, That this President may prove dangerous, and we may be urged to passe Bills upon the Word of some, or any great Person, whose Honor is as much to be respected, as any Promise on my Lord Maiors behalfe. This was generally liked of, but deferred untill to morrow.

Ruled That even in a particuler Bill, when the House is devided, if the No's doe loose it; they must goe forth, and fetch in the Bill: In the Bill of London so ruled; and this held albeit one of the Tellors was Sir Barnard Whitstoone by intrusion, and not named by the Speaker: and yet Mr. Speaker vouched Presidents to the contrary where one of the Tellors was not appointed by the Speaker. Concerning dividing of the House.

The Welsh Gentleman, Master to the Party the last day committed, was now brought to the Barr for serving a *Sub Poena ad reiungendum* on Sir Richard Buckley, and for that the said Writt was served by his direction, he was Committed to the Sergeants.

21TH. MAII. 1606.

Two Bills were reade concerning Fenns: the 2d. reading theref. 202] fore deferred untill to Morrow.[1] Then for want of busines, the House did rise.

22TH. MAII. 1606.

An Act for the more sure Establishment and Continuance of true Religion, having bene formerly sent from this House to the

---

[1] See bills in *C.J.* I, 311, which says they were read the second time this day.

Lords, and now returned with many Amendements were reade.[1]
And for that the Bill is in my conceit a worthy Bill, and the
Amendements and Provisoe very stange; And for that many things
are to be therein observed, I have in the last end of this Booke
inserted the same *ad verbum:*[2] And note, That SIR ROBERT
WINGFIELD did affirme, That at the passing of these Amendements and Provisoe, there were in the Upper House only 8.
Temporall Lords of whom Six, and three Bishops were against
the Amendements, and Provisoe.[3]   Note, the Amendements
came in Paper, and the Provisoe in Parchment. Then the Speaker
asked the Question, thus, As many as think it fitt and convenient
this Bill with these Amendements and Provisoe to be committed
may it please you to say, Yea; To which no man answered Affirmatively. Then it was ruled, That the next Question must be, As
many as thinck it not fitt that these Amendements and Provisoe
be comitted, Say, Nay. For untill some answere be made Affirmatively, there may no Negative Question be proposed. Hereupon
it was ordered, That the 1st. Question should be asked againe,
and some body answer Affirmatively, which was done, and one
only said, Yea: And to the Negative Question, the whole House
answered, and thereby the Bill was dashed.

An Act touching restraint of Excommunication in Ecclesiasticall
Courts. 1? *Lecta*. And generally agreed to be reiected; But
disputed[4] Whether in respect it came from the Lords it should
not have a 2d. reading, but the House doubting some Tricke,
and willing, as it seemed to argue their universall, iust mislike of
the Bill, did cast it away upon the 1st. reading.

23? MAII. 1606.

An Act concerning Logwood alias Blockwood. 2? *Lecta*. ordered
to sleepe.

This forenoone for want of busines was spent with a few unnecessary Motions, touching small Matters.

---

[1] Cf. *C.J.* I, 311.
[2] Neither Harl. MSS 4945 nor the extant portion of the Stanford MSS
contains any such bill. The amendments of the Lords are mentioned in
Hist. MSS Com. 4th Rep. App. 118.
[3] *L.J.* II, 437, records eighteen Bishops and ten lay Lords as present.
[4] See *C.J.* I, 311.

24? MAII. 1606.

An Act for Relief of John Holbich (disherited) by the Extraordinary Amendments of the Errors of a Fyne. 3? *Lecta.*

In this Bill it was ruled, That after the third reading, a Bill cannot be put to the Question of Sleeping, but the Question must be of passing, and it may be, whether the Bill shall be presently put to the Question of passing.

An Act for avoiding Suits touching the Fennes within the Isle of Ely. 3? *lecta.* and upon the Question, reiected.

26? MAII. 1606.

f. 203] An Act against unlawfull Hunting and Killing of Conneys, 3? *lecta.* having formerly not bene committed as a Bill unworthy, was now notwithstanding put to the Question of passing, and upon devision of the House passed by the advantage of One voice only.

Sir John Crooke, Sir Edw[ard] Stanhope, and Dr. Hone brought from the Lords 2. Bills touching Recusants, which formerly had bene sent from this House up. viz.

An Act to prevent and avoide dangers that may growe by Popish Recusants.

An Act for the Better discovery and Punishment of Popish Recusants and the Education of their Children. Which Message in effect tended to declare the Lords Affections to the Bills, to excuse their Amendments and Omissions of things in the Bills, and lastly (to my understanding) That the Bills may sleepe unto the next Session.[1]

SIR ROBERT WINGFIELD moved That some Course may be

---

[1] Bowyer is quite wrong in this. The Lords urged the immediate passage of the bills (*C.J.* I, 312) and James was most anxious that there should be no more delay. Sir Thomas Lake had written Salisbury on May 22: "I have delivered to his Majesty that which you commanded me, and I left him satisfied with it, committing the matter to your discretions. But since, upon my Lord of Canterbury's being with his Highness, who makes doubt that you will not be ready to send down [from the Lords] the Bills of recusants tomorrow, his Majesty conceives that thereby occasion may grow to hold the House longer together, which displeases him; and therefore commanded me to signify to you that, seeing you have made choice of Tuesday, he expects it should be fixed, and no more changes follow, which he thinks would be but a scorn. I did what I could to assure his Highness upon the confidence of your speech; and answered, touching

taken for Punishment of Dr. Parker, who the day before, being
Sunday, had made an Invective Oration against this House at
Paules Crosse, very seditious and Slanderous: Whereupon diverse[1] of the House that were at the said Oration were appointed
to goe up together into the Committee Chamber, and to Collect
and set downe the offensive Speeches, which were delivered by
the Dr. as aforesaid: Which was done accordingly; And MR.
RECORDER Verbally reported what he heard at Pauls Crosse:
Whereupon MR. MARTYN advised That a short Act should be
made, declaring the offence of Dr. Parker against this House;
which some allowed; diverse proposed severall advise herein;
Some wished That the Sergeant should be sent for him forthwith, which was done; Others wished That Sir Roger Aston,[2]
and Mr. Recorder should be sent to his Majesty, not by way of
Complaint, or to disable ourselves to punish the Offence, but to
signify and to make knowne the Iniury: The rather, for that the
Fellowe was the next day being Tuesday by appointment to
preach before his Majesty. Which Message also was sent to his
Majesty. Others desired, That the House should send to my
Lord Chamberlain to appoint an other to preach to morrow before
his Majesty instead of Dr. Parker, which Councell was liked of,
but not put in Execution.

The Serieant did at the Sitting of the House, viz. after dinner
(as I remember) declare that he had bene at the lodging of Dr.
Parker, as he was Commanded, but that some other had more
speed, and advertised the Dr. of this Matter, and that the Dr.
was gone halfe an hower before his coming.

In the afternoone on Tuesday, Mr. Speaker did reade in the

---

the doubt conceived out of my Lord of Canterbury's speech, that it might
be, although you could not be ready to send it in the morning, yet you
might do it in the afternoon, sitting now at both times, and spending so
much time together; and as I thought the Lower House would do the
like. Yet his doubt of any more differing was such as his pleasure was
I should signify it to you, and that he hopes you will prevent any further
delay. I have made bold also to send you the general pardon signed by
his Majesty, which I received from Mr. Attorney." Salisbury MSS.

[1] See names and debate in *C.J.* I, 312–313.

[2] "Now hear you all my news, saving that Sir Roger Aston is become
so popular in the Lower House as they made choice of him and Mr.
Recorder to be sent to the King to complain of one Doctor Parker. . . . ."
Unsigned letter to Lord Dunbar, May 27, 1606. Salisbury MSS.

House a Letter which before dinner he had received from My
f. 204] Lord of Salisbury, to this effect; That his Majesty hath appointed in his owne Royall Person, to heare Dr. Parkers defence
this afternoon, And the Earl wished, That if the House were
possessed of any Particuler notes of this Matter, the same might
be sent to the Court, if not, then Mr. Recorder to attend at the
Court, to accuse the Dr; or in Case the Recorder were not now
present, then the House to appoint some one to attend this
Service:[1] But said Mr. Speaker, Mr. Recorder was then immediatly seene in the Court, and directed to attend, so as there
now needeth no further Order to be taken by this House, but to
attend his Majestyes Good Pleasure.

Touching which busines, his Majesty the next day at the
Adiournment of the Parliament, declared *Inter alia*, That himself
had heard Dr. Parker; That the Dr. denieth some thing, and
other Speeches he Cuppleth with words of Mitigation; and his
expresse words of a Parliament to chuse a King, he affirmeth,
That he meant only by the Parliament of Trees: And said his
Majesty I have committed him to the Private House of a great
Churchman,[2] untill the Cause shall be further heard.

Sir George Coppin, and Dr. Hone brought from the Lords 2.
Bills. An Act for Transportation of Beere. An Act for bringing
a Streame of fresh Water to the North Side of the Citty of London: with signification That their Lordships have provided for
Mr. Colhurst.

---

[1] As soon as the Speaker had received Salisbury's letter, he replied
as follows: "I received your letters some half an hour after 12, and therefore cannot satisfy his Majesty's pleasure to send either the notes or Mr.
Recorder before 11, as is required, whereby his Majesty may be informed
concerning D. Parker's proceedings. But if it might stand with your favour
to the House, to move his Majesty that there may be some time given to
present those notes of information, either this evening or tomorrow morning, it will exceedingly satisfy them, and give them occasion to take great
comfort of his Majesty's gracious favour towards them. Give me leave to
be a mean that his Majesty will vouchsafe them a gracious conclusion in
these parliament businesses, beseeching you to remember that little had
been left unperfected that he had desired, and which will be a good pre-
parative to prepare them against the next session of Parliament." May 27,
1606. Salisbury MSS.

[2] The Dean of St. Paul's. This gave the Commons "great Satisfaction." Unsigned letter to Lord Dunbar, May 27, 1606. Salisbury MSS.

Mr. Recorder in reporting what he heard in Dr. Parkers Sermon, 1st. declared, That his Text was, *Quaerite Pacem Civitatis,* wherein said the Recorder, he dealt as Garnet did in his Booke intituled against lying: Of which the whole Treatise was a Defence of Equivocation: So was his Text for Peace, but his discourse nothing but Sedition. Time being Passed the House arose.

This 26th. day after dinner, the House did sett, chiefely to expect Bills, or otherwise busines from the Lords.

A Message from the King, requiring the Speaker to attend his Majesty, which he did presently, and returned after foure of the Clocke to the House; And then he said That the Messengers that called him would reporte the Cause to the House, who as he said were coming.

Then Mr. Recorder (as I remember) declared That his Majesty understanding that this House had sent unto him, would not take his report before he had heard us; And in Presence of some of his Greatest Councellors, sent for us, and commanded us to reporte what was spoken by Dr. Parker: Which (said the Recorder I did) which the King heard with great Passion; And willed us to say unto you, first, by way of Answer, then by way of Resolution; For Answer, That Though he never used to condemne before he had heard both sides, yet he did hold this which the House had sent unto him to be true; And That he esteemeth f. 205] the words Indiscreete, and Presumpteous, rather then Seditious, yet will he heare how the words can be conioyned, which being disioyned, may be evill interpreted.

His Resolution, That albeit this Case concerneth a Clergyman of the Convocation, and they a Court, which is likely would punish this fault, yet none can so well censure, and punish it as himselfe, which he said he would doe to the content of the House, and therein wills them to be Resolute.

Mr. Iustice Warburton, Serjeant Crooke, and Dr. Hone, brought from the Lords, an Act intituled, An Act for the Kings Majesty most Gratious and Free Pardon. This Act is by Order to be but once reade.

27° Maii. 1606.

An Act for his Majesty Generall Free Pardon, 1° *Lecta* and by Order is no more to be reade.[1]

---

[1] See letter of Coke in *Cal. St. P. Dom. 1603–1610,* 318.

Committees appointed to consider how the Money collected by the Treasurers shall be imploied, and distributed.

The Committees formerly appointed to consider of the Lords Amendements and Alterations of the Bills of Recusants, doe now by SIR HENRY HUBBERT report, that touching the first Bill intituled, An Act to prevent and avoide dangers which may growe by Popish Recusants, the Amendements are few, and such as well may be allowed, and the Bill with them fitt to passe, and upon the question it passed.

Touching the 2d. Bill intituled, An Act for the better discovery and disclosing of Popish Recusants, and Education of their Children in the true Religion; The Lords have taken away the latter parte of this Tytle, and answerablely whatsoever in the Act doth concerne the taking away, or Education of their Children. An other matter altered in the Bill is, That whereas Non-communicants by a certaine Space are by the Bill disabled as Persons excommunicate, their Lordships thinking this Penalty too greate, have inflicted for the first yeare after a certaine tyme coming to Church 20£. for the 2d. yeare 40£. for the 3d. yeare 60£. and so 60£. for every yeare that such Person shall forbeare the communion.

An other Point altered is, That in all Cases where the Bill as it passed this House gave Authority unto two Iustices of Peace to minister an Oath, provided by this Act, unto any Person not communicating, *ut Supra*. There the Lords by their Amendements have added by way of Exception these words (other then Noble men and Noble women) and provided some what in lieu thereof for they have added a Provisoe to this Effect, That in all Cases where the two Iustices of Peace may minister the said Oath to any Person not excepted there, six of the Counsell whereof the Lord Chancellor Lord Treasurer, or Principall Secretary to be One, may minister the same Oath to any Noble Man, or Noble Woman. Also the Lords have provided that no man be impeached for his f. 206] Wives not Communicating. Likewise where the Act did appoint That Gentlemen, and men of quallity shall when they passe over to serve any Prince, being of the Popish Religion, enter bond with Suerties remaining in the Realme, unto such Persons as the Act appointeth etc. The Lords have put out the words (Professing the Popish Religion) and in lieu thereof made it thus (State or Potentate) thereby including all men; And have appointed the Bonds to be such as the Chief Officer of the Port from whence such party doe passe, shall allowe: And such Officer of every such Port to take the Bonds.

After dinner, the Commons came before the King, and the Lords in the Parliament House, the King and the Lords being then in their Roabes, where the Speaker, first made an Oration to his Majesty; Then the King answered in a long Eloquent Speech, containing many Matters: And in conclusion, said, That on a Tuesday himselfe had in Scotland escaped a strange danger of his life:[1] On a Tuesday likewise himself, and the Lords and Commons escaped the Treason of blowing up this Roome with Powder. On Tuesday said he we began againe this Session, and have, God be thancked, passed and done many good things in it; And now on Tuesday I meane to adiourne it unto an other Tuesday in November: And yet I would not have any man thinck me Superstitious, notwithstanding when God hath marked a day, I would have no man to neglect it.[2]

END OF BOOK II

BOOK III
[Harleian MS]

f. 207]   18 November. 1606.

On the 18th. November. 1606. being Tuesday and the day of Adiournment of the Parliament, the Commons did accordingly meete in the Ordinary Place called the Parliament House, at 9. of the Clocke in the forenoone, where Praiers being said as of Course on other daies, The Company sat still about the Space of halfe an houre. Then was reade by the Speakers Direction a Bill intituled.

An Act to make good Grants Assurances and Conveyances made by Corporations and bodies Politick, notwithstanding the misnaming of the same Corporations, 1°. *Lecta.*

After the reading of which Bill, the House continued about halfe an houre more silent, and then the Speaker signified the Kings

---

[1] The Gowry Conspiracy took place on Tuesday, August 5, 1600.

[2] When the King finished, the Lord Chancellor prorogued Parliament until November 25. See the account in *Ambassades*, I, 94–95.

Purpose to be in Person in the Lords House in the afternoone at 2. of the Clock: Whereupon he moved the House to meete here in their House about one of the clocke from thence to attend his Majesty Pleasure and Presence: And so the House having small other busines, did rise, and departed.

After dinner as was before spoken, his Majesty came in Person into the Lords House of Parliament, and being placed under the Estate in his Roabes, wearing his Capp, and Imperiall Crowne, the doore was opened, and the Speaker and the Commons admitted.

All Persons being setled, the Lord Elsemere Lord Chancellor declared the Liberall Grant of the Commons the last Session unto the King viz. of three Subsidies and 6. Fifteenes; He shewed, how slouly the same hath bene collected and paid.

Then he declared the Kings gratious Inclination to consider of such Grievances as were the last tyme presented unto him by the Commons; And required Sir Thomas Smyth, clarke of that House to reade his Majesty Answere[1] to every of them, in Number 16. which he reade accordingly.

Then the Kings Majesty used an Eloquent and very long Speech,[2] which continued an houre and halfe; The chiefe and almost only effect whereof was, to perswade the Passage of the Act and Instrument of the Union: Upon which Point My Lord Chancellor had somewhat touched in his Oration. The Chiefest Argument which his Highnes used was, That this happy Union is already in his Person made by the Singuler Providence of God; That now it only remayneth that the same be confirmed by the Parliament, so as no Splinter may start out; which principally will be by abolishing all old former Lawes of Hostility. Againe he urged, That the greatest Obiection which is the hardnesse and barrennesse of the Countrey, is not materiall, for said he, Wales f. 208] is not so fertile as England, neither are some Shires of England so fruitfull as the rest; And yet no man will say but that Wales, and these barren Shires, are necessary partes of England;

---

[1] See p. 187, note 1.
[2] For the King's speech, see *C.J.* I, 314–315; *Parl. Hist.* I, 1071–75. Part of the speech is in St. P. Dom. XXIII, 65. See also brief descriptions in *Cal. St. P. Venetian, 1603–1607*, 437; *Roger Wilbraham* (*Camden Misc.* X), 88–91; *Ambassades*, I, 433–434.

For the Strength of a Countrey doth not consist only in Wealth, but in the Number and force of able Men: which long Eloquent Oration ended, the King departed, and the Company dispersed.

Wednesday 19th. of November. 1606.

Then Mr. Speaker declared That My Lord Chancellor had from the Clarke of the Crowne a note of the Names of severall Members of this House now absent on Service; Which his Lordship had sent to him, the House to consider what Course may be taken to supply their roomes, or otherwise;

The Names mentioned in the note were these.

Sir Humphrey Wynche, sent into Ireland there to be Chief Baron.

Sir George Carew, Ambassador Leeger in France.

Sir Char[les] Cornwallys, Ambassador Leeger in Spaine.

Sir Tho[mas] Ridgeway, Treasurer at Warrs in Ireland.

Sir Henry Hubbert, since the last Session, made Attorney Generall.

Sir Edward Hobby arose up and affirmed, That where the Party was in Possibility to returne, and uncertaine how long to be absent in which Case he placed Ambassadors, there the House hath not used to receive any new in their Steade: Otherwise he said it is touching Mr. Attorney who is to attend wholie in the Upper House; And quoth he it were good the rest of the Kings Councell were in like Case.

Mr. Speaker moved, That the like Consideration might be had of Sir James Lea Chief Iustice in Ireland. An other Member of the House remembred Sir Oliver St. John, serving as Master of the Ordinance in Ireland. Lastly this Matter was referred to certaine Committees appointed the last Session for the Priviledges; whose names were reade, and a few added to them.

Sir Robert Iohnson moved That a Committee might be appointed to consider of the Statute of Labourers,[1] whereunto Mr. Speaker with Allowance of the House, answered, That a Bill must be drawen, and offered to the House, and so to be proceeded in.

Mr. Speaker caused the clerke to reade the Kings Majesty

---

[1] 5 Eliz. c. 4. *Statutes of the Realm*, IV, 414.

Answer to the Severall Grievances presented the last Session by the Commons, as the same were ingrossed.[1]

f. 214]   THURSDAY. 20. NOVEMBER. 1606.

Mr. Speaker about 8. of the Clock, sent word That it would be Ten of the clock before he could come to the House.

Sir Iohn Crooke One of the Kings Serieants at Lawe, Sir Edw[ard] Stanhope, Dr. Swale, and Dr. Hone Masters of the Chancery, after the Speaker had set a while in the House, brought from the Lords, the Instrument[2] for the Union of the Kingdomes of England and Scotland; which had bene framed by the Commissionors of both Kingdomes, and now was presented to the House engrossed in Parchment, sealed by all the Commissionors of both Kingdomes, except Sir Edward Hobby.

It was somewhat controverted, Whether this Instrument of the Union, should presently be reade; But notwithstanding some mens Earnestnes, and Mr. Speaker urging, it was thought fitt by the House to deferr the reading of it untill the next day.[3]

FRIDAY 21TH. NOVEMBER. 1606.

The Instrument of Union of the two Kingdomes, was reade; which being done, the Speaker recited the Effect thereof, as he useth to doe of Bills.

---

[1] Bowyer here inserts a copy (ff. 208-214) of a "separate" of the King's reply. It begins, "A Memoriall of such Resolutions as his Majesty hath taken . . . . ," and ends, ". . . . he hath made him the Sole and Supreame Gouvernor." Since Bowyer's copy of this "separate" agrees almost verbatim with the copy in *C.J.* I, 316-318, it has been omitted.

There are many copies of this "separate." St. P. Dom. XXIII, 67, 68, 69, 70 (the last corrected by Salisbury); Harl. MSS 299, ff. 23-37; 589, ff. 79-83; 6846, ff. 207-208 (incomplete); Lansd. MSS 486, ff. 106-111; Cott. MSS, Titus F IV, ff. 86-92.

Although James's answer was unsatisfactory in many ways, the House dropped the subject of grievances at this point.

[2] See text of the Instrument in *C.J.* I, 318-323. See also Gardiner, I, 324-328.

Harl. MSS 1314, f. 19, contains a description by one of the English Commissioners of the many advantages that the Scots had over the English in the conferences in which the Instrument was drawn up.

[3] Because "it was somewhat late." *Hist. MSS Com. Buccleuch MSS,* III, *Montagu Papers, Second Series,* 107.

SATURDAY. 22. NOVEMBER. 1606.

SIR GEORGE MOORE one of the Committees for the Priviledges, reported the opinion of the Committees touching the Matter of Supplie of absent Members of the House, thus, Touching Sir Humphrey Wynch sent a Chief Baron into Ireland, the Committees held his Case to be like Sir James Lea, who was sent thether since the first Session of this Parliament, and Mr. Chocke chosen to serve in this House in his Place: which President was the rather allowed heretofore, for that it was alledged That the Chief Iustice and Chief Baron have Patents during their Lives; That the same Rule was given and thought good by the Committees touching Sir Oliver St. Iohn, sent into Ireland Master of the Ordinance; And Sir Thomas Ridgeway Treasurer in Ireland since the last Session: And this Opinion of the Committees allowed by the House.

Then touching Sir Char[les] Cornwallys, sent and now resiant Ambassador in Spaine, Sir George Carew Ambassador in France, Sir Thomas Edmunds Ambassador with the Archduke in the f. 215] Low Countries, it was thus thought by the Committees That none should be chosen to serve in this House in their Places, for that it had bene so ordered heretofore, in respect That the aboade of the Ambassadors is uncertaine and they to be recalled when the King shall please. Lastly, Whether in place and steade of Mr. Attorney Generall called to that Place, and by Writt to attend the Lords House since the last Sessions, there should now be a Warrant from hence directed for a Writt, for choosing of an other in his place here to serve. Sir George Moore reported, it was alleadged by some of the Committees That in 8. Eliz. Mr. Onsloe being a Member of this House was made Sollicitor, and continued here a Member[1] and was chosen Speaker. Likewise that 18? Eliz. Mr. Serieant Iefferies being a Member of the House, was made the Queenes Serieant.[2] Then that My Lord Chief Justice Popham that now is, being 23. Eliz: a Member of the House, was made Sollicitor, and yet continued a Member here.[3] Whereupon

---

[1] D'Ewes, 121.

[2] D'Ewes, 249.

[3] D'Ewes, 280–281. " . . . . and though there was no President in the Case of the Attorney General, yet the reason was all one." Cott. MSS, Titus F IV, f. 93v.

diverse of the Committees think That Mr. Attorney ought to be continued here a Member: But (said Sir George) some of the Committees were of an other minde; Wherefore they left it to the Order and Wisedome of the House. Hereupon the Question was made and propounded by Mr. Speaker, viz. As many as thincke fitt and convenient That a new Member be chosen in place of Mr. Attorney, may it please you to say, Yea, and then *E converso*; But the Voices by the noise being doubtfull, and neither Side yeilding: A Second Doubt arose, viz. Whether the Yea, or the No, should goe forth. Mr. Speaker moved, That the Yea, should goe forth, giving this reason, That Party which seeketh a new thing, is to goe forth. Then quoth SIR HERBERT CROFT, the No must goe forth, for they would have the Kings Attorney to remaine a Member here, which was never seene, and is without President: Herein the House would not agree, and so without concluding any thing in the Point a Silence followed: Then SIR W[ILLIA]M MORRICE made an Idle Speech, touching a Bill by himself preferred the last Session, for to enact the King to be Emperour of Great Brittaine; which moved Laughter in the House; To which mirth, Silence for halfe an hower succeeded: And so the House arose; Mr. Speaker saying it was almost Eleaven of the Clock.

Note, That all this day, the Instrument of Union, lay on the Deske before the Clarke, but not moved by any man to be reade, or dealt with all.

MONDAY. 24. NOVEMB: 1606.

Mr. Attorney Generall came into the House with Mr. Speaker.[1]

MR. FULLER moved, That a Warrant might be directed for a Writt to chose a Member in place and steade of Sir Henry Billingsley who since our last meeting was deceased: Which was granted.

Mr. Speaker moved the like for chosing others in place of such f. 216] Members as were since the last Session, sent into Ireland, viz. Sir Humphrey Wynch, sent thether as Chief Baron; Sir Oliver St. Iohn sent thether as Master of the Ordinance; and Sir Tho[mas] Ridgeway, there imployed as Treasurer; Which was granted.

---

[1] "Hereupon Mr. Attorney finding that upon Debate thereof the Opinion of the House was like to sway that he ought still to serve amongst them, Did of his own accord without any express order in the Case come into the House and serve there." Cott. MSS, Titus F IV, f. 93*v*.

Sir Anthony Cope moved That this House should send up
unto the Lords the Instrument[1] of the Union which formerly we
had received from them: with Signification That the same had
bene here reade, and that diverse had taken Notes of the Particularities in it; And That the Clerk had a Coppy of it; Which
Motion was allowed; And Mr. Secretary Herbert appointed to
carry it up, whom among other Voluntaries, Mr. Attorney Generall did accompany, and returned with him.

From the Lords, Sir John Crooke his Majestys Serieant at Law,
and Dr. Hone One of the Masters of the Chancery were sent with
this Message, That the Lords understood this House had reade the
said Instrument of Union, and how gravely they had considered
thereof, and taken Coppies; Now their desire was That all Expedition may be used in this soe great a busines, doe pray a conference, as speedily as may be, the Number of their Lordships to
be 40. The place the painted Chamber; The tyme to Morrow in
the afternoone at 2. of the Clock, except greater occasions doe
otherwise detaine this House.[2]

Mr. Speaker moved the Question; viz. For a meeting and
Conference *ut Supra*. The voices were doubtfull; Hereupon Mr.
Fuller moved That in respect the Lords are wise and grave, and
have deliberately advised and consulted of the Matter; Therefore
this House should first among Our selves openly dispute, and
discusse it to the End the busines might be well conceived before
we might conferr with the Lords: And he wished that in such
dispute here in this House among our selves every man would
declare his minde; No man to be silent, but every man to speake
though it were but five words, which would be a meanes we should
goe prepared, and meete to good Effect.

Upon this Motion it was resolved, That we should returne word
to the Lords, That at the tyme and place required by their Lord-

---

[1] " . . . . because it was the Authentical Instrument under the Seales
of the Commissioners." Cott. MSS, Titus F IV, f. 93v.

[2] "After Mr. Speaker had declared this message there was a great
silence in the house, so that Mr. Speaker was fain to rise and know the
house's pleasure.

"This word conference made some staggering because we had nothing
to confer of, but to give the Lords meeting and to hear what they would
propound we would be ready, and so appointed 80." *Hist. MSS Com.
Buccleuch MSS*, III, 108.

ships, we would send 80. Committees to attend them, only to heare and understand what their Lordships would propose, and to report the same to this House; who thereupon might advise upon some further Course to be taken herein.

Note That this Answer was not fully an Acceptance of the Lords Message, and Request, but varying from it in the Point of Conference, was notwithstanding returned by Sir Iohn Crooke and Dr. Hone. Which Sir Edw[ard] Mountague said in private to me, ought in this Case of variance to have bene sent by Messengers of our owne. *Ratio patet.*

TUESDAY 25? NOVEMB: 1606.

Diverse Bills were 1? *Lecta.*

f. 217]   WEDNESDAY 26? NOVEMBRIS. 1606.

A Bill reade the 2d. time may be committed, though no Man speake against it.

After a Bill is committed upon the 2d. reading without any Speech had against it, so as the Negative Question of committing have not bene asked, it may be spoken unto.

Mr. Recorder of London SIR H[ENRY] MOUNTAGUE reported[1] what passed Yesterday at the meeting of the Committees of both Houses, thus: After Our Meeting quoth he, we heard what they said: And first the Lord Chancellor said, That Silence in Consultations effecteth nothing: Wherefore he wished that our Commission had extended to speake as well as to heare, and then they should not have doubted but some good would have succeeded: And then he wished That this House would appointe some to conferr with some of their Lordships. Next touching the Manner, he proposed that the Treaty might be of the Instrument either entirely, or devidedly: Devidedly in 3. Points, viz. Repealing of Hostile Lawes. 2. Commerce or Trade. 3. Participation mutually of the Subiects of both Kingdomes, of the Liberties, and Benefitts of both Countries interchangeably. Lastly, he moved That a select Company might be chosen to treate of these Points. Then quoth he, His Lordship remembred to us his Majestyes words, to this effect, That we should with us bring mindes of Indifferency,

---

[1] See the report and debate in *C.J.* I, 325, 1004-05; *Hist. MSS Com. Buccleuch MSS*, III, 108-109.

and Equality, to weigh all things, and to forbeare all termes of bitternes. Then quoth he, The Earl of Salisbury, wished we had brought a larger Commission *ut Supra*: Then touching the handling of the Matter, he did speake also *ut Supra*: And advised That all men in the handling and debating of this great Matter should avoide Partiality, and base Feare.

The Lord Treasurer wished *ut Supra*, That we had brought a larger Commission, and likewise wished That we should deale with the House speedily to resolve, and acquaint their Lordships what we would doe.[1]

MR. MARTIN[2] after his Report ended, moved the House That we should drawe Bills touching the abolishing of Hostile Lawes; and for Commerce: And That we should leave it to the Lords to

---

[1] "Les seigneurs, qui pretendoient faire parler, se trouverent peu contens d'entendre de ces deputez qu'ilz n'avoient aultre charge que d'ouir et de faire leur rapport. Lequel faiet, les Seigneurs furent priez [on Nov. 27. *C.J.* I, 1005], comme plus clair-voians et prochains du soleil, de mettresur leur bureau les deux premieres propositions, se reservans les deux aultres comme moins espineuses. Ce traiet a esté encores moins agreable aux Seigneurs, qui cussent mieux aimé veoir et ouir parler les aultres. Quoi que ce soit, ceste union a la forge et sur l'enclume." M. de la Fontaine to M. de Villeroy, Dec. 6/16, 1606. Paris Transcripts.

[2] Harl. MSS 6850, f. 60*v*, is one of several documents in the hand of Sir Robert Harley.

"Mr. Martin. After Mr. Recorder had made his report of the Lords speches Sir Edmond Grevell speking a distracted and confused speche, Mr. Martin began to this Effect. I would willingly have hard Mr. Speker prposse befor I had hard any man perswade for this time doth desier rather advis of the manner then of the matter and yett he will remember somewhatt ether our silence or our fear hathe lett lye still. For my Lord of Salsbury advised us nether to bring preiudice or bass fear with us. For if any would take exception against the Instrument so it be with modest speche he may. It is the Duty of every man in this great Counsell to speek soe and not in silence to betray his honesty nor in the manner his dutye. And thereuppon desireth all men ther to lay by ther reservations and use ther diligence. The matters to be considered ar 4. Abrogation of Lawes, Commerce, Determining Differences uppon the Borders and Naturalizing. Conference never brought us advantage yett in this it is necessary. His motion is that the first two may be under our care to frame into Bills. And the other two better knowne to the Lords may be ther labor. That so we may walke hand in hand to our best understanding. And that men will not be of that will *Quam si persuasori non persuasori*. And in ther reports thinke that those that doe contradict have not as good ends as any the other."

doe the like concerning the Government of both borders, and Naturalization; For the former is matter wherein many of us is expert, and the 2. latter are best understood by their Lordships.

Sir Francis Bacon.[1]

That this great Matter is not to be treated of in Masse, but in Branches we shall all agree, and the Order, quoth he, I hold best to be by Conference not severally by the two Houses aparte; First, f. 218] because the same was begun in Conference: Next, if the Lords by themselves begin, and settle upon any certainty in any Point, they will afterwards be inflexible, for they are in that Case engaged; Whereas upon Conference, before they be resolved, they are by reasons to be drawen.

Sir Henry Poole moved, That severall daies should be appointed in this House to argue each Point.[2]

---

[1] See this speech as printed in Spedding, III, 303–304.

[2] The rest of the debate is contained in Harley's notes. Harl. MSS 6850, f. 55v; 6842, 5v.

"Sir Hen[ry] Pool. I Cannot speak so well as they that spoke before; Yet my care of the Common Wealth is no less then theirs. The Name is comfortable, to avoid discord, and Hostility, and Union a good work, if we may Effect it. The matter is An Inovation, and deserves a great consideration, and therefore I think we are not ready for a bill, or conference. He therfore wisheth it may be devided into four Branches, as Mr. Martin devided it, and a day Allotted to the handling of every Branch.

"Mr. Speaker. I Crave your Patience, if my memorie give me Leave to Neglect, or omitt any thing that was proposed; the desire of the Lords was for the Matter of manner, not manner of Matter, and that this here is different in opinion and proposition. Here he begune to repeat those that spoke; and omitting Sir Edmond Grevell made Mr. Martin the first. Then recited the Sume of Sir Francis Bacons Speach, and said of that propounded by Sir Hen[ry] Pool, I leave it to your own memories.

"Sir Geo[rge] More. In praise of Union I will not speak, in so understanding an Audience: all knowing it to be the work of god, as the contrary is of the Devil; for when there was but Two men, they were by him devided, Caan and Abel. He moved therfore a Conference but first a Consideration by a Committee. The House disliked his Motion.

"Sir Rob[er]t Jonson. Sure every one here should speak his Conscience freely; I will speak mine. He thinketh the first Division by Mr. Martine, Good, and that we should Consider of the Two first Branches, and Leave the other Two unto the Lords to propose.

"Sir W[illia]m Strowd. It is as fitt for a Bill as that of the Recusancy

THURSDAY 27? NOVEMBRIS. 1606.

MR. FULLER moved, That a Gentleman of this House who only among the Commissioners had not signed nor sealed the Instrument of the Union, might by the House be required to deliver his Reasons of forbearance so to doe.

Then MR. EDW[ARD] HOBBY declared That he tooke himselfe to be the Person entended by the Gentleman that last spake, and said he, during the Commission, I both saw, and heard many things, which then I could not savor, nor can now deliver by reason of the weakenesse of my Memory: And now in the handling of this great Matter, I protest I am not transported with any humour, but I can say, the Zeale of the House *Comedit me*, and the desire of a true Unity so as it may be with the good of the Mother Crowne of England: And I will ever proclaime a *Vae*, yea, an Anathema on him that shall not say, *Ecce quam bonum et quam Iucundum habitare in Unum*: Yet I repent me not of what I have done; and ever shall submitt my self when I shall heare better reasons, and stronger Arguments then at that tyme I did; In the meane tyme I humbly desire That it may be free *unicuique frui Abundantia Cordis sui*: For my owne Part, I never delighted in the Singularity of my Witt, although I have bene taxed in that Kinde, and yet I could have wished to have had Fellowes.[1]

was, by being in Articles, which was the work of our Conference. Then wisheth a Question upon Mr. Martins proposition for the devision.

"Sir Her[bert] Crofts. Moved to Consider among our Selves before a Conference. Here it was remitted over until the Morning."

[1] See *C.J.* I, 325. " . . . . and it was not thought fit he should yield his reason for where the major part have overruled it the rest are wrapped up in silence as in a voider and committed to oblivion." Cott. MSS, Titus F IV, f. 94.

James had written to Salisbury objecting to the words "mutual consent" of the Commissioners in the Instrument, for he had feared "that some of the vainest of the commissioners may start up at the Parliament and may say 'he and he and I gave never our consent but only were overruled by one or two more voices against us'." Undated. Salisbury MSS.

"Au Parlement, les bouches se sont trouvées restreintes, mais non en tous né du tout fermées. Celui que j'ay escrit avoir esté appellé pour rendre compte du refus qu'il avoit faiet de soulzsouie à l'union avec les aultres commissaires deputez pour cest effect deux ans passez, en a respondu et donné satisfaction à ceux de sa chambre, sans rien relascher de son premier advis." M. de la Fontaine to M. de Villeroy, Dec. 6/16. 1606. Paris Transcripts.

Mr. Speaker moved to know the Resolution of the House for answer to the Lords: Whereupon the Serieant was sent into Westminster Hall to call the Lawyers.

Mr. ALFORD, with Mr. BROOKE of Yorke, and Mr. MARTIN wished[1] That this House should deale with the 2. Points con-

---

[1] Cf. *C.J.* I, 1005. The debate is recorded by Harley. Harl. MSS 6850, ff. 55v, 61–62; 6842, ff. 6–7v.

"Mr. Bond. The next day Mr. Bond began to this Effect. He was of opinion, that it would have ended to the good of Both Kingdoms, and the kings content before Christmas, but now despaire of it. Kings that undergo the Greatest burthen, and Councelors that manage the Greatest affairs, can best Iudge, for *Non Omnis fert omnia Tellus.* Neither to every man Appurtaineth Matter of State. The question yesterday was the manner of Handling, which since it is so Inseparable from the Matter I must under favour handle both. The Subiect is to Assure two kingdoms, as one Body to one Head, Already made in the Person of our Soverain, by the Best Blood of both stemms: by Laws first of Love, then of free Interest; all Customes Municipall, always reserved. It is Miraculous, if we cast back our Eys a Hundred years, to see how now zealously Contesting, in this Great Councell, against that [which] the Prudence of our wisest king H : 7 fore-ordered and the wisdome of our Gravest Councell, in the time of E : 6 Endeavoured, so farr as by a Battel; whenas both the Liberties were offered and all things as by his Majestie now desired, were presented to that Nation but prevented by the Suttlety of our Invious Neighbours, the French. The Benefet of this mercifull favour offered by God, I Could amplify by storie, if it were not *actum agere.* Yet this beyond any Contradiction I will say; it is to make that one, that Nature ever so intended, and to put one Shepherd, to guid that flock, that is only folded within the Ocean. Scotland, how much soever now Despised in Imaginations, hath been always able to maintain itself, and hath with us the same religion, which is *sit missimum imperii & vinculum.* The means to perfect this union, Gravely have the Commissioners considered of, and presented and the way to proceed for us, the Lords have reduced to Two heads, either by Conference, with them or by treating among our selves. Of this Last, I heard good projects yesterday. For my part, I wish that of the three first, we may Consider, by three Committees, who dayly may relate their opinions, and Labour to the house. By thus Dealing *membratim*, we shall Hunt out every Doubt, and be well enabled to a father consideration with the Lords.

"Mr. Brooke. I speak less speaking so much of the Matter, it will put us out of the matter of which wee should speak. I have Considered the Two propositions yesterday, of Mr. Martins for Division of the Business between the Houses, and that of Sir Francis Bacon of Conference with the Lords; and this last propounded by the Post Master which I like worst. Master Bacons Argument was subtly propounded, that if we re-

cerning abolishing of Hostile Lawes, and Commerce; And the other two concerning the Government of the borders, and Naturalization to be left to the Lords, but advised That these Matters should be discussed before other Conference should be had, or any Bill drawen.

fered any to be billed by the Lords, we should hardly remove them from their first resolutions; but we find it no new thing, upon good reason to alter their minds. I like best, that first we entertain their bill of Hostille Laws and Commerce, and to Leave the other of highest Nature to the Lords, for they in that matter, Can be furthest that stand in the Bay window, or near the kings Elbow; and where the kings perogative is restrained, to Give admittance, when he shall see them Enabled best for his Service; which restraint being Indeffinite, can best be advised, by those that are near, and have the oracles of Law to Consult withall.

"Mr. Alford. I think we be neither ready for bill, nor conference. The Lords expressed that they had heard all obiections; we none, and therefore, let us desire the Lords to Enter into the Border Causes, and Naturalization, as we into the other; and that when we have well Considered of our Charge, to acquaint them, as they us, with their opinions.

"Master Fuller. We are not ready for any Conference. In Weighty Causes it is best to debate Alternatives, and hear every man Speak then a few Eloquently. One may see more then another, and all surely may see the Affection and Iudgement of the house. I will give mine singly, of every part. To Abolish Hostile Laws is a Iust work, so we do all; but if we Leave any thing, which is not fitt, we shall leave still a memorie of the old enmity. Therefore whither Escuage into Scotland be convenient to remain, it is Considerable; Purchance the like Hostile Law among the Scots may be a stumbling block. In the Preamble to the Articles there is a repetition of all Laws, and priviledges, if the Difference of Priviledges be so many as we have heard, how can there be a conformity. In matter of Commerce it may be prejudiciall; as to have the king by his prerogative to make the Maiors or offices of Towns Corporate, of that Nation and therefore it is fitt that for this Branch, we send for the Merchants to hear their objections. Of Naturalizing the Motion is so hard, that it deserves severall days solemn debate. Before we receive them In, let us seek for places to put them in; London can receive no more; no more can the Trade Towns of England; all occupations are so over-burthened with Artificers. If we bring in Noblemen, see how many must be removed to give them place. Trees removed from a hard and barron soil to a rich and fruitfull will florish fast; but removed from good to worse doe decay and wither, therefore they doubtless will Thrive here; as we doubtless shall wast there. Therefore I could wish everyone to remain In that place, to which Nature hath made his life proper; I therefore Desire, that in this Great matter we debate Thorowly before we conferr to satisfie.

"Master Dannet. Matter of Commerce is Defective; we are restrained

SIR EDWYN SANDYS[1] moved a Conference with the Lords, but not before we have here debated it by Points; But, quoth he, the 2d. Question being, Whether here to be debated by a Committee or in the House, I thinck by a Committee, because there a reply is admitted, which is not here: In the meane tyme (said he) let us send the Lords word That we are not ready for Conference, f. 219] but when we have debated it, then we will conferr with their Lordships touching the Points: And I further thinke That after debate here on every Point, and Conference with the Lords, the Course will be to devide the Points, which perhaps will not seame good.

fishing upon their Costs; they left free to All ours; I wish before this Matter be settled, the Merchants of London be consulted with.

"Sir Nat[ha]n[iel] Bacon. The Lords Expect an Answer, upon that Conference. We may Best distribute the parts; and so we shall goe on in the properest manner.

"Anonimus. [Mr. Gore.] The State of Merchants declined by a reason of Multitudes; This is like to pull it down quite, if here by our Mariners, Shipping and Treasure be divided, purchance our Ancient Enimies shall take new harte to offend us.

"Mr. May. I like the propositions propounded, but not the limitting of this house, by [be in MS] dealing with the Manner, and Matter. Neither both are Equall, nor both alike. I so say a Burthen upon the Hearer a Conference is fitt to Conclude of the manner, and that will not be prejudiciall.

"Sir Ed[ward] Hobby. To Answer the Gentleman that spoke Last against the Distribution propounded; this Course is usuall, and proper, for subsidies and repeals do always so arise, from this House; and are not the Laws of Hostility to be repealed? The other of Commerce and Naturalizing are of State; and ought to grow first out of that other house. For the Two houses are proper for severall uses. He wisheth a Conference to signifie a reason of this distribution desired."

[1] "Mr. Speaker. Mr. Speaker here making a repetition of the Several points ofered this day and the day before and Descending to the question was interrupted by this Speech of Sir Edwin Sands.

"Sir Edwin Sands. I have heard divers Motions, concerning divers opinion concerning the Manner in handling this Great Cause. It is the desire of all to satisfie his Majestie; to fly from prejudice to either Nation; and to make Amity. It hath been an observation that we have usually lost more by one Treaty, then we have got by Two Battles. I pray God this be not so, and in the Conference with the Lords we have rather Lost Ground, commonly then gained. This is a Treaty, and no Conference, because the Subiect is between Two Kingdoms, and tho I am not in Love with Conferences, yet I like of it at this time, so that we may debate

FRIDAY 28. NOVEMB: 1606.

An Act to direct the Proceedings in Causes and Courts Ecclesiasticall *primo lecta*.

Serieant Crooke, Dr. Swale, and Dr. Hone came from the Lords declaring That their Lordships having entred into consideration of this great busines, and having had a Retrospect to the first handling thereof, finde the same was by a Ioynt Committee and therefore do desire continuance of that Course, and to have Conference of the whole, if this House shall so think fitt otherwise their Lordships will proceede as to them shall seeme good in such Points as to them shall seeme fitting; and doe leave this House to their owne Course as they shall seeme convenient.

After these Gentlemen were returned, and called in againe, the Speaker gave Answer, That the House would returne answer by Messengers of their owne, as soone as they could, which should be presently if that so it might be, or if not this day, yet forthwith they would doe what they could.

And afterward by Sir Herbert Croft Answer was sent, That by the last Message, the meaning of the House was not to refuse, or deny Conference, although they had devided the matter as they thought it most fitting, and apt to be handled, and therefore seeing their Lordships doe require Conference, this House after that they have debated the Matters, and enabled themselves to conferr, will willingly ioyne with their Lordships in Conference.

SATTURDAY 29TH. NOVEMB: 1606.

Mr. Speaker moved That the House would take Consideration what Course to enter into touching the great Matters of the Union; Whereupon the House willed the Articles to be reade. Then upon

---

Thorowly before our meeting; for if we settle their demands, by being unprovided of Answers, we shall hardly remove them after. He misliketh the distribution until after the Conference, and not to handle the same by Committees, but in the house. In the mean time to send to the Lords, that we are not ready to conferr, but after we have debated, to send to the Lords again.

"Sir Tho[mas] Holcroft. This will but draw us into a Laboringth and therefore to enter into the business, the way must be to put it to the question, as Mr. Speaker was proposing.

"Of this opinion was Sir Anthony Cope.

"A Message sent to the Lords to acquaint them with our desire that

the Question it was resolved That a Committee should be appointed to treate every afternoone, of the Articles, and to report the next day what they had done. And this Committee to be all the Commissionors, All the Burgesses of Porte Townes, All the Knights and Burgesses of Cumberland, Northumberland and Westmorland, and the Bishoprick of Duresme (in which Bishoprick it was said there was none for the Parliament)[1] and all the House to be present, and have free Speech.[2]

2° DECEMBRIS. 1606.

An Act for the better enabling of Iohn Evelin Esquire to sell Parte of his Lands etc. 3° *Lecta.* Passed.
f. 220] After the third reading, and before the question of passing, The Speaker moved the House, That whereas in the Bill, there is two Blanckes for the Christian Names of two of the Land Occupiers, the same Blanckes might not[3] be filled, which was granted, and being done, upon the Question the Bill passed.

An Act for restrayning the Execution of Canons Ecclesiasticall not yet confirmed by Act of Parliament.[4] 1° *Lecta.*[5]

3° DECEMBRIS. 1606.

MR. HYDE reported the Proceedings of the Committees touching the Articles which concernes Hostile Lawes.

MR. FULLER delivered in the Bill, intituled, An Act for direction of certaine Proceedings in Courts and Causes Ecclesiasticall

---

their Lordships would be pleased to undertake the frameing and Ordering of the Two latter bills (vizt) of the Borders and Naturalization and we the Laws of Hostility and Commerce." *Ibid.*

[1] See W. Notestein, *Journal of Sir Simonds D'Ewes*, 76–77 note.

[2] See *C.J.* I, 324, 326, 1006. "A committee of most [of] the house was chosen." *Hist. MSS Com. Buccleuch MSS*, III, 109.

[3] *Now* is meant.

[4] For points of the bill see *Hist. MSS Com. 4th Report*, App. (*House of Lords MSS*), 118.) A copy of the bill is in St. John's College (Cambridge) MSS, 282, f. 637.

[5] "Thursday about eleven o clock Mr. Speaker went to St. Clements Church with the mace before him to the marriage of the Lady Verney' Daughter to one Mr. Parten of Plumpstead and there was the father of the Bryde, the Clerke and Sergeant were at dynner and had marriage [*blank*] at the Lady [*blank*]." This entry is marked out. C.J. MS, Jac. I, IV, f. 24*v*.

touching Accusations and Oathes Ex Officio: Note the words (touching Accusations and Oathes Ex Officio) were added by the Committees.

One of the Burgesses[1] of Carlile, in a Parliament Speech, declared, That lately some of his Neighbours did buy certaine Sheepe in Scotland, and as they were driving them home into England, the same were seised in Scotland as Confiscate upon an old Law never before put in Execution within the Memory of man: For which the Poore men complaining to the Councell in Scotland, had no other Answer or redresse, but that such buying was against the Law of that Countrey and so no remedy: Afterwards the Parties grieved, came hether and complained to the King by Petition, but their Petition slept with the Master of the Requests; And after long Stay and expecting of Answer, the Parties were forced to depart without redresse, or without money in their Purse to beare their Charges home: Whereas in Queen Elizabeths tyme certaine Scotts men complained of the like, and the Queen commanded Restitution: He desired That some about the King would acquaint his Majesty here with all. The Master of the Requests SIR ROGER WILBRAHAM excused himself, saying That he did particularly acquaint the King with the Petition mentioned, and That the King gave Order, that it should be considered of.

It was moved by MR. FULLER, That among the Number of Hostile Lawes, Escuage might be taken away; Divers offered to speake Pro and Con, but the arguing hereof was deferred untill to Morrow.

It was left to be reasoned with the Lords, Whether it should be enacted, That no Scottish man should be made Bayliff etc. of any Towne Corporate or Citty.

4TO. DECEMBRIS. 1606.

MR. LAWRANCE HYDE reported[2] the Proceedings of the Com-
f. 221] mittees the Afternoone before, touching the Matter of Commerce, viz. That of such Marchants as had bene required to be before the Committees only foure did appeare; That One of those Marchants affirmed that One of the two English Marchants which formerly had bene employed into France according to former

---

[1] Mr. Southwick.
[2] Cf. *C.J.* I, 327, 1007.

Proceedings in the Matter of Union, for Enquiry and Understanding what differences are betweene the English and Scottish
in the Trade of Merchandise, did say unto him, and some others,
That the French corrupted by the Bribery of the Scottish, did
conceale many advantages which the Scottish hath there. That
the said foure Marchants did require 3. things of the Committees
viz. First, to have a Coppy of such part of the Instrument as doth
concerne Commerce. Secondly, to have time untill Monday in the
Afternoone to consider, and informe themselves of the Matter.
And Thirdly, that the Marchant which had bene imployed into
France as aforesaid, and had affirmed to One of these 4. Marchants
as before, might be before the Committees on Monday after
dinner. All which three Points were by the House thought fitt,
and so ordered: And further, That according to the Opinion of
the Committees (which also Mr. Hyde had remembred) these
4. Merchants should on Monday bring to the Committees their
Exceptions[1] to such Matters as they misliked, and also their
reasons in writing.[2]

[1] The merchants presented their objections on Dec. 8. See Gardiner,
I, 329.

[2] A debate on escuage follows. See *C.J.* I, 1007. St. P. Dom. XXIV,
13, is an account written by Wilson for Salisbury. "Escuage hath ben
hottly argued this forenoone my weake iudgment in lawe is hardly able
to poyze whither the arguments pro or contra were most wayghty, lawyers
only disputing the matter. Mr. Fuller the first brocher of thes busines to
daye pulled of his maske and said playnly that it tended to taking away
of wards. His arguments wer very light the most wayghty ones being
the proclamacion & matter of comisseracion that a widdowe depryved of
her husband shold presently (to the redoubling of her greef) have her chyld
taken from her. That it wer against the lawes of god & nature. Which
was answered by Sir Fr[ancis] Bacon that the wisest & best lawegevers
had in the best governed comonwelths ordayned that children shold be
brought up by comissioners appoyntment & not according to the humorous
educacion of the parents. He spake of philosophers, I thinke he ment
Plato and Licurgas.

"Two or three other lawyers which spake for the taking away of the
lawes of escuage grounded ther arguments upon a point of logick viz
cessante causa cessat effectus. Shewing howe escuage was founded upon the
service to the kinge in scotland & wales as against enimyes, which nowe
they can noe more be, & if they shold be rebells all tenures are bound to
that service.

"Those of the other syde proved that escuage by the division was
general & speciall the one was to follow the king in service eyther in

5to. Decembris. 1606.

The Question againe argued, Whether Escuage shall be repealed among the Hostile Lawes: Wherein in all the day was spent.[1]

6to. Decembris. 1606.

An Act for direction of certaine Proceedings in Courts and

sc[otland], wal[es], fra[nce] or els wher, according to the perticular place mentioned, the other whither soever. And it was proved by Sir Fr[ancis] B[acon] that divers tenures by escuage was to serve the kinge in Poytiers & other parts besyds sc[otland] & wales.

"A division of tenures was alledged by Mr. Tate which was tryple that tenures wer eyther from Almoyn, Knyghts service or socag caled in latine 1 *oratores*, 2 *billatores*, 3 *laboratores*. That of all thes though the payment wer uncertayne yett the tenure was perpetuall, though ther was noe use of the service for a tyme as in murage one holdes land to build up a wale of a towne or fortress the wale once built noe use in 2 or 3 hundred yeares, yet the tenure remaynes though the use sleepes, the lyk in escuage.

"The arguments of both sydes wer many which conceyved in general and upon tyme to digest them will deliver them to your Lordship. The most & best that spake was for the remayning of escuage. But the generalest applause was upon them that wold have it taken away.

"At my coming forth Mr. Nanton told me privately that it was voyced in the howse that [*your Lordship* crossed out] my Lord of Salisbury is a furtherer of the matter & wold be willing for the glory of your name that in your tyme of being m[aste]r of the wardes, the wards myght be taken away.

"The ground of the arguments pro & contra I will provide in a breefe against the conference thes being but a iournall taste, howe the game is lyke to goe.

"The matter was left of abruptly & referred till to morrowe, yea said some I wold it myght be to morrowe that wards myght be taken away, yes answered others to morrowe to morrowe, in iest. I heare of noe sitting this after noone."

In connection with proposals to do away with the Court of Wards, M. de la Fontaine wrote: "Selon son gré la maison basse lui donne des barres et restreint ses limites. Mais ces effects semblent s'attribuer à ceux qui parlent le moins, faisant parler les autres." Dec. 23/Jan. 2, 1607. Paris Transcripts.

The financial value of escuage is commented upon in *Ambassades*, I, 475–476.

[1] See *C.J.* I, 328, 1007–08.
"Masters of the Trinity House, Shipwrights and too marchants to attend the Committee (*d.* this afternoon) to morrow in the afternoone." C.J. MS, Jac. I, IV, f. 32.

Causes Eccelesiasticall touching Accusations and Oathes Ex Officio, 3? *Lecta*. Passed. Diverse other Bills were reade.[1]

8TO. DECEMBRIS. 1606.

An Act for Reformation of abuses committed in the Court of the Marshalsey, and for the Limitation thereof. 1? *Lecta*. Sundry other Bills were reade.[2]

9? DECEMBRIS.[3] 1606.

An Act for Explanation of a Statute made the first Session of

---

[1] Carleton writing to Chamberlain describes a speech of this day: " . . . . little or nothing done in the house, onely some ydle fellowes having speaches in store, pickt small quarrels to disburden themselfs of them as Sir H[enry] Poole for one, who slipt owt of a privat bill for the naturalising of a French Doctor into a large discourse of the Union wherin he stiled the Act done by the Commissioners with the title of the Blessed Instrument." St. P. Dom. XXIV, 23.

[2] Wilson's notes for the day are in St. P. Dom. XXIV, 16. "The forenoone was spent in 2 bills that wer Comitted & in 2 reports the one made by Sir Roger Wilbraham of the kings answer to the peticion for the sheep confiscated in Scotland wherin he found him selfe tucht in that it had ben sayd in the howse that some master of requests had smothered it. He reported the kings Answer to be that [he] ever ment ther shold be restitucion and that he did not desyre to lyve to see the king of Scotland wrong the king of England. The other report was by Mr. Martin of the Comittee on saturday and the marriners & Trinityes mens arguments not to suffer any equality to be made in trade betwixt the English & Scotts for that wold in tyme bring all that trad in to the Scotts hands & it wold be to the decay of English shipping & soe danger to the kingdom in dashing the grett ship."

Members of Trinity House had been asked the probable effect of the Union upon English shipping. In their reply (Harl. MSS 158, f. 165) they had violently opposed the Union. The Scotch could build and operate ships more cheaply than the English. New laws should be made to protect English shipping. See *C.J.* I, 1008.

[3] " . . . . Sir W[illiam] Morrice prest hotly upon the motion to have the kings title of great Britany confirmed by Act of Parlement. But he was answeared by one James who concluded a long declamation with this decription of the Brettons, that they were first an ydolatrous nation, and worshipers of Divels. In the beginning of Christianity they were thrust out into the mountaines, where they lived long like theefes and robbers, and are to this day the most base, pesantly, perfidious people of the world. Mr. Hare came soone after with a bitter word against our neighbours, calling them the beggarly Scots, for which he is in danger to be shrewdly

this Parliament,[1] concerning Tanners, Curriers, Shoemakers, and other Artificers occupying the cutting of leather. 2°. *Lecta*. committed.

A Message[2] was brought from the Lords by Serieant Crooke, accompanied with Sir Iohn Tyndall to this effect, viz. That whereas the Parliament was now held chiefly for this great Matter of the Union, which hath by both Houses bene debated; Now for that f. 222] by reason of the Feast approaching, this Assembly is of Necessity to have a Recession; Therefore the Lords desire a Conference, touching the Conference which consisteth on 3. Points, viz. The abolishing of Hostile Lawes, Commerce, and Naturalizing; or at the least, concerning the two first Points, which have so long and much bene debated, viz: The Hostile Lawes, and Commerce; And this to be as soone as may stand with the Occasions of this House.

The Messengers being withdrawne, it was agreed, That where the Lords doe move a Conference, and doe name no day, and place, there this House are to return answer by Messengers of their owne: Also in the Case aforesaid, this House is to referr the tyme and place to the Lords, with this Provisoe (if the Case require as now it did) viz. That before such a time (which now was Satturday at 2. of the clock in the afternoone) they cannot intende the Service of the Conference with their Lordships: And with That Answer Sir Edw[ard] Hobby was sent; by whom the Lords returned answere, That on Saturday at 2. of the clock in the afternoone in the painted Chamber their Lordships would attend the Service of the Conference.

11°. Decembris. 1606.

An Act for Explanation of a Statute intituled An Act of Subsidy

hunted; and thus you may see what extravagancies we have had both pro and contra. . . . ." Carleton to Chamberlain, Dec. 18, 1606. St. P. Dom. XXIV, 23.

"Le Parlement de ce pais nous a representé son nom par beaucoup parler et peu resoudre. L'union ne se peult pas bien coulàre par le fil et l'esquille du nom Breton, lequel aiant faiet par son advocat retentir ses louanges, a trouvé un rude escrimeur qui l'a terrassé et l'a rendu vil et abject aux deux nations." M. de la Fontaine to M. de Villeroy, Dec. 23/ Jan. 2, 1607. Paris Transcripts.

[1] 1 Jac. I. c. 22. *Statutes of the Realm*, IV, 1039.
[2] This was on Dec. 10.

of Tonnage and Poundage made A? 1? Iacobi Regis[1] 1? *Lecta.*
The Statute made 5? R. 2.[2] and 4. H. 7.[3] touching Shipping,
were repealed by 1? Eliz.[4] and this of 1? Eliz. was to endure
but for foure yeares after the Parliament then next to follow:
Which last mentioned Statute being now expired and ended, the
two first, viz. of 5? R. 2. and 4. H. 7. are on foote againe and
revived, per MR. DIKE, but per SERIEANT SHURLEY, quere. MR.
DONETT serving as a Burgesse for Harwich; whereas the Statute
forbiddeth any Marchandize to be carried in Hoyes, or Flatt
bottoms, or other Vessells then such as beare crosse Sailes, now
every Hoye will carry one Crosse Saile, or perhaps two, or if that
way be not used to defraude the Statute, yet My Lord Treasurer
because some Custome is to come to the King, will not for the
Kings Proffitt suffer any Prosecution against such Hoyes.

MR. IAMES of Bristow, If the devises spoken of by the last
Gentleman be not used, yet a *Non obstante* doth dispence with
the Matter.

12? DECEMBRIS.[5] 1606.

Sir Iohn Tyndall accompanied with Sir George Copping, brought
from the Lords 3. Bills, all private, The first was for assurance of
an Advowson of a Parsonage[6] in County Essex from the Earl of
Salisbury unto the Bishop of London, and his Successors, and of
the Advowsen of the Viccaradgee of Cheston in County Hertford
from the said Bishop to the said Earl and his Heires, which Bill
was twice reade the same day and Committed.

f. 223]   13? DECEMBRIS. 1606.

The Bill betweene the Earl of Salisbury and the Bishop of
London was reade the third time, and passed: One of the Com-
mittees[7] declared that they had sent unto the Earl and to the
Bishop, and that both of them had signified their contentment,

---

[1] 1 Jac. I, c. 33. *Statutes of the Realm,* IV, 1062.

[2] *Statutes of the Realm,* II, 18. Cf. report in *C.J.* I, 329, 1009.

[3] *Statutes of the Realm,* II, 534–535. These two statutes forbad the importation of goods except in English ships.

[4] *Statutes of the Realm,* IV, 375.

[5] For Dec. 12 and 13, see *Hist. MSS Com. Buccleuch MSS,* III, 109.

[6] The rectory of Orset. This was to be exchanged for the vicarage of Chestnut. *Statutes of the Realm,* IV, 1133.

[7] Sir Robert Wingfield. *C.J.* I, 330.

and the Bishop said That it is for the Good of his Sea: And the
Earl desired that his Contentment might be signified to the House
with this Condition if it were acknowledged that he gave more
then he tooke.

Sir Roger Astons Bill for the Manior of Soam was reade, and
committed. Sir Iohn Savile desired to understand what was
meant by the word (Tribute) because among other Priviledges
there is by the Letters Patents granted to the Patentees all
Tributes.

15⁰. Decembris.[1] 1606.

Diverse Private Bills were reade.

16⁰. Decembris. 1606.

Sir Iohn Savile moved, That whereas a Bill[2] was Yesterday
reade, which is Preiudiciall unto One Carvile, for as much as the
said Carvile is a Recusant convict and confined, so as he cannot
take notice of this Act, therefore that a Letter might be written
from Mr. Speaker unto him and a Coppy of the Bill sent with it,
whereby he may have Knowledge of the Matter, and day given
untill the next Session, to consent or satisfy the House, which
motion was by the House allowed, as touching the Letters, and
for the other Parte, it was said that at his coming up or sending up
to take a Coppy of the Bill, they would consider of it.

An Act to prevent causelesse Divorce and Separation of man
and Wife, and to continue the Right of Lawfull Marriage, 2⁰. *Lecta.*
And upon the first Question denied to be committed: And upon
the 2⁰. Question throwen out of the House.

On Tuesday the 10th. of February. 1606. the Parliament re-
assembled,[3] on which day little was done; On Wednesday little

---

¹ A conference with the Lords took place on Dec. 15, 16, and 17. See
note, p. 208. The House was adjourned on Dec. 18 until Feb. 11.

² "The Bill for Confirmation of Assurances made of Lands, upon
the Marriage of George Clifton Esquire." *C.J.* I, 331.

³ "The parlement is begun and your schoolefellowes plie it hard, but
do rather yet con theyre old lessons then venture upon new. Only Sir
William Morrice made a motion that this longe wooing might come to
conclusion, and that the King might be wedded to the old widowe Britain.
Most of the time otherwise hath ben spent about his antagonist James of
the Isle of Wight, who being arrested some eight or ten dayes before this
Session, (and the matter brought in question) no man undertooke his

was done; On Thursday,[1] Mr. Speaker moved That such Bills
as at the last Meeting remained committed, without further Proceeding might now againe after the Titles were reade be committed
to the same Committees, and no new Committees appointed to
deale in them, which was done.

Also Mr. Speaker declared That the Order of the House is, that
no Committees under the Number of Seaven should deale with
any Bill, and moved Continuance of that Order which was yeilded
unto.

Upon MR. ALFORDS Motion it was ordered by the House, that
when any Committees have mett upon a Bill, and doe adiourn to
a further meeting on it, that in such Case they shall the next day
in the House Publiquely declare the new time and place of such
their Adiournment.

f. 224]　　　　FRIDAY 14.º[2] FEBRUARII. 1606.

A Bill exhibited by the Knight Marshall[3] was reade, in shew
abridging the Fees of that Court, and to reforme certaine apparent
Miscarriages of that Court: But for as much as the said Bill did
encroach further Power then ever before, therefore the same was
first denied committment,[4] and upon the 2d. Question denied to
be engrossed, and so throwen out of the House.

Mr. Speaker offered to reade certaine Articles which he affirmed
were the Proceedings viz. the Obiections, and Answeres betweene
the Committees of the 2. Houses at the last meeting concerning
the Union.

MR. FULLER declared That he held it not convenient, nor agreable to good Order, that any Notes taken by the Committees at

---

quarrell, nor protected his cause more vehemently then Sir William
Morrice, wherby he hath gotten great honor to himself and his nation,
to be accounted men of goode nature soone pacified." Chamberlain to
Carleton, Feb. 13. St. P. Dom. XXVI, 4°. Cf. *C.J.* I, 1012.

[1] This was on Wednesday, Feb. 11, according to *C.J.* For these days,
see *C.J.* and *Hist. MSS Com. Buccleuch MSS*, III, 110.

[2] This should be Friday, Feb. 13. For Pigott's speech on this day, see
C.J. I, 333; *Ambassades*, II, 87–90, 120–121.

[3] To reform his own Court. Officers were to be duly sworn; they
should be few in number; no one should be arrested without due process
or for small actions under 10*s*., etc. Lansd. MSS 487, ff. 207–207*v*.

[4] "(*d.* Committed to) Reiected." C.J. MS, Jac. I, IV, f. 67.

Conferences should be reade by the Speaker, or the Clarke of this House, nor here to remaine as Acts or Agreements, but should be delivered by some of the Committees trusted namely, for that the same were but their remembrances: Therefore they by way of report should verbally deliver the same to the House to be considered of, wherein for their better memory they might use the help of the said Notes so by them taken at the former Conferences, Which Opinion was allowed. Hereupon for that Mr. Attorney Generall had bene used in the first of these three Points of the said Conference, Viz. for abolishing Hostile Lawes; And Mr. Recorder in the 2d. Point, viz. Commerce, both which Gentlemen were present; And the third Point, viz. Naturalization had not bene in those Conferences dealt with all, therefore it was directed to ease Mr. Attorney as much as might be in regard of the Colde he had taken, MR. RECORDER should reade the said Obiections and Answeres, and MR. ATTORNEY to every Article concerning the abolishing of Hostile Lawes, to yeild the reason, and Mr. Recorder to doe also the like for the Matter of Commerce.[1]

[1] See reports in *C.J.* I, 333–334, 1012–13. The Recorder said that the written articles that he offered contained the agreement of the committees at the conference of December 17 on hostile laws and commerce. The points in the articles were to serve as the heads of a future bill. But other committee-members maintained that they had not agreed to these points at the conference and so the House refused its formal adhesion to the articles. The committees of the House had really been forced into some sort of acceptance by the threats of the Lords at the conference. The conference had been a stormy one. It is described in a letter from Carleton to Chamberlain: "We are broken up this day [Dec. 18] on a sodaine referring the report of all that is yet done till the next meeting which is appointed the 10th of February, and meane time we have liberty to bethinck our selfs what to allow or disprove of such things as have bin agreede on by the Committees at the conferences which have bin many and long and sometimes morning as well as afternoone. .... The Lords at the beginning of owr Conferences were very milde; but ended like the month of March in storme and tempest, which lited heavely on the city of London as not thought a place of that moment, as that the consideracion of the subsistance of it should be put *in equilibrio* of the due regard we ought to have to the general safety purchased to the kingdome by this happy Union. Which came out uppon occasion of owr standing much uppon the honor of owr trade. Wherin honest Nick Fuller was some what too forward saying that the Scots in other countreys were more like pedlars then marchants, for which he was shrewdly chidden; and the marchants having uppon commandement sett downe in writing

The Notes of the Proceedings betweene the Committees was *Ad Verbum* as followeth.

Remembrances of the Conference of the Committees of both Houses, at the Painted Chamber 17th. of Decemb: 1606.[1]

f. 226] After the said Articles were reade, and the reasons delivered as aforesaid by Mr. Attorney Generall, and Mr. Recorder, it was proposed unto the House to consider what should be further done therein; And by some wished that one or more Bills might be framed upon them and the Resolution of the first Commissioners of both Realmes; But the full Resolution of the House was to deale no further in the busines touching the said two Points of Hostile Lawes, and Commerce, but to leave it to the Lords to draw such Bill or Bills, that then this House will afterwards have further consideration.

FRIDAY. 13? FEBR: 1606.

Sir Mich[ael] Sandys his Servant[2] was brought to the Barr, and with him a Serieant of London who arrested him, and the Party that caused him to be arrested since the reassemblye of this Session, and the Matter appeared to be thus; The Party arrested had bene Servant to Sir Mich[ael] Sandys long time, and now of

theyr reasons against community of trade with the Scots, for concluding with a petition that all might remaine as it did with out further uniting which in theyr affaires could breede nothing but confusion, were roundly shaken up by my Lord Chancelor; wherein they holde theyr paynes which they tooke upon commandement, ill repayed. There were given us at the two last conferences certaine mementos against we mett next. As one that perforce we must yeald to many conditions though we foresee we shall be loosers. Then that there is nothing prequired in the instrument of the union which the k[ing] can not doe of himself: and lastly that Scots in state as they are are no aliens. The matter of Escuage which you left so hott in dispute was concluded by the Chiefe Justices in one word, that though the service ceaseth, the kings profit must continue. And thus have you all I can readily bethinck my self of, referring you to Sir Rowland Litton for more ample relation, who hath stayed it owt to the last." St. P. Dom. XXIV, 23.

[1] This is the title of a "separate" containing some of the points discussed at the conference. Bowyer inserts this "separate" (ff. 224-226) at this point. But since Bowyer's wording is identical with that in *C.J.* I, 332-333, the "separate" has been omitted. Other copies are St. P. Dom. XXIV, 20; Harl. MSS 169, f. 209; Lansd. MSS 486, ff. 96-97.

[2] Thomas Finch arrested by Sergeant Harrison at the instigation of Thomas Knight. See Hatsell, *Precedents*, I, 159.

late was become a sworne Attorney of the Common Pleas, and yet Sir Mich[ael] Sandys affirmed to the House, That the Party notwithstanding his being such an Attorney, doth still continue his household meniall Servent, and receives Wages of him. The Serieant excused himself, saying, That he demanded of him that set him on worke, whether the party by him to be arrested were servant to any Member of either of the Houses, who answered Negatively. The Party procuring the Arrest (which first was upon a meane Proces, and then upon an Execution) affirmed that he did not take the other to have served any Member of this House, for that he knew him to be a sworne Attorney. In Conclusion, the Order of the House upon some like Presidents[1] vouched was, that the Party arrested, though an Attorney *Ut Supra*, yet being also a Servant to a Member of this House should be discharged according to the Priviledge;[2] and a Serieant and the other who procured the Arrest to be committed to the Custody of the Serieant of this House for a month, and as much longer as this House shall f. 227] thinck good, but spared putting any Fyne, or damage on either of them by reason of their severall probable Excuses, and afterwards Mr. Speaker said openly, That he would move the Lord Chief Iustice of the Common Plase, That Provision might be, that no Attorney sworne of that Court, should serve any man: So it was agreed that every man at his Perill must take Notice of Persons priviledged.

4.° Martii.[3] 1606.

Sir Edward Hobby reported the Proceedings of the Com-

---

[1] See *C.J.* I, 334; D'Ewes, 642–643.

[2] "All Menial and necessary Servants to have Privilege . . . . *Quare* whether it extendeth to menial and necessary Servants in the Country, or to such as attend the person here." Cott. MSS, Titus F IV, f. 95v.

[3] In the days omitted, the Commons debated the naturalization of the Scots, which was attacked by Fuller on Feb. 14 and defended by Bacon three days later. It was debated whether the Scotch born since 1603 (the post-nati) were naturalized *ipso facto* by the Common Law. The Commons said this could not be so. In a conference on Feb. 25, the Judges maintained their earlier opinion (St. P. Dom. X, 15) against the Commons. The House refused to yield.

For these days, see Gardiner, I, 331–335; Spedding, III, 306–332; *C.J.* I, 334–347, 1013–25; *Hist. MSS Com. Buccleuch MSS*, III, 110–113; *Hist. MSS Com. 14th Rep.*, App. II (Duke of Portland MSS, III), 4. Fuller's speech is in Harl. MSS 6850, ff. 44–45; 6842, ff. 1–2. For Bacon,

mittees[1] viz. Touching such Answer as might be fitt to be sent from this House unto the Lords. And first he shewed, That the Committees appointed were in Number 27. whereof 22. did attend the Service; whose Resolution did consist on two Points.

1. That it is convenient to send to the Lords.

2. To give Advise to the Lords.

In the first Point, to let their Lordships knowe, that we found their Lordships did leave unto us the understanding and Construction of their former Generall Message, in which if their Lordships did purpose to treate of the State of the Post-nati in Lawe, then their Lordships doe know the Opinion of this House, since the Declaration whereof we have heard nothing to leade us to alter the same, but if their Lordships will say any thing therein, we will most willingly attend, and heare what soever their Lordships will say.

2. Secondly, if their Lordships will conferr with us of the Conveniency of Naturalization etc. That is a Matter of State, and therefore we hold it fittest, it take beginning from them that are best acquainted with State Affaires; Notwithstanding if their Lordships will deale freely with us, and open somewhat that may direct, we will attend, and be ready to shew our Councell. 2. Touching Councell to be given, the Committees thincke that we shall doe well to appoint a Committee of this House to consider of the Matter, with such Limitations as may be fitt. Upon dispute[2] in the House it was thought fitt and ordered, That those

---

see Spedding and *Parl. Hist.* I, 1083–95. Certain other speeches are in St. P. Dom. XXVI, 54, 55, 64; Harl. MSS 677, ff. 54–57*a*; 6850, f. 46. For conference on Feb. 25, see *Somers Tracts*, II, 132–143. See also *State Trials*, II, 562; *English Reports (Full Reprints)*, LXXII, 908–917.

"It was delivered as a Rule, that only the Resolution of the House upon a Bill depending was a Judgement of the House. Other Resolutions upon Motions were but opinions. In the case of the Naturalization of the Antenati. 21 Febr." Cott. MSS, Titus F IV, f. 95*v*.

"When a Proviso is offred to a Bill engrossed, which is always in Parliament, after it hath been thrice read the question must be put whether it shall be added to the Bill. And the Question must be put again for the passage of the Bill with the Proviso. 3 Mar. 1606." *Ibid.* f. 96*v*.

[1] On March 2 the Lords asked for a conference to discuss naturalization "in general." Hoby is reporting from a committee appointed to decide upon a reply.

[2] Thomas Wilson writes Salisbury concerning the debate after this

words (but if their Lordships will say any thing therein, we will most willingly attend and heare whatsoever their Lordships will say) should be left out and omitted, whereby though it bē not Inconvenient to heare what the Lords will offer to speake, yet we shall not invite them to speake or treate of that Point.

SIR EDWARD HOBBY was sent with this Message, and reported back; That he had delivered his enioyned Message, which when he had done, the Lords required him againe to repeate it, which he did; and after a Pawse, the Lords willed me to desire this House to sitt a while, and they would send an Answer. And now said Sir Edw[ard] Hobby, I will tell you what is likely to become of f. 228] me; I used said he a Word not used ordinarily of late unto

report: "It was first propounded by him that to daye brought the Message [Sir Edward Hoby], to goe speedily to the business about sending the message. This done ther were some other motions [by Sir Henry Poole] which wer conceyved by some to tend to drawinge the howse to a declaracion upon the point of lawe which to divert Mr. [Recorder] made a speach to drawe on a newe opinion which yett was not conceyved sayinge that as he conceyved the matter, with much disputinge we had quite lost the question. For the question (saith he) amongst us is whither they be naturalized or noe, and the question amongst the Lords whither they be Aliens or noe. That for his opinion he thought they wer nether, but that they wer in a Medium betwixt both, and soe that they were capable of many privledges of the kingdom but not of all.

"He shewed ther was a subiection naturale and a subiect by tenure the first indissolubly bound to his subiection and capable of all priviledges the other not soe, for quitting his tenure he was freed from his bonde. He put the case thus that a scott being (as he is) borne in the kinges allegeance and a natural subiect to the crowne of scottland, coming to dwell heer or purchase land heer the lawe cannot deny him soe to doe for who shall oppose against him? His soveraigne cannot, being borne in his alleageance, non else cann, nor the lawe cannot deny him. Whilst he is heer he is capable of those priviledges which soveraignty geves him which is inheritance or purchasinge or such lyke, but if he departe from hence into scotland or else wher and leave his tenure by quitting his land then he is noe more bound to the subiection of England wher he held but by tenure and not by nature and whilst he is heer he is not capable of those things which the lawes geves. As he cannot be a Juror, nor an officer of the crowne nor a judge etc. nor ought els which the lawe constitutes, but of such as soveraignty brings with it, noe dowbt he is capable of, soe that he is nether Natural nor Alien. Soe he persuaded that as they wer soe we shold leave them & proceed to debate the other point.

"He speech ended, he was taxed of some importunity in that he fell

them, viz. I said thus, The Knights Burgesses and Barons of the Commons House of Parliament have sent me unto your Lordships etc. and so I have said often heretofore, let them that come for the Ports answere it, I am sure the Writts that goeth to the Ports to chuse etc. is *de Baronibus.* Further I said that if they would open themselves unto us, and give us light, we would be ready to attend the Service with them. Their Lordships asked me what I meant by the Service, I told them I was sent a Messenger from the Commons House and had not directions to expound any thing. Lastly, their Lordships desired after Private Conference among themselves, that this House would not rise, but sitt awhile, and then their Lordships would send to you.

This Message was brought by Sir Edw[ard] Hobby after Eleaven of the Clock, whereupon the House staied expecting to heare from the Lords untill it was more then halfe an houre after one of the clock.

Then came Serieant Crooke and Dr. Stanhope from the Lords with a Message[1] to this effect, The Lords haven sent us with this

---

againe to discorce upon that point that had ben soe long in debating & was alredy come to resolucion, & soe the motion was to send the message which being redd it was thought fitt to putt out those words which mentioned hearinge the Lords opinions in the first point of lawe. It was said by some that the Lords had alredy delivered ther opinions by the Judges, but that was contradicted by others alledging that owght not to be taken soe, for then it must be concluded that the upper howse & lower howse differed or wer quyte contrary which was fitt shold be forborne to be conceyved or reported and that therfore it were also well to leave out those words in the message which shold argue a conceite of a diversity of opinion.

"Ther was much a doe in close motions and to the last, to drawe the matter to a declaracion, and that it shold be soe mentioned in the message that it was the opinion of the howse but in the ende it was concluded that it should be termed butt the inclinacion of the howse to that opinion.

"For the rest save those 2 points the message passed as was yesterday concluded att the conference. . . . ." St. P. Dom. XXVI, 70.

[1] Bowyer here inserts the following marginal note: "As the Messenger had spoken the Words (their Lordships) one at the nether end of the House *sonitum ventre emisit;* whereat the Company laughing the Messenger was almost out of Countenance. It is said to have bene young Ludloe; not that this seemeth done in disgrace, for his Father Sir Edward Ludloe before at a Committee fell on sleepe and *sonitum ventre emisit:* So this seemeth Infirmity Naturall, not Malice." Doggerel verses on this incident are found

Message unto you, That the Strength of both Houses consisteth in nothing more then in the Preservation of the Rights of both Houses, therefore their Lordships are very tender in letting any thing passe that is subiect to Misunderstanding; some thing their Lordships received in the Message from this House which they rather thinck was *Lapsus Linguae* in the Messenger, then any Purpose of Evill, or Offence, viz. That the Knights Burgesses and Barons of the Commons Court of Parliament had sent unto them etc. Therefore their Lordships doe thincke good to let you know as One friend may doe an other, That no man doth sitt in this House as a Baron of Parliament, howsoever some Members of this House may be termed Barons of the Cinq Ports. For the Matter their Lordships are very sorry there should be so much Reservations towards them, who doe intend so much Freedome towards you. Next they doe not conceive That this House doth make a Court, but that both Houses together to make one Court. They doe desire That those Words of the Messenger (To attend that Service) may be explained to be a readinesse to attend the Conference touching the Conveniency of Naturalization in Generall, wherein each Partie to declare cleerly what he meaneth; For which Purpose they desire that Satturday in the Afternoone in the Painted Chamber may be appointed at 2. of the clock with the former Committees.[1]

---

in Harl. MSS 5191, ff. 17–18; 4931, f. 10; Stowe MSS 354. The verses are of some slight interest since in them various members of the House make comments in keeping with their characters.

[1] For this message, cf. *L.J.* II, 483. It was probably about this date that Sir Robert Wingfield wrote the following letter to Salisbury: "I am sorry that your Honours of the Higher House did take such an exception of our message, sent by Sir Edward Hoby, who out of abundance of wit, speaking many things pleasantly, might for this have been pardoned. It is taken diversely of our House, for some think that the exception is over curious, considering the placing of the words 'Barons' in the lowest place might have assured you that he meant the Barons of the Cinque Ports, for he left out of what places they all were; for if he had said knights of shires, citizens of cities, burgesses of boroughs, he would surely have said Barons of the Cinque Ports. But I hope your Honours will stay this matter. As for the word 'Court' to which there is exception taken, it is confidently denied by Sir Edward Hoby, and that he used the word 'of Common House of Parliament.' But we think your Honour should deal very nobly with us, to propound some cautions and reservations to

To this the House answered, That to morrow they will send an
Answer, and afterwards ordered that in the meane tyme the former
Committees should meete to consider what answer shall be then
made.

---

be inserted into the Act, if we agree to a general naturalisation of the ante-
nati, as well as of the post-nati of Scotland.

"Whatsoever is informed by the king, I do freely confess to your
Lordship that our House is fully bent to give contentment to the king by
taking away the hostile laws, by admitting of commerce, and naturalising,
with reservation of some natural needful conditions and these but for a
time. Therefore, good my Lord, be you a means, for to move but you dare
I speak, that we may leave off contending about words, and lend ourselves
wholly to the matter for which we are come. I beseech your Honour to
send me the note I delivered you in your passage to the Parliament House,
for I promised it to my friend that lent it, to deliver the same again. For
the matter of law whereof we have already conferred, I think the greater
opinion of our House is to have it quit of all sides, and no more to be
spoken on. There is a business also in our House of the King's displeasure
towards us, and of the dissolving of the parliament, but I hope it is not
true, for I know that the bent of the House is to give the King satisfaction,
being impossible (*sic*) that so great a matter can be concluded without
difficulty and hardness." Salisbury MSS.

Wilson wrote Salisbury on March 4: ".... the message passed as
was yesterday concluded att the conference save that the messenger out
of his owne phantasticality wold need add that *frontispicium* of Barons of
the lower howse & that ambiguous terme of attending the service which
was so rightly noted and resented by the Lords wher as in deed the meaning
of the howse & the words of the message wer that we wold attende ther
Lordships att a conference when they pleasd.

"The Messenger being come into the howse and reportes his owne
message asked what shold become of him that had said the knights citizens
burgesses & Barons of the howse of Commons, Court (he said) he might
have said) and shewed records of parlament that they wer written Barons
& it was accorded by an old baron of the cinq ports that he demanding of
Serient Fleetwood what punishment a Baron of the Cinq ports shold have
for being absent from parlament it was answered as great as any baron
in the land. The messenger said further that he had often in messages
used the same beginning & additions.

"After the Lords message was brought & that therin exception was
taken to the words Barons & Cort, he made a protestation (& many did
iustify it) that he said not Cort to the Lords but howse.

"For conclusion the same Comittee of 20 persons ar apointed to meet
this after noon to consult what answer shalbe sent to morrow to the
Lords." St. P. Dom. XXVI, 70.

f. 229]   5? Martii. 1606.

Mr. Martin reported[1] the Proceedings of the Committees viz.
touching Answere to be returned to the Lords, viz. first, That the
Words (to attend this Service) may be explained a Conference
touching the Conveniency or Inconveniency of Naturalization
in Generall.

To the Exceptions this Answer, first, That this House gave no
Warrant to the Messenger to use the word Barons, but words of
forme were and are usually left to the discretion of the Messenger,
albeit this House doth think, That the said Word is warrantable,
the words of the Writt directed to the Constable of Dover Castle
and the Wardein of the Cinq Ports to chose Members to be sent
hether being (*Baronibus etc*) and the words of the Statute of
9. H. 8.[2] for Election of Burgesses etc. being Barons, without the
addition of Cinq Ports.

For the other Exception, viz: Commons Court of Parliament,
the Messenger doth protest That to his Remembrance he used no
such word, but the word (House): Albeit the Committees doe
thinck That this House is a Court of Record.[3]

Touching the Conference of Naturalization, the Answer to be,
That if their Lordships will freely open themselves in that Point,
then shall such Committees as this House sendeth declare plainely
the Opinion of this House at the tyme and place by their Lordships appointed.

Then the Speaker declared that in the clerkes book of this
House of Presidents, no word is more usuall then the word
(Barons).

This done, the Committees for the Spainish Marchants was put
of untill Wednesday next.

Councell formerly appointed to be heard touching the Bill
concerning St. Sauviours Parish in Southwarke came in the Barr,
and directed that they which are against the Bill should begin.[4]

Against the Bill was said, 1st. That these Vestry Men and their
Gouvernment was setled (as I take it) 50. yeares since, at the

---

[1] Cf. *C.J.* I, 348–349.

[2] There is no such statute. See p. 218.

[3] "But being a Question fallen incidentally, they [the Commons]
will no more dispute, but give answer to the other part of the Message."
Cott. MSS, Titus F IV, f. 97. Cf. *C.J.* I, 348–349.

[4] See *C.J.* I, 349.

Suite of the Parishioners by the Bishop of Winton their Ordinary. Secondly. That their Gouvernment ever since continued Good and Peaceable. 3dly. That they maintaine two learned Preachers. 4ly. That if the Multitude should from tyme to tyme be privy to the Stocke of the Parish, many of the Meaner Sorte would neglect their Labor, and chuse to live on the Common Stocke.

For the Bill were 4. reasons given. First in the Parish are 1500. Householders, whereof are 200. Subsidy Men, therefore no reason that 30. Persons called Vestry men, should only chose Church Wardens, and be Privy to the accompts. 2ly. The Church Wardens are not chosen according to the Statute, which maketh them a Body Politick, and therefore dangerous for forfeiting the In-f. 230] heritance of the Parishioners, being foure or five hundred Pounds Per Annum; For by the Common Lawe, Church Wardens can only take Personall things, not Lands. 3ly. The Church Wardens being but 4. or 6. the 30. Vestry Men spend the Profitts of the Parish Lands, for where at the first the 4. or 6. Church Wardens spent but 14s. Per Annum, now these 30. Vestry Men, by often meeting, spend 40£. Per Annum in cheere and unnecessary Charges. 4ly. These Vestry men having ingrossed all Power in the Parish, doe give out that they are now owners of all, yea they have sold some Parte of the Parishes Inheritance.

The two reasons against the Bill are thus answered, To the first, whereas it is said, That they Maintaine two learned Preachers, the truth is, they have a lease from the King of the Parsonage worth 120£. Per Annum, and they bestowe on two Preachers only 60£. Per Annum.

To the Second, which is, That they Maintaine the Poore, It is answered, That they maintaine not the Poore, but of the Common Collections they are maintained.

The Answer of the Lords was reported to be, First, That their Lordships are content to give Meeting at the day and place appointed: Then touching the first parte of the Answer which this House returned to their Lordships Message, viz. The Excuse; Their Lordships said, they have no Purpose at this tyme to enter into further discourse, albeit their Lordships were not satisfied. Lastly My Lord Chancellor[1] craving Pardon of us, then of the Lords said, That there is no such Statute of 9. H. 8. concerning

---

[1] "My Lord Chamberlain [Earl of Suffolk]." *Hist. MSS Com. Buccleuch MSS*, III, 114.

choice and returning of Burgesses as this House speaketh of, viz. whereby those sent by the Ports, are termed Barons, but touching choice of the Members of this House, there is as his Lordship said, a Statute A? 6. H. 6.[1] and that speaketh not of Barons, but said his Lordship it is therefore good to reade the Booke at large, and not to trust the Abridgement, which in this Case deceived you of the Commons House.

7? Martii. 1606.

Sir Edwyn Sandys reported,[2] That the Committees for this great Conference touching Naturalization had mett, and their Proceedings to have bene with great Paine, but the busines in it self to be so large, That they could not goe thorough the Whole. And we found it true (quoth he) That the Multitude of obiections doth trie out the Truth. After long debate, the Committees thought it fitt and convenient, That in this busines we should swarve from the Instrument agreed by the Commissioners of both Nations to be offered to the Parliament; And to wrappe up the Anti-nati and the Post-nati together:[3] It is hoped That the Lords will not urge us to deale with the Post-nati severally; But if they shall urge us with the Iudges Opinions, First it was by the Com-f. 231] mittees thought fitt That reasons should modestly be given of our dissent in opinion from the Iudges, touching those Post-nati, viz. First That Point is not by the Iudges themselves cleerly agreed, for one[4] of them dissenteth. 2ly. Though the Iudges are alwaies and in all places Reverend, yet are not their words so Weighty when they are but Assistants to the Lords in Parliament, as when they sit Iudicially in Courts of Iustice; For in the latter Case they have an Oath to tie them. 3ly. In all demurrers, before the Iudges speake, they heare Councell on both sides argue, and afterwards upon Studdy themselves, argue and deliver the Law; But here they delivered their Opinions before they heard Our

---

[1] A mistake for 6 Hen. VIII. c. 16. *Statutes of the Realm*, III, 134.
[2] Cf. report in *C.J.* I, 1027–28. St. P. Dom. XXVI, 77, though a report of the conference in the afternoon of March 7, explains certain parts of this speech.
[3] Since neither were to be regarded as naturalized English citizens.
[4] Sir Thomas Walmesley. See *D.N.B.*

Reasons: Therefore we are not so much bound in this Case to their Opinions, as to their Iudgements when they are in their Tribunalls.

A second Point debated by the Committees was Whether the Word Naturalization, shall be used in the Conference, for that the Lawyers thought a new Word, and therefore not determinable in seaven yeares. 2. The word is too Generall. 3. That word maketh a Man Inheritable unto Magna Charta, and then not limitted, nor to be restrained; And therefore it was rather thought fitt we should use the word (Enable). It was hereunto answered, That in the Civill Lawe, the word is used, and it is more fitt to use the Generall Word, then to expresse it particularly. Then by One of the Kings Councell it was said, That the word should never be put into the Act; So it was agreed, That in the Conference, the word should be used with Protestation etc.

They considered what Kinde of Union we meane, and it was said, That there be two Kinds of Union, (viz:) One when two Kingdomes remaine distinct in their Natures, and agree in the Heade. The 2d. is a Consolidation, when two Kingdomes become One in Gouvernment, and this 2d. is that which we desire; But it was remembred, That the Scottish Nation have reserved in the Instrument, all their Lawes, which sheweth that the former Union is that which we are to deale in: On the other Side, the Committees desired the 2d. perfect Union, which though it cannot be done in an Instant, yet the Committees have thought fitt, That by way of declaration we doe shew That we desire the 2d, and that the Scottish Nation be ruled by Our Lawes,[1] and participate all Benefitts with us. And for this 3. Causes may be yeilded.

1. To cut of Idle Speeches, as though the King did desire One Union, and we an other, which is not soe; For it seemeth by the Instrument, That his Majesty desireth a perfect Union.

2. Now if the Scottish will continue to tie us to an Imperfect Union, they must be content to take it Imperfectly.

f. 232] 3. The lesse we yeild to them by this Imperfect Union, the

---

[1] The English feared that the Scots would acquire privileges without being subject to English law.

In these debates, a "perfect" union means a union of the two nations in one system of laws and one parliament. The union proposed by the Instrument is called an "imperfect" union.

more we shall drawe them to the Perfect, when they shall see the Impediment to be in themselves.

It was said, That a great Impediment to this Naturalization, is the French Naturalization: And therefore thought by some that the said French Naturalization is to be broken and waved, for as a Woman, so a Nation cannot stand in firmer Inwardnesse with two men, or Nations.

Whereunto others answered, That we are not to presse that Point of Disunion of Scotland and France, for these Causes, viz.

Hereby we shall hurt them of Scotland our friends, and doe our selves no good.

By pressing them of Scotland to quitt their Immunities in France, we shall advance the Customes and Benefitt of the French King; And we shall hinder and hurt the Kings Majesty here; Because if we hurt them of Scotland, the King our Master must make them Recompence and amends by lessening Customes here.

They Cannot revolt and take parte with France against us, for then having one Head, they are Traytors.

On the other Side was shewed, How better[1] in respect of us, the League is betweene France and Scotland, out of the words of the French Charter, whereby Immunity and Franchise is granted unto Scotland.

Againe, That Charter of Franchises and Immunities is limitted to continue so long as the Scottish Nation doe remaine in the Love and obedience of the French.[2]

Againe, The more they love the French our Enemies, the lesse they love us. Therefore it was thought good by the Committees, that they shall renounce their Incorporation with France but not so resolved to be, but to be proposed to the Lords, to receive further Light from their Lordships.

But to the body of the Matter, it was doubted, whether the

---

[1] Mistake for *bitter*.

[2] "Some priviledges are Communicated during the tyme that they shalbe *Regnicoli* onely. Yet the King of Fraunce hath besydes the Scottish gard of antient attendant on his person, graunted a gard of horsmen all of the Scottish nation. I desire to with drawe the affection of the Scottish nation wholly to us; For considering the ground of their naturalizacion wee have great cause to desire the utter abolishing of their amity with Fraunce, other then by the treaty of peace all Englishmen are tyed unto." St. P. Dom. XXVI, 77.

Scotts shall be naturalized; which doubt was not moved of Hesitation but by Argument to drawe better reason then already is seene; For which Purpose, an honest Gentleman moved an obiection thus.

No Innovation is good in a Kingdome, but either for inevitable necessary, or apparent Utilitie, whereof neither is in this Case.

It was answered, That here is Necessary, viz. To be a Stepp unto a more perfect Union,[1] and also to give the King Satisfaction.

The Committees (said he) I conceive agreed in the most parte, That some Benefitts should be communicated to all the Subiects borne in Scotland, and some not, so long as the Kingdomes stand devided for somewhat must be reserved, and these Reservations to be firme.

f. 233] There grewe a Question, viz. Whether a Dispensation may set at large the restraints; And what force a *Non-obstante* hath?

On one Side, it was thought That a dispensation or *Non-obstante* will set all at large. On the other Side, it was said, That albeit the King cannot be restrayned to grant, yet an other may be restrained, or disabled to take.

It was said, That a Prohibition without a paine, cannot be restrayned, though with a paine it may.[2]

Then the Question was, what we should grant unto them; And hereupon all the Commodities and Priviledges of this Kingdome were put into five Heades,[3] viz.

1. Possessions Reall, as Lands etc.
2. Preferments Ecclesiasticall.
3. Offices in the Common Wealth.
4. Honours.
5. Trades and Sciences.

Now grewe the question, whether we should Proceede in the

---

[1] "Profitable not in Merchandize; that mechanical; but in common Service, Love, Strength." *C.J.* I, 1027.

[2] "The king may dispence by a *non obstante*, with the payne of the statute Lawe, but not with the Lawe, and where a lawe is made without a pecuniary penalty, then the king cannot graunt a *non obstante*." St. P. Dom. XXVI, 77.

[3] The number of things to be granted to the Scots was constantly shrinking. *Ambassades*, I, 440–441.

Affirmative, or Negative Course, viz. What we would grant, or what we would not grant: And resolved, the better Course to be of Proceeding in the particuler Affirmative, viz. What we would grant, and then conclude with the Generall Negative, what we would not grant.

Touching the first, viz. Inheritance, Possessions Reall; Here many Exceptions grewe, viz. If the Scottish Nation inherite here, they will remove their dwelling thither and have their revenues follow; For every man desireth home; And in Scotland they are more free, we were told the Duke of Buckingham[1] did so into Wales, before Wales was subiect to Our Lawes as now it is; by this meanes they shall have the sweete, and avoide the burthens, which were recited to be many, and for the Service of the King and State.

An other Inconvenience in respect of the particular Subiects of England, viz. The Scottish man having here done any Particular wrong, flyeth into Scotland, what remedie for the English Subiect? *Quasi diceret*, None. Hereupon it was remembred, That elsewhere in other Countryes, Priviledges are granted to Strangers, *Dummodo sint Regnicolae*; And therefore thought fitt by the Committees they shall be Inheritable, with Caution to be subiect to all Charges and Lawes.

A third Obiection was, That Scottish men by drawing their Revenues after them in Scotland, will in tyme make themselves Rich, and us Poore: Wherefore we thought fitt, that Ability to inherite, should be *Dummodo sint Regnicolae*. It was to this Point remembred, That a French Bishop was made a Cardinall and went to Rome, his Possessions in France were staied, *Nec Immerito*; For by Comparision, this matter will more appeare; For which f. 234] Purpose, if a man having one Acre of his owne, doe take an other neare unto it of his Neighbour, and shall carry all the Strawe, Soyle, etc. from his Neighbours Acre, and lay it on his owne, thereby will his owne Land be better, and his neighbours made barren. It was answered, That the Duke of Lennox at this day hath the Lordship of Dawbeney in France; But whether of Grace, or Course, *Non Constat*; In Conclusion it was fit this Point of Trans-

---

[1] Probably Henry Stafford, second Duke of Buckingham (1454?–1483).

porting the Revenue from hence into Scotland, should be proposed to the Lords.

Also in the first Point, viz. Possessions Reall, it was moved, whether it be fitt that Scottish Subiects shall be Committees of Wards in England; Wherein was remembred the Inconvenience of bringing up wards by such Committees and the Inconvenience in respect of the Marriage of Wards; which discourse spent much tyme.

Also if One man should be ward in both Kingdomes, which should have Priority. *Quere.*

Agreed by the Committees, That no English Ward shall be brought up in Scotland, but whether Scottish Subiects shall be Gardians of Wards here, shall be proposed to the Lords.

Touching Preferments Ecclesiasticiall, the Committees agreed that the Scottish Subiects shall be allowed the 10th. parte, Except Bishopricks. Also no Scottish man to have two Benefices, nor two Dignities. Also such Scottish man as shall have any Preferment Ecclesiasticiall to be first a Graduate in one of Our Universities, viz. To be a Master of Arts before he be capable of a Benefice, and a Bachelor of Divinity before he shall have any dignity. Also no Scottish man Heade of any Colledge in either University, but to be Capable of Schollerships in such places where the Locall Statutes of the Colledge be not against it.

Thus farr said he the Committees proceeded, not being able for want of tyme to goe further; And we thought that this would be enough for one daies Conference. Yet we entred into the Consideration of the third Point, viz. offices, where we fell into great Doubts; At the first wee conceived it fitt to allow them to be Iustices of the Peace, Sheriffes, Escheators *et similia* but afterwards, we thought it fitt to be proposed to the Lords, Whither the word Iudicature in the Instrument, does not containe and comprehende those places. We divided the Points before fully considered of unto severall Persons that should handle them at the Conference with the Lords.

To myself was assigned the Declaration, That we will deale with the Anti-Nati and the Post-nati together and alike. The 2d. Point touching Naturalization, unto Sir Henry Nevill, and his Associate, Mr. Dudley Carleton. Thirdly, Whether the Scottish Subiects are to be Naturalized, unto Mr. Hedley, and Mr. Holt. Fourthly,

Lands, and Possessions, and carrying forth of Treasure unto Sir Roger Owen and Sir Nath[aniel] Bacon. 5ly. Matter of Wards, f. 235] unto his Majestys Attorney Generall and Mr. Francis Moore. Sixthly, Ecclesiasticiall Preferments unto Sir Iohn Bennet and Dr. Iames. The last Point touching Offices, viz. To under-stand the Lords Opinions, whether Iustices of Peace, Sheriffes, Escheators *et similia* be Officers of Iudicature, was left and im-posed on Sir George Moore and Sir Anth[ony] Cope.

Here because Sir W[illia]m Morrice, according to his fashion offered to speake Idlely, and to discourse of the name of Brittaine, and to make Apologie of some Speeches formerly by himself used in that Matter, and as he said misliked by some, it was said by the Speaker and affirmed by the House, That when any Question or matter is in Speech, if any man will rise and speake of any Col-laterall Matter, the Speaker may silence him; which was done accordingly, and Sir W[illia]m Morrice by the Speaker put downe.

unseasonable Speech.

In the Afternoone at 2. of the clock in the painted Chamber, the Committees of both Houses did meete; at which tyme after an Eloquent Preamble, the Earl of Salisbury his Speech was to this effect, viz: That the Lords doe endeavour a perfect Union with Restrictions: By way (said his Lordship) of Naturalization with Restrictions expressed in the Instrument agreed by the Com-missioners of both Kingdomes to be presented to the Parliaments of both Kingdomes, namely of the Post-nati and the Ante-nati, yet soe as that the Postnati may be Naturalized with Restrictions, but not soe great as the Antenati, which is so thought fitt, though it be but in respect of the Felicity of their birth, and so of their fortune in that behalfe; so all to be naturalized, viz. The Antenati with Restrictions according to the Instrument, the Postnati, with more easie termes.

Earl of Northampton; A perfect universall Union we present, and thereunto such Restrictions as shall be fitt. *Inter alia*, He tooke occasion by discourse to say, and shew that the King doth discend naturally from all Princes that ever did set foote in England, the Romans only Except.

Sir Edwyn Sandys;[1] touching the Union itself, my Lords, we

---

[1] A number of "separates" contain the speeches of the members of the Commons in this conference. Of these, St. P. Dom. XXVI, 72, 73; Cott. MSS, Julius F VI, ff. 105–107*v*; Harl. MSS 6806, ff. 209–210; Lansd.

nothing dissent, we doe differ not *de Re*, but *de Modo*: Our question
is, Whether this be already Wrought by his Majestys happy
coming hether, or to be made by us: In which question we hold,
That Unions of Kingdomes are not made by Law, but by Act
expresse. We are Mylords, by our Commission from the Commons
House, to consider of the Antenati and the Postnati in like degree,
for we have not conceived any reason hitherto, to preferr the
Post Nati before them which served his Majesty long before, and
even in his Coming hither. And first I must propose a Caution,
viz. this word (naturalization) to be a new word not knowne to
our Law; and in the Civill Law it is Generall, therefore we doe
desire that Whatsoever we shall now propose under that word,
f. 236] be no further understood then we doe meane the Same.[1]
There be, said he, two Unions, one perfect, The other Imperfect;
And we find that the latter, viz. the Imperfect Union is proper
to our present Treaty, and to that which is proposed in the Instrument, whereby the fondamentall Lawes of each Kingdome is to
be preserved; Yet we doe desire That the perfect Union which is
a Coniunction under one Law, and Gouvernment may as tyme
shall affoord be wrought betweene us: In the meane tyme wee
thincke it improper that all Commodities etc. should be imparted
to them, which by their owne meanes stand severall, and not
consolidated unto us. Againe, we doubt, That if at the first, we
shall imparte and grant all Priviledges etc. to them, this Imperfect
Union may hinder them and keepe them from seeking the perfect
Union by us desired; For if at the first wee grant unto them upon
this Imperfect Union all benefitts, they will *Acquiescere* and goe
no further; whereas we are perswaded, That if at the first wee
now deale Liberally with them, though not wholy, they will both
see Our Love by that which wee shall grant, and enter into Consideration of the Impediments that doe hinder them from enioyeing
the Residue, and then finding such Causes to be from themselves,
they will remove the Same.

MSS 486, ff. 66–67 are practically identical. St. P. Dom. XXVI, 78, 79,
are different accounts. Bowyer's account is an independent one. Notes
have been made from St. P. Dom. XXVI, 73 and 78, when they add anything.

[1] "The Civil Law hath Degrees of Naturalization; but the Common
Law hath not so." St. P. Dom. XXVI, 73.

Sir Henry Nevill handled the Inconvenience unto us of the Confederacy betweene Scotland and France: And first he offered to be considered, Whither it be safe for us to entertaine into our Bosomes them whom he shewed to be so fast annexed to an other Kingdome and People.[1]

Whether fitt to imparte all Benefitts to a Nation having the like in an other Kingdome.

Whither we may entertaine the Love of this Nation in Generall, before they have put of the Love of France, to whom they are ioyned.

Mr. Hedley[2] devided the Benefitts of Naturalization into five heades, viz. 1. Lands. 2. Preferments. 3. Offices in the Common Wealth. 4. Honours. 5. Trades and Sciences. And as we would be glad said he to communicate unto the Scottish Nation Many Priviledges, soe would we likewise desire to have security that they shall not possesse that which we reserve for ourselves;[3] And that

---

[1] "Ground of their Confederacyes, which for the time they drewe from Charles the great but for the occasion we fynde it by necessarie inference both out of their leagues and mutual Acts of Naturalization to be their enmitie against the Crowne of England begunne by .H. 2 to induce the marriage with his sonne Francis which alliance was made *contre les Anglois les auntiens et communs enemys de l'un et l'aultre Royaulmè*. And Monsieur Seravyn said that the cause of the privilege of that Nacion must not be drawne to example for others." St. P. Dom. XXVI, 78.

"Treaties made not onlie betwixt the Kings but between the Kingdomes and people." St. P. Dom. XXVI, 73. "And therefore a *quaere* whether the Kings coming to the crowne hath dissolved that or no." St. P. Dom. XXVI, 78.

"The same obligacion still mainteyned and contynued, because they Do still receave and enioye the reward and recompence thereof by their Priviledges in France.

"The Scottish Nobilitie bound to ioyne with the King of France against any King whomesoever opposite to the King of France; and to referr the Arbitrement to the King of France in case of Doubtfulnes or question of the Succession." St. P. Dom. XXVI, 73. "And the French King obliged to aide such a one for King in Scotland, whome the greatest part of the Nobilitie shall receave, which how dangerous this may be we may guesse by the example of Richard 3." St. P. Dom. XXVI, 78.

[2] Mr. Crewe gave this speech. *Ibid.*; *C.J.* I, 1028.

[3] "And if they [the Lords] demand why we swerve from the instrument which leaveth the Praerogative unbounded we answer the saving of Praerogative that goeth only to the Ante-nati and if we deale only with them we would not swarve for one generation but relye upon the

my Lords is the Effect of as much as I am by direction to say, leaving the Particulars which we are willing to grant, and wherein we thinck fitt to disable them, to be declared by others that are to follow me.

Sir Roger Owen, wee are willing they shall be Inheritable to Lands, but not to carry the Revenewe and Profitts into Scotland; And to that Purpose he remembred, That a French Bishop was made a Cardinall at Rome, and thereupon his Possessions in f. 237] France were seised; And other Matters he remembred, before delivered by Sir Edwyn Sandys, by Report in the Commons House.

Sir Nath[aniel] Bacon,[1] spake so lowe, That he was not to be heard where I stood.

Mr. Francis Moore[2] handled the Matter of the Wards as before was by Sir Edwyn Sandys opened in the Commons House by way of Report of the Committees Proceeding.

Sir Iohn Benet Dr. of Lawe, presented the Inclination of the Commons House to communicate Ecclesiasticall Preferments *Ut Supra* by Sir Edwyn Sandys in his Report before mentioned.[3]

King's Commission but the other concerneth all posteritie. So the King's word bynding but himself, we must provide for his posteritie." St. P. Dom. XXVI, 78.

[1] "Sir Nathaniell Bacon. 1. That they may be subiect to the same Taxes and payments as English. 2. That they may be Liable to the Lawes and iustice of England, as if they were resident heere." St. P. Dom. XXVI, 73.

[2] "Mr. Francis Moore. Concerning Wardes. Caution to be had for their 1. Education. 2. Landes. 3. Marriage. . . . .

"The refusall of a Wardes marriage to a Scottishman or Scottish-woman shall not be so penall as the Law makes it for English.

"That some convenient order may be taken for restrictions in the matter of Wardes, Lest by this occasion the Wardes should be inticed to verie unfitt marriages, which were verie inconvenient." St. P. Dom. XXVI, 73.

[3] The Scots were not to become chancellors nor commissaries when these officers were also ecclesiastical judges, nor to become judges of the Prerogative Arches, nor to obtain Deaneries having jurisdiction. St. P. Dom. XXVI, 78. "That they may have Deaneries, Treasurershipps, Archdeaconries, Chauncellorshipps, Benefices with Cure, and all other such places as have no Judicature." St. P. Dom. XXVI, 73.

The Scots were to be excluded from the masterships of colleges in "Cambridge, Oxford, Eaton, Winchester, Westminster, Manchester." They were not to be masters of hospitals. St. P. Dom. XXVI, 78.

And first, That we would except from the Scottish Nation Arch-
Bishopricks and Bishopricks, for they are Barons of Parliament,
and have also Offices of Iudicature; But they may have Arch-
deaconryes, Chancellorships etc.

Sir George Moore proposed to the Lords, Whether the words,
Offices of Iudicature in the Instrument, the Places of Iustices of
Peace be comprehended.[1] *Quibus dictis et Intellectis*, the Lords
arose, giving at that tyme no Answere, or Resolution, nor Opinion
in any Point so as above proposed: And so the Conference brake
up, and Wednesday the 11th of this Month afterwards appointed
to meete againe.[2]

11TH. MARTII. 1606.

Absence
Clarkes Fee

Mr. Speaker moved That upon every Lycence given to any
Member of this House, the Clarke of the House may have his
ancient Fee, which was affirmed to be 17s. 8d.[3] and granted.

Moved by SIR HENRY POOLE, That no Knight nor Burgesse,
doe departe with leave, before he hath paied the Ordinary duty
to the Collectors appointed by the House, viz. a Burgesse 5s. and
a Knight 10s. which was so ordered.

Agreed That if two stand up together to speake, the Speaker
is to determine who first arose.

Serieant Crooke and Dr. Stanhope Knights from the Lords
declared, That the Points delivered to the Lords at the last meeting
by the Knights and Gentlemen of this House were so many, and
so weighty, That their Lordships who were Committees could not

---

[1] And sheriffs. "The like question made of Coroners, Feodaries,
Undersheriffes, and Escheators. . . . .

"The whole end & scope of their Message was 1. Dutie to the King.
2. Care of the English. 3. Love to the Scotts.

"Desired of them, that as the Titles are united in the Kings person,
so the affections of all the Subiects might be united among themselves.

"Sir Edwin Sandes. 1. A protestation that they onlie propound these
things in raw and imperfect sort; but that they are not to conclude, or
binde the Howse. 2. That they Desire not to be excluded heereby from
propounding any farther or other reasons, or doubts that they shall finde
heereafter." St. P. Dom. XXVI, 73.

[2] M. de la Boderie writes that Parliament is accomplishing very little.
Ambassades, II, 120–121.

[3] A mistake for 6*s*. 8*d*. "Anciently but 2s. 6d. was due for a Common
Burgesse." Cott. MSS, Titus F IV, f. 97.

hetherto make Report thereof unto the Lords in the Upper House; so as consideration not having bene of the same, their Lordships doe desire, That the Conference intended this day, may be putt of; And likewise their Lordships would have desired Friday to be appointed for this Conference, but that day being appointed, and necessarily to be imployed for his Majesty other Service in London, they doe desire that the Conference which should have bene this f. 238] day, may be appointed on Saturday, if it may so stand with the good likeing of this House; Whereunto was agreed, and the calling of the House deferred untill Monday, then to hold Peremptorily.

SIR EDWYN SANDYS reported to the House the effect of the Conference last had with the Lords,[1] thus:

Touching the Conveniency of Naturalization, their Lordships have had Consideration of the forme and of the Matter to be dealt in.

Touching the forme, the manner of their Lordships dealing with us at the last Conference, he noted that the Lords made long and learned Speeches, commending the Union in Generall, but for Particulars, referred us unto the Instrument, with this, That if any Occasion of addition were, they would ioyne with us; We (quoth he) on the other side, declared our selves in Particular, according to Our Instructions given us by this House, to which the Lords replyed not, but tooke day over; Therefore the Committees of this House much lesse would reply at that tyme, nor doe now thincke good to reply hereafter, before we have heard their Lordships; Yet at our next meeting not to heare meerely, but with Protestation etc. to adde or diminish as occasion etc. and in such Sorte to explaine any thing that shall seeme mistaken, and to adde what shall be necessary. He conceived That the matter is double, viz. Generall and Particular. The latter seemeth the very worke; The Generall is only [blank].

In this busines, the Committees have thought fitt to be considered,

1. What Persons are to be united.

---

[1] Sandys is reporting from the committee that met the Lords on March 7 and that subsequently drew up a plan of procedure for the next conference of March 14. The date of this report is March 12. Cf. C.J. I, 1029-30.

2. What Kinde of Union is desired, and fitt to be made.

3. What Impediments on the Scottish Side are to be removed.

4. What Security is to be had for that which wee will grant, and the restraining of that which we will not grant, but reserve.

It was moved among our selves the Committees thus; What if the Lords shall proceede in their owne Course to urge a difference betweene the Anti-nati, and the Post-nati, and thought fit that then we are not to argue it, but to heare and report: Otherwise if the Lords will permitt us to hold on Our Course, wee will then maintaine Our Positions.[1]

Touching the Union, wee did present to the Lords two Unions, viz, one perfect,[2] the other Imperfect; shewing further that we desire the former, though the Instrument doe appoint us, and restraine us to the latter. Our Committees among our selves inquired how wee shall iustify that the Impediment of the perfect union is in the Scottish Nation; Whereunto was answered, that out of the Course and words of the Instrument, it will be proved, for *Inter alia*, whereas we have provided for Continuance of the f. 239] fundamentall Lawes of this Kingdome only in the Preamble, on the Scottish Parte, those words are in the body of the Instrument with these words further (otherwise we cannot be a free Monarchie)[3] which we construe a distinct Kingdome.

One Impediment to be removed was also said to be the French Incorporation, which is Reciprocall betweene Scotland and France; Which was said to be from France to Scotland so long as the Scotts shall remaine *Sub Confederationa et obsequio Regis Franciae*, which so happened because the French King having made this Incorporation absolute, it required Confirmation of the Courts of Parliament, and in the meane tyme, Scotland made an Incorporation to the French absolute, and then the Acts of Parliament in France limitted the Kings Charter unto Scotland *ut supra*.

upon the
Mariage betweene
France and Mary
the Mother of
our now King

It was alledged That the present Usage is contrary to the Right; For at this day it was said, That the Scottish Guarde in France is supplied by French, and that the Scottish are not there Inheritable, but are driven to particular Letters of Naturalization.

---

[1] See Spedding, III, 333, notes 2 and 3.

[2] "Union in Law, in Government, in Privileges, etc., a perfect Union." *C.J.* I, 1030.

[3] See the Scotch Act in *C.J.* I, 319.

Whereupon I found the Committees thought it fitt That by way of Proposition the Scottish Naturalization should be considered.

The fourth Point concerned the Security of Restriction viz. That the Scottish Nation shall take no more then wee shall think fit to grant; and that they meddle not with such things as we shall exempt or reserve to our Selves. And herein the Committees yeilded reasons why we should insist on Security, viz.

1. The Restrictions are necessary even for the Scottish men themselves, for a perfect Union is best for them, *Ergo* Restrictions which may shew them the want of that which is best for them, will soonest drawe them to it, and is best for them.

2. If the Lords require why wee desire Security for Observation of the Restrictions, which doe oppose the Kings Prerogative saved by the Instrument of the Union; It may be answered That if we are to treate only of the Ante-nati, and to restraine only them, wee then would take and relie on his Majestys Promise conteined in the Instrument for all those Ante-nati will be passed and gone in an age, but the Post-Nati are to have Continuance for ever, and the Kings Worde dieth with his Naturall body, to which though wee all wish Continuance ever to the end of the world, yet we doe well knowe, That it is subiect to death even as all other Creatures.

So we determined to insist upon Security; And then to understand from the Lords what Security which we have reason to expect from their Lordships: For That in the Case of Purveyors, they seemed able to devise unto us a meanes to binde the Prerogative upon Composition, which they urged.

f. 240] We proposed to their Lordships five things Considerable in the Union. 1. Lands. 2. Preferments. 3. Offices. 4. Honours. 5. Trades and Sciences.

Touching Lands we moved two Provisions;

1. That such Scottish men as here shall buy Lands, doe not carry our Treasure, viz. the Revenue of their Lands away thether.

2. That we might have some remedy devised against Scottish men which doe wrong here to an English Subiect, doe afterwards flie thether into Scotland.

We observed that in the Instrument among Lawes of Hostility to be repealed, the Statute forbidding Transportation of Treasure is not mentioned. Wee moved That in the Clause of Iudicature,

Offices mentioned in the Instrument, the State of Iurors may be considered as a maine Branch of the first Point concerning Lands.

The Second Point being Preferments Ecclesiasticall, wee thought good to adde to this a Defalcation for Places having Iudicature annexed to them. Unto our former Provision touching Colledges, we likewise added Winton, Eaton, and Westminster; And also Headships of Hospitalls; Also no Scottish Man to have two Benefices, nor 2. dignities, but only One Benefice, and One Dignity: And every such Person to be Master of Arts in One of our Universities, before he be Capable of a Benefice, and Bachelor of Divinity before he have any Dignity.

Thus farr wee have proceeded, now said he, we desire to understand the Pleasure of the House for Distribution of Matters and Points against the next Conference. For our owne Opinions, wee thinck the French Matter well imposed on Sir Henry Nevill, and Mr. Dudley Carlton; The rest to be committed to Sir Maurice Berkeley, Sir Iohn Bennet Dr. of Law, Mr. Brooke, Mr. Crewe, Mr. Headley, Mr. Alford, and to a Seaventh (innuendo himself) if you shall not be pleased to spare him: And thereupon by the House ordered That the Seaventh should be added.[1]

Also by the House Mr. Headley is appointed to reporte the last daies Conference, and Mr. Recorder, and Mr. Hyde to report the next daies Conference; And the Point whether Iustices of Peace and such like, be offices of Iudicature, referred to Sir Anthony Cope.

SIR GEORGE SAMPOLE,[2] moved That the House would send unto the Lords, signifying great disease and Inequality the House is in at a Conference, by standing so long bare, and to desire Provision in that behalfe may be made.

f. 241] SIR THOMAS HOLCROFT moved That the Lords be dealt with, That no Strangers not being of the House doe come in, or be present at the Conference.

MR. ALFORD seconded Sir George Sampole, and moved That for as much as diverse ancient Gentlemen of this House have bene and are necessarily to be used at the Conferences, who are not able to endure the long weary, and unseasonable Meetings; For whereas heretofore the Course of Proceedings was by Bill, so as

---

[1] An eighth name, Sir George More, was added according to *C.J.*
[2] Sir George St. Paul. *C.J.* I, 1030.

when any Conference was required the Same was only for Satisfaction, and examining some one Point: Now the whole body of
the busines is of late discoursed and debated at Conferences, which
maketh the Attendance long, therefore some order may be taken
by the Lords; the rather for that divers of this House have after
conference found themselves sicke and lame long after; That
therefore Provision may be made for our more easy sitting when
we shall attend any such Service. Hereupon it was directed by
the House that the Committees for the Priviledges shall consider
what Message may be fitt to be sent, and upon what grounds, and
in what Sorte.

SATTURDAY 14. MARTII. 1606.

MR. FULLER reported[1] to the House the Opinion of the Committees for the Priviledges to be, That a Message be sent to the
Lords, to desire Provision for the more ease of such Persons as
this House shall from time to tyme send to conferr with their
Lordships upon these reasons, viz.

1. For that their Lordships House and this House doe make but
one House.

2. Untill 6. E. 3.[2] The Lords and Commons were one House,
and did set together.[3]

3. After the first Severing of the Commons from the Lords,
for long time the Manner was this, That House that for Resolution
in any Point did desire Conference, was accustomed to send unto
the other, desiring some certaine Number, which commonly exceeded not 12. to be sent unto them, so that small Number of
Lords coming to the body of the Commons, it is not likely the
whole Commons did stand or were bare in reverence of so few sent
downe to them.

4. At the often Meetings of the Commissioners of these 2.
Kingdomes, England and Scotland, touching this Union, and the
framing of this Instrument since proposed unto us, all the Committees of all degrees did sitt etc.

---

[1] Cf. *C.J.* I, 352, 1031.

[2] See *Rot. Parl.* II, 66–67.

[3] "And none bare headed nor standing." St. P. Dom. XXVI, 84.
This manuscript is an account by Thomas Wilson of the episode in
question.

5. The Lords doe present but themselves, viz. every man his owne Person, How great and honorable soever he be, but of the Commons, every man is a body Representative, either of a whole County, or a Burrough at least.

6. All Commissioners of the Peace at quarter Sessions, and at f. 242] Assises, are equall, and the meanest Gentleman in Commission sitts on the same Bench covered with the greatest Earle being all equally Councellors.

7. To the obiection, That it hath bene heretofore as now it is, etc., Answered, That heretofore Conferences were only upon Bills digested before hand, and in that respect brief, but now the body and every particular of the busines is to be debated Pro and Con, by the Committees which draweth the Service long. The Resolution of the Committees for the Priviledges therefore was, That some Person of accompt *vid*: Sir Francis Bacon, should be sent to the Lords forth with only to desire their Lordships That for as much as diverse ancient Gentlemen of this House, who are necessarily to be employed at Conferences, cannot endure to stand in such Sorte as now they doe, therefore their Lordships will be pleased to take order for our more ease at such meetings: And to say no more, except the Lords shall require upon what ground or reason this House doth now first seeke alteration of the Order and fashion heretofore used, and then Sir Francis Bacon to deliver the reasons aforesaid.

Mr. Speaker craving leave to be heard, proposed to the House, Whether it be not probable and conceived by every man, That this question touching more ease at Conferences among us, hath bene related, and is well knowen to the Lords; which for because in his owne Opinion he doubted not, therefore he moved That the House would consider, whether it may not be better at this tyme, seeing we are so speedily as this afternoone to meete with the Lords, therefore to forbeare this Message in Expectation that of themselves the Lords will prevent us, and provide for the ease of the Committees which wee shall send, which said he if it so take, is best, otherwise, if the Lords take no notice of your Purpose herein, then upon their next demanding of Conference, this motion will perhaps be more seasonable;[1] Whereunto the House enclyned, and did forbeare to send *ut supra*.

---

[1] "This is likely to come in, to day [Wilson is writing the week after

The Conference[1] with the Lords after dinner was in the Painted Chamber at 2. of the clock, to this effect, viz. Earle of Salisbury,) I will use no Preface but a short Parenthesis, which is no more but to let you knowe Gentlemen how sensible the Lords are of the Inconveniency and Incommodity which some special Persons among you coming to conferr with us doe endure; We doe therefore move you, That your selves will not oppresse, or thrust one an other in this Place, wherein wee doubt not but you shall find more ease.

f. 243] We will now (quoth he) give you such Answere to your Obiections, as presently doth satisfy us.

We will hold as neere as we may, the Order of the Instrument framed by men, whome we trusted not with an Acre of ground, or a flocke of Sheepe, but with the Common wealth. The Points first proposed in the Instrument are, the Abolishing of Hostile Lawes, and Commerce, of these two at this tyme wee are not to talke.

The third Point only which is Naturalization, is now in debate, and proposition betweene us. And herein first is to be handled, the Post-Nati with Restrictions, to which you shall receive Answere particularly to every of those Points which you at the last Conference proposed: But (said his Lordship) I doe not tell you That we will speake of nothing else.

The Points by you offered as considerable in the Matter of

March 14] if a message be sent, & offered for remidy to Consideracion of the Lords. It was propounded twise on Satturday by one man at 8. a clock and after at 10. when the house was full. Many would have had thes reasons and allegacions before mentioned, remembred to the Lords. Other wished it shold be propounded but in generality & the inconvenience only alledged to the Lords with out adding the reasons." St. P. Dom. XXVI, 84.

"The House hoping the Lords would take notice of this complaint and redress, did nothing more therin. . . . . It was afterwards complained of to the Lords, but no redress nor answer." Cott. MSS, Titus F IV, f. 97v.

[1] See report of conference in *C.J.* I, 1032. "Mr. Holt made report of the first day's conference with the Lords, which was Saturday fortnight; and Mr. Recorder made report of the last day's conference, which was Saturday sevennight." *Hist MSS Com. Buccleuch MSS*, III, 114.

"Les deux Chambres hautes et basses ne se peurent accorder, pour le moins en apparence; car sois main le Roi a opinion qu'elles ne sont que trop d'accord." *Ambassades*, II, 136. See *ibid.* 136–139.

Naturalization, (said his Lordship) are these viz. 1. Lands. 2. Capacity of Ecclesiasticall Preferments. 3. Honours. 4. Offices Temporall. 5. Trades.

Touching the first, Lands, wee are resolved to grant to all the Scottish Nation, Ability to purchase Inheritance.

Touching your restrainte that the Treasure raised of Lands be not transported in Specie into Scotland, to this we doe not assent, for wee doe thincke That they shall gaine nothing by Transporting it thether, because the Standard being Equall in both Kingdomes, if men will be diligent here, others will never be desirous to transporte Treasure thither.

And whereas you say, That they will convey the Treasure coming of their Revenue here, into Scotland, and makeing their aboade there, will not be taxed for the Common Service here: Wee on the other Side doe thincke That by the removing of their Residence unto Edenburgh, they shall be no more freed of Taxes here, then if such Persons shall remove from hence to Newcastle.

The third Obiection is, That a Scottish man doeing a wrong here, and flying into Scotland, here is no remedy against him, in which respect you desire that such Person shall be tied to their Personall aboade here, as doe here purchase Lands.

Wee doe assent That a meane shall be devised for that Inconvenience: And likewise for Transportation of Money out of both dominions, there shall be a meane devised to make it as penall out of Scotland, as it is out of England.

f. 244] Touching Ecclesiasticall Preferments, wee thinke untill a perfect Union be wrought by tyme, and Oppurtunity, it is not fitt that any of the Scottish Nation be Archbishop or Bishop; neither Deanes, Archdeacons etc. so farr as the said places be within the worde, Iudicature, which must receive Construction.

Touching Plurality of Benefices, and Dignities, wee think it fitt, that Scottish men have no more then One of each, so farr forth as the same One of each Kinde may enable the Party to live honestly. Wee assent the Scottish shall be quallified as you say: Also that they be not Heads of Houses, wee assent: That they be not fellowes of Colledges otherwise then you have said, wee assent. For the Number of Benefices to be in the totall impartible to the Scottish Nation, whereas you allowe the tenth throughout England, wee assent, so farr as the Presentation is in the Power of yourselves, but such as are in the Kings Power, it is fitt he dispose of them at his Pleasure.

Touching the Freedome of the Scottish Nation in France, wee thinke fitt the debating thereof be at this tyme deferred; not but that it may be easily answered, but for that yourselves have reade the Instrument, and wee have not had tyme to consider of it.

Touching the Matter of Wardes wee are loath they should have **Wardes** Education of Scotland, if Scottish men should have Committments; And herein you doe but speake before us. Further you would not have wast done by Scottish Committees, if you reade the Condition of Committments, you shall see the Religion and Conscience of them that committ them. Touching Marriage of Wards, wee agree, That refusall of a Marriage tendered to be had with a Scottish Subiect, and marrying with in Age, shall not be penall.

Ante-Nati, ought not in our opinions to be Iustices of Peace.

Sir Edwyn Sandys,[1] If in our Grant, we have not care soe to provide, that there be enough both for them, and us, Our Bounty may be our Baine, and the Felicity of the Receivors may prove

---

[1] Thomas Wilson had been instructed to make a report of this important speech to give to Salisbury. He wrote Salisbury on March 15: "I have bene with some of my frends, and amongst other discourses taking occasion to speake of the generale commendacion that is geven to Sir Edwin Sandys his speech the last day, I thought to drawe them to some perticuler recytall of some points, but I fynd ther memoryes not ready upon the sodayne, but upon a convention betwixt us every one to charge his remembrance in recaling and setting downe the perticularityes of the 2 last conferences and then to confer them together, I hope to gather somewhat more from others then myself can yett calle to mynd upon this last perticular. This some of them have promised we shall doe betwixt this and tomorrowe at night and soe ther will not be the least suspition of that I aym att.

"The point which your Lordship demanded of me touching the priviledg of naturalizacon of scotts in France whether it be taken away or noe, thes are the allegacions and reasons pro et contra. [A long list follows]." St. P. Dom. XXVI, 87.

St. P. Dom. XXVI, 85, is Wilson's report of the speech. "The effect of the Re[*blank*] made Answeare delivered to the Lords at the last Conference. [These words are in the margin and are crossed out.]

"Collections out of Sir Ed[win] Sands Speach before the Lords.

"The introduction was to shew the great trust committed to the house

the Misery of the Grantors. Wee treate not of the Preferment of such as have deserved well of his Majesty specially, but of a Multitude of People. And wee are but Conduits to convey Our conceipts, and I am sorry, That it is my fortune to deliver any thing displeasing to your Lordships and dissent is alwaies displeas-
f. 245] ing. Wee are (quoth he) tied to the Imperfect Union, not by our owne choice, but by the Act of Parliament made by the Scottish Nation, and the Proceedings of the Commissioners accordingly.

In our Act it is said by way of Declaration, That this Union shall be done without Alteration of the fundamentall Lawes: Their Act hath that enacted in the body of the Act, and it is

---

of Commons by the whole commonwealth, that accordingly we were to proportion our Care and Warines to the waightines of the busines.

"The waight, expressed in 4 considera[ci]ons.

"1. Naturalisation extendeth not to one limme or branch of the king-dome but to the whole body.

"2. It concerneth not one kind or degree of benefits or privileges but all this realme can afford.

"3. It is not communicated to a few onely uppon desert, but to a great and populous nation.

"4. It is not for tyme onely but for perpetuity, and therfore we are as well to foresee what State of commonwealth we transmit to posterity as we looke back with contentment uppon that wee have receaved of our Ancestors.

"The waight of the cause hath bred our warines in proceeding. Yet such a warines as hath not made us backward in duty to his Majesty or in the furtherance of the service which we have shewed by our freedome in delivering our opinions and propownding owr dowbts.

"The warines chiefly shewed in the restraint of such as spake before theyr Lordshipes who were not licenced by the house to deliver any thing of theyr owne sence but as they were instructed. And they were but as conduits to convay such matter to theyr Lordships as had bin before prepared.

"Answeare to the difference putt betwixt Ante nati et post nati.

"The Cause of our dissenting from them in this point to proceede of the consideration of the kind of Union wher of we now treat.

"An imperfect Union, likened to a crooked and knotty piece of wood which requires much hewing and paring before it can be made fitt for use.

"The cause of this imperfectness in the Scottish nation, by inserting this clause into the body of theyr act that theyr fundamentall lawes and privileges should not be altered, and that therein they have expressed theyr meaning to be, to stand a free Monarchie.

"Our desire of a perfect Union which with consent of the Scottish

thereby further enacted that they will stand an absolute Monarchy; which wee construe an absolute Kingdome.

Wee doubt not but by the Assent and Assistance of your Lordships, wee shall tender such a forme of this Imperfect Union, as your Lordships shall well like of. *Nimia Amicitia est Causa Odii*, and therefore the Proverbe well saith, Love little, and love long. Our House is of this Opinion, That the Act of Union now in hand is not necessary, but Honourable. Our Purpose is, That if your Lordships will not give us leave to handle the Ante-Nati and the Post-nati both alike; wee will humbly give your Lordships Audience,[1] but not any Answere.

This spoken, the Chief of the Lords at the upper end bending their bodies, and putting their Heads together over the boarde did conferr long in that sorte together; And then the Earle of

---

nation might be affected. And by the direction and ayde of theyr Lordships such a one might be sett downe as would be both honorable and profitable to both nations.

"The imperfect Union would worke a contrary effect to this owr desire.

"1. It would hinder the perfect Union, because a desire once satisfied doth there rest.

"2. Partaking in liberties and privileges and standing still divided kingdomes and different in Parliaments lawes and customes may in time breede difference of affections, and be a cause of hatred not love. Exemplified by a consideration of friendship betweene particular persons *nimia amicitia* (when there is difference in nature and conditions) *causam dat odii*.

"Conclusion. Not fit to grant perfect privledges of naturalisation Unlimited, to an unperfect Union. Therfore by order from the house no yealding to a difference betweene the ante nati and post nati, not uppon any Jealosy of the Lords meaning but to give no assent to the reason of this defference expressed in the instrument and therfore unless we might treat of them both together we would humbly give theyr Lordships audience but no further proceede in conference.

"[*On side*] And this act of naturalising a nation being no act of necessity but voluntary and free. Therfore no act of the law but of the king and state."

Lansd. MSS 486, ff. 65-65v is a short and almost unintelligible account of this speech.

[1] Thomas Wilson wrote: "Concerning the using the worde Audience by the gentleman on Saturday they [the Commons] excuse it by imporpriety sayinge he shold only have said that they had noe further commission but to heare their Lordships with out replying unless they wold proceed on both alyke." St. P. Dom. XXVI, 84.

Salisbury spoke to this Effect, It was resolved by my Lords, That more should speake, and better able then he that had spoken; But now wee have resolved to give the Lower House no such Conference as shall beare the Title of an Audience, for there is much difference: Wherefore since this day is rather a Narrative, then a Conference, therefore wee will shut it up without giving reasons untill wee may meete on a Conference, not an Audience, with this, that wee never meete with them who are like to take a dissent for displeasure. And wee will acquaint Our House with your Answers, not doubting but they will give us further direction in this busines.

MONDAY THE 16TH OF MARCH. 1606.

The Clerke after that he had said Praiers, declared that the Speaker was sicke, and thereupon further meeting of the House was put off untill Wednesday next.[1] Likewise on Wensday,

---

[1] The Speaker was ill but the Government was very glad to delay debate in the House for a few days. It was feared that the Commons were about to pass a resolution declaring invalid the opinion of the Judges on the naturalization of the Post-Nati. On March 15 Salisbury wrote to Sir Thomas Lake, the secretary of the King: "I have received this night, at 8 of clock his Majesties letter to the Lords [of the Council], and imparted it accordingly. So have I also his verball message by Sir Roger which he delivered clearly and particularly, as it was expressed in your Letter. Of which I thought fit to give you notice, that his majesties mind may not be in doubt of any mistaking. His Majesty rightly noteth that, to which indeed, the House is most inwardly affected, which is to get some such definite Sentence pass in the howse, of the invalidity of the Judges Resolution, as may make them daynty herafter to judge the question, or make the judgement less acceptable, for which we were so wary, as this day Mr. Speaker had his direction to remember his Provisionall order in case it should be offered, wherof there is some more then ordinary disposition. But therof his Majesty may rest secure; for first bona fide the Speaker is not well. And when we heard his Majesties message, we thought to make this use of it. First I did send to know how he did. Who sent word, he was afraid he should not be in ease to come to the howse, and yet would straine himselfe, if I thought it would hinder the King's service. Wherunto My Lords agreed that I should make this Reply, that we had no hast for any thing yet these 2 or 3 dayes, being to report and consult, before we would send to conferr, rather expecting that the Lower Howse would feele their owne ommissions and send to explane themselves. But for his coming abroad my Lords did not only presume to warrant him to stay, but rather would command him not to adventure till he were better,

diverse being assembled in the House after Praiers,[1] the meeting
for the same Cause was putt of untill Friday following. On which
Friday being the 20th of March,[2] after the Clarke had ended
Praiers, Mr. LAURANCE HYDE declared that Mr. Speaker being

as that which they knew his Majesty (of his gracious care of his health)
would impose upon him, wherwith he seemed comforted, and sent us word
he would stay for 2 or 3 dayes. In the meane time we will be doing that
which we think fittest for his Majesties princely ends. And as their is
any cause, send againe to his Majesty having thought it only my duty
at this present to commend my humble service with this short advertisement." St. P. Dom. XXVI, 91.

"The parliament men that were in the house went to a sermon to
Westminster." *Hist. MSS Com. Buccleuch MSS*, III, 114.

[1] By Wednesday the Speaker was better but was kept away by the
advice of the Council. Salisbury wrote to Lake: "For that which you
wrote by Mr. Thellwall, I may not hide it from you, that in this point,
of the difference betweene Postnati & Antenati there is a great heat of
spirit kindled to decide it by a question in the Lower howse. Wherof, as
long as I am doubtful and doe but consider, either what such an affront
would be for the present, or what a preparation it will be to make judges
dainty to judge it, or when they have done it, to make people less reverence
it, the consequence whereof, could neither be good for this present time,
nor for herafter. My Lords, I meane such of us, as wrote the letter to his
Majesty, have all thought it the safer way to prevent all causes. And
therfore although it is most trwe, that the speaker is not so ill as to be in
any danger yet having heard, how much they murmured at his abscence,
he was resolved to have come forth today, and sitt an hower, had not I
sufficiently prepared him in that point. Neverthelesse his Majesty may
please to secure himselfe, that either his sicknes shall sufficiently or arti-
ficiently keepe him with in or if he doe come abroad, there shall be a
provisionall stay of any such shrewd circumstance of Alienation of mens
mindes. So as his Majesty shall not need to alter any purpose of his
coming, for wee will not be overtaken in that kind. That his majesty
persuadeth himselfe of our care in this, is an argument of his gracious
disposition." St. P. Dom. XXVI, 91. March 18, 1606.

[2] Salisbury wrote Lake on the 20th: "For the matter you wiste of
[the possibility that the Commons might declare the Judges' opinion
invalid] know this, it is too incertaine a thing for us to devine what you
will doe once in your congregation. But if it were in my case I would not
suspect that they will doe so irregular a thing. Yet it is trew that in this
case I thinke his Majesties care necessary to which you may only say
[to the King] that the Speaker's absence is of it selfe accidentall by sick-
ness and surely, Monday will be the soonest, and against that he shall
have his provisional directions." St. P. Dom. XXVI, 91.

For these days of the Speaker's absence, see *C.J.* I, 353-354; 1031-32.

f. 246] yesterday reasonably recovered, came downe into his dyning Chamber, and tooke cold, whereby in the Night an Accident hapned unto him (viz) a Loosenesse, by which not being able to goe abroade, he desireth forbearance untill to Morrow: Hereupon the House gave further Order to spare further meeting untill Monday following.

MONDAY 23° MARTII. 1606.

Speaker Sicke

On Monday 23. March, after the clarke had ended Praiers, MR. BROOKE declared That Mr. Speaker found himselfe not well in State to goe abroad; And even at this Present there is one with him to administer Phisicke unto him, whereby, he shall not be able to goe forth of his chamber, in which regard he desired to be forborne untill to Morrow, which request the House yeilded; and it was moved[1] That some Course might presently be thought on which wee may hold in Case the Speakers health should not permitt him to supply the Place: Whereupon the House gave Order the Committees for the Priviledges should consider, Whether the House may not choose a new Speaker for the Cause aforesaid, and what Course is to be holden in Case of the Speakers Sicknesse; for which Matter the Committees were required to meete in the Committee Chamber in the Afternoone: And likewise the Committees for Examination of Greivances complayned on by the merchants against the Spaniards, were appointed to meete in the House this Afternoone.

FRIDAY 27. MARTII. 1607.

From the Lords came Dr. Stanhope and Dr. Swale, declaring That their Lordships purposing this Morning to send unto this House a Message, doe desire they will forbeare to arise in the meane tyme; which motion was yeilded unto by the House; [*blank*].

An Act concerning the Sale of Parte of Wallers Lands for Satisfaction of 500£.—and odd money, unto Warrein, according to a Decree in the Chancery, which was this day offered to be 3° *Lecta*; And upon a Petition exhibited on the behalfe of Waller, It was ordered, That Councell shall be to morrow heard at the

---

[1] By Sir Robert Wingfield. *C.J.* I, 1031.

Barr on both Sides, with this Provision, That at the third reading, no Councell be hereafter heard to any Bill.[1]

Serieant Crooke and Dr. Swale from the Lords declared That f. 247] when the Lords did last send their Committees to conferr with the Committees of this House touching the Naturalization of the Scottish Nation in Generall, as the Same is devided into the Ante-Nati and Post-Nati, only the Point of Conveniency, without so much as pointinge at the Matter in Lawe was entended, and that without Preiudice or Conclusion to either House by any thing that then might be spoken, which tooke no Effect because the Committees sent from hence had no Power to conferr, but to heare; Now their Lordships Knowing this House to be as desirous as themselves to finish this Great Worke, doe desire an other Conference, touching the Conveniency of Naturalization of the Scottish Nation, both Ante and Post Nati; And to this End the Conference to be free and liberall, That the reasons of difference may be propounded and discussed on both Sides, without dealing with the Matter in Lawe, or advantage to be taken of any thing that shall be spoken, nor either Partie to be bound by anything there to be spoken, but that thereby the Inclination of both Houses may be understood, to the End that Bills may be drawen accordingly by both Houses. And because Easter approcheth, soe as the Houses are likely to have a Recession for a tyme, therefore their Lordships doe desire an Answer as before is spoken, as soone as conveniently may be.

These Messengers being withdrawen, MR. LAURANCE HYDE[2] spake to this Effect, viz. That it is fitt and comely for us to give the Lords Answer, and meeting, alwaies with this, That wee remember Our former Proceedings, and doe now what we shall thinck fitt with that Gravity as beseemeth us; Wherein he thought it convenient we should remember our former Resolution, upon great Debate; Which was, to deale with the Ante-Nati and the Post Nati together, and (said he) I doe assure myself, That the Kings desire and Ours is all one, namely, to worke the perfect Union, as being best for both Kingdomes, which is only by making ourselves one and the same body, and that is only to be done by a Subiection to the same Lawes: To this perfect Union we

---

[1] Cf. *C.J.* I, 1033.
[2] *Ibid.*

shall sooner attaine by an other Course then by that which hetherto we have laboured in: For hetherto we have held our Selves to the Instrument, which is a hinderance to that we desire; And we have spent a yeare and proceeded little; For the Scot- f. 248] tish Nation have reserved them selves to continue a Free Monarchy they have saved their fundamentall Lawes, their Liberties, Priviledges and Rights, which being done no perfect Union can be had: And I am perswaded That the Commons and all the Scottish Nation except some few greate Persons That have Liberties unfitt for Subiects, as Power to pardon Treason, Felony, murder, Manslaughter, and other like, would gladly yeild to the Subiection of Our Lawes; And in this Case stoode Wales whilst the Earles Marches held their great Liberties and Powers, and never were united untill by H. 8. they were discharged of all such Regallities, and made even as wee, thereby partici- pating all Priviledges and Advantages with us, and are since as good Subiects as any of us. Againe wee have by Petition sought redresse at his Majestis hands of many Grievances, this may be a meanes to obtaine our desire therein when happily his Majesty the rather to give that Nation Encouragement to come to us, may be pleased to ease those burdens of which we complayned: And there is no Doubt, but if the Scottish Parliament will renewe and enlarge their Commission, wee may in farr lesse time debate and conclude a perfect Union for the good of both Nations then we have already spent in dealing in this Imperfect Union.

His speech being ended, the Messengers from the Lords were called in and dispatched thus, That this House had entred into Consideration of their Lordships Message, but the time being now much spent, cannot presently resolve, but as soone as con- veniently may be they will send Answer by Messengers of their owne.

Satturday. 28. Martii. 1607.

Whether fitt for the Comons according to the Lords Mes- sage, to conferr in Point of Conven- iency of Naturali- zation of the Scot- tish Nation, with- out distinction of Ante and Post Nati

Mr. Dudley Carleton[1] began with a Preamble to this Ef- fect, viz. So long as Matter of Law was in hand, I thought fitt for myselfe a man in that Kinde meerely unlearned to be silent, and during that dispute I heard many learned and grave Speeches; Now that Course being finished, and that we are come to treate of Matter of Conveniency, I hold it necessary for myself among

---

[1] For the following debate, cf. *C.J.* I, 1033–34.

others, to declare what I conceive: We finde by the reporte of
the last Conference, That the busines hath bene much furthered
by the Labor of the Committees, and how the same hath bene
hindered by the Strict Commission which went from this House
f. 249] to treate, whereby our Committees were restrained and
limitted to treate only of Naturalizing the Scottish Nation, wholy
together without distinction of the Ante Nati and the Post Nati;
Now it is by the Lords required, That wee should againe conferr with a more liberall Power to distinguish and sever the
Ante from the Post Nati, and to examine whether in reason
they be not to deale with all by way of Restrictions, in severall
Degrees and fashions.   For my owne Parte, I thinck no Inconvenience if wee treate first of the Post Nati, and in their Naturalization to adde what Restrictions we shall thincke good, and
afterwards in the Consideration of the Ante Nati, to adde what
more wee shall likewise find fitt and convenient; with this Protestation to be both here registred and declared to the Lords,
That this is done without admitting them by Law more capable,
then the other, but to reason only in Policy and Conveniency. I
have heard the Lords say and some alsoe heard affirme, That of
five Points required to be imparted to the Scottish Nation by this
Naturalization, the King of himself may doe fower, and then it
is a good bargaine for us to grant somewhat of our owne, thereby
to wynn the King to be pleased to tie even his owne hands; Yet
with all my Opinion also is, That first we looke and provide for
security to enioy, and for performance of such Restrictions as
shall be agreed on.

Dr. Duncombe; We are tied in Honor and in Iudgement to
maintaine that we have done; And I take it, though no solemne
Iudgement have passed in open House, for distinction of the
Ante and Post Nati, yet wee limited heretofore our Committees to
treate no otherwise then with[1] distinction, therefore in Effect we
have Iudged it, therefore I thinck it is fitt for us, now to expect
Bills from the Lords, and not spend the tyme in Conference; and
to that Purpose I wish Answer to be returned to their Lordships.

Sir Maurice Berkeley; We received a Message from the
Lords etc. Now the Question is what answer is fitt to be returned:

- *Without* is meant.

If the question now were, whether there should be a Difference betweene the Ante and the Post Nati, I should Perhaps make no difference, for wee are I thinck all satisfied That in Law they are in the same State, and *non distinguendum ubi Lex non distinguit*; f. 250] For my owne Parte, I doe not see how wee can in matter of Conveniencie make a difference betwixt the Ante and the Post Nati, but we shall give Countenance to the Opinion of the Lords and Iudges in the Point of Law; For wee shall admitt that for Inconvenience which the Iudges have set for Law, and they will be the forewarder to put their Opinions in Execution: (To this he might have added, That if the Lords differ from us in matter of Conveniency, as the Judges doe in Point of Law, then both Points are in a Sorte ruled against us, because the Opinion of the stronger and mightier is that way, and upon Contestation what Course of Decision, *quasi diceret* who Knoweth not by whom) But say Sir Maurice the question is, whether wee shall heare and conferr with the Lords of the Matter of Conveniency; I thinck that as wee have to my Understanding satisfied their Lordships in the Matter of Law, so wee shall likewise give them Satisfation in the Point of Conveniency, and thereby also discourage the Iudges to putt their Opinion in Practise, and this Conference to be without Conclusion, and with Reservation to doe afterwards as wee shall see Cause.

Sir Herbert Croft

I thinck That before Conference, it will be convenient that among our Selves wee consider of the Matter of Convenience, and this to be in the House, not by Committees; For as I doe confesse that in Committees by short Arguments many times truth is beaten out, yet I have observed, That in Committees when every man may reply, some speciall Persons of Place by speaking often, and countenance doe prevaile more then by their reasons: And touching the maine Matter of the Question, I thinck the Ante Nati are in favour and grant as much, and more to be respected then the Post Nati; For wee see their deserts, of the other wee cannot iudge, and againe one Age will end that which wee give them; But the other is perpetuall to them and their Seede. In processe of discourse he came to say, That wee deale with a Nation that in their Treaty doe give to us merely nothing, and our giving them any thing is not the way to bring them to us, but to hinder the Perfect Union so much desired.

It is said That this perfect Union cannot be done presently, but must be wrought by tyme, and further occasion. I thinck f. 251] otherwise, for if the Scottish Nation have that sincere Minde to come to us, as wee doe towards them, it may as speedily be done by renewing, and enlargeing the Scottish Commission, in such Sorte as was yestersay spoken; And this will be done in tyme convenient, before the Points of Hostile Lawes, and Commerce yet undecided, be determined and setled; And in any other Course wee shall never Compasse the perfect Union, for if they may enioy all Benefitts here, and remove the Profitts of this Place and themselves in Scotland, they will never be in Court, nor neare here about, the charge and Subiection being much greater in this Kingdome then there. Againe, wee ought to be the more carefull, for that wee may make a Law, which wee can never undoe, but the Scottish Nation is not tied to a Negative Voice, but may doe and undoe at the Pleasure of the Parliament without the King;[1] So as if wee have not a perfect Union, they of Scotland will stand able to enioy what they have taken, but not bound to yeild either Profitt or Obedience further then themselves from tyme to tyme shall please. I doubt not but if his Majesty did understand our great desire of this perfect Union, he would not mislike it. To conclude, I would not admitt a Conference with the Lords, before that among our Selves wee have debated the Point of Conveniency.

Lastly, I could wish That this House would thinck upon some Course to make knowen to his Majesty how much wee desire this perfect Union.

Sir Francis Bacon.[2]

In my desire, I doe wish a perfect Union, for that would be an unfallible Argument that wee shall never sever; Againe *Dulce Iugum ubi tractus non est impar;* And if our Subiection be heavie, their Libertie is certainly dangerous; and this Union is not Impossible, for there is great Correspondency already betweene Our Lawes and theirs, for the radicall Lawes are all one, only

[1] This was untrue. See p. 252.
[2] See this speech as printed in Spedding, III, 335–341.

they have some Addition of Latine and French, viz: of the Civill
Law, and the French Customes; But this is not the tyme to worke
this desired Union.   One observeth, That the Woman which in
the old Testament did represent the Church, had a Garment of
many Colors, but that Christs Garment was without Seame, so
as *sit in veste varietas, scissura ne sit,* difference may be in Lawes,
great Contrariety may not be. I thinck that before you have removed
the marke of a Stranger, you shall never bring in unity, for no
f. 252] Birde or Beast is taught any thing before you feede him.

Then he disputed the Conveniency of Naturalization of the
Ante, and Post Nati, with distinction, *vid:* In severall Degrees;
And said he, where men are to be naturalized by the Pole, it is more
fit to naturalize with favour the man growen, then the Infant; But
not soe in the naturalizing of a Nation; And in the latter wee may
see how much the Astrologers respect the tyme of Birth, for by
that they gather the disposition and fortune of the Partie.   It is
one thing to be a friend, or Subiect, and an other thing never to
have bene other; and therefore if it were to denize, or naturalize
Aliens, I would not doubt but to perswade for to give more unto
the Flemings that never were our Enemies then to the Spainard,
that now are our friends, but lately were other: So to the Ante-
Nati, who never were but Subiect to our King, me thinketh
should more liberally be given, then to the Post Nati.

Sir John Crooke, and Dr. Swale from the Lords brought a Bill
to make the Lands of W. Cardinall subiect to pay 500£—heretofore decreed in the Court of Whitehall against him.   Which
Messengers being departed, the House bent themselves to the
busines before in dispute.

Sir Robert Wingfield

Thought it not fitt to speake of the Matter at this tyme, for
said he, The Question now is, whether wee shall give the Lords
a Conference, or not: And I think wee may conferr with their
Lordships, for in my conceite it will not hinder, nor impeach our
Opinion, whereof I still am, *vid:* That there is no difference
betweene the Ante and the Post Nati.

Sir Roger Owen

The natural Philosophers observe, That when Birds moult
their feathers, they are not well; Surely I finde diverse of our

Members absent; Wee have moulted even of them whom wee
imployed in our last Conference; A longe discourse he made,
shewing great reading, and touching the Matter, he concurred
with Sir Herbert Crofts, *vid:* To argue it here in open House;
And in Point of Conveniency said he, there is no difference
betweene the Ante-Nati and the Post Nati. St. Augustine borne
after Christ, wished he had bene *Ante Natus,* to have seene
f. 253] *Christum Incarnatum;* And doubt not but the Post Nati
of Scotland will wish they had bene borne *Ante,* to have seene
the Crowne set on the Kings Head. Our Union, and the Mysti-
call Unity differ, for in Ours there is *Unus,* but not *Unum,* for
the Kingdomes are severall, and the King one, but in the Mysti-
call there is *Unum,* but *non Unus;* for the Persons are distinct.
Growing out of one Speech into an other, he said, In France and
Spaine, when diverse Provinces and Kingdomes have come together, Commissions have gone forth to reconcile the Lawes, and
where a difference hath bene found (in the Case of France) it
hath bene ordered That the Lawes of Paris, and (in the Case
of Spaine) the Lawes of [*blank*] shall direct, and guide the Lawe;
from hence he shewed the necessity of reconciling the Scottish
Lawes to Ours: In which discourse, by passing through many
things, and reasons, with much Variety, he spake to this effect,
viz, The Iudges have affirmed the Lawe to be, that the Post
Nati are Naturalls; if that doe so stand, then repeale the Lawe
we cannot, if otherwise that our Opinions already conceived
against the Iudges be right, then declare the Law as is desired
we may not; And to conferr of this Point with the Lords, as I
take it, we ought;[1] My Councell is, That wee waite on his
Majesty, and to shew unto him our reasons why both in Law and
Conscience wee make the Ante, and Post Nati, all one.

MR. BROOKE

The Question is now no more, but whether we shall give the
Lords Conference, or not; To grant an absolute Conference, I
known not what to say; To denye I thinck it not good, rather I
wish to grant a Conference, and to leave it to the discretion of the
Committees, whether they will replye, or not. This Motion was
received with a General and Universall mislike.

---

[1] *Ought not* is meant.

Sir Anthony Cope

Thought good to answere, That the House being so small and empty, and the Feast of Easter neare, whereby it is likely, That some Adiournement will be of the Assembly, that therefore farther Conference and dealing in this Matter be deferred untill it shall please the Kings Majesty, that the House doe meete againe; And this Motion was well entertained Generally.

f. 254]   Mr. Attorney Generall,

The Question is, whether we shall give Conference to the Lords to dispute of the Ante or Post Nati with these two Cautions, viz, 1. That the Point of Right be not dealt with all. 2. That nothing that shall be spoken doe binde us.

1. He shewed (with reasons not very forcible to perswade) That without note, or touch of Inconstancy, wee may conferr as is desired.

2. That we ought so to conferr, for that otherwise, all this yeares Labour is lost, in Case wee departe, *Re infecta*. Therefore you may if you please (said he) allow Conference; at which if their Lordships shall propound newe things, as is likely they will, then may the Committees well require tyme of deliberation; But if otherwise their Lordships Propositions be such as the Committees shall conceive may be presently answered, then to use their Discretions.

Sir George Moore

That wee ought to conferr as is desired, but more with Variety of words and earnest Protestations (now growen too frequent) then with Argument or reasons not before used, or forceable to perswade.

Monday. 30. Martii. 1607

Sir John Higham,[1] moved the House, That their Lordships should be answered, That this House will consider of their Lordships Message touching Conference, and at out next meeting give them answer how wee will conferr.

---

[1] The Speaker had moved what answer should be given the Lords on the question of conference.

MR. ALFORD,

Our last Conference did breake of because wee would not conferr of the Ante and Post Nati severally and distinctly. Now
their Lordships move a Conference in the same Point and fashion:
Wee have heard no reason neither from the Lords, nor among
our selves to induce us to change our Mindes; It were therefore
Levity in us now to entertaine Conference in a Course Contrary
to our former Purpose: Afterwards, having amplified this Matter,
he concluded with him that spake last, viz, To returne word to
the Lords, that at our next meeting wee will give them answere.
f. 255] The Serieant of the House brought a Letter from his
Majesty[1] to the Speaker; The Effect whereof Mr. Speaker
delivered unto the House thus; His Majestyes Pleasure is to
speake with you before breaking up of this Assembly; And because he understandeth how empty the House is, and likely to
be fewer, his Highnesse Pleasure is, That no man departe before
you have attended him; Which he is pleased shall be to morrow
in the afternoone at 2. of the clock at the Court, and no farther
Proceedings in this busines which you have now in hande to be
had in the meane tyme.

MR. ALFORD,

Moved, That Sir Francis Bacon, and Mr. Recorder might be
appointed to take notes of the Proceeding before the King.
Others thought that not fitt, in regard that Mr. Speaker is to be
there present, who is fittest and proper to informe the House if
occasion be of any thing passed in his Presence.

Mr. Speaker,

Said, That Report is only to be made, when certaine Committees or Persons are present, but when the whole House is present, there ought to be no Reporte, for what should Reporte be
made to a man of that which himself heard.

Warrein and Wallers Councell[2] were called to the Barr; and
first the Councell of Waller who opposed the Bill for Sale of
Warreins Lands for Payment of five hundred and odd Pounds
decreed against him in Chancery, was heard.

---

[1] This letter was written by Salisbury. See *Hist. MSS Com. 3rd
Report*, App. (Phelips MSS), 281.

[2] See names in *C.J.* I, 1034.

Then for that Messengers from the Lords, Viz, Serieant Crooke and Dr. Hone were at the doore, the said Parties and their Councell were withdrawen: Which Messengers being then admitted brought a Bill from the Lords for Comfirmation of Certaine Lands to All-Soules Colledge in Oxenford; who being departed, the aforesaid Parties and their Councell were called in againe and heard; And afterwards the Bill was put to the Question, and passed.

On this Monday in the afternoone, I rode forth of Towne, so I was not with the rest of the House before his Majesty on Tuesday; But the Effect of his Majesties Speech was as I have received it by Tradition, and Reporte.

f. 256] On Tuesday In the afternoone the Commons came before the King in the great Chamber at Whitehall, at which tyme his Majesty used a long Speech[1] for furtherance of the Union, in such Imperfect Sorte as by the Lords was proposed, declaring That himself did affect and desire greatly Union Which is so much urged by the Commons, but that the same cannot be compassed on the Suddaine: Wherefore he persuaded That which is presently required, as an Inducement to the other. Then he shewed his owne Power in the Parliament of Scotland, to exceed his Power in this here; affirming That he hath there a Negative Voice as here; and that there, nothing may be handled in Parliament, but such Matters as be proposed within Twenty daies of the beginning, and delivered to an officer to whome it appertaines to receive the same, and who is to present the same unto the King, and then is it in the Kings Power to appointe which and what matters shall be dealt in, and such as he disalloweth are never so much as motioned. Lastly touching the League betweene Scotland and France; This I received by report to be the Effect of his Majesties long Speech, which it were needlesse here

See this Speech at large in Printe.

[1] The text of this speech is to be found in *C.J.* I, 357–363; McIlwain, *Political Works of James I*, 290–305; *Somers Tracts*, II, 117–132; *Parl. Hist.* I, 1099–1115; Lansd. MSS 513, ff. 16–41*v*. Part of it is in St. P. Dom. XXVII, 2. See descriptions in Wilson, *History of Great Britain* (1653), 37–41; *Cal. St. P. Venetian, 1603–1607*, 488; *Hist. MSS Com. Buccleuch MSS*, III, 115; *Ambassades*, II, 142, 164–169; M. de la Fontaine to M. de Puysieulx, April 1/11. Paris Transcripts. It was without doubt an excellent speech. See favorable comment in Gardiner, I, 337. After the King's speech, Parliament was adjourned until April 20.

to set downe at any more large, for that the same is in printe, and and of the more Credit because as Sir R. C.[1] told me on the 20. of Aprill the King commanded Sir F. B.[2] and Sir H. M.[3] Recorder of London (for that they had at the time of the Speech taken Notes) that therefore they should now set it downe, which they did accordingly upon their owne Notes and Collections of Mr. Fr. I.[4] and bring the same to his Majesty who perused and perfected[5] the said discourse, and gave Order for the printing of it.

20TH. APRILL. 1607.

The Commons House being by former direction and Commandement of his Majesty to reassemble; The Speaker here presented himself about 9. of the Clock, where diverse of the Commons (as were affirmed by One who seemed to have Counted the Persons present) to the Number of 53. or thereabouts, did appeare, and after an howers Silence, Mr. Speaker reported the State of the busines of the House, thus, viz.

Ten Generall Bills passed.
Private Bills passed Nyne.
In the hands of the Committees [blank].
Remaining ingrossed Bills, five.

f. 257] Bills once reade, Seaventeene.

Bills brought in by the Committees and nothing yet done in them, five.
Bills dashed, two.
Bills reiected at the second reading, fower.
The Tytles of all which Bills, he also reade.

---

[1] Sir Robert Cotton.
[2] Sir Francis Bacon.
[3] Sir Henry Montague.
[4] Probably Mr. Francis Crane, Clerk of the House of Lords.
[5] Salisbury wrote Lake on April 16 to report to James some news from the Continent: "Yet lett not this take any time from the worke of his speach wherein the speedy printing, after it is done, shall supply any other losse of time." St. P. Dom. XXVII, 9.
M. de la Fontaine writing to M. de Puysieulx seemed to think that the printing of this speech did more harm than good. May 1/11. Paris Transcripts.

Mr. Marten,

That wheras to morrow is by former Order appointed to reade the Bill for drayning of the Fenns, That at the Suite of One that followeth the busines, the House would be pleased to heare councell set forth the said Bill before the same should be reade, whereunto was answered, First That it is not likely that the reading of that Bill will hold to Morrow; Againe That Councel is seldome heard, but only where there is opposition to the Bill. Lastly, that before the Bill be reade, Councell by the Order of the House is not to be admitted.

21. Aprill. 1607.

When the House had set an hower and halfe, and determined to deale in no busines, not so much as to receive daies unto Committees,[1] there came from the Lords Serieant Crooke and Dr. Hone, who brought a Bill for the Confirmation etc. of all Lands, Tenements Rents etc. heretofore conveyed, assured, demised etc. to the City of London;[2] whereof when the Speaker had after the departure of the Messengers reade the Tytle, the House cryed away with it; Howbeit it pleased them to cease that Motion and to suffer it to stay.

27. Aprill. 1607.

The Bill for drayning of the Fenns in Cambridge Shire, the Isle of Ely, and other adioyning Countyes was secondly reade, and thereupon ruled, That by the Custome of the House, Matters of Importance are to be discussed openly in the House before the same be committed; and so was this Bill argued in the open House, and Ordered That Councell as well for the Bill as against it shall be heard in the House on Wednesday next, and in the meane tyme it was not committed.

---

[1] "The house was still so thin, and St. George's Feast drawing on, we advised to adjourn the court till Monday." *Hist. MSS Com. Buccleuch MSS*, III, 115. "Court adjourned by reason of the small number. (20 Apr.) (27 Apr)." Cott. MSS, Titus F IV, f. 99.

Days assigned to several committees, according to *C.J.*

[2] "To several Companies within the City of London, and to the Mayor and Commonality, and Citizens, of the City of London."

Sir Francis Barrington

Moved,[1] That the House would appointe a tyme to proceede in the great busines of the Union; Whereupon the House agreed to meete to morrow at 8. of the clock, and at 9. to enter into that busines; and ordered that the Speaker should cause all the Law-f. 258] yers of the House who are not now in the House to be then present, and all that are present to take Notice hereof.

28. Aprill. 1607.

Sir Edwyn Sandys[2] in a long learned Speech, said to this

---

[1] The Speaker had directed this motion to be made. He wrote to Salisbury: "After my attendance this morning upon your Lordship I overheard some speeches that passed between some gentlemen sitting behind me, whereof taking notice I took opportunity to approve the same, and thereupon there was a motion made by Sir Francis Barringham, from whose mouth I held the same not distasteful (both in respect of the time and his former declared inclination), the substance whereof was, that in respect of our long sitting, which had expended both our time and powers, that now we might descend into consideration of the great cause of the Union, before we intermeddled or dealt with any other cause whatsoever. Whereupon it is resolved and ordered that we shall tomorrow by 9 o'clock enter into debate thereof, omitting all other causes; wherein if there be aught that your Lordship shall think fit for his Majesty's service by me to be observed, I beseech your direction therein." April 29, 1607. Salisbury MSS.

[2] Sandys boldly moves for a union of the Parliaments and laws of the two countries. He wishes an act declaring the consent of both kingdoms in such a union and for commissioners to prepare it.

For his speech, see *C.J.* I, 1035–36; *Hist. MSS Com. Beaulieu MSS, Montagu Papers,* I, 50. This speech in the hand of Sir Robert Harley is among the Harley Papers belonging to the Duke of Portland.

"Sir Edw Sands 28 April 1607.

"He was rased by the kings speche wich was to him and may be to us a pathe to procead on.

"King divided his speche. Matter 1. perfect union. 2. somthinge for a preparatione. Manner. What preparatione fit to effect it.

"He devided the first part wiche is for a perfect union into 2 considerations.

"1. What is a perfect union.

"2. Wither the perfect union be more behouffull a consideration.

"A perfect union must be *unus rex unus Grex una Lex* and this followeth the simetry of man and cours of Natur whic[h] maketh one head, one body, one soull.

Effect; The King by a wise and learned Speech hath stirred us up
unto a Proceeding in the great Union, so long and so much already

"Then he considered what parts we had alredy attayned to. Wich was
the first.

"1a. *Unus Rex*. by the .2. royall stemmes in one hous.

"To this he proposed an obiection and answer to it. 2 fold.

"Obiection. This union is but in the person of his Maiesty and may
deterrior in his issue. So did that of H. 8. in England and that of Hen.-2.
for the hous of Valois in Franc.

"Answer 2. 1. Kings promis the Lin of Scotland to Follow England.
2. Common fatte to all kingdoms and therfor to be born withall.

"2a. *Unus Grex*.

"This he described to be a uniform concurrance in one and the sam
principall Action wich is (making lawes for Goverment) and this must
be by making us on[e] parlament.

"His Resolve out of this was that kings goverment by law was only
in his one person.

"Making of Lawes ar communicated to the people in all iust gover-
ments.

"3. *Una Lex*.

"This he maketh the Naturall work of the former .2. for on[e] Law
cannot be but by on[e] people and Effects cannot be wher the necessary
causes ar away.

"He[re?] he labored but but very much perplexedly to prove that
thought ther wer on[e] and the sam Law in generall, yett it wer two in
the Individuall, respective to the severall Countres. His Example was
that if James the first had planted all English Lawes ther and abrogated
the rest yett wear not the[y] and we all under on[e] Law under on[e]
parlament on[e] Jug on[e] Chancelor one Seall. And the defect of som
of thes wilbe in the imperfect union a mayme to the exicution of Justic
in ether kingdom respectivly.

"Her he fell uppon 2 Consideration or Advises.

"1. To co[n]sider what Lawes mor fitt to be alyk in this union wherin
he agreed the Criminal Lawes only for somtims Civill or Customa[r]y
ar divers in the best united Stattes.

"2. Out of the kings Spech to revew our lawes and reduc them in
regard of the people to mor order and certinty. Wherin in a digression
he collected that the heavy hand of god in thes latt plages, inundasions
ship wracks, and wrongs to us by our Lat reconciled Neighbours was to
punish us for not giving a certen Law unto the people.

"And thus far he proceded to perswad a perfect union only.

"2a. Part wether behooffull to hav a perfect union.

"3 reason to shew it. 1. King desiereth it by his speech. 2. Lords by ther
Eloquent orations much in commendation of union wich cannot hav ther
end but in the perfect union. 3. Our desier signified by two messages sent
by him to the Lords wich he insisted uppon for .2. reason.

debated here among us: And therein his Majesty did deliver his desire in two Parts, viz. 1. The Matter. 2. The Manner.

"Reason. 1. Impossibilyty to govern with out this union and this agreed with the kings spech. 2. Behoufful to both Nations. 1. Strenght. 2. Eas of Burdens.

"1a. Strenght. For the[y] ar inlarged by ours as we by thers. And althought Greatest kingdom ar not allwayes best yett by reason of our now great Neighbours mor necessary.

"Her he reiected as no reason that of shutting the back dorrs for this wear shutt long befor this when we left our right in Franc by the Sword and wore it only in our title.

"2a. Eas of Burdens. Many hands mak light worke.

"Perticular reason why beneficiall to the Scotts this perfect. 1a. Gayn by being united to a rich Nation. 2a. Avoyding the danger of being a province.

"Arguments of disadvantag by them allegged and answered. 1a. By this union the[y] shalbe but the Northern part of our kingdom. Resp. So we but the souther part of thers and this is the faut of Natur and not of the union wich we could wish now otherwis for the mor Equalyty. 2a. This will tranfer from Scotland the seat of the kingdom. Resp. 1a. This will fall out no worse in the perfect then in the imperfect union. 2a. I may say with Bisshop Islip in his *Speculum regis* that in the tim of H. 3. the person of the king was lyk a good Angell, But sinc purveanc cam it hath not ben so. *Procull a Iove procull a Fulmine.* I mean of the purveors.

"Discommodityes we shall receav by the perfect union ar not to be helped by us nor the Scotts to be blamed for them but Natur.

"Conclusion of this 2. part was with .3. commendations of the perfect Union abov the Imperfect.

"1a. Facility. Not trobeling us with post or antenati, French Alianc. Leaviing of Burdens provisions reservations, restriction of Commerc and Ministeriall goverment for it is not fitt in any union New men should com to be governor etc.

"2a. Possibility of Redress. If any thinge shall be amiss. For this Act of the Imperfect union is in Natur of a Leage, not admitting alteration but by consent of both partyes. And I pray god our gayn by leages be not fatall to us.

"3a. No precedent of the imperfect Except that of Franc and Scotland but many of the other.

"His conclusion of this part that the perfect union is with les troble and with mor benifit.

"2a. Part of the Matter.

"The preparation his Ma[jes]ty desired was in 2 respects 1. To have a progression. 2. To avoyd disreputation.

"Our Satisfaction to him may be to the 1a. To procead to abrogatt Hostill laws and therin to giv reputation to the Instrument. 2a. To pass now an Act to authoric commissioners to prepare matter for a perfect

The Matter, he declared to be a Perfect Union.

The Manner, That we should at this Session frame Ourselves to a Preparation for it.[1]

And to these two Points will I frame my Speech.

And first it is necessary to shew what the Perfect Union is. Then how wee shall prepare Our Selves for it in this tyme.

Therefore as the King termeth it, the perfect Union is, That there be *Unus Rex, Unus Grex, Una Lex.* And better it cannot be expressed; So as it is truly said, A divine Sentence shall be in the Mouth of the King.[2] Now let us consider what parte of this Union we have already obtained, and what is yet behind.

The first Branch which is *Unus Rex*, we have already. I will yet mention one obiection which perhaps as yet remaineth a Doubt in some Mens Mindes, and then I will cleere it: And that is, that this first Branch *Unus Rex*, is only in the Person of the King and of his Posterity, but may end by Possibility, as we see the plentifull Issue of H. 8. here in England, and of H. 2. in France have both fayled. But this I cleere, first upon the Kings Promise who hath said, That he will take Order That if his Issue fayle, yet the Crowne of Scotland shall ever follow the Crowne of England; But if this be not, yet we are but Subiect to the Universall State and Case of all Mortall things, Change.

The 2d. Parte of this Union is *Unus Grex;* This is not yet with us, for it is not *Unus Grex*, untill the whole doe ioyne in makeing

---

Union. For that being effected Commerc and Naturalising ar necessaryly · consequent. And this is answerable to the cours of the world wher Duty must precead and rewards succead. But if ther be a necessity layd to procead further in this imperfect work I wish it to be bounded to years in wich tim the perfect may be accomplished. And under Condition that if the Scottish Nation shall oppos it that then the former shall stand voyd.

"2a. Of the kings division wich was what preparation fitt. Respon. He wished that reasons for the perfect Union and the Facility ther of might be collected and Humbly presented to his Ma[jes]ty.

"Sr. Ed. Sand." Harley Papers.

M. de la Boderie wrote: "Chacon croyoit que ce que ledit Roi avoit dernierement dit a ceux de la maison basse [on March 31], dut les avoir fort amollis. Depuis qu'ils se sont rassembles, l'on a vu tout le contraire, car il y en a eu qui ont parle plus hautement que jamais." May 5/15, 1607. *Ambassades,* II, 223.

[1] By passing the measures before the House.

[2] Prov. 16: 10.

Lawes to governe the whole; for it is fitt and iust, that every man doe ioyne in makeing that which shall binde and governe him; and because every man cannot be personaly present, therefore a Representative body is made to performe that Service.

The third Branch of this Perfect Union is, *Una Lex.* Which also is not yet betweene us: For untill there be one Parliament there cannot be One Law: And being One Parliament, in tyme there f. 259] will be One Law: Yea, in the meane tyme, though Scotland would give up their Lawes and take Ours, yet it were not one Law, but the like: Not one Individual law though One in Kinde; Therefore One Parliament is necessary: For though they that have the same Lawes, yet if One Greate Seale be not currant in both Places, One Chancellor and Officer to send to both, whereby a Scottishman wronging a Subiect here, and flying thither may be sent for, it is no Law. And now were it good for us, as the King wished, to take opportunity to reviewe Our Law, for whatsoever is the Cause, the Lawes are not in so high Reputation as heretofore; Let us therefore reviewe them, and make One Parliament.

The next Point is, Whither this perfect Union be behoofefull and desirable: And sure desirable it is, for his Majesty hath shewed his desire, the Lords theirs, the Commissioners of both Kingdomes theirs, and wee our desire, Yea, myself from this House twice delivered your mindes herein to the Lords, and I protest, I speake my owne hearts desire, and upon the same Protestation I doe not know any man that hath spoken in that Course, but spake as he thought. And here it is not amisse to reviewe the reasons that may move this perfect Union. And First, To the King it is more behoofefull, for he shall more easily govern both Kingdomes when they are united and subiect to One Lawe, then being under Severall Lawes.

To both Nations it is behoofefull, first in regard of Strength, for thereby we shall be encreased by the accesse of Scotland, and Scotland encreased by our Accesse. And albeit I am not of opinion that the greatest Kingdomes are generally the happiest, yet now for as much as our Neighbour Countries are so growne, I thincke it fitt for us to be so also. And I doe not hold the shutting of the backe Doore to be any reason to encrease the good which cometh to us by the accesse of Scotland; For I understand that thereby is meant the takeing of the Scottish aide and assistance from

France, for now wee have no question with France as anciently wee had, when our Kings claymed some parte, Yea all that Kingdome as their Inheritance.

To this reason of Strength, I will add a Second, which is, Ease of burdens; For when two Nations ioyne in charge, the same will be more easy, and so must Scotland ioyne with us when the same Lawe and Authority doth rule them, and us.

To the Scottish Nation in particular it will be behooffull, for thereby they shall be benefited by participating with us all Manner of Preferment.

f. 260] It may be obiected That it will be preiudiciall to the Scottish Nation for that they shall be but a Northerne Parte of Our Kingdome, who are now a Kingdome of themselves. That is herein satisfied, That wee shall be but a Southerne Parte of their Kingdome.

An other disadvantage to Scotland may be pretended in this, That here will be the Residence of the King. To that may be answered, That so it will also be in the Imperfect Union. And further, I may remember what in a written Treatise[1] directed by the learned Arch Bishop Islip to the King, was said, when he diswayded the King from using Purveyors and Purveyance, viz, That whereas the Presence of the King is a Comfort to the People, now saith he of late by the Grievance of these wicked Instruments the Purveyors, your accesse is to every place dolefull and heavy: So with the Kings Presence immediatly doe follow many Burdens and Grievances.

To returne to the Point, The perfect Union is more easy to be effected then the Imperfect, and so shall wee not neede to treate of Ante and Post Nati, nor of Restrictions, nor to be troubled with assurance of Performance.

A Second Commendation is Possibility of Redresse of Errors.[2]

A third is of Presidents; For of this perfect Union the Presidents are Infinite, but of the Imperfect, for my Parte I remember none but the Combination betweene France and Scotland.

To conclude this second Point, I thinck this perfect Union more behoofefull, then the Imperfect.

The third and last Point, is Preparation to this perfect Union,

---

[1] *Speculum regis Edwardi.* See *D.N.B.* under Simon Islip.
[2] By a common Parliament.

and this is that whereunto the King inciteth us, and it is fitt first that some what be done; And next, That Nations about us doe not despise Our Proceedings.

And I thinck That both Points may be satisfied: And first is to be considered with respect to the Instrument: And therein first the abolishing of Hostile Lawes, wherein it will be no disreputation unto the Commissioners to amende that which they by mistakeing of the Lawe in some Pointes, have done amisse.

The second matter is Commerce; This is a Benefitt, and ought not to preceede Dutie: Howbeit upon hope of the Scottish yielding to our Lawes which maketh the perfect Union, I could willingly move, That in some Sorte it doe preceede, namely in this Sorte, That wee grant it to them for a time, the grant to f. 261] stand, or else to cease: And againe a Punishment upon the Scottish if in the meane tyme they misdoe; And a Commission to certaine selected Persons to treate with the like Persons of the Scottish Nation for effecting of this perfect Union.

Mr. Speaker standing up, desired to be licensed to speake, and then declared That this Proiect now offered is new not heretofore moved, either in the House, nor at any Committee, which said he, I take to be the Cause of the Present Silence, I must leave it to your Considerations, whether you will deliberate hereupon untill to morrow, or now to dispute of those Matters which have already beene dealt in.

Sir Tho[mas] Holcroft.[1]

Moved, That the House would proceede where they last left before Easter, viz. To dispute and resolve, whether they will have Conference with the Lords touching Naturalization in Generall, or what distinction betweene the Ante Nati and Post Nati.

Mr. Speaker reade the last Message from the Lords to the Purpose moved by Sir Tho[mas] Holcroft, and the Answere, which was, That the House would enter into Consideration thereof among themselves, and then returne their Answer.

Sir Herbert Croft.

It is Mr. Speaker as you have remembred, but with this Addi-

---

[1] For the following debate, cf. *C.J.* I, 1036.

tion, That wee did enter into Consideration of the Matter, and having begun therein, yourself stood up and signified the Kings Pleasure, that wee should forbeare to doe any thing further, therein before we had attended and waited on his Majesty. Now Sir You tell us That the Motion or Proiect offered by the Gentleman that first spake is new, and therefore you wished it should be advised upon, and not dealt with presently; Sir I am not in this, of your opinion, for alwayes, as from tyme to tyme wee have found rubbs by difficulties, so still wee have had recourse unto wishing and devising how this Generall and perfect Union might be compassed; Therefore I think the Proiect offered by the first Gentleman for a perfect Union, to be good, and I could wish That the King might cleerely understand our desires and Mindes, namely how much wee are stalled with the Imperfect Union, and how much wee desire the perfect Union; And likewise our Desire f. 262] to take a Course presently to further it, without any minde to use this as any diversion of doeing somewhat in the Imperfect, which to my understanding is not a Steppe but a hinderance to the perfect: And therefore I doe wish Mr. Speaker, that your Self as our mouth should deliver our desires and our reasons unto his Majesty, and the same to be prepared to your hande by a selected Committee. I doubt not but the Scottish doe desire the Imperfect Union, thereby to enioy Benefitts with us, which when they have perhapps will be backwards in the Perfect.

And seeing our last dispute was broken off by the Kings command, I could wish that his Majesty should understand our desire to doe somewhat towards the perfect Union as he desireth, and hath incited us: That wee think the Course we were in of the Imperfect, will hinder it; And our devise, or Proiect such as was offered by the first Gentleman, to doe somewhat towards the perfect in such Sorte as before I moved.

Sir George Moore.[1]

Moved, To conferr with the Lords, only to heare what reasons they can give us to change our Mindes in treating Generally of the Ante and Post Nati together.

Sir Henry Poole, went with Sir Herbert Crofts; And so this

---

[1] "Sir George Moore: The imperfect no Impediment to the perfect." *C.J.* I, 1036.

dispute upon the Speakers Motion, (the tyme being spent) was put over untill to morrow.

29. APRILL. 1607.

SIR ROBERT WINGFIELD.[1]

Moved, That by 3. Bills, one for abolishing Hostile Lawes; The 2d. for Commerce; The 3d. for Naturalization and Restrictions, Entrance be made towards the great Union, untill the perfect doe come. Yet he concluded That he wished a Conference with the Lords about the 3d. Point, viz: Naturalization.

MR. FULLER.[2]

First, he commended Sir Edwyn Sandys his Motion yesterday made, allowing his difference, That it is not enough to have the

---

[1] "S. R. Wingfild. Many hars a fott hindereth sport or a fresh har· 4. matters yesterday proposed. 1. great union. 2. imperfect. 3. Resons to be collected. 4. conferenc with the Lord[s].

"1. He approved the sam but no fitt tim to consider it.

"2. Imperfect. Entrance or Satisfaction. Hostill law. comerce. Offices etc. No hindrance to the great union if in a mesure.

"This imperfet fitt to be now treated on but by bill better the[n] conference ether generall or secret.

"3. Reasons. Lyketh the proponder but not the proposition. Reason is because his maiesty knoweth all the reasons alredy.

"4. Conference. King plasur by messag not to proced not at all but for a time and therfor we may procead." Harley Papers. For this and following speeches, cf. *C.J.* I, 1037.

[2] "Mr. Fuller. All wish a good end. A good plot laid yesterday. He moved.

"A union must be one court.

"*Unum unitum* distinct Con[di]tions[?].

"Not lawes one but law making all one.

"If community of Benefitt then charg of law.

"Alyk in subsedy but by parlament wich they may deny if severall.

"If *unum* cannot be then preparations.

"Consider lese preparations be not Hinderanc wich may of both sids.

"Re[asons].

"Resons on the[ir] sid. Rights granted cannot be opinions to a perfect. The[y] mor fredom. Our welth and the[ir] fredom maketh them better then our laws.

"[Reasons on] our sid. Not in favor but in hatt if it draw away the hart[?]. Ordnanc of god to live by labor. If any by gift or favor goe

like Lawes, except the Lawes be made in One and the same Parliament, and that he proved by the difference of *Unum, a Unitum,*

beyond, his fellow will make his rom better then his company. Therfor the[y] to liv by thers we by ours.

"Ther liberty of Commerc in the North. All trad of Northern Curssys at depe by reason of libertys under ratt[?].

"London great Custom Subsidys yett subiect to purveanc borne, etc. Scott[s] not to the latter if the first. Therfor the[y] cannot com to the Markett in equall degree. This makes a hart burning.

"We lyk in the Surkett when lawiers goe in equall degrees.

"2 arms to one head the right learn his own offic etc. True *unus* bredeth love.

"Benifitts to them only. Thes 4 years no English to any offic ther. Her the other way led to welth mariag offic. If the gayn holly thers lett ther law procead.

"The[y] will say our hast in our law with Franc was to hasty. To this we may say ther caus may be with us[?] in to much hast.

"Union fit in Somthing as Hostill lawes.

"Therfor a law ether from us or the lords.

"For conference. Not fitt he thinketh for 2 reasons. 1. The end wither we can make a lawe secuer wich we cannot for if the[y] hold the postnati be as they hold what law can we mak. Ether we tak from them or wrong the prerogative. Then if purveanc cannot bind the prerogative then what will the Jugges say in this.

"Settell the law that they ar not and then what we doe we doe of grac and favor.

"No disgrac to Jugges for Juges ar for law not for statt so fitt.

"*Amicus plato sum Socrates sed maxime patria.*

"Therfor he wisheth a selected compan[y] to gather reasons to win the Jugges.

"Not fitt to lett reason rest uppon memory but to be wrighten for [*word illegible*].

"Good ground if sett down to iustify[?] our actions.

"Ob. The king may doe it by his prerogative.

"Ans. The king may parden felonys yett not so much to mak the statt[?] a denn of thevs.

"Honor to strangers but not so to hurt the statt.

"The king will not doe.

"He thinketh that denisens cann by [no] wright sit in parlament for so so many may be admited as will o[*blank*]. So as the king cannot giv awa[y] the part so not the wright to the Subiect.

"He then adviseth to proced to Hostill laws.

"For Commerce to hav a committy.

"And for Naturalising to draw in wrighting our reason[s]." Harley Papers.

heretofore used in this House by a learned Civilian: For it is *Unitum* if they have our Lawes, but not *Unum* except the same Court make Lawes for them and us. Then the Question is, What f. 263] and How the Preparation shall be to this *Unum*, this perfect Union. I thinck, said he, it must not be such as hath been moved by some, For if wee give them great Priviledges it will hinder on both Sides: First, They having already of their owne Greater Free-domes then wee have, when they shall have also such, as wee grant them alsoe, then having both they will never come nearer to us: Likewise on our Side it will hinder, for when One man doth gaine but Equality with an other, and both live upon indifferent termes all goeth well on: But if one Person by extraordinary favour or otherwise, over gaine or eate out his Fellow, the other how good soever his disposition be, will repine and be discontented; It hath been in this place already proved, That the Scottish Nation with such Priviledges as they have now, have gotten all the Trade of Roan for Kersyes:[1] In my calling, if One Practiser doe by favour, or Gifts, or other meanes, get all the doeings at the As-sises, though he be a man otherwise without offence, yet for this Cause, the rest had rather have his place then his Company.

There is Benefitt say some by this Union; It is true, but the whole Benefitt is to the other Side; For I doe not heare of any English preferred there; Therefore the Profitt is theirs; Let them first make their Law for this Union, and let not us begin; If they say, That in such Course they were overtaken in their Act of Con-federation with France, and therefore the burnt Childe dreadeth fier, then wee may well say, *Felix quem faciunt aliena Pericula Cautum.* Yet let us doe somewhat, let us make a Lawe forthwith to abolish Hostile Lawes, and this not by Conference, but by Bill; For Conference is not the way, for wee are not to conferr on the Conveniency of that, for which we cannot make a Law that may be firme or good: For so long as the Lords hold the Naturali-zation of the Post Nati, wee can make no Law to be good; For as wee find Conveniency, wee must take somewhat from the Post Nati, which is their Right, Yea, and from the King parte of that which he claimeth as his Prerogative: And what will then follow, marry when the Parliament is done, the Iudges that heretofore

---

[1] "The trade at Diepe wholly in their Hands." *C.J.* I, 1037.

told us, that the Lawes made upon so good ground touching
Purveyors can not bind the Prerogative; will they not also tell
us That our Law for restrictions will not binde the Prerogative?

But say some, the most of this which is required, the King may
doe of himself? That I say wee are not to argue, neither is it
f. 264] materiall. Wee Know that the King may pardon Felony
etc. The King may make a denizen, but not to sitt here; But yet
the King wee must thinck will not pardon all, nor so many Felons
as that the Kingdome may swarme with Thieves, nor bring in so
many Strangers as that this Country may by them be overrunn.

Touching the abolishing of Hostile Lawes and Commerce, if it
be thought good to doe any thing, let it be by Bill, but let us
first conferr touching such a Bill.

Touching Naturalization, let certaine Persons selected be appointed to collect the reasons of our Iudgement, and deliver the
same unto the Clerke, That from thence perpetually a reason
may be given of our doeings to posterity touching the Proiect of
Sir Edwyn Sandys concerning this perfect Union.

Mr. Marten.[1]

The King may make any Man denizen and plante him, if the
Countrey will choose him, in this place. The Proiect offered
yesterday is not to be entertayned, for it cannot take good Effect
etc. No doubt but the granting of Priviledges will allure the Scottish Nation to come to this perfect Union; For otherwise if they

----

[1] "Mr. Marten. Question now wither proced for a conference with
the Lords or for a messag to the king for a perfect union with our reasons.

"Mr. Fuller will have a union and the[y] no union and then a union.
For a perfect union then not for commerc and then for Hostill laws.

"To desier what cannot be had is no procedenc. Lett us proced to a
beginning. Hostill laws ar determ[in]ing in the kings. Move must be to
mak a union wich must be participation of benifitts in a degree. Therfor
some statt of Commerc yett not to have it by ther privileges to our
preiudic.

"Temple not bilded by david thoug his desire. But it had a beginning.

"Mr. Fuller obiecter. Security. His reason that purveanc could not
be by the Jugges be bound.

"Reason. Such provi[s]ions may be to inable them to tak benifitt conditionall and we may restraine the king.

"The king may doe. But for the obiection of Felons or Trad the cass
is not all one. For to give to them places wher he was born is no un-

come not to it, they are likely in tyme to become a Province, which is more heavie then any Commoditie to be granted them can countervayle.

MR. ALLFORD.[1]

The great difficulties which will incurre when wee shall fall into the Consideration of Restrictions to be annexed unto the perfect[2] Union, was, as I take it, the reason of the new Motion yesterday concerning the perfect Union. And this Union I wish and like of the Proiect; For although by Union wee shall reape no Profitt, nor have no *Quid Pro quo*, yet if they come to our Lawes, they become our selves, and wee give to men of our selves, which will be an Answer to the Countrey and Satisfaction to our Consciences.

SIR FRAN[CIS] BACON.[3]

In abolishing of Hostile Lawes, and in a Generall Union wee all agree, and it hath been said That by these two, our Reputation is

---

reasonable thing. Then it is best to confer to some that wiche we may doe for our go[o]d.

"Proposition proposed unseasonable and may bred to us loss and increase them and us hart burning.

"To mak Scotland a provinc is not to be contervaled by any benifitt the[y] receave wich must be untill the perfect union. And therfor the[y] will desire it." Harley Papers. Cf. *C.J.* I, 1037.

[1] "Mr. Alford. The cause that moved the proposition yesterday is the many restraintes cautions etc. etc. and to offer distastfull cautions to a princ is ill. Wich by reason of our answer we must doe.

"To tak away benifitts when the[y] hav tasted is bitter.

"When under our law we giv not benifitts to strangers but to our own pepell.

"Nothing can gett love better then to admitt them to be as our selves.

"So no temporary union but the perfect." Harley Papers.

[2] *Imperfect* is meant.

[3] "S[ir] Fra. Bacon. No elaborat Speches in term from lawiers.

"Full consent but a differnc uppon the conveanc.

"Hostill lawe. One people *unus grex.* Approvd to of all parts.

"2. Perfect union with preparation or subseque[n]c.

"Ob. If benifits granted then we give a way the adamant.

"Res. If we granted all it wer so but we mean to qualify all.

"Man but forbidden one tree desier it as much as all.

"Tree of Honor in the midst of the garden withholden will draw.

"Som reservation may be until the perfect union.

"I fear not *amycus dicitur qui non admittitur hospes.*

saved, in that wee have herein granted much: It is well moved,
but it holdeth not, for hereby wee shall but Kill dead Lawes, and
begin in a new Course of a perfect Union by new Commissions,
and so doe no more in the first, then is already done; and by
f. 265] the 2d. loose a Parliament of 4. yeares past, whereof one
yeare hath bene spent in Sessions: I doubt the Interim, for in
the meane tyme whilst this new Commission is in hand, and Execution, if wee looke not on them, France and Spaine, will looke
and worke on them, and so wee shall be further off hereafter from
the perfect Union then now we are.

Likewise for Commerce the State now standeth at the worst,
as the Law now is, for if by Port Cocket, commodities passe
into Scotland, and from thence into other Parts, then shall the
Scottish Merchants be able beyond Sea by reason of the small
Custome in Scotland, and Priviledges there, especially in France,

---

"Proposition yesterday to proced to hostill law and a commission.

"Resp. On[e] to litle the other to far for shall all this tim be spent to
repele a dead law or renew a commission.

"Incorporation the work of age and not so sudden.

"Som Stepp for *non progredi est regredi.*

"Naturallis[e].

"This taketh away the mark of strangers. For thoug we look not
uppon them so yett Franc may and Spa[in].

"For Commerce it is infinet wich to us disadvantagous.

"No remidy for transporting our commoditys under collor to ports
frenc[h] por[tuguese].

"Corne to Spayn may be no law aga[in]st.

"So Coyne and Bullion.

"Privilges of Franc to them an[d] until we doe somthinge is hevy
uppon us.

"Prerogative may be bond.

"In purveanc is the binding of the King.

"In this the capacity of the subiect for the king cannot giv to him but
to him as he may tak.

"This was but a digression and as in Poetts the best part of the workes
so was that of lawe reveuing.

"Lawes revuing under the decemvir.

"So by Solon.

"So by Justinian. So by Alpho[n]so in Spayn. So almost in Ed. 1.
for when lawes goe a ded the[y] grow to a Chaos.

"The king shewed the way when he stirred the watter with his stepps.

"Adviseth to fall to digesting of some bills." Harley Papers.

to sell better then others, of which will follow that which wee feare, and partly feele, the decaye of our Merchants.

Touching the Security, I mistrust it not, for wee are not now to binde the Prerogative; but to disable the Subiect, for the King can grant no otherwise then the other can take.

This new devise of a new Commission to treate of a perfect Union, is but *Digressio*, so is that of refining Lawes, and yet I think it spoken *Ex Candore Animi*, and to shew much Arte.

And touching reviewing of Lawes, the like hath bene in diverse Countries, and in Manner here in the tyme of E. I. for from him wee had most of our Fundamentall Lawes: So I wish wee may leave this Digression, and fall to our busines by Bills or otherwise, and beate the wind no more.

Sir Roger Owen.[1]

No Obiection yet why wee should not proceede in the Proiect of the Generall Union, if the Proposition be understood. It is the Intention of the King to come to the perfect Union, so it is

---

[1] "Sir Ro. Owen. Mantayneth the proposition of the generall union. Nether if understood ther can be any obiection.

"1. Intention of his Ma[jes]ty.

"2. Intention of us not by aversion. No new question.

"3. Then answer of Obiections.

"1. By his speche printed and not the so devid[ed?] union. The king pesse *faciam eos in Gentem unam. Henricus Rosas regna Jacobus.* A golden sentenc to that purpose.

"2. Our offer[?] may by for divertion new matter and if we divert away the golden work *faciam eos in gentem unam.*

"Wishes transparant smile of Jubiter make a man. *Mell in ore mell in corde.*

"Propounded anciently to be subject to our lawes or religion. So the matter ancient but the manner herin by conference or otherwise.

"3. Instrumentall union. No imperfect union offered but Scotland. Resp. That is not so for the[y] ar *regnicoli* recipricall. So long as the[y] wer under franc.

"2. Ob. Disgrace to the lords. Resp. The[y] did it uppon a resolution of Jugges of the post nati. Nether the[y] loss the[ir] labor by the Hostell lawes. And the provisions will serve for the perfect union.

"3. Not possible. Respon. It is feacable. Lett any may [*man* is meant] put in a grund against the perfect that is not mor in the perticuler than I will yeld.

"Owing money from out of Scotland to obey law no parlam[en]t[ar]y Com[m]iss[ion] can help.

Ours. That it is the Kings Intention, it appeareth by his Speech printed, and if we put our hand in our purse, and can feele a 20s–Peece of Gold, wee may reade on it, *Faciamus eos in Gentem Unam;* And upon the xs–peece, *Henricus Rosas coniunxit, Regna Iacobus*: Therefore I think the Gentleman spake in this Kind did not use Aversion, nor diversion.

The Matter yesterday proposed is not new here, for it hath beene often moved That they come to our Lawes. Now the Question is, whether wee shall proceede with the Instrumentall Union, or with the perfect Union: And I thinke That this Imperfect and Instrumentall Union is not to be proceeded in. I say as before I have said, That in all the world is never found any such Imperfect Union; And although some say, Yes One, viz: betweene Scotland f. 266] and France, yet I say that was Generall and Perfect.

An other Obiection is the Reputation of the Lords which offered this Instrumentall Union; I say to them, it is no disreputation, for the Proceeding and offer was upon the Iudges Opinion touching the Post nati. Neither shall these Lords and Commissioners loose their Labour, for the Hostile Lawes shall be abolished, and the Lords in the Instrument wherein they have handled the Imperfect Union, will serve for our direction in the perfect. It is Impossible say some, to worke so speedily this perfect Union, I say it is feisible, and therefore Let any that cometh after put any one Difficulty, or Inconvenience in this

---

"Fighting the Duelle we loss goods. Bind not the[m] her.

"4. Ob. Long a doing. Respon. A shorter lin will effect this. Respect the note *Brevissima extentio a puncto in punctum.*

"5. Ob. You may doe bothe. This to follow the other. Resp. If this may be as soon don it is a thing of popery to goe to saints wher we can go to christ.

"For the tre is paradice. Resp. If the[y] com into our garden will the[y] gather our weeds for so the[y] account our lawes.

"6. Ob. Why should not you be subiect to your lawes may the Scots say. Resp. Ther lawes ar not so fit for a monarchy wich is fittest for our pollyty and the[y] therby wilbe [*word illegible*].

"7. Ob. Carying away Coyn Corne. Resp. If the lawes now will not bind how will ther be new.

"England liethe better for trading into Spayn Corne.

"Therfor fitt to mak our reason to his Maiesty to pursue his desier for the perfect union. If we cannot satisfy them then lett the lords put in ther bills." Harley Papers.

perfect Union, which shall not be more in the Imperfect, for none that went before have done it. But I will shew you One in the Imperfect, viz: I sue a Scottish man to an Outlarie etc. and he goeth into Scotland etc. Againe an English man figtheth with a Scottish man here in England etc.

It may be obiected, That this perfect Union is a long worke? I answere, as little tyme will doe it as will worke the Imperfect; Ours is *Recta Linea*, therefore nearer then *Linea Curva*.

It may be asked why wee should not first doe the Imperfect to give the King content, and after have the other. In answere, It is no good Course to goe about, when we may goe the next way: And in truth, grant them the Imperfect, and they will never come to the other.

An other Obiection is, That if wee doe not now proceede touching the matter of Commerce, wee are at a Preiudice *Ut Supra*.

To this I say, as the Law now is, they cannot transport into Scotland by Port Cocket as hath been spoken off; And if the Law now in force will not tye them, then will not new Lawes hold them. As for transporting corne, if they carry it into Spaine, they must buy it here; and here the Money will staie. Againe, England lieth betweene Scotland and Spaine, and so our Merchants can best transport thether.

MR. RECORDER.[1]

The question is the Order of Proceeding, not the Matter, viz. Whether wee shall begin with the perfect Union, or the Imper-

---

[1] "Mr. Recorder. Order of the union not the matter. We must goe to the top by steps. We agre in the end perfection. It was proposed wither a precedent. In Aragon to Castill ther was a participation of benifits befor a union. Can a man in a day chang a statt of a commonwelth and mak a parl[ia]m[en]t. Is it as easy to doe this as to agre one point of commerc.

"If it wer only to give them benifitts I should wishe it but it is to restrayn them that the[y] may hav given them.

"For Hostilyty it is agreed.

"For Commerc we stand uppon much disadvantag. For so they by the privilges of Franc. etc. Restraining them the benifitts the[y] hav.

"If we lett this point of Commerc allon untill a perfect union we shall never recover the losse.

"Fram the bills and put in reservations and hear the speches then." Harley Papers.

fect? I think That unto great Matters wee come not but by stepps:
f. 267] It hath beene said, That in no Kingdome this Imperfect
hath begun, or proceeded; I am no State studied man, but I
thinke the Union of Arragon, and Castile began with Participation
of particular Benefitts. Wee are at an afterdeale touching Commerce, *Rebus Sic Stantibus*, as now they doe; Let us frame Bills
with Restrictions, and not expect the perfect Union.

Mr. Attorney Generall[1]

The Question is, whether wee shall proceede where wee were, or
take an other way, which for the present wee conceive to be the

---

[1] "Mr. Atturny Hubburt. Poynt now wither by the former stepps
or to take an other way.

"Perfect union preferd befor the unperfect no man doubteth.

"Perfect union desird is a consolidation of .2. kingdoms in one that
the[y] may so forever remayn.

"How we stand bond by our former proceding. For if we wer only by
the commissioners then the[y] wer but directeryes to us.

"But now we vary from our selves and not cross the commissioners
but our selves. *Ratione* that act that gave authoryty gave by intimation
order not to medell with fundamentall lawes. If we shall then intend the
alteration of thos then we vary from our selves. And if the[y] had had
as fre a commission the[y] would hav proceded to the perfect.

"Was this for .2. years sinc the commission this poynt of perfect was
never thought of in all thos conferences. Will it not argue levity in us.
Will it not giv the Scots suspicion of being deluded. And how strangers
will tak it we know not.

"You say the perfect is that the King desireth. So doe we. We speak
not against on an others desier but the means for it.

"*Faciam eos in gentem unam* it is in the Futur tenc. It is not presently
to be done.

"I say it is not [*now* is meant] impossible for if in .3. years we can not
attayn this litle how many 3 years to the holl.

"For Collecting reasons I lyk it not. My reason is we have not thoroughly debated any part of this union so then as it wer sequestring our
selves from the Lor[ds] hous to proced to a new thing.

"He thinketh a thing of Necessity that somthing be done now.

"Fredom of Commerc will bring gayn to them and we se if ther be
no order the[y] will trad as the[y] doe now to our great loss.

"And this law may give the king a fitt answer to ther Suttes to say
he is bound.

"To use some cautions in thes things to be granted to bind them to
admit the perfect he lyketh wel but to procead in the mean time." Harley
Papers.

better way. The perfect Union to be most desirable, no man doubeth, but whither this be the tyme and Course to seeke it as is proposed, is the doubt: And I thinke this is not now seasonable: Let us consider how wee stand bound by our former Proceedings; For if there were nothing to binde us but the Proceedings of the Commissioners, then that were to be controlled by them that gave the Authority; But I say wee shall crosse our selves if we take this new Course: For the same Act of the Parliament that gave the Commissioners Authority to prepare, though not in the body of the Act, yet in the Praeamble, it sheweth that the Fundamentall Lawes are not to be abolished: And upon that did the Commissioners proceede, for I thinke if you had given them that Power that now you offer to the new Commissioners, they would I am perswaded have willingly accepted it. This Commission was sped A?̊ 1604. and pursued by Conferences accordingly, albeit sometymes words have bene cast out to the effect now offered; But it worketh not Our Disreputation, yet it will give Iealousy to the Scottish Nation, that having done nothing these 3. yeares in the Imperfect Union, we will delude them in our new Proiect, and Forraigne Nations will hold it but a Stratageme to delude the Scotts, and doe nothing.

It is obiected That the King doth desire the Perfect Union; True, but He hath also shewed, That he doth not think it fitt to be done presently.

The word on the Kings Coyne is obiected; *Faciam Eos in Gentem Unam*, but you must consider, That *Faciam* is the Future Tense. f. 268] I think to alter our Course, will give no hope of campassing our desire; For if in these 3. yeares wee have done nothing in the Imperfect Union, surely in 3. tymes 3. yeares wee shall doe nothing in the perfect.

If wee shall take the new Course to begin with the Perfect Union, yet will it not be fitt so to doe by gathering reasons, and presenting them to the King; For hitherto we have done nothing, but by Conference with the Lords, and if now wee shall sever our Selves from them, we shall give the Occasion of discontent. Then he rann the former Course, to declare the Inconveniencies of Commerce in the Interim etc. and the like he affirmed of Naturalization.

Lastly, he moved, That wee might proceede with our former Course without dealing with any new Matter.

Mr. Speaker[1]

He remembred briefely the Speech of Sir Edwyn Sandys and Sir Herbert Croft, and Sir Roger Owen, *Vid*: That the reason of this new Proiect for a perfect Union should be collected and delivered to the King, to maintaine the Inclination of the House to that Generall Union. He shewed that that Course would crosse all our former Proceedings, and therefore moved to treate with the Lords in Prosecution of our former Course.

30. Aprill. 1607.
Sir Robert Wingfield

From the Committees brought into the House the Bill for the restraining and declaring the Iurisdiction of the Marshalsey, and for Reformation of abuses in that Court:[2] He shewed that the Bill had beene formerly committed, and for want of Lawyers upon a Motion the House recommitted; That this second Committee at which many Committees meet, and heard Councell of both Sides, did thinke good the Bill should sleepe, and a new Bill to be exhibited for Reformation of abuses, and therein the Iurisdiction of the Court not to be dealt with all.[3]

On the other Side it was informed, That the first Committee upon good deliberation, did think good to maintaine the Bill f. 260] for restraining and limiting the Iurisdiction of the Court; And for lack of tyme did not proceede to the Residue of the Bill which concerned Reformation of abuses, and that the Pro-

---

[1] "Mr. Speaker. The Motion now is for manner not Matter. The on[e] sid desire red a collection of reson to shew the king ther desire to procead to the perfect union. And if his maiesty be not herin satisfied then to proced to the other. The other sid taketh this proiect to cross commission our selves and our 2 years conferences. Wher of 2 hath recom[en]d[ed] a reparing to bills and the .3. we mad offer to deall with the Scotts as with our brethern. etc. Now wiche I leav to your consideration to procead in." Harley Papers.

[2] The provisions of the act are in Lansd. MSS 487, ff. 205v–206. All laws about the Marshalsea should be enforced; the Court should try certain cases only if both parties were of the King's House and other cases only if one party were of the King's House; officers exacting unlawful fees should be imprisoned and anyone imprisoned contrary to this act should receive treble damages.

[3] The committees objected to the act because it benefited lower courts rather than remedying the abuses. Lansd. MSS 487, ff. 206v–207.

ceedings of the first Committee was never reported to the House, and without their Privity was the Motion made for addition of more Committees, which was as seemeth done by some one of them, with further Purpose, and unorderly done. Lastly, That the Parties which follow the Bill, doe desire to be heard in the House by Councell, and there to have the Bill censured. Hereupon it was agreed, That the Proceedings of the first Committee ought not to have bene reported to the House, because they concluded nothing; Yet the Motion of an addition so made indirectly was not liked; And in Conclusion Satturday was appointed to heare Councell on both Sides in open House.[1]

It was agreed to stand with the Order of the House, That when any Member doth purpose or move any thing to the House, he is to have his Answer before any other Man move any other Matter.

MR. BROOKE.[2]

Commended the Motion of Sir Edwyn Sandys, but thought it unseasonable, insomuch as it was not moved sooner; And now

---

[1] Cf. *C.J.* I, 365, 1038. The Commons proceeded with the bill of which the committee disapproved and passed it. But it failed in the Lords in spite of a petition from the Commons (Harl. MSS 6803, f. 125*v*).

[2] "Mr. Brook. This day turn a wildernes into a gren feild.

"Against the proposition to present to the king the reason of the perfect.

"One parlament mak one law easily.

"Welth must goe into Scottland by trafeck and lands her[e] and then we cannot comand it unles by parlament in time of need.

"Not to follow the proiect now. Ob.

"If benifits befor lawes the[y] would not take [*word illegible*] but our reasons.

"Hinderanc of the perfect.

"A union of gold if we walk in the first.

"Comens with matter and after find an easier etc.

"No disgrace to alter.

"King knoweth all. etc. I lyk his speche not his reason because he is head of both.

"Secur the kings pleasure by his negative voyce and ther we must by our.

"2. reason to doe somwhat.

"1. Scotts commerce. The king hath not by pattent forgiven custom. But the[y] may transport as from port to port and so oppen that Custom.

"2. Jugges ar of oponion for the most part (butt one lyk Paphnutius

(quoth he) wee have spent so much tyme in an other Course; And the King who hath a Negative Voice, will not like it: Therefore somewhat is to be done for two Causes, the One alledged yesterday by a Gentleman,[1] the Other not yet touched: The first, the Inconvencience of the Interim unto Our Merchants in matter of Commerce, as things now stand: The 2d. the State of the Question betweene the Iudges and us. If wee doe nothing, it will be easy to trye the Naturalization of the Post Nati by course of Lawe,[2] and when some Iudgements shall be entered of Recorde, wee cannot encounter it with an Entrance here in the Clerkes Booke; Therefore some thing must be done and whether by Bills or Conferences is the doubt; And though I like better of Bills, yet I think as wee have hitherto proceeded in the former Points of Hostile Lawes, and Commerce, so wee should in this Point of Naturalization, by a Conference with the Lords.

MR. HOLT.[3]

f. 270] When I heard That new Proiect, I was much perplexed untill I heard the Obiections, and the Obiections confirmed me in allowing the Proiect.

---

but I fear he shall not as P. turn the holl consel). Jugges leav ther own opinions if the[y] try a postnati and leav 2 or 3 records of it. How shall we revert it. Not by our clarkes book. It is but an erthern pott to a brasen.

"Manner wither by Bills or conference.

"Not rip for Bills. Hostill lawes the wayse way. Commerc we have entred into and somwhat of the first part of Naturalization.

"Therfor to consider ether Bill or conference but I lyk the latter." Harley Papers. For this and following speeches, cf. *C.J.* I, 1038.

[1] Sir Francis Bacon.

[2] Exactly what happened. *State Trials*, II, 559.

[3] "Mr. Holt. No reson to reiect the last proiect. Perplext befor he hard the obiections. That confirmed him.

"Obiection 4 against the new proiect. 1. los of labor. 2. Disgrace. 3. Repugnant to our selves. 4. [*blank*].

"1. Labor hath bin generall for a union that we pursue and speciall for a perfect union.

"No loss if we had herby delivered us from many agrievances of lawe and stat. But we gayn by getting such a resolution for a perfect union.

"To bring out this pleding[?] to lett all be burnt.

"2. No disgrace. No power the[y] had but instrumentall. The comiss[ioners] but proxys. We had the determ[in]ant power. They have done ther labor worthyly now we ar to exicut our own power wich was

The Obiections are in Number fower, viz.

1. Entertainment of this new Proiect in the losse of all our former Labours.

2. Disgracefull to the Proceedings of the Committees, or Commissioners formerly imployed.

3. Repugnant to our Selves.

4. We shall hereby discontent the King, and crosse his desires. To Which is answered,

1. If we incline to this new Proiect, we have not lost our former labors; First we have by the passed disputes and Conferences been resolved of many doubts in Lawe and Policy. Againe in that we have grown to a resolution and love of a Generall Union, our Labor is not lost.

2. We shall not disgrace our Commissioners, for to them wee committed but a deliberative Power, not definitive, which was reserved to our Selves; They have done their Partes, they have deliberated and proposed, if now wee shall determine of their Propositions, wee doe our Selves Right, and to them no wrong.

3. Wee shall not hereby be contrary to our Selves, for our first purpose was to preserve our Fundamentall Lawes, if the perfect Union proceede, wee Keepe our Purpose.

4. We doe not discontent the King, nor crosse his desire, for his desire is a perfect Union, and that wee seeke hereby, and if wee seeke a perfect Union, then the further wee wade in the imperfect, the more we wander in Error.

So all obiections already made are but Apparitions, therefore I thinck That either wee ought to embrace this Proiect, or some Course towards it.

---

to determine ther labors. Then yf ther actions should sway ours then they hav all and we do a disgrace to our selves.

"3. No contrariety. Our first resolution was a preservation of our fundamental lawes. Is not that is [*in* is meant] this continued for in this we only intend a review no abollysh.

"4. Discontent of Discent from the king resolution. Resp. We do agre with his desir. His desier is a perfect union. So ours. His expedition. So ours. It is a harmony.

"To have the perfect union is the way of perfection. To have the other is perdition.

"All propositions against is [*it* is meant] but apparitions. Therefor to embrac it." Harley Papers.

Mr. Wentworth,[1] Contrary;

And first said he, all changes in State are dangerous, and to make one of two perhapps may have Inconvenience; For already this House is as great as one Speaker can moderate, as one roome can containe, as wee can heare One the Other speake; Therefore if wee shall proceede in this new Proiect, Let us first consider f. 271] of Particularities, least when wee have moved the King in it, afterwards wee finde upon Argument cause to alter our owne mindes and desires.

Mr. Dudley Carlton[2]

I wish not the perfect Union, first because it is not likely to be effected: Againe no Argument hath bene used against the Imperfect, but it holdeth against the perfect. But the Commissioners you say shall provide against these Inconveniencies, I aske you How? Why, it must be by Restrictions, and then it is not perfect; So as if we proceede in that, wee must resort againe to this Imperfect, and when wee have engaged our Selves to the

---

[1] "Mr. Wentworth. Not fitt uppon generall motions to imply a generall consent of parlament.

"Changes of setled estatts dangerous. Then to chang Cuntry must be full of perill and must look for long work.

"Making the houses all on[e] is not to secur power. The Speker can hardli rull this and the rang of this is of the holl statt.

"Consider the proie[c]t first in perticular not in generall and not to goe to the king before we hav agred.

"Therfor to procead as we did in the last sessons." Harley Papers.

[2] "Mr. Carlton. That with sundrie of you what to propos is the union as resolution of our selves.

"We left at a messag from the lords that we should continue our conferences touching Naturalising. Now what our answer should be must be our discours and nothing els.

"Many men many minds.

"Som Bills. The down right blow is a bill.

"Skirmishe is our conference and as yett fittest.

"Security to be considered first.

"Som would hav Collections of reason and put into your mouthes. Kings lyk not (d.replyes and) well.

"Adrian disput my doctrine. Good not to argue with him that can comand so many legions.

"The king spech was to the lords as well as to our selves. Why should we tak uppon us the holl. Yett it poynted to us in the delay. Lett us

King in this perfect Union, and shall not be able to performe it,
wee loose our Labor. Where some have said, That there can but
One Example be shewed of the Imperfect, I say in the World,
unlesse in Case of Conquest, no Union was at the first perfect.
The Examples alledged are Lituania and Poland, Portugall and
Spaine, Britany and France, Scotland and France. To those the
truth is that Portugall and Spaine have distinct Parliaments, so
hath Lituania and Poland. Of Britany and France is the most
doubt, yet Brittany within these 3. yeares held a Generall Councell of the States, when none was held in France. So as this Imperfect is also of us to be labored; And herein wee ought to be
well advised in makeing Restrictions: Here be some Gentlemen

proceed and then he is answerd to our duty. Effects will better satisfy
then protestations.

"So[me] say that this now is no divertion.

"Pick arguments out of his maiesty spech to the perfect union not fitt.

"He doth not mak the perticuler affections of men the affection of the
Laws.

"I bind my wishes under possibility.

"Not one argument proposed against the perfect union as wel as the
other.

"Planting tres in this.

"Offices—in this.

"Transmigration into the plesenter part. In this.

"Commiss[ion]ers may help this other.

"Then wher is the perfect union.

"So that in the end when we com to this perfect concluding we must
hav recors to the imperfect.

"2. Examples. Marvell at som gentellmens great undertakens. On
one hand the other non[e]. Traviell around the world you shall find non[e]
but by conquest and the[y] wer first imperfect.

"Lituan[ia] Polan[d]. Brit[tany] Fr[a]nc. Portugal Spa[in]. Franc
Scotland.

"Port[ugal] Spaine. Distinct parlam[en]t. Lituania and polan[d] doe.
Brittany and Franc yett Brittany holdeth a severall parlam[en]t. Then
are thes imperf[ect]. For *una lex unus grex unus rex.* Wer not thes offered
for the imperf[ect].

"*Neque relinqui tota res nec perstringi potes[t].*

"This is a truc befor a peac. To see that thes two bodys shall tak no
hurt until the perfect.

"2. ingred[ie]nces[?] offerd.

"Restrictions what you pleac and not to be dispenced with a [*blank*].

"Lords hav interest we wel as we. And .3. years hath bin spend in
this cours." Harley Papers. Cf. *C.J.* I, 1038.

are Enemies to long Speeches, if they concurre not with their owne Sence, but I hope they will be no Enemies to reason. I think we should proceede in the Course wee are, the new Proiect to be reiected, yet the good will of the Gentleman that did offer it, to be embraced and comended.

Mr. Lau[rence] Hyde.[1]

The Motion of the perfect Union was no digression, and I think it ought to be followed, and I think it easier to be compassed then the Imperfect, I speak what I think; I doe desire all present, That the King be not informed That any man hath *Mel in Ore et Fel in Corde*, for himself he heareth us not etc. Though I think the perfect soonest done, yet I doe thinck it to be done presently; I doe not think it Preiudiciall to the Honor of the Commissioners, much lesse of the King. Touching the busines, this Course is no diversion, no frustrating of our former Labors.

f. 272] Let us confirme the abolition of Hostile Lawes; Let us communicate further to the Scottish nation as may be thought fitt but with this, Viz, So as if the perfect Union doe not succeede within a tyme, this to be voide; For if wee should not hope the perfect Union to follow, I would not yield to the Imperfect, and in this doeing, wee doe not give words, for wee give them presently substantiall Kindenesse, all upon hope of a perfect Union to follow. I am for the perfect Union, yet not to give over this as a Preparation.

Touching the Conference I would have it continued, but in such Sorte as formerly wee did resolve, *Vid:* without distinction of the Ante Nati and Post Nati.

---

[1] "Mr. Hid. Perfect union no digression. Mor easely compased. Not *Mell in ore Fell in corde*. If he did not think it he would not be commended.

"Reason. Easier to be compassed. [*blank*.]

"Not that it should be in hast.

"Nor to ta[l]k and doe noth[ing].

"Nor to dishonor ether his majesty or the Comiss[ion]ers.

"To goe to bills conditionall to de[c]line in years if the perfect be not.

"And use them not as brothers but as our selves.

"Giving somwhat will draw on the perfect union.

"Security for restrictions.

"No conferenc with the lords unles the[y] may goe all on[e].

"The temporary benifitt until the perfect will detering the perfect union." Harley Papers.

Mr. Yelverton.[1]

By way of Preamble declared his owne Innocency, and the wrong done him by Reports, adding this, If the Viall of wrath

---

[1] "Mr. Yelverton. If the viall be in a princes hand it had powerd uppon my head if he had not ben a merciful man.

"Differnc great. Not 2 of on[e] mind.

"I was and I fer shall ever be against the imperfect union.

"Yett if this statt to effect the perfect I should assent to it.

"But that that is now a foot is most dangerous to our statt.

"No disgrac to the commiss[ion]ers nor to our proceding.

"King spech and preambl of the commission a perfect union.

"You gav the Commiss[ion]ers authority to treat for the good of both kingdomes.

"The words wer the [*words illegible*].

"This proposition taketh no fundamenta[l] lawe away.

"Propositions now a foot ar not good for both kingdom[s].

"Propositions ar .3. Hostill la[ws]. Co[mmerce]. Natur[alization].

"1. No opposition. The Hostill lawes wer a wall the[y] could never scall. The[y] geat much by it but why we should desier any of the .3. I see no reason.

"Ob. Crossing of our own proceding. If your hounds hav taken a wrong sent direct them.

"If in bills.—The[y] had bin reiected.

"Ob. Lett us not shilp [*slip* is meant] this opportunity. etc.

"Ther can be no security. And that safty that shalbe proposed will bred enmity.

"What oppression can com but it must be through his maiestys hands. Nether with out him can the[y] bear up ther sutts.

"He never will do us wrong that ar his best born thoug not his first borne if we complayn.

"Differs from Mr. Hid for a tim to be sett downe.

"If we shall now give them Ken[g]ly apparles and then strip them out of it will be no way to love.

"This is no stall but a stand.

"Adam one tree.

"Restrictions bind them on[e] part all the body wilbe unquiett.

"Security cannot be but in the pening of the act.

"In purveance the king could not be bond.

"Mr. Bacon differenc. Incapacity.

"If the party be mayd incapable the king may give them capacity. By his pattent.

"But this is not bettwen subiect and subiect.

"For Commerc. Restrayn them and the king may mencion this act the thing any desyer.

"Actt to a tim certein.

might have bene put into the hande of a Prince, it had bene all powred on me; But the King is to be honoured for his Mercy and Iustice.[1]

Touching the Matter, It is growen to a Suspicion, least by this new Proiect wee loose our Labours past; I ever was, and I feare ever shall be, though reason may alter me, against this Imperfect Union. The perfect Union is no disgrace to the Commissioners nor Crosse to our former Proceedings. The Commissioners Power was to consider and to propose to us, but our Power to determine.

The Law is like the Firmament Over the heads of the Scotts, it is honorable for us. The Commission was to treate for the good of both Nations, but in the Imperfect Union, is all for the good of Scotland, nothing for the good of England.

The Abrogation of Hostile Lawes is granted, the Scotts have gotten by that. This new Proiect is no Crosse to our owne Proceedings as hath bene before declared.

"Then when you shall strip them of what you gave what good can grow of this.

"Port of Dover to a tim. Has it not bin continued longer.

"Bilding Battelment. Condition is easily in an other parlam[en]t.

"If conditionall who shall plead the condition not performed.

"Perchanc you shall not se the record that breacheth the (*d.* pattent) Act.

"Naturalisation. I think no man nedeth to repeat.

"*Eadem persona* not *idem rex.*

"*Stat lege Corona.* The law maketh him King.

"If the law be with them god forbid to abrig them.

"Why restrayn Northern Englishmen we then the Southern.

"Castell and Aragon was but communication of privileges and wer under on law.

"Not lyketh conference. If you plac som in the forfront they ar not willing for.

"Som of us hav felt it.

"To proced to the perfect union.

"For doing somthing. Doe Hostill lawes. Not the rest.

"3 years tossed on the seas we se a dov[?] elight[?].

"Lords send down ther bills that that is so difficult *in vaga questione.*

"No mor conferences.

"I fear the bill will want strenght when it is delivered and will hardly hold up his head." Harley Papers.

[1] See *D.N.B.* under Sir Henry Yelverton, and *Archaeologia,* XV, 27–52.

By way of obiection, it is wished that wee slipt not this occasion of doeing ourselves good; Nay I say wee shall doe Our Selves hurt, for wee can doe our Selves no good this way: For your Restrictions cannot be secured, but your Restrictions and Security will be hereafter hurtfull. The hurt which is feared if wee proceede not with this Imperfect Union but leave the Matter at large as now it standeth, is farr from me to doubt, for it cannot be, but through the King, whom I will never mistrust. I shall not easily be drawen to the last worthy Gentlemens Opinion, for if f. 273] wee shall cloath them like us, and we shall take it after from them, it will breede a Mischief; for restraine them, and they will think themselves as bad as ever and they will I feare breake loose. The Restrictions and Security must be by Parliament, and the Iudges have already given a deadly blowe. They cannot be bound by the Statute of Purveyors; Yea said a learned Gentleman but we will make the Persons of the Scottish incapable; to that I say, That if you disable betweene Person and Person, the King cannot dispence, but against himself he may. A Gentleman would have this Statute for the Union to be Temporary: You may remember That the Statute for the Peere of Dover[1] was but for 3. yeares, but it hath continued 26 yeares. Then a Condition he saith will helpe: It is indeed the safest way, but it will not be so for us; for who shall pleade it; Perhapps you shall not see it;[2] A Condition is but a Battlement, and an other. Parliament may be ledd to take away the Condition when the building shall stand.

Touching the Post Nati and the Ante, I think no difference, if the Post Nati be naturalls wee cannot restraine them, for then are they Northerne Englishmen.

In Consideration what the Question shall be, I am against Conference, it hath done no good, and if you place some in the Forefront they will not speake, wee have found it. The perfect Union is no diversion, for it was in his Majestys first Statute.

Then goe to it by Bill, wee are all agreed to abolish Hostile Lawes, therefore we have not sett Idle. For the other two Parts, Viz: Commerce and Naturalization, wee have spent 3 yeares, and alwaies hetherto continued in much Doubts; Therefore let

---

[1] 23 Eliz. c. 6. *Statutes of the Realm*, IV, 668. This was to have lasted seven years.

[2] "Perhaps you be restrained from Sight of the Patent." *C.J.* I, 1038.

the Lords send downe their Bills to these two Points, and when
we have their Bills, wee will passe them if they be fitt.

1ST. MAII. 1607.

SIR ROBERT WINGFIELD.[1]

I was for the perfect Union, but he[2] that spake last except
three yesterday hath seduced me (here the House smiling) he
corrected himself, and said, converted me; The reasons whereby
I am now led are, The Encrease of Religion, Content of the King,
The Greatnesse of the Kingdome. And touching the Manner I
did perferr Bills, but now I preferr Conference, because wee have
f. 274] begun in the other two Points of Hostile Lawes, and Commerce, therefore I wish the same Course to be held and continued.

MR. SOLLICITOR.[3]

Nothing perfect which hath not had his tyme to begin, and
grow to Fullnesse, this is a rule, and the Course of Nature, and

---

[1] Cf. debate in *C.J.* I, 1039.

[2] Mr. Dudley Carleton.

[3] "Mr. Solicitor. Hostill laws and repelling is sayd a donation to the
Scotts. As the law stands we ar under penaltys. And therfor to repeall
them is to put a yoke from our own neck.

"Commerc concerneth the Merchants craft.

"Cariing comoditys out of Scotland.

"This Hous the hole body by representation. Many porte town[s] have
send hither that ben marchants. Many marchants her of the House.

"Securyty. Shall not we as well trust his maiesty as well as our
(*d.* prog) Ancestors hav his progenators.

"He that moved gave me Satisfaction in his loiall duty to the King
that he would do no harm to the sub[ject].

"King prerogativ restrained and changed by parlam[ent].

"By pattent make a Bishop.

"Charter in King John to give fre Elec[tion].

"That by Magna cart[a]. Merton etc.

"Baron by grand sergeany the king may raiss his relief as he wo[uld]
but by Magna Carta it is bond. So it was in Ranulf Glanvill befor that
bo[und].

"Cutting tres. Restraning by Magna carta.

"Statut restraneth the king prerogative in purveanc.

"Shall we disable men to take office. Obj. The King may dispenc.

"I say wher ther is any disability by act of parlam[en]t the king can
not dispenc.

Order of Mens Actions: Fruit by no tree is brought forth in a
day, but must begin of a budd; So all Arts and Sciences have their
beginning and progresse. This perfect Union is *Finis Ultimus,* but
wee are diversly distracted in the Course; For my owne part, I
know it is the Cause of my Countrey, and therefore I have hitherto
sett still and observed what hath bene said. It is said, and truely,
That perfect Union is Love, but what hope any Countrey will
suddainely leave, or change their Lawes. Lawes must be altered
in *Melius,* and *Sensim,* which cannot be but in tyme, therefore
this perfect Union is like Plato his Idea.[1] Shall wee use a new
Commission to inquire of means to this perfect Union? Alas
what Incouragement shall they take when they see the Labor of
former Commissioners laid aside? Three things have by the Commissioners beene proposed to us: In the first two, wee have made
a good progresse, and conferred to good purpose; In the latter wee
have done lesse. It is said That the abolishing of Hostile Lawes
is a great Donative to them, no it is good to us on whom the
Penalties doe lie, for as the Law now standeth, wee loose life for
carrying a horse into Scotland etc. In the matter of Commerce
much Labor hath beene spent, and it concerneth most of the
Marchants, whose Arte I understand not; But to my Understanding, the Carrying of Commodities into Scotland over Land, the
easy Custome there, and thereby the transporting from thence
upon easie termes, be the Inconveniencies, and are to be provided
for, whether the Union proceede or not: And I think the Bill
for that Matter ought not to proceede from the Lords, but from
us, wherein let us have the advise of Marchants.

What Security? If a Penalty, the King may remitt it; If a
penall Law, the King may dispence with it; And may not wee
trust the King as well as our Ancestors trusted his Ancestors.

"43. Eliz. in my lord cook leases by Clergymen. Ecclesiasti[cal]
persons contrary to Statut 13. El. had mad leases. The Jugges resolve
the leases void. The reson is becaus the leasers wer uncap[able?] and if
the Queen could hav despensed this exception with the[m].

"Mak the Jugment voyd wher authoryty can mak that good that was
not god.

"God forbid that we shoud se the day that lawiers shold not dar to
plead the law." Harley Papers.

[1] "Excellent in Imagination only; *non in rerum natura.*" *C.J.* I,
1039.

Touching Naturalization, the Question hath bene moved what Security may wee have for the Restrictions? I am cleere of f. 275] Opinion, That the Kings Prerogative may be bound by an Act of Parliament. Anciently the King might constitute a Bishop *Per Traditionem Annuli et Baculi.* 6. E. 3. etc. but there was a Charter in Parliament which is an Act of Parliament[1] etc.

The Kings Prerogative was, That if a Baron died holding of the King, the King might seise his Relief as he pleased, and this was taken from him by the Statute of Magna Charta cap. 2? The King might have cutt downe the Timber of any Person to build Shipps But by the Statute of Magna Charta C.21. this is taken away. Many of these I could enumerate, but it hath beene said, What Course shall wee take? By disabling the Persons? If so, the King will dispence with it; I say no, the King cannot; For where a disability is laid on the Person by Act of Parliament, the King cannot dispence with all. The Statute of [*blank*][2] Elizabeth prohibits Bishops etc. to make leases longer then 21. yeares, or 3. lives; Afterwards diverse Ecclesiasticall Persons made long leases to the Queene, and adiudged, That for as much as the Persons of Ecclesiasticall men were disabled to make such leases, therefore the Queene could have no such lease.

If touching Places of Iudicature, Restrictions will not helpe, make the Iudgement before them to be voide, and *Coram non Iudice.*

To conclude, Having spent much time, let us redeeme the tyme; For the 2. first Points, I beseech you, Let us have Committees and Bills drawen forthwith: For the latter I leave it to your Wisedomes.

Mr. Speaker.

I have received Letters, whereby I am commanded to let you Know, That whereas his Majesty understandeth that there are severall Constructions of his late Speech, his gratious Pleasure is, That no further dispute be had before you shall have attended his Majesty, which he requireth you should all doe to Morrow in the Afternoone, at 2. of the clock in the Great Chamber at the Court.

---

[1] Possibly a reference to 9 Ed. II. Stat. I. c. 14. *Statutes of the Realm,* I, 173.

[2] 13 Eliz. c. 10. *Statutes of the Realm,* IV, 545.

2? Maii. 1607

Councell on both Sides concerning the Bill for Limitting the Iurisdiction of the Marshalsey, and Reformation of abuses in that Court, came to the Barr, viz, Mr. Warre for the Marshall, Mr. Goldsmith for the Bill against the Kings Marshall, and putt to the Question, Whether they should be heard this day, or deferred.

After dinner the House waited on his Majesty in the Great f. 276] Chamber at Whitehall, where I had no Conveniency to take his Majestys Speech,[1] only I observed generally, That it consisteth in 1. An Exposition of his former Speech. 2. An Answere of Obiections.

For the first he declared That in the Course of his former Speach, he meant a full Union, not a perfect Union. Then, said he, The first Obiection is, 1. What gaine by this Union shall come to England?

This is answered, That this place is the Seate of both Kingdomes etc. 2dly. you have Peace. 3ly. By the Addition of a strong Nation to you.

Against the first Commoditie hath bene said, yea, but *Procull a Iove, procul a Fulmine.* I answere, if my Presence be a burden I will make you an offer, I will make my abode one yeare here, an other in Scotland; or I will abide at Yorck being in the Middle Place of the whole Island; Or after the fashion of the ancient Kings, both of England and Scotland, I will ride circuit about the Countrey, and I am as able to doe it as any heretofore.

Then it is obiected, what Security shall wee have of these Re-

---

[1] For this speech, see *C.J.* I, 366–368; *Parl. Hist.* I, 1115–19; St. P. Dom. XXVII, 14. The editor has seen a copy of a manuscript containing another version of this speech. The manuscript is among the Phelips MSS preserved at North Deighton Manor, Wetherby, Yorkshire. See also *Ambassades*, II, 223–224.

The speech was in a scolding tone and quite inferior to the speech of March 31. It did, however, have an effect on the Commons. "As his Majesty has very wisely flattered the small fry with soft words and shown his displeasure in vigerous terms against the great, who were seducing the others to oppose his will, it is hoped that he may at last effect that union of the two kingdoms which he so ardently desires." *Cal. St. P. Venetian, 1603–1607*, 494. James had privately scolded some of the Upper House whom he thought were opposing the Union. *Ambassades*, II, 199–201.

strictions, for say you, wee can have none by reason of the Kings Prerogative? Herein I am not able to resolve you; For first I am no Common Lawyer. Next you will not believe the Iudges; But if I can give you no Security, why seeke it you, for then you were better take the Honor of a Prince, then to leave the Matter to the Course of Lawe which the Iudges are to resolve, who are to iudge your Lives, and your Lands, and whose Opinion you Knowe already in this Pointe.

Wee are not now to consider, whither a Union etc. for it is done, *Res non est integra*. Wee must now provide that all occasions that may hereafter divide the Nations may be taken away.

But you will say, the Lords at the first argued their good liking to a full Union. It is true, But they entended it by way of Preparation, and accordingly the Commissioners proceeded, and if it be not farr enough the fault is yours that would not grant so large a Commission as I then pressed.

It is enough That the Hostile Lawes are abolished? Why they are dead already, and the Order now to doe it, is but a Shaddowe, for it were ridiculous to punish an Englishman for selling a horse in Scotland, or a Scottish man for flyeing.

If Bills come among you, no hope say some of you that they shall passe? To this Ominous Prophecy, I can say nothing, but I hope it will not prevaile with you; And I doe wish you, That as I have not hetherto wronged any, so you would Consider I am a f. 277] man subiect to Passions, made of flesh and blood, and therefore I pray you stirr not your King too farr.

Love me little, and love me long, say some of you.[1] Nay Love me much, and love me long, for small things doe decay quickly, therefore love much, and doe much, though not vehemently; doe it quickly, the season of the yeare, your owne Harvest even inviteth you to dispatch, let your Affection and Love to your Prince appeare; You have no Foole to your Prince, if you have any doubts, Lett me Know it, and goe forewards so as you may redeeme tyme, so as your Neighbours may see your Love towards me; So as you may reioice in me, and I glory in you; And still be doeing untill you have come to the End; And tempt not my Patience with frivolous discourses and delayes, who ever have striven to overcome you in Patience.

---

[1] See speech of Sir Edwin Sandys at a conference on March 14.

4.º Maii. 1607.

Mr. Speaker[1] first makeing a Briefe Repetition of the Kings Speech, offered from his Majesty a Bill intituled An Act for the continuance and preservation of the blessed Union of the Realmes of England and Scotland, and for the abolishing and takeing away of all Hostile Lawes and Statutes, and Customes that may disturbe or hinder the same.

Note that the first Statute in this Bill mentioned to be abolished was one Statute made 5.º R. 2.[2] for passing into Scotland out of England, and also Order or Provision for Tryall of passing from Scotland into other Partes by English Subiects without Expresse Lycence.

The 2d. was the Statute 4. H. 5.[3] touching Letters of Reprisall, or Letters of Mart.

The 3d. a Provisoe in the Statute of 33. H.8.[4] for Keeping handgunns etc. by Inhabitants within [*blank*][5] Miles of the borders of Scotland.

The 4th. a Statute made 7. R.2.[6] for transporting Victualls etc. Armour etc. into Scotland.

The 5th. a Statute made 21. H.6.[7] touching Man Slaughter.

The 6th. a Statute made 7. H.7.[8] commanding Scottish men to avoide out of England.

---

[1] "Mr. Speker. No expecta[tion] of a relation wher the wholl hous is cale[d].

"Yet .2. Caution. Direction.

"1. In respect of long time in disput to leav matter now of discours and draw our selves to the tru certa[inty?].

"2. Now we underst[and] his Ma[jes]ty pleasure to procead to an end proscribing nether matter nor manner but expedition.

"And from his Ma[jes]ty a bill oferd as a preparation.

"An Act for the continuance and preserving of the blessed Union of the realms of Engla[nd] and Scotland and taking away all the hostel laws." Harley Papers.

See *Hist. MSS Com. Buccleuch MSS*, III, 115–116; *C.J.* I, 1040.

[2] *Statutes of the Realm*, II, 18.

[3] *Statutes of the Realm*, II, 198.

[4] *Statutes of the Realm*, III, 835.

[5] Twelve miles. *Ibid.*

[6] *Statutes of the Realm*, II, 35.

[7] Mistake for 31 Hen. VI. c. 3. *Statutes of the Realm*, II, 363.

[8] *Statutes of the Realm*, II, 553.

Then one Statute made 23.H.8.[1] and the like 1.° Elizabeth[2] for conveying horses, etc.

One Statute made 1.° and 2.° Philip and Mar:[3]

Lastly One Statute made 23. Elizabeth[4] prohibiting Lands to be let to Scottish men.

f. 278] Then it maketh voide by Generall words all other Lawes, Statutes and Customes made etc. against Scottishmen as Enemies.

Lastly it warranteth a Commission to be directed by the King unto 10. English, and 10. Scottish men to heare and end all Causes yet depending according to Borders Lawe and committed betweene the last Treaty 1596. and 1597.[5] and the death of the late Queene, not concerning life nor Member.

5.° Maii. 1607

The Councell[6] for the Bill against the Encroachment of the Marshalsey, and on the other Side for the Marshalsey being both at the Barr, were withdrawen, and the Speaker proposed which Councell should begin; acknowledged That generally he that speaketh against the Bill ought to begin and so ordered to be now done. The Bill was intituled thus, An Act for Reformation of Abuses in the Court of Marshalsey, and for limiting the Iurisdiction thereof. Much was spoken on both Sides, after all was heard and the Councell withdrawen, ROBERT BOWYER said That two things had from the beginning drawen him to like the Bill, which not having bene hitherto answered, he continued his Opinion, Viz. The words of *Artic[uli] Super Chartas*,[7] are, That the Marshall Court *desormer ne tient Plea de Franck tenement, ne de det, ne de contract;* So as said he it doth not say a Man shall not bring any such Action to recover Freehold, nor Action of debt, nor an Action upon the Contract, for then an other Action perhaps, as now is used, *Vid:* Action of *Trespas sur le Cas* upon *Indebitatus assumpsit*, might have lien, and *sic in caeteris;* It

---

[1] *Statutes of the Realm*, III, 380.

[2] *Statutes of the Realm*, IV, 367.

[3] 2 and 3 Phil. and Mar. c. 1. *Statutes of the Realm*, IV, 266.

[4] *Statutes of the Realm*, IV, 663.

[5] *Cal. St. P. Dom. 1595–1597*, 269; *Acts of the Privy Council*, XXVI, 202.

[6] See the names and debate in *C.J.* I, 369, 1040.

[7] *Statutes of the Realm*, I, 138.

saith the Court shall not hold Plea of Freehold, or debt, or contract, so as whatsoever the Action be, if any of those be the
Matter of Action, that Court cannot hold Plea of it.

It was moved, That the Court of Marshalsey shall direct or
send out no other Processe then was used in the tyme of [*blank*][1]
and granted by the King, then said One, shew me That the Proces
now used in your Action *Sur le Cas*, upon *Indebitatus assumpsit*
was used in that Court before the said tyme of [*blank*] and I will
be against the Bill, otherwise not.

WENTWORTH, *ad idem*, and said he, the Title of the Court is
Placita Serenissimae Aulae Domini Regis, etc. Againe in Drapers
Case[2] in Kings Bench, It was holden by all the Iudges except the
Lord Chief Iustice, That the Court of Marshalsey should not hold
Plea in an Action of the Case upon *Indebitatus Assumpsit.*
f. 279] And the Bill being put to the Question, passed.

Sir Iohn Popham then also Steward of the Marshalsey, and his grandsonn Mr. Warre then his deputy.

11. MAII.[3] 1607.

The Bill for Lymitting the Iurisdiction and reforming abuses
in the Court of Marshalsey 3.° *lect.* and passed.

12. MAII. 1607

Resolved, That he which reporteth the Opinion of the Committees is also to relate the reasons of the Committees.

The Committees of the Bill of Clothing brought back the Bill
and with it a Provisoe, That inhabitants being Freemen of Hereford, Lempster, Bewdly, and Coventry, may cloth not having
beene Apprentices to that Trade, notwithstanding the Statute;
This Provisoe was put to the Question, whether it should be added
to the Bill, and ordered Affirmatively; thereupon the whole Bill
and Provisoe was engrossed. Then the Matter was whither the
Question should be upon the whole Bill to passe, or might be on
the Provisoe only. Some would have the whole Bill recommitted,
but it was ruled, That after a Bill is engrossed, the same cannot
be committed, but either in open House, or in the Committee
chamber, sitting the House, either one line, or more may be
stroken out, or added at the Pleasure of the House.

---

[1] 28 Ed. I. *Ibid.*

[2] *English Reports (Full Reprints)*, LXXII, 898; LXXIX, 75.

[3] For days omitted, see Appendix B.

Sir Herbert Croft, moved That for as much as this Provisoe was brought into the House by the Committee first as a distinct thing, and by the House ordered to be added, therefore now the Question cannot be upon this Provisoe, but must be on the whole Bill: But ruled That in this Case, and generally in all Cases, the House may take away after a Bill is engrossed what, and how much thereof they please and upon the Question, this whole Provisoe being at the last 12. or 20. Lines, was stroken out.

From the Lords Serieant Crooke and Sir Edw[ard] Stanhope brought a Bill intituled An Act for Restitution in Blood of the Sonns and Daughters of Edw[ard] Windsor.

This House sent up to the Lords a Bill intituled An Act for Reformation of abuses in Ministers and concerning Subscription. And an other intituled An Act for Reformation of abuses in the Court of Marshalsey, and for the Iurisdiction of it.

13? Maii. 1607.

Sir Edwyn Sandys[1] reported the Proceedings of the Committees touching the Complaints heretofore exhibited by our Spanish Marchants, and of their Grievances.

f. 280] Mr. Brooke a Member[2] of this House is deffendent in a Personall Action, and Issue ioyned, and to be tryed on Satturday next, the Deffendent is warned at his Perill to be present or else a Tryall to passe against him, it was moved what in this Case shall be done. Answered by the Speaker, That he had in like Cases written diverse Letters to the Iustice of Assise to stay such suite, and hetherto had heard no Complaint further, and so was it in this Case ordered.

Ruled, That if a Sub poena he served on any Member of this House, he must bring the Sub poena into the House before he can have Priviledge.

15? Maii. 1607.

Mr. Speaker moved, That Sir John Boys a Member of this House being of Councell with a private Bill in the Lords House may

---

[1] For the difficulties of the Spanish merchants, see Gardiner, I, 340–354. Notes of Sandys' report are contained in C.J. I, 1044; St. P. Dom. XXVII, 19; Harley Papers.

[2] The member is Mr. Francis Bullingham. Brooke is informing the House of the case. See C.J. I, 373, 1044.

with the good favour of the House be accordingly permitted; and shewed That himself in 27. Eliz. was so admitted in a case betweene the Lord Dacres, and the Lord Norrice;[1] But because the House was not now full the Resolution of the House was deferred.

16. Maii. 1607.

Sir Edwyn Sandys was sent from this House to the Lords to acquaint them with the Complaint of the Spanish Merchants and our desire to exhibite a Petition to the King as well for restitution and amends for wrongs past, as for prevention of future Iniuries to be done in such Course as his Majesty shall think fitt; and therein to desire their Lordships to ioyne with this House; and coming back he reported his doeings, and that the Lords after some pause answered that the Matter of this Message is somewhat strange and very weightie both for the Matter and the Order; whereunto their Lordships cannot presently give answer, but they would debate it among themselves, and send answere by Messengers of their owne as conveniently they might.

18. Maii. 1607.

Serieant Crooke brought downe a Bill from the Lords for the Establishing of the Possessions of Ferdinando late Earle of Derby. Councell[2] came to the Barr in the Watermans Bill.

Sir John Higham moved That a Petition[3] might be framed by a selected Committee on the behalfe of certaine Ministers, and delivered to his Majesty by the Speaker; Whereunto was answered that by the Speaker it might not be delivered.

17. Maii.[4] 1607.

f. 281] Mr. Speaker delivered from the King, That his Majesty had understood of a reporte divulged not only in and neare Lon-

---

[1] D'Ewes, 317. No mention of name of counsel. Another precedent cited (see *C.J.* I, 373) concerned a matter of title of honor. "But note that the Title of Honour is decidable only in the Upper House, and not to be meddled withall in the Nether House. And therefore more reason to admitt them to be of Counsell in that Case, wherein they cannot be Judges, then in any case which is to pass both Houses." Cott. MSS, Titus F IV, f. 101.

[2] See *C.J.* I, 375.

[3] See *ibid.*

[4] The correct date is May 19.

don, but also in many Parts of the Country, wherewith he findeth himselfe Exceedingly grieved, not with this House, but with the Matter: *Vid;* That which is published and made Common of an undue and violent Course of Proceedings by the Commissioners of both Kingdomes in the remanding of Barrow backe into Scotland, and his Execution there; and herein said he, his Majesty is exceeding tender and grieved, and would be more grieved if there were iust Cause: His Majesty therefore being desirous to cleere this Question not to you whom he understandeth to be already satisfied, but that you may the better satisfy the Countryes where you dwell, doth desire you to heare a Minister of Iustice in those Parts, namely Sir W[illia]m Seaton, that having out of his mouth heard the truth of all the Matter, you may be the better able to satisfy the Countryes where you dwell.

Hereupon Sir W[illia]m Seaton was called for into the House by the Serieant with his Mace, as a token of Honor, not as an offendor, then it was putt to the question, where he should stand; Some said at the Barr, others *Econtra*, for that he came not as an offendor, others maintained the first opinion.

[Stanford MS]

f. 31. a]   [19 Maii 1607]

Hereuppon Sir Will[ia]m Seaton was called for into the howse
by the Serieant with his Mase as a token of Honour not as an offendor, then it was put to the question where he should stande:
Some saied at the barre, others *econtra:* for that he came not as an
offendor: others maintained the first opinion because Mr. Attorney
generall Mr. Cooke coming to deliver unto the howse the case
touchinge certaine of the offendors in the gunpowder treason against
whome in their absence an act of their attainder was to passe, did
stand at the barre.[1] This confirmed divers in that opinion who
added that he might have a stoole as Mr. Attorney then had and
my Lord of Hertford at an other tyme and my Lord Marques
had.[2] To this Mr. Speaker replied that Mr. Attorney used the
stoole only for his ease whilest desposicions and the like weare
reading, not when he spake, and that the Tow Lords spake not
[at] all, but came in with their Counsaile who spake for them,
and concluded that it became not anie subiect to speake to this
assembly setting. In conclusion it was ordered that the Serieant
with his mase should bring him within the barre 2 or 3 steps and
there he should stand by him: whilest he delivered his mynd and
then conduct him forth againe.

Sir W[illiam] Seaton being brought and accordinglie standing
in the howse the Speaker declared unto him his Majesties pleasure
viz. That having herd of the fame of Barrowes triall and execucion
to be somwhat disorderlie, and for that the same is in herd sort
bruited heare in England, hath signified his princelie pleasure that
you, one of his majesties ministers in that place should heare declare what the truth of the proceedinge in that cause was, not as to
a companie doubting or beleeving anie such rumor as hath ben
spred concerning the same, but to enable this howse and the
particular members therof the better to satisfie their countries
therin when they shall come downe where they dwell therefore
etc.

[1] 29 April, 1606. See p. 139 and *C.J.* I, 301.
[2] *C. J.* I, 210, 214. "Lord Marques" appears to be a reference to Lord
Henry Seymour, the younger brother of the Earl of Hertford.

Sir W[illiam] Seaton being a veary tall bigge man of a bold countenance speach and spirit having used some preamble: saied to
this effect:[1] viz. When his Majestie had directed his commission[2]
unto divers persons of both Kingdomes under both his seales giving
equall authoritie, wee agreed that none of us should deale in
matters of iudicature but where they knew the Lawe, and so the
offendors to be subiect to the Lawe where the offence was committed, and to this the King agreed and accordinglie wee have delivered at Carlisle and Newcastle 30 of our nacion all executed,
and have receaved out of England but 16 or 17: whereof have ben
executed but 7. The Lerd of Barrow had committed 4 or 5 felonies
in Scotland since the Kings coming, for some of theis he left the
country and went into Flanders, and since returned: The King
directed that some few of the comaunding offendors should be
delt withall and this man being a principal party that offended,
was sent unto us into Scotland: The order of his triall was this
(for I am not only willing to give an accompt of my doings but
to suffer iudgement for anie thing which I have doon in anie matter
as his Majesties minister). I saied unto him being before us: Lerd
of Barrow you are accused for your life and I will conceale no thing
from you that our Law will allow you for your advantage: Therefore I let you know that you maie have a prolocuter. I to have none,
saied he: well saied I then you have libertie to speake against the
triors, and then to the fact. I to have saied he no Scott my Judge
nor my trior. I told him that would not availe him. Wee have
saied I a warrant from your King and ours to iudge you, still he
f. 31. b] saied nothing, but he would not be tried so: Then I called
for the Inquest and said, Lerd of Barrow, I am your frende and you
have ben at my howse, if anie of the Inquest have doon wrongs to
you or your wife, or contrary wise if you have wronged anie of
them, saie it, he shall not passe on you, he aunswered I will saie
nothing to them but against the whole, well said I then blame your-

---

[1] Sir William Seaton "spoke in that place about half an hour relating
the particular of the proceedings wherein he gave the House good satisfaction." Cott. MSS, Titus F IV, f. 101*v*.

In his rough notes, the Clerk wrote, "*Quaere de* Mr. Bowyer for the relation." *C.J.* I, 1046.

[2] Rymer, *Foedera*, XVI, 504, 609. The names of the commissioners
are contained in St. P. Dom. XXVIII, 28.

selfe: There was laied to his charge 14 or 15 things all olde saving fowre:

1. The first for stealing of a mare.
2. The second for stealing 4 mares from Alex Hume.
3. For taking certaine hides from a Scotch man.
4. For six horses from the Lord of Everston.[1]

1. To the first he aunswered that he was innocent but the owner that had lost the mare came to him and desiered him to make enquiery after her and to helpe to her againe, which saied the Lerd of Borrow I did although I neaver knew or was acquainted with the taking of her: then I asked him who was the theefe but he woulde not declare it:

2. To the second matter of the 4 mares he saied it was doon in the late Queenes time, I willed him to prove the time. He did it not but saied as before that the Scotts loved him not. I willed him yett to speake against any of his Jury.

3. To the matter of the Hides, he saied that he tooke them as unlawfull goods to be carried out of England into Scotland and such as weare forfeited the halfe to the King the other halfe to the taker. I asked him why he had not then paied the Kings parte into the Exchequer he aunswered that he made restitucion of the whole: yea saied I that restitucion sheweth a wrongfull taking: yea saied he you prevented mee and made mee make restitucion: why saied I the restitucion was by your wife according to our direccion when you weare in Flanders and wee could not get you: aunsweared that indeed his wife did it by our direccion without his knowledge:

It seemeth the prisoner was remaunded not knowing with what he should be charged, and the tyme should have ben proved against him.

4. To the fourth matter, as I remember Sir W[illiam] Seaton declared nothing.

20 MAII. 1607.

M.r. Speaker came early to the howse before the company was in anie sort full and adiourned the court untell that day senight viz. wensdaie 27 *Maii:* So the expectacion of the howse to have had a report of the proceedings of the committees in the bill for abolishing hostile lawes and of the new added proviso against the remaunding of prisoners was frustrate: *Ah ha Convive spes ubi ves-*

---

[1] Perhaps Evertown, Dumfriesshire, or Edgerston, Roxburgh.

tra iacet: so in this some doubted Arte. For it is thought that as well the reformacion of the saied bill by the Committees, which first was drawen by Mr. Attorney nlot without direction and helpe etc: as this proviso brought in by Mr. Fuller and disputed by the Committees at large: was not acceptable:

27 Maii 1607.

A long bill sent downe by the Lords for the establishing of the Castle honors and mannors etc. late the Enheritance of Ferdinando Earl of Derby was red *primo*.

f. 32. a] The howse calling for a report of the proceedings of the Committees before the last adiournement, concerning the bill for abolyshing of hostile Lawes; Mr. Speaker stoode up and saied[1] he had somewhat to deliver unto the howse from the Kings Majestie: But first saied he I humblie praie you for my owne particular, give mee Leave to speake for my purgacion concerning a bruite published in the towne. It is divulged that I shoulde this day senight past without the pleasure and consent of the howse adiourne the parliament untell this daie with purpose to prevent the putting of the matters then in dispute to the question, and to take the advantage of this morninge to put it to the question before [the] companie should be come to towne.[2] It is true that the howse hath power to adiourne the setting for a time and it is as trew that the King hath also a roiall power to adiourne and on Tuisday I had direccion from the King to adiourne the parliament and so I did the next day: Touching my purpose therin I protest I had no such entent as before I remembered to be since bruited and therefore I disclaime from your favor herein and appeale to your Justice whether eaver I have put anie thing to the question but in full howse.

From his Majestie I am to saie this much: His Majestie hath herd of the Report before mencioned and doth conceave the same to have ben delivered abroade by such as beare no good mynde towards him nor the state. And commanded me to assure you in the woorde of a King, he neaver ment it, with this protestacion Before my Kinge. etc:

---

[1] Cf. his speech in *C.J.* I, 376.

[2] "That at the next meeting few might be present but such as His Majesty was sure would yield to his pleasure." Lansd. MSS 486, f. 122*v*.

Secondlie his Majestie commanded mee to tell you that in this particular as in all others he hath no entent to gaine to him selfe anie thing nor to the nacion from whence he came, but to the fartherance of Justice, and he hopeth you do so to, and that you desier not to maintaine,[1] wherefore the order to be taken herin he leaveth to your selves. Lastlie his Majestie taketh notice of the generall absence of the members of this howse and he holdeth it dishonorable to him selfe, to this howse, to the busines, that so manie shoulde be away at the handling of this matter: and he will ioine with you in anie course you shall finde out for reformacion: And touching the matter in question he willeth you to take some fit time to heare and dispute and resolve it:

This being spoken the howse resolved to morrow morning as the clocke shall strike nine to enter into dispute of the busines.

28 MAII 1607.

SIR GEO[RGE] MORE reported the opinion of the Committees for the priviledgs touchinge reformacion of absence of the members of this howse and thereuppon ordered that the howse shalbe called on this daie senight. A bill entituled an act for better attendance in the commons howse of parliament was this daie 2do. *lecta* and committed unto the former committees and some few others, who are to meete on Satterday next in the Exchequer chamber.

SIR H[ENRY] POOLE moved that whereas this howse having heretofore[2] sent to the Lords for a conference touching the complaint and greavances of the Spanish merchants ther Lordships had sent no other aunswere but that they will send aunswere by their owne messengers which perhaps maie be on a soddaine, and forasmuch as our committees are not yet so fully furnished to all points as uppon farder advise with some merchants they may be, therefore for their better enabling and preparing to meete with the Lords and to aunswere all obiections therefore the said committees and the merchants may againe meete *ad quod non nemini responsum*.[3]

The bill of Inmates committed, to be considered in the temple hall on tuesday.

---

[1] *Not to maintaine offenders* is meant.
[2] On May 16.
[3] "Committee for Spanish Wrongs, to meet To-morrow." *C.J.* I, 1046.

Abolishing hostile
lawes.

Remaundinge of-
fendors inter-
changeably.

f. 32. b] Sɪʀ Fʀᴀ[ɴᴄɪs] Bᴀᴄᴏɴ reported the proceedings of the committees in the bill for abolishing hostile Lawes.[1] thus:

The bill saied he was allmost finished, but beinge neere the shoer was anc[h]or[e]d untell a question might be heare proposed to the howse, and your direccion understoode. Wherin I will first deliver the question, then the argumentes which weare used on both sides, and afterwardes a mocion that was made and because if my memorie shoulde be unfaithfull to mee, I may be so likewise to you therefore I will otherwise then is my custome take the benefit of my paper.

And first I must let you know that 3 things weare agreed and no parte of the question:

1. First that thes 2 Realmes shoulde not be used for sanctuary to crimminall persons of either countrie.

2. Secondlie that if an Englishman offend in Scotland and be there taken before he recover England, he shalbe subiect to the justice of that Realme *et econtra:*

3. Thirdlie if a Scottch man offend in England[2] and be pursued and taken on fresh suit I conceave that that is not the cas that for the crime and person concurre.

---

[1] The bill was committed to the whole House on May 7 (*C.J.* I, 371). The committee met several times between that date and the adjournment on May 20.
Cf. the report and debate in *C.J.* I, 376, 1046–47. This report and many of the debates during the rest of the session have to do with the trial of persons committing violence on the border. It was common for Englishmen and Scotchmen to cross the border, commit some crime, and then fly for safety to their native country. The bill before the Commons provided that such persons, upon arrest, should be remanded or handed over for trial to the authorities of the country where the crime was committed. Thus Scotchmen offending in England would be tried in England and vice versa. The Commissioners for the Union had desired this as providing swift trial for offending Scots. But the House of Commons opposed the trial of any Englishman in Scotland. They feared that the innocent would suffer along with the guilty, for an Englishman once in the hands of the Scots would probably be convicted in almost every case. It will be seen that the Commons held firm on this point and that the act as passed prohibited remanding under any circumstances. See Gardiner, I, 337–339.
[2] Bowyer means a Scotchman who had offended in Scotland and then fled to England. See *C.J.* I, 1046. Such an offender would naturally be remanded.

The cas is simplie thus.

An Englishman doth offend in Scotland and returneth into England (not taken in fresh suit) what course shalbe taken with him and so *via versa;* considering that marshall Lawe is ceased, and herin there seemeth to the Committees but 2 courses.

1. The first that the Malefactor be remanded to the place where he offende.

2. Secondlie that Remanding cease and the offendor to be tried in England *et econtra.*

Now next I am to deliver equallie the reasons as they passed on both sides.

First for the Remanding 7 reason weare alleaged: viz.

1. A Rule in state that when you will make an alteracion you do it with the greatest congruity with the former that maie be: And the marche lawe was, that uppon truice daies an offendor convicted was remitted unto the warden of the place where the offence was committed,[1] therfor now a Remaunding must be continued in proporcion etc.

2. Secondlie this Remaunding hath congruitie with the Lawe of Nacions, as it is in Artois and Picardy which are only in league and contract each with other, and there the offendors are transmitted. *ut supra:*

3. Thirdlie Severity is to be expected where the offence was committed by cause the lawe of that place was offended, and those countrie men wronged, whereas in the offendors owne countrie Remissenes is likelie to be founde. Theis be both extremities, and the lesse hurtfull as now things stande is severity: and for England it is more expedient by cause the offences of the Scottish are more frequent and greater than ours in respect their borders are more neere the hart of their contrie than ours are to the body of our countrie, so as he who hath doon an offence can more easily draw him selfe out of their borders and have more kindred and frends in the middest of their realme then *econverso* ours have.

4. An exception to a new triall to be devised in England, and the difficultie [of] said triall, for if the Judges come but once a yeare, men that do prosecute against an offendor must waite long

---

[1] Nicholson and Burn, *History and Antiquities of Westmoorland and Cumberland,* I, xiv; Walter Scott, *Border Antiquities,* I, cvii–cxii.

and have seldome dispatch and the troble of bringing witnesses to the place where the Judges set wilbe greate.

5. Example is most and best if this be where the offence was committed.

6. The Indictment must be *Contra pacem domini Regis Coronae* etc: wherin may be inconvenience to admitt both to be but one Kingdome and to have but one Crowne over them.

7. There hath in 4 yeares now last past of the Kings raigne not above 7 ben remaunded which have ben executed and so the feare greater then the hurt.

f. 33. a] On the other side against Remanding weare given five reasons. viz.

1. First the inequalitie of the Lawes in the two Kingdomes. For the Law of Scotland[1] is more severe and lesse favorable to life then ours: viz. in sixe points.

Heare in England two Juries are to passe upon a man for his life the one of 24 to indictment him, and the other 12 at the least to trie him uppon his arraignment. Whereas in Scotland there is onlie the latter.

In England all the iurors must consent, whereas in Scotland the odde voice is casting: though it be but one more then those that would acquite the prisoner: so one mans vote sheddeth one mans bloodde:

The third disadvantage and inequalitie is in the use of witnesses and prosecutors, for heare the prosecutors and Jury come before the prisoner and the evidence is openlie given in the hearing of the prisoner and standers by: but in Scotland the prosecutor sheweth not him selfe, and the evidence is given to the Jurors in private, no man not the prisoner hearing by what or what it is, unlesse the prosecutor will offer himselfe to come face to face before the prisoner.

The prisoner may have his peremptory challeng to the Jurors and likewise his legall challenge uppon cause, heare in England but not so there:

In England clergie is allowed to the prisoner, not so in Scotland:

In England you can not endanger the life of an accessorie before

---

[1] St. P. Dom. XXVII, 42, contains a description of criminal trials in Scotland.

you deale with the principall, least after the accessory be executed the principall uppon better matter alleaged in his defence be acquited. But in Scotland the[y] will trie the accessorie first, uppon pretence of this policy: that the Accessory who receaveth and abetteth the principall is commonly the better man, and the maintainor of the other:

Yet in Scotland the prisoner hath greate advantages, first he maie have an advocate, also he may challenge the Judge: and not so in England: (it seemeth hereby and by his generall delivery that he graced the Remanding opinion, for to thes 2 may be said that in England if anie matter in Law happen the prisoner ought to have councell and for matter in fact, himselfe is better able then anie counceill to answere for him selfe: To the second maie be saied that the Judge is entended indifferent and setteth as Gods minister and was not appointed by the King for this or that triall only):

2. The seconde reason against Remanding was this: *Pr[a]estat nocentem absolvere quam innocentem damnare.* Which is a greate reason at this time for they are in hott blood whilest the Feudes are fresh:

3. The third is a reason of state, viz. if remanding be allowed, how good soever the Justice be, it wilbe otherwise conceipted, for people shall not understande the proceeding but by reporte:

4. Fourthly This is not nor may not be the cas only of guiltie persons but of others also who are cleere, for it will not suffice that a man neaver hath ben in Scotland, for that notwithstanding he may be questioned as a Receavor, and remanded also as a principall uppon complaint without direct profe: and to this was added the easie procurring of wittnesses in Scotland:

5. The fift and last reasons was a Retortinge of the reason of Example for the example woorketh best reformacion when the punishment is among them, where the offence grew, and from whence the offendor came and this saied he is the best that I can remember and carrie awaie of that which was delivered.

The third parte said he of my gererall distribucion was the mocions that weare made in this cas which weare seaven:

1. First that if Remandinge stande it should be the restitucion or remitting to be uppon fresh suit.

2. Before Remanding be, if it shall stand, that there be Inquisi-

cion and examinacion whether the matter pretended be preignant, and therefore this to be first enquired by an Enquest of English iurors.[1]

3. If this inquisicion be not thought fit yet that by magistrates some examinacion be had of the truth of the fact, obiected against an offendor:

f. 33. b]   4. This Remanding to be restrained unto the 3 counties[2] adiacent which weare marches.

5. That if a remanding shalbe, yet the prisoner to have *Medietatem nationis*.[3]

6. That if a Remanding shalbe yet wee shoulde be Suitors to the King for Cessation.

7. To pray a conference with the Lords in this point of Remandinge:

The question of forme after this matter of substance, was whether this provision of Remanding shalbe annexed unto the bill of abolishing Hostile Lawes or framed by it selfe, or with some other hereafter. Against ioining or adding it to the bill was alleaged our long sitting and desier to rise, and this point requiereth deliberacion, On the other side was saied that to abolishe hostile lawes is but *actum agere*, and before the next opportunity to deale in this provision of Remaunding, the liefe of manie subiects maie be questioned.

SIR ROG[ER] OWEN. The questions among us at the committee weare twoo.

1. First whether as the Lawe now standeth a man having committed felonie or treason in Scotland and being returned and abiding in England may by such commissions as are already sent foorth be remanded and sent back into Scotland:

2. And secondlie what remedy:

To the first I saie negatively, and first not by the Canon Lawe, for a Bishop of two Sees cannot draw him that hath offended within one of his diocesse to aunswere it in the other and so in the two Kingdomes. Then not by the Civill lawe for by that lawe the King cannot alien his subiect unto an other King or Crowne, (for which

---

[1] "Some Inquisition in Nature of an Indictment." *C.J.* I, 1047.

[2] Northumberland, Cumberland, and Westmoreland.

[3] "If a Trial in Scotland, then half of English." *C.J.* I, 1047. A reference to the composition of the jury.

purpose he cited authorityes) much lesse in theis two Kingdomes
for then wee shall transmitt a subiect not only to subiection to an
other crowne but to an other law whereas in other countries the
civill law for the most parte doth governe all: It is saied that
Artoys and Picardy do use or have used to remande *ut supra.*
I aunsweare, that this may be by confederacion and contract not
by civill Lawe. And touching the Territories of Spaine I saie it is
not all one for they weare originallie all one kingdome and then
severed and now againe become under one. Againe although in
Spaine and those territories, there be severall Chauncellors, yet is
there one generall Chauncellor over all: And if in anie particular
or rare cas anie province want a particular Law, the same resorteth
unto the civill law by which Spaine itself is governed: But for
Granado the King of Spaine cannot send them foorth *ut supra*
for their triall.

Againe this cannot be by commen law for felony committed in
Scotland is no offence heare: *et econverso:*

Likewise for 12 other reasons:

1. It is against Magna carta: *Nullus* etc. *capiatur imprisonetur*
etc. *aut utlagetur aut exuletur aut aliquo modo destruatur nec super
eum ibimus, nec super eum mittemus nisi per legale iudicium parium
suorum.* etc.

2. It is against the statute of [*blank*].

3. It is not triable there:

4. The mischeife of remanding a man uppon surmise.

5. The offences are not alwayes alike, for that may be felony in
Scotland which is not so heare and *econverso:*

6. No man can waive or forsake his native lawes, *ergo* neither be
put from them.

7. A Scottishman is not aunsweareable heare because he is an
alien, *et econverso:*

The other reasons I observed not:

Sir Danyel Dun began first to prove Remaundinge by such
Commissions as aforesaied lawfull by the civill Lawe, but at the
first Mr. Speaker interrupted him craving leave of the howse so
to do, and then request him and all the companie to forbeare the
dispute of that point, for saied he you all understand my meaning
and do conceave whom it concerneth (*inuendo* the Kings Majesties

proceeding in granting such commissions). Then D[aniel] Dun proceeded to prove Remaunding *ut supra* necessary. first

1. That satisfaccion be made to the Commen wealth where the offence was committed and consolacion ministred to the party hurt. f. 34. a] 2. Secondlie Example, as before on the same side was alleaged, and for this second he alleaged a text out of the Civill Lawe, and heare he was entering into the lawfulnes of remaunding, but was interrupted by Mr. Speaker as before, with approbacion of the howse.

3. Difficultie unto the party iniured if he be driven to seeke recompence in an other country. Next for the matter of forme he thought it most fit if Remaunding be taken away that it be doon in a law by it selfe.

In conclusion after much variance for making of a question, It was uppon a question cunning[ly] perswaded by the Speaker, ordered that the former Committees should consider of somme course of triall and punishment of felonyes murders *et huius[mo]di* committed *ut supra* without Remaundinge:

From the Lords Serieant Crooke and D[octor] Hone brought a bill for assurance of the howse and certaine lands of Theoballs by the Earl of Salisbury unto [the] King and of others in Exchange from the King to the Earle:[1]

28 Maii.[2]

I was absent.

---

[1] St. P. Dom. XXVII, 31 is a draft of this bill.

[2] A mistake for 29 May. Thomas Wilson wrote an account (no doubt for Salisbury) of the proceedings for the day:

"This daye was nothing done of moment this morning.

"The bill for assurance of Tiballds and Hatfeld etc. had his first reading.

"Thre bills sent up to the Lords who were upe before they came.

"The bill of starch dasht the howse (being not above 100) devided about it.

"In the afternoone att the Comitte.

"They have disputed and agreed upon thes points.

"1. To make all English accessoryes of fellonyes done in Scottland to be principales, for that happily the principale being in Scottland cannot be found and the lawe of England (as it nowe is) permitts not to proceed against an accessorye untill the principale be condemned.

"2. To take away the clergye from all thefts done in Scotland by

29 Maii:[1]

Nothing doon but the bill of exchange betwene his Majestie and the Earl of Salisbury for Theoballs 2do. *lecta*.

30 Maii[2] was Sonday.

Primo Junii 1607.

The committee for the bill of abolishinge hostile lawes mett[3] and in that bill was agreed and sett downe an order for execucion of Justice and triall of felonyes doon by Englishmen in Scotland where the offendors recover England:[4] and this to be doon without remaunding, against which course of Remaunding in this bill is speciall provision.

---

partyes taken in England for that they wold else be too frequent the place of refuge being soe neer and noe clergie allowed in Scottland.

"3. To take away all peremptory challenge of Jurors unless only the number of fyve, wheras by the lawe of England a man upon his lyfe may peremptorily challenge 20. The reason of this was for that if every man myght peremptoryly challeng 20 besids those he shold challeng upon cause ther wold be great difficulty to gett soe many V£ men as wold try a man.

"4. That thefts done in Scottland and tryed in England the party shall only lose lyfe and goods but nether corruption of bludd nor forfayture of lands.

"It was moved by Sir Edwin Sands that the Scothmen tryedd in England shold have advocats and counsell to plead for them alledging the hardness of our lawes in that point in regard of all the lawes of christendom and howe in Venice the most Eminent persons tooke upon them that office to defend such as were accused of Capitale crymes wherin he seemed he wold wish that liberty permitted all over England. But that was answered by Mr. Atturney to be the removing of a corner stone and soe it was put off to the tyme when ther shold be a tretyng of the conformitye of lawes of both Kingdomes.

"The conclusion was that Mr. Atturney and others shold frame all thes and the precedent poynts into forme and adioyne them to the bill of hostile lawes by Monday next, which bill shold then be brought into the howse." St. P. Dom. XXVII, 30.

[1] A mistake for 30 May.

[2] A mistake for 31 May.

[3] In the Court of Wards. Meanwhile nothing was done in the House, though the Speaker and a few members were there.

[4] The prisoners were to be tried in the three northern counties of England before the ordinary Justices of Assize as if the offense had been committed in those counties.

Mr. Yelverton. Notwithstanding a law thus passed forbidding remaunding and providing a course of triall in England a Commission may hereafter be graunted to remaunde as before, viz. with a *Non obstante* and the only way to prevent it is to adde a penaltie on such as shall remaund or send any person backe into Scotland contrarie to the effect of this act. Hereuppon some moved to have it fyne and Ransome, others agreed it should be *Premunire*, but after argument the Companie enclined to make it felony notwithstanding the opinion of the Kings counceill who affirmed that his Majestie might licence such remanding though it weare by this act made felony because it is not *malum in se* but *malum prohibitum:* but the Company reiected that opinion and enclined to the other:

2 JUNII. 1607.

In the forenoone about 8 of the Clocke the Committees for the bill of abolishing hostile lawes mett in the court of wards and there having spent 2 houers, about 10 of the clocke Mr. Speaker sent the Serieant to entreate the committee to come into the howse, and the companie being accordinglie in the howse Mr. Speaker declared to them that he had a message to deliver to them from his Majestie which his highness was pleased to deliver saied he to mee in wrighting and to signe the same with his owne hande and then Mr. Speaker red it, and so againe read it the second time and so delivered the same to the clerke of the howse whereof the coppie followeth.[1]

f. 35. a]   3 JUNII 1607.

Bill of hostile lawes. Committee. The committee for the bill of abolishing hostile lawes and providing a new kind of triall of an englishman which having criminallie offended in Scotland recovereth England without Remaundinge, did meete in the court of wards in the forenoone, and

---

[1] Bowyer here inserts a copy of the King's message. The editor has not reprinted Bowyer's copy, since the original is found in *C.J.* I, 377–378.

In this message James allowed the Commons to prohibit remanding in the act, but expressed his displeasure at the proposal that remanding in the future should be regarded as felony. James considered this proposal as a slight upon his own past actions. The Commons yielded, and the act as passed prohibits remanding but contains no provision for disobedience.

after some varietie of opinion and uppon the question proposed,
did resolve that the prisoner who is in such case as afore, to be tried
in England for felony etc. alleaged to be doon by him in Scotland
shalbe allowed to have witnesses swoorne herd for his purgacion:[1]
uppon theis reasons, first for that it was affirmed and by Sir Rog[er]
Aston saied that the Law of Scotland is so: Next bicause by this
lawe wee take from the accused divers advantags which the law
of England doth allow in cas of felonies: viz. Clergie: allso that
wee make the accessorie triable and to suffer death before anie
proceeding against the principall which is otherwise by the law
of England in cas of felonye. *Et huius[mo]di*.

Before this was concluded divers argued contra: and some proposed proiects some tending to a meane course: viz. One[2] moved
that Whereas if exception be taken to a iuror before he be swoorne
2 or 3 being formerly swoorne on that iuray shall trie whether the
iuror now challenged be indifferent. So let the Jury trie and pronounce whether the witnesse produced be fit to be herd: otherwise
a lewde person may be acquited through the testimony of the like
person: Sir Edwyne Sandys moved that no domesticall witnesse
might be swoorne or herd for that such may be presumed favorable:
nor any defamed or detected person. But this and the like notwithstanding it was resolved as above said that such accused person
should be admitted to have all witnesses swoorne and their credit
referred to the Jurors.[3] After dinner the Committee met againe,
at which time Mr. Fuller moved that this act might not rest uppon
woords of enacting against Remaunding, but that to avoid all

---

[1] This is a point that will constantly recur in the following debates.
According to the English law a prisoner accused of felony could not have
the witnesses on his behalf put under oath. This meant that the jury,
if so disposed, might slight the evidence of the prisoner's witnesses because they were unsworn. The Commons proposed that in border trials
these witnesses should be sworn. They gained their point with certain
modifications. In these debates the word "witnesses" should be taken to
mean "sworn witnesses."

For arguments used in the House from June 3 to June 5, see a document
printed in pp. 314-318 note.

[2] Probably the Attorney, Sir Henry Hobart, who made a similar
motion in the House two days later.

[3] That is to say, the jury should decide what evidence was worthy
of belief.

danger of Commissions to remaunde with *non obstante*, this
statut might farther also have woords of declaracion that the law
is so as now wee make or ordaine it against Remaunding. Heere
Sir Fra[ncis] Bacon remembered the dispute yesterday in the howse
touching the unlawfullnes of such commission: and Mr. Speakers
mocion to staie that argument and allso to prevent a gentleman
f. 35. b] that would have aunswered that point as in the Civill
lawe. Allso Mr. Attorney told Mr. Fuller that wee weere past that
point and that therefore he might not by the order go backe to it.
To which the Committee agreed:

4 JUNII.

Committee.   A few of the Committee mett in the morninge in the court of
wards, to whome Sir Fra[ncis] Bacon from his Majestie delivered
a message touching the clause of admittinge witnesses to an
Englishman having offended in Scotland *ut supra* to this effect:
His Majestie hath understoode of your care to provide by a dew
course of Justice here in England to punish such English subiects
as having committed felony in Scotland shall escape into this
realme, his Majestie doth likewise understande of your resolucion
to allow the person accused witnesses for his purgacion and this his
Majestie taketh notice that you did hold fit in regard that you
conceaved the Law to be so in Scotland: He is fullie perswaded
that no one man in this companie will take *patrocinium latrocinii*
for those weare his woords. Wherefore he commaunded mee to
saie unto you from him that uppon his owne knowledge the Law
of Scotland is not so:[1] and that the triall of felones there is not
according to the civill law but by Jury as heare in England: He
farther commaunded mee to tell you from his Majestie that this
clause will do more hurt by encoraging malefactors then all the
rest of your severitie in the residew of the act will do to restraine
them and so his Majestie wisheth you to consider accordinglie of it.
    Sir H[enry] Poole: moved that it was now out of the power of the
committee to alter or varie from that which they have formerly

---

[1] See a paper describing trials in Scotland that the Speaker read to
the House on this day, June 4. *C.J.* I, 378–379. See also St. P. Dom.
XXVII, 42, which contains a much fuller account of criminal procedure
in Scotland. The *Calendar* (p. 360) states that this paper also was read
to the House. But the present editor finds no proof for that opinion.

done, and therefore wished that proceedings shold be reported to the howse as they now stand and this withall if it shall so seeme convenient.

Mr. Leuckner moved that forasmuch as the committee was yesterday greate when this point was resolved and now is veary small that therefore notice may be given to the howse what busines is now heare in hand to the ende the Committee may be more full. Which mocion was liked and Mr. Leuckner being sent accordingly manie came foorth of the howse into the Committee. Then Sir Fra[ncis] Bacon delivered the King's message againe.

Mr. Fuller. I was not yesterdaie carried to allow witnesses *ut supra* by the Law of Scotland but in Justice, for albeit generally witnesses are not herd heare in like cas yet is not the Law of England against hearing of witnesses for there is no one booke or cas in all the Law, to that effect. Againe the only reason of the contrary Usage is for that witnesses should not be herd against the King, and yet in accusacion of Forgery, Periury *et huius[mo]di* which also is for the King witnesses are examined for the defendant, and otherwise an innocent man may be condemned with out defence, so as Justice is for admitting of witnesses in this cas and the Law not against it. Only an encrochement upon the Law is to the contrary and therefore seeing the profes against the accused are to be of an other country, yea likely of his enemyes with whome he and his blood have had fewdes and seeing the profes against life ought to be more strong and cleere then those for life, I thinke wee ought to allow thes witnesses.

Mr. Jones. The Common Law doth not take witnesses for purgacion from the accused of felony for by the Common Lawe an appeale of robbery or murder lieth for the party robbed or for the next of Kyne of the person murdered: and if within a yeere and day such appeale be not preferred the King may endict the offendor: and in the Appeale the defendant may *de iure* have witnesses examined for his defence and the King's attorney shalbe of counceill with him. If the appeal be not persued and at the King's suit the party be endicted, hear witnesses are not taken by law from him, but it is encroched, and if the party be acquited in the appeale it is agread barre to the Indictment.

f. 36. a]   Mr. Carleton. Of necessity wee are to referre this matter to the howse for where it is saied that the opinion of the committee was and did grow uppon an Error, viz. a conceipt that the Scottish law was so, surely Sir W[illiam] Seaton in the howse saied that he asked Borro whether he had anie witnesses to testifie for him, yea whether anie advocate to speake for him. Therefore it is good to acquaint the howse how that point of law is now retracted by a message from the King and then if the howse will referre it to us to be considered of, wee may safely dispute it.

Sir Rog[er] Owen. Surely Sir W[illiam] Seaton did deliver in the howse as Mr. Carleton hath reported, and yesterday Sir Rog[er] Ashton did allso affirme the law of Scotland to be that the accused *Ut supra* may have Witnesses examined for his defence and pur- gation, but seeing his Majestie hath testified otherwise now commeth the question whether wee shall dispute it againe or certifie the howse: and I thincke wee ought to report it to the howse. For when a Committee hath decided anie matter by a question, it doth bind them as a question in the howse doth the howse, and you Sir Fra[ncis] Bacon being in the chair are as the Speaker in the howse.

Mr. [*blank*] was sent to desier Mr. Speaker not to arise butt to set untell the committee might come to him into the howse.

Mr. Attorney. The King saith on his Knowledge that the ac- cused *ut supra* by the law of Scotland cannot *de iure* have wit- nesses examined for him, Sir W[illiam] Seaton saied that himselfe being a iudge did in favor aske and offer Baro to have witnesses herd. Thes two agree and may be both trew. But let us fall to the question, whether wee the Committee may alter that which wee have doon, and resolved by the Committee not to go backewards but to report the matter, as it now standeth to the howse and there the same to be ordered:

Sir Fra[ncis] Bacon. I was by his Majestie commaunded to de- liver the message to the Committee and having so doon I have dis- charged my duity and cannot deliver it anywhere ellse from the King except you will commaund mee to repeate it in the howse: wher unto he was required by the Committee. Theruppon the Committee leaving that point, and for their better understanding herd the whole bill readde over: and then arrose and went into the howse: SIR FRA[NCIS] BACON reported[1] to the howse the

---

[1] Cf. his report and the subsequent debate in *C.J.* I, 379, 1048-49.

proceedings of the committees in the bill and desiered that the whole bill and not only the alteracions might be readde. Then he shewed that the Committee hath referred 2 things backe unto the howse, The first the preamble, The 2d. matter in the close of the bill. The first thus: Where the woords be The happy unyon already begoon in his Majesties person: Some thought fit that for honor some other woords weare added, as, Grounded, or Vested, Planted, Inherent: or such like: and the same in the foote or ending of the bill.[1] The other matter referred to the howse by the Committee is of more weight: viz: Some would that the prisoner for his life of whom the dispute now is, shalbe allowed witnesses, to testifie for his purgacion and innocency and it is trew that some of the Committees did encline to allow witnesses in that case uppon this supposicion that the law is so in Scotlande, but since that time yesterday Mr. Attorney be[ing] out of the way uppon other service, his Majestie called for mee, and commaunded mee to signifie to the Committee his woords touching this matter which I did accordingly and thereof am not to saie at this time anie thing to the howse from his Majestie, but the Committee have directed mee to make declaracion of the same heare unto the howse, which is this. His Majestie commaunded mee to signifie unto the Committee that his highnes taketh notice of the clause offered for admitting Witnesses to the prisoner *ut supra* etc: which he allso understandeth was by a perswasion or opinion that the Lawe is so in Scotland, wherefore he doth assure you uppon his owne knowl-
f. 36. b] edge that the law is not so there, and that there trialls are not after the civill law but by Jury as heare. Againe if you admitt this clause his Majesty sayeth that it will do more hurt by givinge impunity then all the rest of your care and severity by the act will do good.

Mr. Speaker. I thinke it not the order for mee to move the two points of woords and matter before the bill be readde, and it is moved that the whole bill be read once, which if you allow, I desier to know your pleasure. Wheruppon it was ordered that the whole bill shoulde be readde:

Uppon Sir Fra[ncis] Baringtons mocion Mr. Speaker declared the order of the howse to be that if the Committee differ,   Committees differ.

---

[1] The suggested change was not made.

and uppon a question it is overruled among themselves they cannot afterwards do the contrary: but in that case the howse may
differ from the resolucion of the Committee.

SIR JOHN SHIRLY moved the howse to consider that the clause
for witnesses to be herd etc. agreed on by the committee, may be
adde[d] unto the bill before the bill be redde. Mr. Speaker. It
ought not to be argued whether it shalbe added or not before it
be first put to the bill, and so it was agreed:

Report of Com-
mittee.

Allso uppon an other occasion it was ruled that not everything
spoken at the committee is to be reported to the howse but all and
only such things as the committee shall direct to be reported.

5 JUNII 1607.

Committment and
speach after.

After a bill is committed uppon a generall mocion anie man
maie speake, but not after a bill is committed uppon a question
affirmative and negative:

The point was argued whether the partie tried in England for a
robbery doon in Scotland uppon this new offered law, for abolishing hostile lawes and triall in England of felonyes doon in Scotland,
the defendant or party tried or arraigned shalbe allowed witnesses
generally was this daie disputed.[1]

---

[1] See debate and division in *C. J.* I, 379, 1049. St. P. Dom. XXVII,
44 is a collection made by Sir Robert Cotton of arguments used in the
House from June 3 to June 5, chiefly on the latter date.

"The Speeches in the Commons House of Parliament concerning that
Clause in the Bill for repeal of Hostill Lawes, for Admitting the Accused
to have Witnesses on their part to be Examined uppon Oath contained
either

"1. Arguments (1) For the inserting of that Clause. A. (2) For the
rejecting of this Clause. B.

"2. Propositions for some middle or indifferent way to be held. C.

"3. Motives for a Petition to be made to his Majesty. D.

"A. Arguments for inserting the Clause. Answers to the Arguments.

"1. Arg. In cases of greatest Importance it is more requisite to admitt all means to discover the Truth, than in the smallest. And to respect
a Man more in the Interest of his life than of his beast. But in Question
of Lands, Goods etc. being of farr less value, than life, we admitt witnesses,
Ergo.

"1. Resp. In favor of Life the Law doth presuppose, and not in other
Cases, that Men will bee more prone to forswear themselves, and therefore to prevent Perjury, doth not admitt of witnesses, which reason may

SIR ROB[ERT] HITCHAM the Queens attorny: negative, not alleaging anie reason worthy the setting downe.

MR. WEINTWOORTH affirmative: And he resembled it to the cas of the appeale: for if a man bring an appeale of robbery, or of murder in both which cases the life of the defendant or

move us more against this Clause, if wee respect the place where by the Confession of Sir Henry Witherington forswearing is so frequent.

"2. Arg. Where there is like to be an Extraordinary pursuit of Blood, there it is fit to use any unusuall means of Justification. But upon the Borders, by reason of the Malice of their bloody Feuds it is like to be so. Therefore to admitt the Prisoner his Witnesses though it be extraordinary. And not by putting the life of an Englishman uppon the Oath of a Scott, make Justice to be a means to execut private Malice.

"2. Respon. No fear of the Prosecutors Malice when the Judg and Jurors are English.

"3. Arg. Whatever is not against the Laws of the Kingdom, of Nations, or of God, cannot bee taxed either with Injustice, or Innovation. But the allowing of this Clause of witnesses is not against etc. *Ergo.*

"3. Respon. It is against the Common Law, For no witness is allowed by that Law but upon oath. But no witness is in Cases of this Nature allowed to be sworne Therefore no witnes is allowed by Law. And according to the Civill Law, if you give the Delinquent advantage of witness, you must by the same to the Magistrate, of Torture.

"4. Argum. If in prosecution of a Felon by an Appeall the Law alloweth wittnes, why not in an Indictment. Since the change in form cannot alter the quality in Matter. But in an Appeall the Law allowes the Prisoner his witnesses. Therefore etc.

"4. Respons. The reason is not alike, for in an Appeall the Sute moveth from desire of Revenge in the Party wronged: But the Indictment from a grand jury can intend no Malice. Therefore in an Appeall the Law admitteth the accused not onely Witnesses, but Counsell that he may have as good a Defence as the other hath an Accusation, which no Man holdeth fitt in this Case.

"5. Arg. All Judgement is Gods, and therefore it is fit wee make our Rule of Judgement according to his Law. But his Law doth allow wittnesses to the accused. Therefore etc.

"5. Resp. First there is no such express Text. Secondly the Morall and not the Judiciall Law of the old Testament, out of which they force this, is left to rule us by.

"6. Arg. Of Necessity for the preservation of the honour of our Justice wee must admitt the Prisoner his wittnesses uppon Oath. For since the Law alloweth the Judg without Oath to take Knowledge of a Testimony for him, and that his Sentence may be lead thereby contrary to the Testimony uppon Oath produced by a Scothman, it would give

appellee is in question, as well as uppon indictment and arraignement, the defendant or appellee maie produce witnesses and yet
in those cases if he be acquite[d] he shall not afterwards be called
in question by way of indictment at the Kings suyt.

Sir H[enry] Montague Recorder of London contra: for there is

some Imputation in that Nation to our Justice. And show of apparent
injury done unto him.

"B. Arguments against the inserting of the Clause. Answers to the
Arguments.

"1. Arg. Since our endeavour is to work an Union, wee must to effect
that, as near as we can, reduce our Lawes to Uniformity. But to admitt this Clause, is to make a contrariety, where there is already a conformity. For by the Law of Scotland in Causes Criminall witnesses are
not allowed (noe not *sub arbitrio Judicis*). Therefore a way to hinder,
and not further our Worke.

"1. Resp. That it is not so in Scotland as is alledged: Reason giveth
us a Cause to thinke, but greatnes of Authority standeth against us.
And in this *Sententia Imperatoris* must bee *Sententia Juris*, since the Law
may bee in his Breast, but if it had been of the common Law a Question,
we had no reason to believe it. But that admitted, the erecting of this
Clause doth rather hinder, than advance Equality. For since the Law
of Scotland permitteth the Delinquent Counsell which is not here, it is
fit, wee counterpoise it with some other advantage which may bee this.

"2. Arg. No Alteration of Fundamentall Lawes can be without perill
as appeareth by that *De donis conditionalibus* in Edw. I. time Cause of
much Tumult. But admitting witnesses in this sort, is altering of Fundamentall Lawes. Therefore etc.

"2. Respons. First as well in favor, as in prejudice of the Party accused
we have in this Act already without contradiction altered the Common
Law on the one Side, taking from him his Clergy, and peremptory Exception, on the other Side giving him security of not forfeiting Land, or cor-
rupting blood. Secondly no general Rule can be in Government and new
Offences must have new triall. And so making that an offence, which the
Law now maketh none: in regard of the Place. For it is not *contra
Coronam et dignitatem* of the King of England, but of Scotland. It is no
alteration of an old Law, but taking away of the border Law.

"3. Argum. Where Justice is more favorable, than in any other
Country, there needeth no Addition of Grace. But the Justice of England,
which proceedeth by Indictment (accusing none but by Verdict of 24,
condemning none but by particular Jury, admitting none against the
Prisoner uppon Oath, and disabling the proof at the Judges discretion by unsworn Testimony, who doth, as Bracton sayes, plead for
the Prisoner *Ne Christus crucifigatur et Barabus liberetur*. And in all
other Causes but of this nature is tied to Judg according to evidence,
but in this, as the Judges agree in Hen. 4. time, he may by his particular

a difference, for the appeale is an accion of Revenge, *ergo* as iust
to allow witnesses for defence as for accusacion. So is not Indictment. And in other countries they use Torture to wring out
confession from the defendant: other reasons are theis.

Knowledge informe his Judiciall) is with far more lenity than that of
other Countries, that alloweth Torture; Therefore.

"3. Respons. You will make so much of Discretion, you will make it
an Idell.

"4. Argum. Whatsoever shall take away the Remedy for punishing a
perjured Jury, is not to bee approved. But this Clause that giveth Evidence on both side, doth either perplex the Jury, or thereby give them
a colourable Excuse whereby they may avoid the Censure of the Starr
Chamber. Therefore.

"4. Respons. The Answer to this was that Juries are as well brought
into the Starchamber for triall of Lands etc. wherein witnesses are on
either Side produced, as in trying of Lyfe, that admitteth but the one.
To this Mr. Speaker replied, that the Starchamber sentenced no Jurie
in regard of his Verdict, but for corruption by Bribery, or the like.

"5. Argum. No Law is Just that giveth more advantage and Incouragement to bad Men to offend than to good Men to prosecute. But the
admitting of this Clause will do so. For by the Oath of their Confederates
and Kindred acquitting themselves with him against the Just Accuser,
because *Crimen imposuit* an Action of the Case, or Conspiracy, and so
discourage him from prosecuting Law and Justice.

"6. Argum. It is most injust to give to Men prone to offend more
advantage of Impunity then to those that are usually most apt to obey.
But to give to the dissolute Borderers the benefit of witnesses (who by
reason of Situation and Custome have Theft and Murther almost for
nature, and therefore ought to have a more severe Law. For there are as
well *Leges loci* as *Temporis* and *Misericordia puniens* as *pariens*. For to
cutt off him that cannot live but to offend, is to give mercy to them that
live well) and not to the Gentry and Nobility of the more civill parts, is
to doe so. Therefore.

"7. Arg. The King cannot challenge any of the Jury, but the prisoner
may peremptorily. Then if you allow him his Challenge, and his witnesses,
you give him an advantage of the King, and if you admitt the King to
challenge witnesses, you shall make it as infinite as of Juries.

"8. Argum. If the Delinquent be admitted Witnesses for his Offence
done in Scotland only, which is so as the Clause now standeth, wee shall
incourage them to rob there onely, which is Injustice. And if for Equality
(which wee cannot blame the Motive arising from our selves) the Scotts
shall by a new Law admitt the like to their Borderers, then will the Disadvantage rest wholly on our side for their rapine will be more uppon us
by reason of their greater penury, And their tryall lesse in Justice by reason
of their Perjury.

1. If you admit witnesses for the prisoner you bring in Periury.

2. The defendant or prisoner will bring in one or two frends to sweare for him and in that case though sixe sweare directly against the prisoner yet if the Jury acquit him, as it is most likely

"C. The Propositions for some indifferent course to be held in admitting the Prisoner his Witnesses upon Oath.

"1. To leave it to the free choice of the Jury, whether they will admitt any, and those they shall admitt to swear.

"[Response]. No reason to insert this as a new Law when the Law already leaveth to the Jury's discretion the admitting or rejecting of such Testimony.

"2. If the Jury be bound by this Law to hear Testimony uppon Oath for the Prisoner, then in this Law to leave the Choice of the Wittnesses they will hear to their election before they are sworn. For to lett the credit of the Witness rest uppon the discretion of the Judg who is for the most part a stranger in the Country, is not so fitt as to refer it to the Jury, who by inroulment must better Know the Partys, and since the Law doth make them in Question of Exception Triors of themselves.

"3. Not to leave the Choice to the Jury, who will receive all in favor of life nor to the Judge, who is not acquainted with the Persons, but to take a middle way, which is that All freeholders shall bee received without Triall and the other left to the Judg and Jury.

"[Response]. This cannot bee since uppon the Borders there are few or no Freeholdes all their Estats being tenant rights a Kind of Copyhold.

"4. To make this Clause a [*blank*] untill the next Session.

"D. The Petition was expressed in a Speech by Mr. Yelverton to this Effect.

"That before his Majestys Message to the Commons this Clause was received *nemine contradicente*. And therefore perswaded that we might (as the Children of Israell prayed to their God to speake to them no more in Thunder, but by the voice of Moyses) be humble Petitioners That the voice of our God uppon Earth may no more sound unto us at the penning of a Bill. In two clauses of this Act hath his Majesty interposed his honor in the one, his reason in the other; His Honour which is rapt about his Scepter as being drawn in question for his former proceedings by addition of the penalty. But since no Man can so sensibly discerne the blemish of reputation as he whom properly it concerneth, I wish to have all dispute of the penalty barred. As for his reason it must be like his coin, it must have weight. For the point of honor, desist, for his reason, weigh it. None of his Gold but I may weigh it, before I take it. His reason is of great power and staggereth any of us, stopping some from speaking at all, or speaking causeth them that they are not resolved at all. Lett us therefore be Suiters that the Voice of our God uppon Earth may no more in this House be heard, but to infuse his reason into such Vessells of flesh as wee are. Thus shall wee maintain our Priviledges etc."

thcy will, you cannot punish them by anie course of Law for that they had evidence to leade them to that which they did, though apparantly false:

3. You thinke such offendors not woorthy of Clergy, also you hold them as dangeros that in that case the accessory shalbe tried before the principall yea though the principall be not apprehended or delt withall: *ergo* this favor of witnesses is not fit to be allowed them.

4. You change the Lawes, which was so deare to our predecessors that they said *Nolimus leges Angliae mutari*.

f. 37. a] Mr. Fuller. At the committee I was of opinion that witnesses in the case now in hand ought to be allowed and by that which I have hetherto herd I am confirmed in my opinion. This day and every daie at our coming into this howse wee pray that Gods law maie direct us in makinge our lawes, The Law of God doth allow witnesses in the like case, *ergo* wee ought to make our law accordinge: *ergo* but to right, Equity is indifferent, *ergo* equall witnesses, and by the rule of law Lyfe, Dower and libertie are favored:

In an Appeale witnesses are allowed to the defendant, Yea saie you but this is for the King: I Replie *ergo a maiore* witnesses are to be allowed to the defendant. For an Appeale is betweene partie and partie in which the Judge and other persons are indifferent, but heare the King is party, the King shall have the whole forfeiture and the Judges are the Kings *ergo* more fit in cas of an indictment to have witnesses allowed the prisoner.

Mr. Attorney moved as before at the Committee, viz. not all witnesses to be without exception to be allowed, but they to be tried by the Jurors and by them to be allowed or disallowed.

After several speaches the question was made by the Speaker thus: As many as will have this clause of allowing witnesses to the prisoners altered Say yea: and *econverso:* and uppon division of the howse, the Yea lost, and the clause stoode unchanged:

6 Junii 1607.

The act for abolishing hostile lawes 3° *lecta* engrossed, and passed and sent up with others unto the Lords.

8 Junii 1607.

Serieant Crooke Sir Edw[ard] Stanhope from the Lords declared that their Lordships having heretofore receaved from this howse a request to conferre touching the greavances of the Spanish merchants have entered into consideracion, That their Lordships are equallie sensible with this howse of the greavances of state, And forasmuch as the particulars are contained in the petition[1] which they conceave is directed to the King and parliament which as yet they have not seen but their Lordships will ioine with this howse in consideracion thereof: and in suyt unto his Majestie on the behalfe of the peticioners as shalbe fitt: with this that their Lordships do desire this howse should understande that their aunsweare hath not ben deferred upon any neclect of the mocions of this howse, but by reason of other more weightie affaires: but now their Lordships wilbe ready to ioine with this howse in consideracion of the premisses when [they] shall first have seen and considered of the peticion which their Lordships desier may be sent unto them.

The messengers being withdrawen, Sir Edwyne Sandys in whose hands the said peticion remained spake to this effect: The peticion containeth two things One a narracion of greavaunces, and the Other, A proposicion for amends or reformacion which second is allso set downe in two points, The first to revive an olde statute,[2] the latter the making of a new law: The first point which consisteth in a narracion of greavances the Committees embraced and considered of, the second which containeth a proposicion for amends they would not deale with but thought good to leave the redresse unto the King: the peticion I have not now heare, but to morrow I will bring it.

After some speache it was agreed, *nemine contradicente*, that the peticion shalbe sent whole unto the Lords by messengers of our owne with report of as much touching the point or matter of redresse as hath ben in that behalfe delivered by Sir Edwyne Sandys: and aunsweare presently to be sent to the Lords by their messengers that to morrow the peticion shalbe sent unto their Lordships which now is not heare:

f. 37. b]   9 Junii 1607.

Sir Edwyne Sandys. This parliament hath much favored the selling of private possessions wherin the gravity and honor of [the] howse hath ben ever to have regard to wrong no person: now uppon

---

[1] The petition of the merchants is printed in *C.J.* I, 341–342.
[2] 4 Hen. V. Stat. II. c. 7. *Statutes of the Realm*, II, 198–199.

the bill for selling the possessions of the Earl of Derby it hath ben
doubted whether certaine lands being therby assumed to the heirs
males, certaine to the daughters[1] and heirs generall of Ferdinando
late Earl of Derby, and certaine on Other persons, whether the
proviso which after all that cometh in the ende of that act be
sufficient to save the rights of others entende[d] not to be preiudiced
by this act: and herin some doubt or scruple was amonge the
Committees. Wherefore he moved that some provision may be that
the generall provision may be sufficient to releive and provide for
all persons saving such as are expressely excepted:[2] Rich[ard]
Strowdes cas[3] was that notwithstanding the privilege of the howse
he was called in question for speaches by him used in parliament,
and was acquitted and a law in the same bill that no man shall
after the parliament be called in question for his woords used in
parliament. And accordingly he namely Sir Edwyn Sandys delivered in a bill intituled An act to prevent fraude and wronge
doinge in private acts of parliament.

Serieant Crooke and Doctor Stanhope from the Lords declared
that their Lordships have considered of the bill sent unto them from
this howse for abolishing hostile lawes and committed the same.
That the Committees have conceaved some doubts uppon the bill
which they likewise conceave maie best be cleered by a conference
with a committee of both howses, which they have reported to the   Conference.
Lords in the howse, and theruppon their Lordships do desier a
conference with this howse as soon as convenientlie maie be either
this after noone at two of the clocke or on thursday at the same
hower in the painted chamber, the Committee of their Lordships
to be in nomber fiftie: Thes messengers being withdrawen: SIR
ANTH[ONY] COPE moved that the first meeting of our committees
with the Lords should be only to understande and heare their
doubts not to argue: and then a second meating to conferre of the
points which wee should so find to be doubted by their Lordships:

Mr. Speaker. The course moved by Sir Anth[ony] Cope hath ben

---

[1] Ferdinando, the fifth Earl of Derby, had left his daughters as
coheiresses with his younger brother William, the sixth Earl.

[2] Sandys pointed out a general danger in private acts of Parliament,
"where an Act passeth, in the Body for the Settling of any Estate, and a
Saving cometh after, which doth no help." *C.J.* I, 381.

[3] 4 Hen. VIII. c. 8. *Statutes of the Realm*, III, 53-54.

used where the matter of which the conference must be, is new to us, and moveth from the Lords but where it is uppon [a] bill from our selves it hath not ben the use:

Hereuppon the messengers weare brought in, and aunsweare by them sent that uppon a gracious message heretofore receaved from his Majestie[1] the howse hath appointed to call the howse this after noone, but they will attend the service of Conference on thursday at 2 of the clocke in the painted chamber: as the Lords requier.

Sir Edwyne Sandys was sent to the Lords with the peticion of the spanish merchants, and this message viz. That this howse receaved the peticion as conceaving the same after his Majestie, to be exhibited unto their Lordships and them selves and have considered of it as far as they can do and do find the greavances and wrongs complained on to be exceeding greate, as the same uppon hearinge of one side only do appeare, but havinge no power to convent or deale with the other side viz. the Spanish Ambassador, have thought it duitie to referre the Reformacion to his Majestie to whom the care to relive his people doth appertaine, and to that purpose have desiered that their Lordships will ioine in peticion with this howse, and therefore according to their Lordships message have sent unto their Lordships the said peticion.

Committees. Uppon occasion of a bill concerning salers and Marinors returned into the howse by the committees Mr. Speaker delivered that when a bill first cometh into the howse it is the part of the Speaker to make a briefe therof: so when a bill is committed and alteracions made the Committee is to alter the breviate accordingly and so to returne it.

Committees. SIR H[ENRY] POOLE moved that in lieu of divers committees for the bill of coppies[2] which are out of towne others may be added, and certaine Committees left out that are parties and officers. Wheruppon it was ruled that Committees whom the matter of the bill doth concerne shall not be left out but continued according to manie former presidents. To the 2d. point it was aunswered that if there be enough remaine in towne no supplie shalbe in lieu of the

---

[1] The King's message of May 27 called attention to the poor attendance in the Commons.

[2] The bill to prevent clerks from charging exorbitant rates for copies of legal documents.

absent, and the Committees names being red there appeared enough in towne.

In the after noone the howse was called.

f. 38. a]   11 Junii[1] 1607

Sir H[enry] Poole moved[2] for the company of the armourers 2 things: viz. 1.º that some maie be appointed to draw a bill against the next cession for their releife and the maintainance of that trade, 2do. that the Lords may be moved to wright their Letters into the countries to set men at libertie to buy wheare they can best: wheruppon the howse resolved that no man by lawe can be compelled to buy of anie person and that no subiect ought farther to flie then to the lawe: Againe wee ought not of this howse to seeke to anie subiect: To the first point it was agreed to be against the order of the howse to give order in one cession for drawing of a bill against the next:

Sir Fra[ncis] Bacon reported[3] the conference had yesterday with the Lords thus: The conference was entered into by the Lord Chauncellor, he began with a civill and kinde commendacion of the temperate labor of this howse, then he declared the cause of this conference viz. to cleere doubts not many in nomber but weighty, Namely in nomber 4, First by the bill as now it standeth in case of high treason, if the fact be acted in Scotland by an Englishman, it is triable only in the 3 ioining counties Northumberland Cumberland Westmoorland which faults have hetherto ben thought fit to be tried in the Eye of the Kingdome not in anie remote country: 2do. Whether when hereby wee have drawen the nomber of peremptory challenges to five, our meaning be to allow this nomber or any for treason which the law alloweth not as it now standeth, 3º Whether wee do entende anie Pier of this realme offending *ut supra* be to be tried otherwise then by his Piers, 4º Whether we do entend that any person offending in treason *ut supra*, shalbe allowed witnesses.

And it is trew that the same greate person did glaunce at the

---

[1] The correct date is June 12.

[2] See *C.J.* I, 382.

[3] Cf. the report in *C.J.* I, 1051–52. The Lords put forward certain preliminary objections to the bill for trials on the borders, as it had been sent up from the Commons.

generall clause of witnesses but that was more stoode on afterwards, as I will shew:

It was aunsweared by some of us that wee coulde not divine or foresee what doubts their Lordships woulde propose and therefore wee could not deliver what led the howse to set down or give passage to those points but wee must speake *ex re nata:* againe, that it is impossible where manie reasons are given, to report or set downe what led every man to his opinion or to concurre with others. And as Pindarus saed many times *maius non dicta quam dicta movent.* And that many in this howse who speak not are as wise as others that do speake. To conclude it was saied that whatsoever should now be spoken, by anie of us must be taken as private opinions. And because the Lords did generallie runne uppon the matter of treason, it receaved this aunsweare: That as the matter standeth, our eyes and the occasion of the bill is cast most on the matter of felony which is that which is feared on the borders, not so much treason, which not being feared was not endeavored to be corrected by this lawe: Touching the 2d. doubt it was saied by us that the meaninge of the howse was not to give anie challenge in case of treason, nay the woords as they now stand in the bill do not yeld it, for five challenges are allowed only where challenge lieth: 3° touching the trial of Piers it was saied by us that as Patricide had not punishment provided etc. so wee did not conceave nor doubt that anie Pier would commit such felony as might be within this bill. 4to. Touching wittnesses to be allowed to the defendant in treason: it was farre from our meaning or thought to give anie ease or incoragement to offendors in that kinde. Then 2 speaches weare used by 2 greate persons who commonly sett at the upper ende of the table (the Earls of Salis[bury] and Northampton). The first speache maie be devided into an 1. Introduccion. 2. Argument. 3. Advice.

f. 38. b] 1. First he saied that in the wisdome of this howse he had ever observed either a constant resolucion of defence, or an inclinacion to harken to farther reason when it was offered, He said he assured himselfe that neither the howse nor anie of the howse did incline or meane anie aleviacion in case of treason. Nextly he saied that wise men entendinge their minds wholy on the maine do often times let passe lesse matters, which others do observe, and he saied that so it might be with this howse and yet this might be *felix culpa*, for it might give their Lordships occasions to put us in mynde somwhat of the clause of witnesses in generall, and this he saied might be without offence or unkindnesse, as this howse amended latelie in a bill¹ sent hether from the Lords the attributes of Highnesse applied to the King, and Majestie to the Queene.

2. Next was his Argument, consisting on 3 variances and 3 inconveniences in this bill for abolishing hostile Lawes: Touching variances he alleaged them in this, viz. he saied that wee varie in the Ende, the principall, the Lawe. Our ende he saied is love, but this wee varie from: which he proved by Barrowes speeches to his soon att his death, who then seeing his soon present to weep reproved him for it, saying See this bravely revenged: Secondly [he] saied wee varrie from our principall, which is tendernesse over the innocent, for he saied our course is contrary, for where wee would provide to preserve a few supposed innocents from the doubt of severitie of Justice wee expose manie innocents to the violence ot malefactors. Thirdly wee varie from our Lawes, nay from all lawes, for in perplexitie of Evidence where the Iudge is to give sentence of life or death our Law taketh away witnesses from the guilty, The civill law doth torture the delinquent, If wee take away the one, wee should settle the other:

The first inconvenience is, that no malefactor will stirre foote out of doares to do any villany but he will sett and prepare witnesses for his purgacion and so in short tyme there will be ready a standinge Crew of damned witnesses.

The 2d. inconvenience is that there wilbe continuall calumniacion of all verdicts.

The third and last inconvenience is, touching the nature of the time; His Lordship saied he doth not doubt but tyme will woorke out all greavances betweene the nacions. He gave for example Portuigale and Spaine, for saied he I neaver herd a Portuigale speake of a Spainarde without a [*blank*] and I thincke a Portuigale cannot saie the *pater noster;* and therefore seeing this law must be perpetuall he thought it inconvenient for a temporary inconvenience:

q[*uaere*] how this was applied for I could not take it.²

---

¹ The bill for the exchange of Theobalds for Hatfield between the King and the Earl of Salisbury. See *C.J.* I, 376, and *Statutes of the Realm*, IV, 1133.

² "The Disease so violent, as not to fit to weaken the Remedy." *C.J.* I, 1052.

3. The advise which his Lordship used was, that some mitigacion might be had of this clause touching witnesses: but the same not to be referred to the iudge, who is but one, who is but a stranger, who is to greate to beare out his owne doings, but to the jurors, who are 12, who are neighbors, who are not [too] greate to beare out their doings.[1]

The Earl of Northamptons speach devided it selfe as the former into an Introduccion, Reasons, Advise. His Lordships introduccion was to this effect, That as when the woorthy Woorkeman represented a perfect picture to the view of manie, One found one fault and other an other and one in the shoe: so said his Lordship in this exact well penned bill somwhat in the shoe latchet maie be loose and found by mee: etc.

His Lordships reasons weare 4: viz: *primo* by this course in this clause wee drive ourselves from our owne entente and ende: and in an other sort then hath ben spoken for our meaninge being to unite our selves viz. the 2 kingdomes lawes wee do herby disunite our selves in lawe in this point.

2do. If they of Scotland should conforme and unite them selves to us in this, yet is this contrary to both our selves, who both have made profession not to change our fundamentall lawes.

f. 39. a]   3.° Our tendernesse towards our owne contrimen doth remaine and appeare though this clause be stricken out, for yet are wee then in better cas then Scottish men for they heare not the witnesse.

4to. By allowing witnesses this greate inconvenience will ensue, viz. that every corrupt Juror may have a proppe to beare out himselfe for when such a corrupt Juror hath the color of an oath on both sids he is not punishable.

Then he concluded with a monicion that wee woulde make some triall of this lawe.

After this a replie was made by 2 of our companie, one a gentleman of great universalitie (Sir Rog[er] Owen) the other a veary learned gentleman Mr. L[awrence] Hyde. Which was aunsweared

---

[1] That is, that the jury should be empowered to refuse to hear a witness, if it regarded him as unfit to give evidence. This suggestion was later approved by the majority of the Commons, though certain members strongly opposed it.

by 2 greate persons, one a chief Judge towards the spirituall lawe[1] the other towards the commen Lawe[2] but my tables saied Sir Francis Bacon weare full: and so pleasantlie he ended his reporte:

Mr. Speaker declared that he conceaved the pointes doubted by the Lords and the inconveniences in the bill as now it standeth to be That whereas treasons doon out of the realme in anie forraine countrie are triable in anie countie of England now by this bill treason committed in Scotland is triable onlie in the 3 adioining counties viz. Westmoorland Northumberland and Cumberland.

2. Whether having drawen peremptorie challenge in case of felony by this bill unto five which is a farre lesse nomber then the common law alloweth your meaninge be to allow any such challenge in treason.

3. 3° Whether a Pier of this Realme offending against this law shalbe tried by a common iury.

4. Whether a person accused of treason triable by this statute, shall be allowed witnesses for his defence.

5. Whether witnesses are to be allowed in anie case within this statut without distinction. Then the farder dispute of this matter was deferred untell the next day:

12 JUNII[3] 1607.

When the Committees do amend and do adde a proviso the first question is for the adding of the proviso and the second uppon the whole bill. *Proviso added by Committees.*

Sir Rob[er]t Bretts peticion[4] exhibited to the howse was readde, wherof the point was uppon the priviledge of the howse, to this effect: viz: Sir Ro[bert] Johnson, since the beginning of this cession of parliament exhibited a bill in the Eschequer chamber against the Peticioner and urged him to aunsweare and whether now Sir Rob[ert] Johnson being a member of this howse may by priviledge therof staie Sir Ro[bert] Brett from proceeding in the cause was proposed: and ruled after some small speache on both sides that Sir Ro[bert] Johnson shoulde have priviledge. *Priviledge to stay suits:*

---

[1] No doubt the Archbishop of Canterbury.

[2] Probably Sir Edward Coke, now Chief Justice of the Common Pleas.

[3] The correct date is June 13.

[4] The petition is in *C.J.* I, 383.

Touching the matter yesterday proposed and partlie disputed[1] concerning the bill for abolishing hostile Lawes betweene this realme and Scotland MR. FRA[NCIS] MOORE declared that uppon the last conference with the Lords, he conceaved that the meaning of this howse was not to take away or to debarre that treasons doon in Scotland may not be tried in anie county of England nor to limit such triall to be only within the 3 adioining countyes of Westmoorland Northumberland and Cumberland: likewise I thincke this howse did not meane to take away from the nobility triall by their Piers. And so touching the 2 next points wherefore I do wish wee should spend our dispute uppon the first point viz. of Witnesses. f. 39. b] MR. DUNCOMBE. Let the Lords know from us that if they please to amende anie thing they have power so to do, and then if they send it to us wee will argue it:

MR. WENTWOORTH wished that where wee last mett with the Lords unprovided to answer them so now wee should send unto them for a 2d. meeting to satisfie them in such things as wee did and do hold stiffe, and for the rest their Lordships seeing the weekenes of our grounds and that some things slipped as it weare *sub silencio* may be encorraged to amend them. Least if they should amend or alter that which wee shall stand on, the bill be dashed. SIR H[ENRY] POOLE *ad idem*.

SIR ROBERT WINGFEILD. Wee cannot go to a question uppon a bill except wee had it from the Lords but wee may enter into dispute of the matters proposed by the Lords and theruppon signifie our inclinacion to their Lordships: SIR H[ENRY] MONTAGUE *ad idem*.

MR. YELVERTON. For the points of treason I woulde not have us saie, we ment it not, for the woords beare it, but wee maie signifie our inclinacion to admitt alteracion therin if the Lords thincke there may be danger in it: In the matter of Witnesses I did observe by the report, that the 2 woorthy noble men[2] did not move this as a doubt fit to be cleered, but argued against that whole clause, which I will neaver assent unto, and therefore I will nowe deliver

---

[1] See the debate in *C.J.* I, 383, 1052. "Much disputed, whether [to wait] upon the Amendments, to be sent down by the Lords; or to dispute now, and prepare Reasons for a Conference; and not to decide it, but to offer Reasons in a Second Conference."

[2] The Earls of Salisbury and Northampton.

my opinion beforehand for I woulde be loth hereafter to dash the bill: now by the bill witnesses are allowed to the prisoner for his purgacion, uppon such reasons as the howse like of: It is now desiered that the Jurors shall allow or disallow such witnesses viz. to heare or not heare them as they shall thincke good: this I cannot consent unto: for if a Jury shall refuse to heare a witnesse that weare blooddy, if the Jury allow such a witnesse it sheweth partiallity.

Mr. Brocke. I hold it not for our gravity to acknowledge an error, so likewise I know that wisdome was not borne in us, therefore I wish this aunsweare to be made viz: That if their Lordships do conceave that in this bill is anie ease or advantage given to anie person that shalbe tried in case of treason, It is farre from our meaning to give comfort or encoragement to anie such offendor. Touching the other point which concerneth Witnesses, the same hath ben disputed and thoroughly debated among us and thereuppon resolved and the iudgement of the howse passed, therefore how farre this howse maie admitt anie alteracion herin wee must leave it to their Lordships wisdomes.

Heruppon it was ordered that Mr. Brocke with the former committees shall betwixt this and monday attend Mr. Attorney and set downe in wrighting this his proiect and agreed that the aunsweare must be delivered to the former Committees of the Lords which did open to the committee of this howse the doubts aforesaide, but in this sorte, viz. this howse is to send unto the Lords signifieinge that wee have entered into consideracion of the doubts which the Lords committees from that howse delivered unto ours and wee are ready to give aunsweare from this howse to their Lordships said committees at such time and place as their Lordships shall please to appoint and Mr. Attorney appointed to deliver this message.

15 Junii 1607.

It was opened that the Committees did not meete at Mr. Attorneys chamber to agree and set downe the aunsweare to be sent to the Lords touching the bill for abolishing Hostile lawes, but it appeared that Mr. Brock of and by him selfe had set downe the effect of his owne mocion or proiect in that behalfe: whereuppon it was ordered that the Committees should presently go up into the

Committee chamber and agrea on it, which they did as Mr. Brocke had set downe: whereuppon Mr. Attorney was sent to the Lords with the said answeare and to say farder that our aunswere will not be long: whereuppon the Lords returned woord that their Committees should be ready this afternoone at 2 of the clocke in the painted chamber and farder desiered this howse to sett a while f. 40. a] for that their Lordships will anon send aunsweare touching the peticion concerning the Spanish merchants which they formerly receaved from this howse: afterwards came Dr. Stanhope and Dr. Hone from the Lords declaring that the Lords had considered of the said peticion and do yeld to a conference accordingly touching the same: which they appoint this after noone at 2 of the clocke in the painted chamber, after the other conference: which this howse accepted: And because the committees of this howse for both causes are not the same, therefore the committees which formerly weare appointed in the spanish busines are added to this:[1] and of them Sir Edwyne Sandyes cheifely appointed to speake herein, then the Committees went into the Committee chamber to consider and distribute the partes: as they ment to handle them:

16. JUNII. 1607.

Peticion against Jesuits: etc. Non-residents etc.

Peticion notified secretely to the King before reading in the howse and stopped: etc. *Ut plus postea* 3 leaves after.

SIR W[ILLIAM] BOULSTRED. Whereas a peticion[2] was desiered to be exhibited by this howse to his Majestie for the better execucion of lawes against Seminaries Jesuits and priests, etc. Which peticion was referred unto certaine Committees who accordinglie have taken paines therin and penned it and brought it into the howse againe[3] my suit is that it maie now be readde.

Hereuppon Mr. Speaker[4] delivered that his Majestie hath taken notice of this peticion and holdeth the contentes to appertaine unto him selfe which he will eaver regard and therefore willeth

---

[1] See committee lists in *C.J.* I, 324, 326, 344.

[2] See the petition and interesting debate in *C.J.* I, 384–385, 1053.

[3] The committee was appointed on May 18, and it brought in the petition on June 11.

[4] The Speaker wrote to Salisbury: "This day suddenly and unlooked for was the petition which lately was offered to your Lordship's view called for to be read, which I endeavoured to suppress by declaring his Majesty's pleasure that no further proceeding therein should be had, but was notwithstanding much urged to be read as otherwise greatly tending to the

that this howse do deale no farther in it: Sir Fra[ncis] Hastings. It is no doubt in his Majesties power to redresse the fault, and it seemeth by our course which is to seeke it of him and from him that wee so hold it, It is not a fault in us to seeke of his Majestie in good sort, And therefore consider how this matter hath proceeded. First heare in the howse was a mocion for a peticion to be made *ut supra*, this was allowed and a Committee appointed to consider and draw such a one and to offer it to the consideracion of the howse, The Committee did meete accordinglie, Consulted, have framed a peticion, the order is the howse should heare it, and so to allow or disallowe it. Then is it in his Majestie to yeld or not to yeld it, and for order sake I thincke it ought to be readde:[1]

Mr. Speaker. No peticion is to be made unto the King contrarie to his direccion otherwise of a bill. Therefore 13 Elizabeth[2] this howse purposed to make a peticion to the Queene, shee tooke notice of it and sent woorde she would not be peticioned. Likewise [*blank*] Elizabeth[3] a peticion was framed by this howse to be exhibited to the Queene for the execucion of the Duke of Norfolk, and the successe as the former:

Mr. Wentwoorth. Wee cannot take notice of the Kings pleasure by you as our Speaker, for so you go not to his Majestie Speaker.

absolute breach of their privilege, which they conceive to consist in preferring of bills and informing of their grief by petitions; where I was driven to oppose at several times 10 or 12 speakers, being not backed by the speech of anyone; and in the end not without the distaste of many who misliked that myself should so often oppose their proposition, drew them that a committee should to-morrow in the afternoon view and report to them what hath been herein warranted by former precedents. I find the most part of them have no liking of the matter in the petition contained and yet have and will exceeding press the reading thereof, and so then to stay any further proceeding therein, for that the committee by order of the House have drawn and returned the same to the House and therefore ought to be read, for the House yet taketh no notice of what is therein expressed. I fear me I shall not be able to keep the same from reading, but then I strongly assure myself the same will be suppressed, wherein I humbly beseech your Lordship's direction; for I find the best affected to the King's service strongly bent for the reading thereof." June 16, 1607. Salisbury MSS.

[1] "Against the Liberty of the House, not to read it." *C.J.* I, 1053.
[2] D'Ewes, 167, 180.
[3] 14 Elizabeth. 1572. D'Ewes, 206–207, 214, 220.

but some of us with you. Againe as yet there is no peticion of the howse, for the howse hath allowed none, therefore his Majestie can take no notice of anie such peticion. Allso Sir you saie that the King is not pleased to be peticioned for execucion of the Lawes etc. for him selfe is willing to see the same doon: but in this peticion is also matter for which there is now no lawe, namelie that his Majestie wilbe pleased not to dispence with Nonresidents, likewise that the Bishops be pressed not to admitt or allowe insufficient ministers, which power is in them for they may reiect and if the Ordinary do not repell an insufficient clerke the Metro- f. 40. b] politane maie and ought to reiecte him, and from such a certificat no Appeale.

Mr. FULLER. I was a Committee for the framing of this peticion, and I do affirme that in it there is no thing for which this howse hath not hearetofore passed one or more lawes, and because they have not taken effect let us do our dutyes which is to seeke to the King in such order as may become us.

Mr. Speaker wished that the Committees for priviledge maie this afternoone peruse the presidents, and to consider whether by them it doth appeare that a peticion is to be readde where the King forbiddeth it.

Mr. DUNCOMBE. Sir all your presidents wilbe uppon a peticion of the howse prevented by the Kings direccion but this is not yet a peticion, but a thing in mouldinge, and when it is readde then if it be not allowed nor thought fit to be proceeded in I will give my voice to suppresse it, but let it be first readde:

SIR EDW[ARD] GREVILL contra, for, saied he, if wee marke the ende it wilbe labor lost if wee reade it, and allow it and afterwards the King reiect it.

Mr. ALLFOORD remembered that our peticion for the merchants trading into Spayne was lately reiected[1] and now likewise this, therefore he wished that presidents be considered and that Sir Rob[er]t Cotton and Mr. Bowyer, may bring foorth such presidents as are best knowen to them, to thend that if our priviledge do so beare, wee be not preiudiced, if otherwise, wee offende not.

Mr. Speaker. The presidents be that when a peticion hath ben

---

[1] On June 15 the Lords refused to join the Commons in presenting the petition to the King. See report on June 17.

in framing, before the howse hath herd and allowed it the com
mandement hath come and stopped it.

Heare manie called to have the said peticion reade, others to
putt that by called for a report of yesterdayes conference with the
Lords:

SIR FRA[NCIS] BACON finding the voice of the howse to continue
for reading of the peticion, moved that some others might be
ioined to the former committees and theruppon the howse named
Sir Ro[bert] Cotton, Mr. Bowyer, Mr. Tate, Sir Maurice Berckley then the names of the Committees being read Mr. Bowyer
was one, Mr. Wentwoorth, Sir W[illiam] Boulstred *et alii* weare
added.[1]

MR. GOOD after a preamble against Detractacion, and with
protestacion of Love and loialty *inter alia* used woords to this
effect, If the arrest of one member be held with us an impeache-
ment of our liberties, what shall an arrest of the whole howse be?
especiallie by the King? But shall I hereby taxe his Majesties
proceedings? no, for I do not interprete his Majesties message as a
stoppe by displeasure, but rather he doth as a kind father that
doth not hide from us what will displease him and what he would
have us do.

f. 41. a]   17 JUNII 1607.

I was called out of the howse by Mr. [*blank*] who brought mee
a message of honorable favor from [*blank*] shewing much favor
towards mee etc.

SIR FRA[NCIS] BACON reported[2] that at the last meeting with
the Lords it was delivered to their Lordships that this howse
conceaved their doubts to be 4 concerning the points of treason
and the fift to be touching the generall clause of witnesses con-

Report of a Con-
ference.

---

[1] These names and others were added to the committee for privileges.
See *C.J.* I, 1053.

[2] Bacon's report is printed in Spedding, III, 347-361. It is also found
in St. P. Dom. XXVII, 53. St. P. Dom. XXVII, 54, contains an outline
of the speech of the Earl of Salisbury, which Bacon was reporting. See
also Gardiner, I, 340-354.

Bacon was reporting a conference that took place on June 15. He
had opened the conference by delivering to the Lords the message suggested by Mr. Brooke on June 12. Then the Lords took up the question of
Spanish grievances.

tained in the bill. To the 4 first it was aunswered that if the Lords did conceave that the bill as now it standeth doth anie way lessen the punishment or give ease unto treason of anie kinde, it is farre from the entention of this howse to make the cas of traitors better then they founde it, or to mollifie the punishment, neither had this howse anie purpose to preiudice the Lords in point of honor, or to innovate the course of ther Lordships trialls.

Touching the fift that it was no new question, but that which heretofore had ben proposed, disputed and determined, uppon the question, therefore how this now may alter or varrie from that, is left unto the wisdome of their Lordships to consider, and heare said the Reporter, my parte of dew might cease, for of that which followeth I was neither nominated a Reporter nor appointed a speaker. Trew it is I tooke noates for my owne stoare and provision and them I am ready for your better service to imparte unto you, if so be your pleasure. Whereunto was aunsweared by the general voice, Yea: then he thus proceeded,

The first speach was undertaken by the principall councellor of estate[1] I meane of matters of estate, In good faith Mr. Speaker it contained a worlde of matter but how I shall make therof a globe or a mappe I know not: In the beginenge, he saied, he woulde discharge us of all replie, because they had no warrant to dispute and he wished it might be with like brevitie, which he foresaw could not be, then he desired a benigne interpretacion.

His speeche consisted of three partes: viz.

1. First as the peticion was exhibited by the merchants:
2. Secondlie as it was delivered to this howse.
3. Thirdlie as it was commended by this howse to the Lords: The first point he subdivided viz:
1. First the persons of the merchants.
2. [blank].[2]

In their persons he gave eight observacions.

First a greate regard of their profession and therin their great indurance etc. And of merchants a second sort which suffer lesse and are commonly as riche as the other.[3]

---

[1] The Earl of Salisbury.

[2] "The matter and parts of the petition." Spedding, III, 348.

[3] "Others that lyve att home upon certayn gayne. Less to be regarded." St. P. Dom. XXVII, 54.

An other note in the persons of merchants he observed, viz: that their informacions are subiect to misenformacion viz. from their factors, and in this kind he vouched one Leeke,[1] who complained to the Lords of the takinge or arrest of his ship and desiered an asper letter, to whome was aunsweared, beare a while, what will you saie if no such thing be happened to hir, and that shee safelie returne shortlie, which so happened. Thirdlie he observed in the generall person of merchants, that they are apt to intitle the state in their particular greavances wherof they have sence.[2] In this particuler he saied the merchants of Spaine have some cause of complaint and the same doth encrease but that them f. 41. b] selves are, if not causes, yet accessorie, for he saied that the taking away of the Monopolie of that trade or companie by this howse[3] at their suyt hath brought in confusion in that trade and therby their suits in Spaine more frequent and woorse followed then heretofore. So as except a Leageir Ambassador lieng there for causes of state shalbe turned into a factor for merchants their suits cannot be followed.

3. The third observacion [*blank*].[4]

4. The 4 observacion, that merchants in this Course have inverted the due order, or order of duity in addressinge themselves to the foote and not to the headde.

5. Lastlie he noated that they swarved from their owne direccion of their peticion. For [*blank*].[5]

The matters of their peticion are three *vid*. Complaint of 1. Wrongs in fact. 2. In Lawe, as inequalitie of Justice in Spaine. 3. Remedy, which they requier, by Letters of marte.

In their trade they complaine of 3 wrongs, viz. Wrongs in the trade to 1. Spaine. 2. The Indyes. 3. The Levant Seas. Wrongs in fact.

---

[1] Possibly George Leake, a merchant in the last years of Queen Elizabeth.

[2] "Seekers to drawe the great bargaines of the Kingdom and the treatyes to have dependency upon their petty matters of trade." St. P. Dom. XXVII, 54.

[3] 3 Jac. I. c. 6. *Statutes of the Realm*, IV, 1083.

[4] Two points omitted by Bowyer are (1) that the wrongs were not as great as the merchants claimed and (2) that it was presumptuous in them to ask for things that might lead to war. Spedding, III, 349–350; St. P. Dom. XXVII, 54.

[5] For the petition had not been presented to the Lords but only to the Commons.

Spayne.   His Lordship pitied their wrongs in Spaine and yet he offered 4 extenuacions: First that their wrongs there are only in delays and not in uniust iudgement. Theis delaies said his Lordship are somwhat to be attributed to the nature of that people, A prowde people and such are commonly dilatory and wilbe waited on. Againe the multitude of merchants there, the distance of countries there, etc. A third extenuacion he alleaged in the tymes, viz. a new reconciliacion so as yet not setled course. The 4th extenuacion he used, was, for that said his Lordship, the causes of theis wrongs are sometyme offered by ourselves in coloringe Flemish goods, sometime directlie and sometime unwillinglie, as if an english cloath receave so much as dye in Flaunders, by the agreement it is out of the peace.[1]

Indies.   Touchinge the Indies, The Spaniards keepe that trade as a treasure locked up from all confederates. But yet the Kinge of England woulde not in the Treaty be expressely excepted, and on the other side the King of Spaine woulde not have it expressed lawfull, so it was left at large, but yet if the King would admitt a right in the King of Spayne then amends should be made.

Levant Seas.   f. 42. a] The wrongs in the Levant stand uppon two particulers. The one, The arrest of a ship called the *Triumph*,[2] in Scicilia. The other in Sardinia of a ship called the *Vyneyarde*, which was for carrieing powder to the Turke. And for this the French founde fault with the Ambassador of our King there remaininge.[3] Here endeth the wrongs in fact.

Legall wrongs.   Now touchinge the Legall wrongs. Aunsweare was made that the Lawes of Spayne wherewith wee finde our selves greaved, are not new, nor made for this purpose. Perhaps they are harsh and have of the Moores somme what: So our lawes of the Admiraltie are not reputed abroade easie. And the King of Spayne hath wrightten to a Corrigidoares in favor of the English.

Remedy. Letters of marte.   Lastlie the remedy desiered by the merchants is by letters of

---

[1] The English were bound not to bring any products of the Low Countries into Spain. Rymer, *Foedera*, XVI, 621–622.

[2] The name of the ship was the *Trial*.

[3] The Venetian ambassador speaks of complaints by several nations, though he does not mention the French. *Cal. St. P. Venetian, 1603–1607*, 318.

Mart. This said his Lordship is vaine, for in that course,[1] first the merchant greaved must complaine to the Keeper of the privie Seale etc: Then having no redresse he must resort to the officer of the greate Seale and so obtaine Letters of Marte, wherefore he concluded that the state remedie is better then the statute course. Secondlie this remedy by Letters of Marte is pernicious, For the stoppe of spanish goods in England is a trifle, the stoppe of the goods of English merchants in spaine is inifinite and so the exchange is pernicious.

Now as the peticion was a thinge offered to this howse he declared that this course of entertaininge peticions of private wrongs which might tende to so greate consequence of breach of peace with so greate a Prince is dangerous for it soundeth [*blank*].

To some touch of iniustice [*blank*].

Also to touch the Kings prerogative supreme to which it appertaineth to order such things.

For the first, it weare uniust to yelde the merchants peticion, for wee had herd but one parte viz. the complainant.

For the seconde that it weare against the Kings prerogative:[2] *ut supra* he made good by divers presidents *ut*, 18 E 1.[3] a complaint by the Commons touching uneaven waights, the parties sent to courts of Justice. Againe *eodem anno*[4] A complaint against the Earl of Flaunders, *Rex nihil aliud potest* but by request to the Earl of Flaunders. 14 E 3 The Commons request that certaine Covenants may be entered into betweene the King and the Earl of Flaunders aunswered [*blank*].[5]

18 E 3.[6] The Commons weare greaved with merchentes strangers.

43 E 3.[7] The Commons complaine that their trade with the

---

[1] That is, by the Statute of 4 Hen. V (*Statutes of the Realm*, II, 198), which the merchants wished to have revived.

[2] "Of an absolute determination and power of concluding and making war and peace." Spedding, III, 356

[3] *Rot. Parl.* I, 47. Lansd. MSS 486 (f. 125) mentions these precedents and adds, "*Quaere* of Mr Fuller for the Precedents." Apparently Fuller took notes in the conference as well as Bacon.

[4] *Rot. Parl.* I, 61.

[5] The King would do as he saw fit. *Rot. Parl.* II, 113.

[6] *Rot. Parl.* II, 149–150.

[7] 45 Ed. III (so in Spedding, III, 357). *Rot. Parl.* II, 306.

Esterlings was not uppon equall termes, and request the Esterlings may find suerty to entreate the English merchents in their
country in such wise as they are heare, Aunswered thus, The same
so hath and shalbe done, as neede shall requier.

50 E 3[1] the commons requiered remedy against the subiects
of spayne. Aunswered thus the King will wright his Letters.

Eodem anno[2] the merchants of Yorke in parliament desier that
where the lord of Arcle and Corkham in Hollande hath staied 36
Samplers of their woolls to the value of 900£ supposing that the
King oweth him money for his service in Fraunce and will neither
for the Kings letters nor other meanes deliver their woolls, that
Magnum Con- therefore they may have licence to staie the shippes of the same
cilium. Lord at Callaice or in England until they be paid and aunswered
to the value. Aunswered: Let it be declared to the graund counceill
and they shall have remedy according to reason.

17. R. 2.[3] in parliament the Commons weare by the Lords requiered to advise in matter of peace or warre to be concluded,
and the[y] refused to deale therein as not appertaining to them.

To thes purpose see allso 10. R. 2.[4]

f. 42. b] The third inconvenience, is in matter of policie of estate.
This is a secreate of Policie, for no King will enter into warre, but
he will first consider of his abilitie how to disioint the Prince with
whome he is to warre, and thes consideracions are so secreate that
Kings are not only not willing to imparte the same to greate
counceills, but do therwith acquaint not all but some select persons of their private counceill.

Now come wee to this peticion as it is commended from this
howse to the upper which was short yet gracious viz. their Lordships do make a good construccion first of a generous opinion in you
said his Lordship of the Commens howse of the Kings abilitie to
right his subiects, next out of a tender sence in you of the merchants
harmes and thirdlie[5] etc. (which I could not take).

---

[1] *Rot. Parl.* II, 346.
[2] *Rot. Parl.* II, 353.
[3] *Rot. Parl.* III, 315.
[4] *Rot. Parl.* III, 215. But here the Council and not Parliament declined to advise the King. In 7 Richard II (*Rot. Parl.* III, 170, 171) the
Commons refused to advise the King concerning a treaty with France.
[5] The willingness of the Commons to assist the King in his future

Secondlie his Lordship did assure us (saied Sir Fra[ncis] Bacon)
that that King which in treaty of peace with Spaine did beare
such a hand as that he rather gave termes then tooke them, that
he would not recall his people servinge against Spayne,[1] will not
be backwarde as occasion shall serve to undertake an honorable
warre: Lastlie the King can do no more to urge the King of Spaine
for our merchants then he hath doon, nor the King of Spaine promise more amends then he hath doon which must be expected.

There (said the Reporter Sir Fra[ncis] Bacon) succeeded a second speach[2] of an other Lord, who first commended the merchants as good members, that bring in what wee waunt and carrie
foorth our aboundance he termed them Neptunes almesmen and
Fortunes adventure[r]s. He gave five reasons why their Lordships
cannot ioine with us in this peticion.

Earl of North-
ampton.

1. This howse, saied his Lordship, *inuendo* this of the Commens,
according to the first institucion consisteth of Knights and burgesses who are not fit to handle matters of state.

2. *Ordinacio belli et pacis summi Imperii.*

3. If the King should intende anie such matter he will not be
prevented by the Commens.

4. It is not our parte to prevent the King of honor but as Joab
being ready to take a towne[3] did forbeare so to do, but sent for
David etc. least the honor of that victory might otherwise fall on
himselfe:

5. By our solliciting and inciting the King it might be inferred
that the King did so sleepe in the sobbs of his people that it weare
needfull to awake him by a parliament. His conclusion was noble,
viz. That if the state shall so requier, their Lordships will not only
spende their breath to perswade warre but their wealth and blood
in persecucion of it.[4]

---

foreign policy. Spedding, III, 359. Nevertheless the Lords declined to
join the Commons in presenting the petition to the King.

[1] See Gardiner, I, 209–210; Rymer, *Foedera*, XVI, 619.

[2] This was a most insulting speech, which Bacon toned down in his
report. See Gardiner, I, 353–354.

[3] Rabbah. 2 Samuel 12: 26–29.

[4] The Commons accepted Salisbury's arguments and did not debate
the matter further. But the Speaker feared that they would. He wrote to
Salisbury on June 16, "The report of yesterday's attendance on your
Lordships will be to-morrow presented to the House, wherein I am com-

Calling the howse. The calling of the howse, which formerly was appointed to be this afternoone is now putt of, for that the committees for producing precedents touching the exhibiting of peticions to the King, and his Majesties prevencion by way of taking notice therof before hand, and signifie his pleasure to the contrarie, are at this time to meete.

Revealing Secrets. The Committees mett, at which time Mr. Allforde desiered satisfaccion touching a president *tempore* H. 6.[1] vouched this parliament that one of the Kings servants was putt out of this howse for revealing unto the King matters in debate. From whence he inferred that the King can take no notice what is heare in handling before it be perfected and sent to him.

Speaker. f. 43. a] Sir W[illiam] Twisden. Wee cannot take notice of the Kings message for it cometh not by our mouth the Speaker, as our Speaker.

Sir Edwyne Sandys. 8 Elizabeth[2] it was moved amonge the Commens to deale with the Lords to ioine with them in suyt to the Queene, that shee woulde marrie, and declare Succession, this continued in discource divers daies *notatu digniss[imo]* the Queene sent two severall commaundements not to proceede, and afterwards that message or commaundement not to proceede was by hir revoked: this he found in the iornall booke of this howse remaning with the Clerke, which being by him readde, some of the Committees labored to put a contrary construccion uppon the message of countermaundement of the first commaundement, for maintenance wherof there was some small showe of reason by reason of some unaptnesse in the setting downe of it, but being considered, weighed, and debated was conceaved cleerely by the Committees, to be as Sir Edwyne Sandys had vouched the same.

---

manded, if they be not satisfied with your Lordship's answer, to make known unto them his Majesty's express commandment that they forbear therein any further to proceed, which I much believe they will obey, and not proceed in any petition, but to stay them from talking thereof I doubt herein as in the former [the petition on religious matters, which the House wished to have read on June 16], and therefore, if I may not offend, I would wish they might spend their breath in speech, so that they proceed no farther." Salisbury MSS.

[1] The editor can find no such precedent.

[2] *C.J.* I, 76–78; D'Ewes, 128, 130.

At this Committee on the other side was saied that 14 Elizabeth[1] *Speaker.*
The Speaker signified the Queenes pleasure that no bill should be
exhibited touchinge religious matters but such as the clergie should *Prerogative to*
first allowe, *Nota* no authoritie or proofe produced herof. The like *restraine.*
vouched 13 Elizabeth[2] but not proved. Allso was vouched 20.
R. 2. the Commens blamed for medling with the Kings howse
14[3] etc. Also 21. R. 2. n. 44[4] how subiects are tied to the King
etc.

18 Junii 1607.

Mr. Speaker havinge attended his Majestie at White hall came *Peticion against*
into the howse halfe an hower after nyne of the clocke. *Jesuits, Semi-*
naryes, and for
Sir Fra[ncis] Hastings offered to report the opinion of the *silenced Ministers.*
Committees of priviledgs touchinge the readinge of the peticion,
before respected or deferred uppon the Kings message, and concerninge the Kings Letter or rather warrant to the Speaker for *Speaker.*
such message as he delivered[5] for leavinge out the clause of
penaltie uppon such as shoulde remaund offendors, to be entered or *Message.*
not entered by the clerke of this howse, but Mr. Speaker in a low
voice stopped him: and all the absent members of the howse weare
sent for into Westminster hall: who beinge come, Mr. Speaker
declared that from his Majestie he had a message to deliver, which
was this morning given him by his highness for his better memorie in wrightinge viz. The Kings pleasure in substance this, that
wheras heretofore his Majestie beinge given to understande of a
peticion in the howse containinge [*blank*] matter did, saied he, by
mee signifie his pleasure to staie Your farder proceedinge therin
not meaning therby to surprise you in anie thing belonging to
you, nor meaninge to lose anie thing that from his progenitors
appertaine unto him, and since havinge understoode that the
said peticion had not ben redde in the howse wherby the howse
might take notice of the contents, commaunded mee this morninge
to bringe the peticion to him and having redde it, doth find it to

---

[1] D'Ewes, 213.

[2] Elizabeth "would not suffer these things to be Ordered by Parliament." D'Ewes, 185. See also D'Ewes, 180.

[3] Haxey's case. *Rot. Parl.* III, 338–340, 407–408. The accusations and
demands of the King are in paragraphs 14 to 16.

[4] *Rot. Parl.* III, 357–359.

[5] On June 2.

consist on two partes, The one to move his Majestie to give direccion to his Judges to take order for execucion of the Lawes against
Jesuits Seminaries etc. The 2d. touchinge libertie for certaine
preachers heretofore silenced. His Majestie willed mee to lett you
know that for the first you shall not neede to spurre a runninge
horse for he doth ioine therin with you, and did on Sonday was
senight before he herd of this, give order to the Judges to proceede
touchinge those persons accordinge to the Justice and severitie of
the lawes. Touching the 2d. his Majestie saieth that this parte of
f. 43. b] the peticion containeth no other matter then that
which his Majestie from you by mee heretofore receaved[1] and
therto gave his aunswere resolute, and therfore how farre he may
now by you be farder pressed he leaveth to your wisdomes. His
proceedinge therin was not only after his owne disposicion but by
advise of his councell and of the Bishops, and of all the Judges of
the Kingdome being both privatelie and publiquely called therunto
in the starre chamber. He wisheth that you woulde remember his
aunsweare then given you, his Majestie no way Entending to
surprise you by the direccion given but willing to deale openly
freely and at large with all his subiects willed mee to saie that his
Majestie understandinge that this peticion hath not yet ben redde,
shall no waie be offended that it be redde: Which accordinglie was
redde:

MR. WENTWOORTH[2] moved that forasmuch as wee have receaved
aunswere from his Majestie touching the first and the last points
of the said peticion viz: concerning Jesuits, and touching silenced
ministers, but touching the middle point namely Nonresidentes
wee have had no aunsweare, wee shoulde therefore make peticion
unto the King in that point.

SIR RICH[ARD] SPENCER, moved to forbeare anie farder to
deale in this peticion uppon divers reasons: SIR JAMES PERROTT
with Mr. Wentwoorth uppon divers reasons.

MR. ALFORD moved that the peticion as now it standeth maie
be put to the question, and so orderly suppressed, for saied he now
and not before it is ours.

SIR RO[BERT] WINGFEILD moved that the peticion maie sleepe.

---

[1] On May 14, 1606. See p. 167.
[2] For this debate, cf. C.J. I, 1053.

SIR FRA[NCIS] BARRINGTON. Wee having doon our duities and the Kings pleasure knowen I wish the peticion should sleepe.

MR. MARTYN moved that the clerke maie enter the Kings message for our enioyeing our priviledges.[1] SIR FRA[NCIS] HAS-TINGS being to report the proceedings of the Committees touchinge this peticion, did omitt so to do because the matter is ended by the Kings message now delivered by the Speaker. The 2d. point referred to the same Committees was concerning the letter heretofore sent by the King to the Speaker touching the matter or clause of penaltie in case of Remaundinge, which he reported thus viz. that the Committees do conceave the said Letter to be only private to you Mr. Speaker for helpe of your memorie in so long a message, and therefore to be redelivered backe to you, and not to be kept nor entered by the Clerke in the iournall[2] and therwithall Sir Fra[ncis] Hastings gave it backe to Mr. Speaker. *Clerke Priviledge.*

Kings letter touching penalty, on Remaunders.

SIR THO[MAS] HOLCROFT moved that at such time as there commeth anie thing from the King or in question touching the priviledges, the clerke do enter nothing, but that some for that purpose appointed by the howse do first survey and peruse it:

19. JUNII. 1607.

It[3] was moved by SIR RO[BERT] WINGFEILD and seconded by MR. ALLFORD and after by SIR EDWYNE SANDYS that accordinge as Sir Tho[mas] Holcroft at a committee wished and yesterday in the howse moved, No entrance shoulde be made by the Clerke of this howse of any matter which may concerne the priviledges of *Entrances by the Clerke.*

---

[1] The *C.J.* contains merely a brief statement of the substance of the message.

[2] "Committees to consider whether it were fit that a Letter from his Majesty containing a Sharp reproof of the House touching the matter of remanding Malefactors should be entred in the Clerks Book. Report that they held it not fit. Whereupon it was so Ordered." Lansd. MSS 486, f. 125. Nevertheless, the clerk entered it under the date of its delivery (June 2).

[3] In the back of the book of the Commons Journals MS, Jac. I, III, there is written a copy of the following passage of Bowyer's diary concerning entrances by the Clerk, as well as another passage dealing with the same subject on July 3 (q.v.). The following words are written at the beginning of the copy: "Extract from a Manuscript Journal formerly belonging to Speaker Williams—communicated by Charles Williams Wynn, Esq., Member from Montgomeryshire to me Chas. Abbott, Speaker 1804." This copy contains numerous misreadings of the original.

this howse, nor any message or letter from his Majestie but the same be first perused and allowed by the Committees for priviledges or by such of them as the howse shalbe pleased to appoint therunto. This course Mr. Speaker much diswaded Saieing, First the Clerke in the parliament time taketh only short noates and after the parliament doth perfect and enter the same, so as in the parliament such things are not to be perfected, and when the cession is ended nothing can be doon by survey or allowance of anie: Againe in all courts, saied he, the Judgs do only deliver the orders and the Clerks do enter them, so likewise heare the Clerke is to be trusted, but the Replie of MR. ALFORD and SIR EDWYNE SANDYS pervailed wheruppon it was ordered that no such enterf. 44. a] ance as aforesaide shoulde be made before the same be perfected and allowed by the Committees of priviledges, and they are on monday next in the court of wards to meete and the clerke to bring his booke of such enterances or noates as he hath made or taken this cession which is by the said Committees to be perused and reported to the howse whether anie and which are to be Continued or left out.

20 JUNII[1] 1607.

High Commission.   MR. FULLER with a high commendacion of a bill which he held in his hand to be of as greate importance as anie that hath ben read this cession, preferred a bill concerninge the High Commission grounded uppon the statute of *primo* Elizabeth:[2] the title of which Bill saied he is, An act for explanacion of one branch of a statute made *anno* 1° Elizabeth intituled an act to restore to the crowne the auncient iurisdiccion over estates ecclesiasticall and spirituall and abolishinge all forrayne power repugnant to the same.

In the course of his speach he shewed that this act of 1 Elizabeth is the ground of the High Commission: that the Commission at every renewing encrease[th] and encrocheth more power and more, is such as by the Law is not warrantable nor can be graunted, yet because that act of parliament establisheth such power in the Commissioners as the King by his Letters Patent shall give them, some hold it good. He shewed how manie statutes or offences

---

[1] June 23 is the correct date.
[2] 1 Eliz. c. 1. *Statutes of the Realm*, IV, 350. A clause of the act empowered the Crown to issue commissions for punishing ecclesiastical offenses.

against how many statuts the High Commission doth enquier of and punish: viz. of 2 acts in *primo* Elizabeth: one other in 5. Elizabeth: one in 13. Elizabeth, tow in 35 Elizabeth and of all theis by oath of 12 men or of the party himselfe. Manie other matters he added which I could not take, and their authoritie is to enquier and punish the premisses either accordinge to the lawes or to their discrecion, and the Commissioners or 3 of them to find out by what meanes to enquier of the premisses etc. Their power to commaund and imploy sheriffs etc. To take recognicauncs of the party accused etc. To inflict punishment, to distraeine etc. To iudge of matters of *premunire* which by the law is reserved onlie to the Kings Bench, for iustices of peace or of assize can only enquier of such offences and not proceede but onlie to certifie the Kings Bench. Nextlie what three of them do accordinge to their discrecion is finall, for there lieth neither Error nor attaint, and their proceeding is strange. I moved saied he the last terme in the Exchequer for 30 persons fined at 30£ apeece all except one att 20£ and one at 10£ only for not apparance, and theis fines extracted into the Exchequor: Cole a ministers cas I moved in the Kings Bench which was this: The High Commission sent a persevant for Cole being a preacher in Hamshire, this persevant woulde not suffer him to make himselfe readie, but tooke him awaie as he found him and offered to tie his leggs under the horse belly, but that neighbours woulde not so suffer him, notwithstanding when he came thorough a towne he led his horse by the head like a traitor: Mr. Speaker interrupting him contrary as some conceaved to order, moved thus, If a patent be to execute lawes accordinge to discrecion is not this voide? wherto Mr. Fuller aunswered thus, I moved this terme to have had in this case a Habeas Corpus for I held the lawe to be as Mr. Speaker saeth but the Judgs aunsweared that if there be an act of parliament to warrant such a patent it is good; then my booke is that wee must come to the parliament.

f. 44. b] The coppie of such noates as Mr. Fuller for his rememberance had collected and held in his hand when he delivered the premisses, viz.

   1 Elizabeth.[1] An act restoring to the crowne the auncient iuris-

___

[1] 1 Eliz. c. 1. *Statutes of the Realm*, IV, 350. Fuller was listing the statutes that the High Commission was empowered to enforce.

diccion over the estate ecclesiasticall and spirituall and abolishing all forraine power repugnant to the same.

2 Elizabeth.[1] An act for Uniformity of commen praier and service of the church and Administracion of the Sacrements.

5 Elizabeth.[2] An act for the assurance of the Queen's Majesties roiall power over all states and subiects within her dominions.

13 Elizabeth.[3] An act to reforme certaine disorders touching the ministers of the churche.

35 Elizabeth.[4] An act to retaine her majesties subiects in their due obedience. An act to restraine popish recusants to some certaine places of aboade. For publishing of false tailes, Rumors etc.

2 Jac:[5] An act for the due execucion of the statutes against Jesuits Seminarie preists Recusants etc.

f. 9.[6] Power to enquier of all the premisses offences and contempts against any of the statuts by oath of xii men or oath of the parties, of all sedicious books contempts, Conspiracies, private Conventicles, false rumours or tales, sedicious misbehaviors, slanderous books, lybells, Wrightings, Woordes and saieings published invented or sett foorth to be published invented or set foreth by any person or persons against us or anie our magistrates officers or ministers or others whatsoever contrarie to the foresaid lawes or statutes or anie of them, or contrarie to anie other lawes or statutes of this realme ordeined for maintenance of religion or tending to the depraving of them or anie of them.

All affraies quarells ether in Church or churchyards or Uppon anie ecclesiasticall person.

f. 11. Allso take order by their discrecions that all penalties uppon the statuts of *anno* 1 Elizabeth maie be leavied uppon the goods and lands of the offendors by way of distresse.

To heare and determine and punishe adulteries fornicacions mis-

---

[1] 1 Eliz. c. 2. *Statutes of the Realm*, IV, 355.
[2] 5 Eliz. c. 1. *Statutes of the Realm*, IV, 402.
[3] 13 Eliz. c. 12. *Statutes of the Realm*, IV, 546.
[4] 35 Eliz. c. 1 and 2. *Statutes of the Realm*, IV, 841, 843.
[5] 1 Jac. I. c. 4. *Statutes of the Realm*, IV, 1020.
[6] The remainder of this copy of Fuller's notes is written in another hand, not Bowyer's. Fuller in this part of his speech was abstracting portions of the latest ecclesiastical commission, which had been issued in 1605. (St. P. Dom. XII, 66, 67.) This commission followed very closely the ones issued in the last years of Elizabeth.

behaviors and discords in mariages and all other greavous crimes and offences, Which are punishable or reformable by ecclesiasticall lawes according to the tenore of the lawes on that behalfe, or accordinge to your Wisedomes consciences or discrecions. Anie three of you devise waies and means for the triall and serching out of.

f. 12. Full power to accorde such punishment to every such offendor by fine imprisonment censures of the church or other lawfull way, or by all or anie of the said waies as to your wisedomes and discrecions or anie 3 or more of you as aforesaid shalbe thought meete and convenient.

To call before you all and every offendors in anie the premisses and all such as by you or anie 3 of you or more shall seeme to be suspected persons in anye of the premisses and every of them to examine uppon their corporall oathes touching every or anie of the premisses.

If any disobey your orders decrees or commandments in anie thinge touching the premisses, to punish by excommunicacion or other censures ecclesiasticall or by fines accordinge to your discrecions, or to committ the same persons so offendinge to ward, ther to remain untell he shalbe by you or anie three or more enlarged, or by all or any the said meanes according to your discrecions.

If any be sued for the offences aforesaid at the instance of any they have power [to] award him coastes; for parators.

f. 45. a] f. 15. Power to commande all and every sheriffs, iustices, and other officers and subiects within this realme in all places as well exempt as not exempt by your letters or other proces to apprehend or cause to be any person or persons which you shall thincke meete to be convented, and to take such bonds for their appearance as etc. or commit them to prison.

fo: 16: Power to take recognisance of the partie accused for the performance and accomplishment of such orders and decrees as to you or any 3 or more of you shall seeme reasonable:

f. 16. Power to appointe messengers with allowaunce of such fees etc. f. 17.

f: 17. To appoint a receavor of all such fines and sommes of money as shalbe assessed:

f: 22. Power to execute the premisses notwithstandinge anie appellacion perroracion priviledge or exemption, any our lawes statuts proclamacions, other graunts priviledges or other ordinaunces which be or may seeme contrarie to the premisses notwith-standinge.

f. 22. Commaundement to all iustices of peace, maiors, bailiffes etc. to be aiding and assistinge to the Commissioners etc.

5 Elizabeth c. 1.[1] The offences there are *premunire* and iustices of assise and iustices of peace have onely power to enquire and certifie the kings bench and there to proceede, yet etc. [*blank*] not to be impeached but uppon such testimony as the iurie shall thinke meete.

35 Elizabeth c. 1. The punishment in this statut is abiuracion as for felonye and declared before whom it shalbe made.

35 Elizabeth c. 2. The forfeiture is losse of all the goods and Chattells of the offendors and of his lands duringe life.

35 Elizabeth c. 2. Onely such as be suspected to be semynarie priests or massinge priests may be examined whether he be a Jes-uyte or seminarie or massinge priest.

But by this Commission they may examine every person upon anie of the matters in the said statuts.

They may levy by distresse all ther fines.

They appoint receavors.

They may set fines at ther discrecion. Ther discrecion with[out] limitation, and make decrees by discrecion.

What they doe appeareth by those for whome I speake one[2] be-ing imprisoned 9 monthes: his offence supposed for complaining or furthering complaints to the parliament howse.

Laid[3] for conventicles.

W. Coulder at the black bull in fleetstreate[?].

And the last day of the last terme I moved for 20 persons fined for [*blank*].

1. Jac. c. 5.[4] All statuts made against Jesuites seminarie Priestes and those which concerne the withdrawinge of subiects

---

[1] Fuller was here showing that the powers of the High Commission went far beyond the powers provided in the statutes that the Commission was authorized to enforce.

[2] R. Maunsell. Fuller's defense of Maunsell and Ladd led to his own imprisonment and to the famous quarrel over prohibitions between the lay and the ecclesiastical courts. See Gardiner, II, 36–42. See also a pamphlet published in 1607, *The Argument of Master Fuller in the Case of T. Ladd and R. Maunsell.*

[3] Ladd. See the preceding note.

[4] C. 4.

from ther due obedience takeinge the oath of obedience and recusants shalbe put in due execucion. Manie statuts *sub* etc.

Forfaitures[1] for such as send their children over seas to seminaries. The child to be disabled etc. if he returne not within 4 monthes.

No person to passe over seas without licence except merchants mariners etc.

As theise things are verie inconvenient so they are unlawfull.

For such commission without statut of noe force:

The statut[2] hath noe woords to etc. but the last viz. [*blank*].

These cannot be construed for to expound thintent of the makers.

The title of the act, for restoring to the crowne the auncient iurisdiccion and abolishinge foreine power repugnant to the same. viz.

The preamble to reforme heresies etc. which by ecclesiasticall power was to be reformed.

The trew power ecclesiasticall ther in fact.

The Church of christ, wherin god setteth amongst the assemblie of gods and the iudgment is gods and he is with them in the cause and in the iudgment therfore to expounde that Christs church should be governed by the law of Antechriste is hard construccion uppon such indefine woords.

f. 45. b]   25 JUNII 1607.

Mr. Fullers bill touching the high commission exhibited on tuisday entituled An Act for reformacion of one braunch of a statut made *anno* 1 Elizabeth entituled an act for restoring the Crowne etc: *primo lecta:*

By this bill was requiered *inter* [*alia*] thes woords in the act of *primo* Elizabeth viz. (Accordinge to the tenor and effect of the said Letters patents) to be voide.

Statut 2. H. 4. c. 15.[3] tending to enlarge the authoritie of Ordinaryes long since abrogated.

SIR GEO[RGE] MORE returned a bill intituled An act for the es-

---

[1] Provisions of the statute cited above, though inaccurately stated.

[2] That is, the statute of 1 Elizabeth, upon which the High Commission was based.

[3] *Statutes of the Realm*, II, 125. The famous "burning statute," which gave churchmen powers to act against the Lollards. Fuller declared that this statute could not be made a legal basis for the powers given to the High Commission.

tablishinge of the possessions of Ferdinando late Earl of Derby, with a speach to this effect, viz. Yesterdaie the Committees mett and spent from 2 untell 7. There was counceill for the heir male likewise for the heir generall and ther weare some of the purchasers and though few weare there of counceill with them yet every committee was a counceillor for them: Then the amendements weare redd and the bill put to engrossing.

Dr. Stanhope and D[octor] Swale from the Lords brought the bill formerlie sent up by this howse for abolishing of hostile lawes with some amendements and addicions.

Uppon Mr. Speakers mocion the Amendements, Addicions and takings out weare readde. Of which being many one was After the woord (Theft), put in (Buggery) *linea* 79. An other was *linea* 88, after (Of) and before the woord (Witnesses) put in the woorde (Such): then followed many more amendements.

The addicions do conteine in effect a reference of the allowance of witnesses to the Jury or the moste parte of them[1] and for triall of Noblemen by Piers.

Amendement of the Lords Additions. To the point of triall of witnesses by the Jury, Which as the Lords had so set downe that the iury in their descrecion should allow or reiect witnesses, the Commens added woords to this effect, viz. (Uppon their Oathes)[2] to allow or reiect witnesses: *Nota* an amendement of an addicion. An other amendement by the Lords was thus After the woorde (Witnesses) put in the woord: (Only).

26 JUNII 1607.

The bill exhibited by Mr. Fuller touching the proceeding by the high Commission 2do. *lecta:* and committed this afternoone in the court of wards.

Mr. Speaker remembered where the howse left yesterday in the bill for abolishing hostile lawes. And among the Addicions and amendements doon by the Lords this was one, After the woorde

---

[1] It will be remembered that the Commons had inserted a clause in the bill allowing prisoners to have their witnesses put under oath. As suggested in the conference on June 10, the Lords added a provision that the jury should be allowed to reject witnesses whom it regarded as unfit to give evidence.

[2] This amendment was not made till June 30. Bowyer must have written these lines after that date.

(Justificacion) putt in theis woords (as hereafter shalbe allowed).

Then he readde the Addicions touchinge witnesses pro et contra, and the triall of nobility by Piers.

Heare was *altum silencium*. Then Mr. Speaker did put the howse in mynde that there is but 3 courses, Either, said he, you must be pleased to dispute it, or to committ it or to put it to the question. Wheruppon it was committed, the whole howse to be committees in this place this after noone but not uppon a question. *Speaker.*

Sir W[illiam] Stroude moved that being but 10 of the clocke, the Speaker might departe and the howse presently to proceede by committee, of this point divers opinions arose wheruppon the question was made whether now or in the after noone. *Committee.*

Mr. Dyet. In the fore noone no Committee in this place: Sir Fra[ncis] Barrington, the Speaker neaver left us all settinge. Mr. Speaker *econtra*. *Committee.*

Mr. Carleton. I herd divers take exceptions to the bill who now are absent, therefore I wish wee should not now proceede, untell such persons be present that wee maie satisfie them. Mr. Speaker *ad idem*.

It was put to the question, and the voices being doubtfull and the question put againe the No prevailed. *Question.*

Mr. Martyn desiered a resolucion, whether a matter being ordered by a generall consent without the question or any No: this be binding so as the howse cannot alter their purpose afterwards. Mr. Speaker. It is not bindinge before the question, and No: to which the f. 46. a] howse seemed to assent. *Order without Question.*

After dinner members assembled in the howse, The voice as I and others conceaved was for Mr. Fuller to take the chaire, and some on Mr. Attorney. Mr. Fuller modestly refusing, (*ut est moris*) Mr. Attorney offered himselfe to it. Then the question was whether all the bill or only those parts should be reade where the alteracions weare and agreed the Alteracions only to be readde. The first alteracion was thus viz: After (offences) leave out theis woords (of treason, misprision of treason, petit treason, concealement of treason) and put in theis woords (of Coniuracion, Witchcrafte, dealinge with wicked and evill spirits).

Mr. Fuller. The preamble will have no Remaundinge, and therefore an other course of Justice was to be devised, and now when you come to provide a course of Justice you except Treasons etc. so as Remaundinge in that cas, is inevitable.[1] Sir Geo[rge] Moore. The entent appeareth as Mr. Fuller saieth and yet wee did not put in witchcraft, Buggary *et alia*, and as the Lords have put in more therin then wee did so they may take away some others. Mr. Attorney. A clause afterwards towards the ende of the bill doth cleere it which is, to this effect, viz. That no man for any offence doon in Scotland shalbe remaunded, there to receave his triall untell both the realmes shalbe one in lawes and governement.

Sir Fra[ncis] Bacon newly Sollicitor.[2] There is a provision by the statut of H. 8.[3] for triall of treason doon in Scotland, *ergo:* not necessary here to be mencioned. Mr. Fuller. The statut of 13. H. 8.[4] limiteth leases by Deanes and Chapters and other ecclesiasticall persons to be only for 21 yeares and adiudged not to extend to Bishops, because insomuch as the statut began not with them being the cheifest, wherby it was presumed they weare ment to be at large as before and therefore the statut of 1 Elizabeth[5] provideth for Bishops to be in like sort restrained. Mr. Attorney. I reverence their opinion that do doubt as I woulde have them to regarde myne, I do not thincke that by disputacion wee can cleere it, wherefore some other way must be founde. Sir Roger Owen. I will not iudge the lawe, but I saie uppon Mr. Fullers cases and others that have ben put the other way, When the preamble is one way and the body of the act an other, the Judges have a court of Equitie in them to do as they thincke good.

This point being doubtfull the Committee did incline to amende it in such sort as they might which by the better opinion (as I con-

---

[1] The Lords had taken treason out of the list of offenses for which trial was provided in England. The Commons therefore feared that there might be remanding in cases of treason, in spite of a general statement that prisoners were to be tried in their own country. The Commons later added a clause definitely prohibiting remanding for treason trials.

[2] Bacon had become solicitor-general the day before, June 25, Doderidge receiving the post of King's Sergeant.

[3] 26 Hen. VIII. c. 13 (*Statutes of the Realm*, III, 509) and 35 Hen. VIII. c. 2 (*Statutes of the Realm*, III, 958) both provided for trial of treason committed out of the realm.

[4] A mistake for 13 Eliz. c. 10. *Statutes of the Realm*, IV, 544–545.

[5] Obviously another mistake. See the debate on June 27, in which Fuller repeated his speech and other members pointed out errors in it.

ceaved) was thought could not be but by conference, and so was this point left to farder consideracion.

The next amendement was to this effect viz: Whereas our bill was generally witnesses to be allowed to the accused for his cleering: The amendement is (is witnesses as hereafter etc.) and that was explained by a proviso after added by the Lords to this effect, *vid.* that the witnesses should be such as the iurors returned to trie the prisoner or the most parte of them should uppon their Consciences and discrecion thinck good, Lawfull, and sufficient in the Lawe.[1]

Mr. Fuller. Manie offences doon beyond the seas are heare triable, Allso 2 Jurors swoorne are to trie a Juror challenged, and they may do it without inconvenience for they are to trie only his indifferency which doth easily apppeare by kindred etc. but heare you will have the Jurors trie the truth of a testimony before they heare it, which is most dangerous, for the witnesse allmost allwaies is to them unknowen, so as they can iudge but of his utward appearance. Againe often times a base yea a vile person may shew such reason of his knowledge and of that which he saieth, that may make his testimony apparantly true and unaunswearable. Againe 2 iurors that trie a third whether indifferent or not, do it uppon their f. 46. b] oathes and heare you will have the Jurors or the most parte of them allow witnesse or disallow them only uppon their conscience and discrecion: Next he argued uppon the equitie of witnesses in case of life more then in anie other civill cas. Circumstances said

---

[1] Many of the following speeches oppose the rejection of any witness by the jury. Nevertheless a large number of the Commons approved the Lords' amendment (which stands in the act as passed). On June 16 the Speaker had written Salisbury: "I have dealt and conferred with many concerning the point of witnesses in the bill of hostile laws, and do find them much inclined that if your Lordships restrain the clause to such witnesses as the jury shall allow of on the delinquent's part, and that they shall also be at liberty to refuse such witnesses as are offered on the accuser's part which have been in blood feud or malicious action with the delinquent, that then the same will readily be assented unto; otherwise, I conceive some doubt of the success thereof. I understand that Sir Henry Witherington doth much labour the passage of the bill, although the witnesses should be abridged, affirming that if the bill should be overthrown, himself and many others were in danger of undoing thereby. I was myself this afternoon to have attended your pleasure, but failing thereof, I hope your Lordship will excuse this my long discourse." Salisbury MSS.

he do serve the truth of witnesses and if you will reiect him before you heare him, then you refuse the examinacion or consideracion of his saieinges. Mr. Duncombe. The proviso is not indifferent for when the person standeth for his life, the witnesse against him is Scottish unknowen to the Jurors in which regard they cannot understand what exceptions are iustly to be taken to them: Againe if they would except to such witnesses, it would be saied, why it is for the King, this bringeth a terror. Againe if such witnesse sweare false he is gone backe into Scotland, and no remedy against him. On the other side a witnesse for the person is terrified with the Starre chamber, and being reiect no hurt or preiudice followeth to the Jurors who only by indiscrecion have reiected him. Mr. Holt. This triall is uniust, therefore I marvaile any man will saie he seeth no cause of obiection unto it: For this kind of triall is meerely arbitrable; and by whome? eaven by the Jurors for they may admitt or refuse witnesses by discrecion and the triall is by witnesses, yea and by parte of the Jurors, which is the Scottish triall where the Englishe is by all the Jurors. And so the triall of witnesses being by the Jury the triall of fact is in like sort by the Jurors, *ergo* the fact is triable arbitrably by the Jurors, which is woorse then before wee weare, for that was arbitrable by the Commissioners which is more honorable. Mr. Wentwoorth. The Lords are heare contrary to themselves for they say in the preamble, (For avoiding of periury etc.) and yet a defendant charged in the starre chamber for periury or subornacion is allowed witnesses. Testimony uppon oath is allowed in Appeales, but not say you in Indictments: I saie no difference: Yea in an indictment the lawe doth allow witnesses, and they are admitted and herd when the Judge in discrecion thinketh fit. Neither doth anie booke denie it *Et quod non lego, non credo:* Sir Ro[ger] Owen. (Sir[1] I know there maie be exceptions to this whole clause of witnesses yet I will reserve it for the howse, I will now only speake of it as a clause that commeth newly from the Lords and wee must) I thincke this clause of witnesses without preiudice for first, The starre chamber is no matche to this case, for there the Clerke is he that must refuse if anie witnesse be reiected, but heare the Jury is iudge and allower of the wit-

---

[1] The words in parentheses are crossed out. They are the first words of the next speech.

nesse, and therefore it is more like to the triall by the Civill lawe, where the Judge is Judge of the fact and maie reiect the Juror. Mr. Yelverton. Sir though I know there may be exceptions to this whole clause of witnesses yet I will reserve it for the howse, I will now only speake of it as a clause that commeth newly from the Lords and wee must compare your amendement and this clause together, your amendement is only of witnesses on the parte of the delinquent and those they will have to be such as be Good, Lawfull Sufficient: Our law doth not determine that, for he that hath ben a theefe may nowe be none, and he maie be false of his fingers that is trew of his tongue: well Sir this then wilbe tried not by the Jury but by the Judges: what Judges? not Judges of assise, but such as the King will make Commissioners, who may be no Lawyers. A-gaine a man Excommunicated or owtlawed is not *Legalis* and yet wee have overruled it heare that a person owtlawed may be wise, and a good member of this howse. Allso the exception unto wit-f. 47. a] nesses is uppon suggestion not uppon oath, which I take to be unequall: Farder it will breede corruption, for in their dis-crecion they maie allow witnesses. Againe it breedeth hart burning for the most parte maie allow or reiect witnesses, then if 7 will allow and 5 will not, when will they agrea in their verdict? for they which will allow a witnesse, will beleeve him *et econtra: Sicut audio sic iudico* saieth Christ[1] so it is not the sight but the hearing of a witnesse that must leade the Jurors, wherfore I am against that clause:

Sir Fra[ncis] Bacon undertooke to aunswere the cheife obiections made by Mr. Yelverton, his aunsweres to the two first I tooke not: The third obiection was for that such allowing or reiecting of witnesses by the Jury is not appointed to be uppon oath. Though it be not saied to be uppon oath yet saied he, it is set downe to be such as shall appeare unto them etc. which woord (Appeare) I take must be by oath. The fourth obiection is, that it cometh to neere to the Scottish law: for the odde or casting voice doth it. I aunswere, The odde voice among the Lords in the starre chamber doth it, and they are as it weare the Jurors *Judices faciendi* and in challengs of a Juror, the most of them which are formerly sworne do trie: The fift obiection is, that disagreament is wrought hereby among

---

[1] John 5:30.

the Jurors, I aunsweare it is not strange for Jurors to disagrea. The sixth obiection is the power given to the Jurors: this is likewise aunswered that it is not strange to see a Jury potent and therefore 3 persons having severall issues to be tried, one saied God send mee a good cause, the 2d. wished a good Judge the third a good Jury.

27 JUNII 1607.

The long bill for setling the enheritance of the mannors etc. of Ferdinando late Earl of Derby was redde.

After dinner the Committees did meete for the bill of Hostile lawes.

Mr. Attorney in the chaire delyvered that it is agreed of all parties that no remaundinge shalbe, now the question is whether this clause doth sufficiently provide for that. The doubt is for that heare is no provision against remaunding in cas of treason and allso other offences are put out by the Lords *ergo* conferring the preamble with the residew, Remaundinge maie be for theis offences.

Sir Fra[ncis] Bacon Sollicitor made shew to repeate for the informacion of such lawyers as weare not yesterdaie present the obiections then made and to aunswere them, but I tooke it not. Mr. Fuller breifely repeated his owne reasons yesterdaie given *videlicet* 3. *Primo* Where the statut against Receivors[1] doth in the preamble declare the meaning to be against the King's officers, though the purvey be generall (All Receivors), yet it was holden to extend only to the Kings officers. 2do. A cas of periury upon a statut of like nature. 3° the cas of ecclesiasticall leases omitting Bishops[2] etc. He concluded that because all parties did agrea that no Remaundinge should be, and this as now it standeth is at the least doubtfull therefore wee shall do well to thinck of some course how wee maie amende it. Mr. Diggs. The statut of Elizabeth[3] was construed as Mr. Fuller saieth, not to extend unto Bishops not only uppon the reason by him remembered but for that *anno* 1 Elizabeth[4] there was a law to the same effect in force against Bishops and therefore now needelesse: Mr. Attorney added that Mr. Fullers opinion was conceaved uppon the reading of the abridgement

---

[1] 7 Ed. VI. c. 1. *Statutes of the Realm*, IV, 161.
[2] 13 Eliz. c. 10. *Statutes of the Realm*, IV, 544–545.
[3] *Ibid.*
[4] 1 Eliz. c. 19. *Statutes of the Realm*, IV, 381–382.

title Leases: but in the booke at large Bishops are named in one parte and not in an other for they seeme left out of this parte *de industria*, viz. because as Mr. Diggs saied there was a lawe then *in esse* to that purpose. Mr. Brocke. Treason must be understoode of such offences as are heare treason and not such as are treason in Scotland and not heare.

f. 47. b] Mr. Crew. The particuler reason in the preamble doth not exclude the generality of the purvey coming after, Yet I could wish that the woord (whatsoever)[1] weare added to the end of the generall purvey: heare he vouched the opinion of Dalison the Judge uppon the woord (such entry)[2] and yet it hath ben since taken that the woord (such) do[th] nothing. I do wish that if there be anie other occasion to attend the Lords, this woorde (whatsoever) may be added, or other order taken for explaining and making the matter cleere. Mr. Hyde. Though the preamble be speciall I thinck you may make your purvey generall, but I thincke it wilbe good for the satisfaccion of all men to adde the woorde (whatsoever). Mr. Tate. If there had ben no inducement, I would have ben of opinion that the purvey had conteined all offences but the inducement beinge, for that there is provision for punishment of offences so as there now no more necessity of Remaundinge, I now thincke the purvey not generall enough, therefore I wish that the inducement be taken away and so the law will be generall.

Agreed that the Committee shall first resolve whether the faults suspected or doubted shalbe amended and herin first to see whether and how to amende it. And then to argue or intimate to the Lords our entent in that behalfe. Mr. Attorney moved that first wee should see how it maie be amended before wee resolve that it shalbe amended, for if you first resolve it shalbe amend[ed] then if it cannot be amended, you have resolved against the passage of it as it is.

Hereuppon it was determined that against monday morninge presidents shalbe sought whether and how amendements in this case maie be and thursday the opinion of the Committees with

Amendement of the Lords Amendements or addicions.

[1] He wished the act to state that there should be no remanding for any offense "whatsoever." This word is used in the act.

[2] His interpretation of 32 Hen. VIII. c. 33 (*Statutes of the Realm*, III, 788). Dyer, *Reports* (ed. of 1794), I, 219.

such course as they shall thincke fit herin to be reported to the howse.

The next point being concerning witnesses was a litle handled, first Mr. Fra[ncis] More thought it well as it now standeth: Sir Fra[ncis] Bacon, thought it better now for the English offendor then as wee sent it upp to the Lords and if it be not well yet not [so] much amisse as that the whole bill should die for it: Sir W[illiam] Twisden. The power to allow or reiect witnesses is left to the Jurors to guide by their discrecion whiche I thincke should and ought to be by rule and the woord (Appeare) is a doubtfull woorde and setteth not downe anie certaine course how. Allso favor and malice are hidden things and must be disclosed by circumstances; I like well the Jurors to have the allowance of witnesse, but I wish it to be by rule of matter apparant. Mr. Crew. The woord (oath) doth not referre to the Jurors who are to allow or reiect witnesses, but to the witnesse that is to be herd, viz. that he shalbe herd on oath.

29 Junii 1607.

The Committees met in the court of wards about the bill of hostile lawes returned from the Lords before the setting of the howse, and afterwards in the howse MR. ATTORNEY reported[1] the proceedings of the Committees thus: viz: First that the Committee agreed the clause concerning wittnesses as it standeth,[2] together with the inducements of that clause. Next: that the putting out of theis woords (high treason: misprison and concealment of treason etc.) breadde a doubt, not so much for the putting out of those woords as for the inducement: for some doubted that though the woords in the purvey be, (that no person shalbe remaunded for any cause) yet because the greatest offence viz. treason, is not expressed and smaller be expressed before the generall woords, therefore that Remaunding remaineth for those greate offences, in which respect the Committee thought good that by woords of explanacion it should be expressed that Treason, etc. should be expressed, but before they would conclude, they resolved to see presidents whereuppon a gentleman that hath best opportunity and most understanding in ancient presidents shewed

R[obert] B[owyer]. f. 48. a]

---

[1] Cf. the report and subsequent debate in *C.J.* I, 388, 1055.

[2] Thus retaining the clause that allowed the jury to reject unfit witnesses.

to us of the Committee presidents of tow kindes, viz: Firste that wee have added a schedule to the Lords schedule: and secondly that wee have amended the Lords amendements. Within the second is our cas thought to be, For though the Lords have not altered the woords of our bill in this point, but taken away the woords (Treason etc.) yet therby they have altered the sence of our bill in that point, therefore wee may amende it as their amendement: and hereuppon the Committee farder thought good wee should conferre with the Lords to signifie unto them our purpose or inclinacion to amende: least if wee do it afore without their privitie, wee thereby hazard the bill: Then he declared to the howse, How, and in what, and in what woords the Committee held fit to alter the bill.

Mr. Speaker moved, to know the pleasure of the howse, whether according to the opinion of the committee wee should send to the Lords for a conference and to signifie unto them our entent to alter their amendements.

Mr. Anth[ony] Cope. That all witnesses be herd, and not to leave power to the Jurors to heare or reiect a witness. He shewed that Deuteronomy wee must search before wee iudge[1] which cannot be but by hearinge witnesses: Three differences he madd betweene Jurors and witnesses, Jurors ought to be without 3 exceptions viz. he must not be false in woord and deede: 2do. not furious and revengefull, 3° not corrupt: And theis are not requisite in a witnesse for his testimony is but to enforme the Jury, who may beleave as they see cause for if they find by circumstances that a bad fellow saieth true they may beleeve him *et econtra:* Then he held the Jurors most unfit of all others to allow or reiect a witnesse, for Juror[s] ought to long to be informed, and to heare all that they can, and it will follow, that if the Jurors may heare only such as they please, they may without danger of their oath condemne whom they list, for they are sworne no farder then their evidence, and heare they may choose whether they will heare anie evidence other then such as they presume wilbe to their mynde.[2]

Sir Geo[rge] More. The power to heare anie witnesse without oath is not taken away but provision that none shalbe swoorne but

---

[1] Deuteronomy 1:16 or 17:9.
[2] "That this Point might be opened at the Conference." *C.J.* I, 1055.

such as the Jurors shall allow: The law of God is that wee admitt
no false witnesse and this referring the allowance of witnesses
unto the Jury, is the way to avoide false witnesses and periury,
and the Jurors uppon whose conscience and oath it lieth to passe
uppon the prisoner is fittest to examine, and reiect or allow a
witnesse: MR. WENTWOORTH alloweth of Conference for amendements, and that the clause of witnesses is to be altered, and that
when wee do go to the Lords, forasmuch as their Lordships have
sent us woorde that herin wee have varied from the law of other
countries and from our owne law, I wish their Lordships should
be informed that wee have not varied *ut supra*, and shewed his reasons which weare sundry uppon this grounde, that (Life is to be
favored) more then any thinge else) but in other cases witnesses are
allowed *ergo* heare. MR. YELVERTON. I know I am suspected to
[be] against the bill, and so I am for I see reason so to be: The
howse enclineth to a conference with the Lords touching some parte
of this bill, and I thincke wee ought allso to conferre uppon the
point of witnesses, otherwise when the bill cometh to passage, I
shall except and protest against it.

   MR. FULLER. All witnesses are to be herd, otherwise the mischeife wilbe this, wee must expect the like law in Scotland, and
this will follow, a scottishman when he shalbe once heare reiected
and not herd, will saie at his returne, why should wee go into England to accuse, wee cannot be herd, and then wee maie not expect
to be herd there, by which meanes Justice will faile. MR. DUN-
COMBE protesting his love to the bill yet with Mr. Yelverton.

Many privately   SIR EDW[ARD] HOBBY. I cannot thincke that anie man speaking
misliked this   against this clause, or for conference on this point doth love the
braine-sicke tax-   bill, but doth secretely endeavor under a faire shew to over
acion of others.   through the bill. I was against the Instrument of the Union, as It
was drawen, but I am for the bill: The bill addeth nothing to the
King in commodity nor honor but to the subiect of England: And
if there weare nothing but the repeale of the statut of 5. R. 2.[1]
I would give my voice to it.

   f. 48. b] MR. HOLT. First against Sir Edw[ard] Hobbyes indiscrecion: Next he shewed that this clause of reiectinge witnesses
maketh the triall of life arbitrable, for truth and evidence cometh

---

[1] *Statutes of the Realm*, II, 18. One of the hostile laws.

from witnesses, if then in discrecion witnesses may be reiected the truth may be arbitrably reiected. And the Italian proverbe turned into english is this, Shew mee with whome you go, and I will tell you what you do, then, if I may choose the witnesses I do choose the evidence. Sir Fra[ncis] Bacon Sollicitor. They that spake against the clause of witnesses and for the bill, spake no doubt their mynds, But for that the first gentleman enterposed the law of God, which I neaver heare but it sinketh into mee: I saie in Deuteronomy is no such thing, and the greatest truth that eaver was, was interdicted to be testified by an unworthy witnesse for when the Divell[1] would have witnessed of Christ, Thou art the soon of God, he was forbidden by Christ himselfe.[2]

Ultimo Junii. 1607.

Mr. Attorney reported[3] that the commission yesterday given to him and other messengers sent to the Lords was to declare unto their Lordships the consideracion heare had of the bill of Hostile Lawes and likewise touching the same to conferre with their Lordships if occasion should be offered. Accordinglie said he I delivered your pleasure and after we weare a while retired the Lords called us in againe and requiered present conference with us which was in the painted chamber. Wee declared that this howse hath had consideracion of the amendements, and of the clause annexed of newe to the bill, that this howse did conceave in one point a difficultie, and did allso determine not to alter without their privitie to the end that the bill that was so deare to them and to us might proceed the better: Wee shewed that wee conceaved the Kings gracious meaning and the resolute purpose of all parties to be, that no englishman for anie offence or cause shalbe remaunded into Scotland there to be tried: and that wee did conceave that wee had passed the bill accordinglie, but as their Lordships have altered it ther arriseth some difficultie for they having mencioned only smaller offences, wee doubted the generall woords after will not include Treason, and the other greater offences ommitted: Wee

---

[1] Luke 4:41.

[2] The House resolved upon question to confer concerning the clause of remanding, but not concerning the clause of witnesses.

[3] Cf. his report and subsequent proceedings on the bill of hostile laws in *C.J.* I, 388–389, 1055–56.

farder told them that as there is cause of amendement so wee have
Amendements. sound precedent, that in us is power to amende it, yet wee thought
good to acquaint their Lordships with it and to do it with their
assent wherto they agreed in all points.

The bill for sale of coppihold lands[1] was *primo lecta* and manie
cried away with it, Sir Ro[bert] Johnson stoode up to speake and
by a frowne of Mr. Speakers did set downe againe, and being called
up by the howse, he arrose and said, to this effect, It is a strange
conceipt that the misdemeanors of stewerds cannot be reformed
without sale of the lands, and, said he, I have wrightten herin as
much unto my gracious soveraign as any man of my hert, and if my
proiect may be followed if I do not remedy this fault let the King
take my head. But herof I shall speake more at the second reading.

Speaker. The clerks man that wright the bill for abolishing hostile lawes
was called in to wright the amendementes in the howse: which being doon Mr. Speade[2] did reade the schedule added by the Lords
touchinge witnesses, and then offered to putt [it] to the question.
Mr. Hyde. The exceptions which have ben taken to this proviso
carrie weight: Shall the Jury on discretion without oath reiect and
allow witnesses? This is of moment and well moved, and the
parties ought to be satisfied, whether it so be as now it standeth,
and I thincke it is so: The oath of the Jurors is; You shall trew
delivery make, betweene the Kinge and the prisoner att the barre.
The Jurors surely may without danger of this oath preiudice
witnesses. Therefore I would have that wheras the woords be that
the Jury (accordinge to their conscience and discrecion) seeing wee
find wee may amende, I would have added (Conscience oath and
discrecion). This was well allowed by the whole howse. Afterwards Mr. Speaker moved that the woords should be (Accordinge
Amendements of f. 49. a] to their conscience and discrecion uppon their oathes).[3]
addicions. And determined that the woords (uppon their oathes) shalbe
added in paper and fixed on the margent of the bill, and so sent
upp to the Lords by them to be engrossed, for it was agreed

---

[1] A bill "For the Confirmation of all Letters Patents, and Grants, to
be made by the King's Majesty, of any Copyhold Lands, etc." *C.J.* I, 388.

[2] Mr. Speaker.

[3] Thus altered, the Commons passed the amendments of the Lords.
The bill became law without further change.

that the Text of that proviso being the Lords, they are to engrosse the amendement.

Mr. Speaker declared that the Lords desier that the Parliament drawing to an ende this howse woulde sett in the after noone which was assented unto: Allso that the committee for the bill of patents are to meete after dinner in the court of wards. Mr. Alford desiered that this bill maie sleepe for the manie difficulties.

1 Julii 1607.

The bill against the use of horsehides etc. by showmakers etc. allso the Bill to enable John Good to assigne a terme unto his Majestie being yesterdaie in the after noone sent from the Lords to the Commens who then weare in nomber besids the Speaker but 20 persons: and now but 17 weare *primo lecta*. Allso both those bills 2do. *lecta* and committed.

A bill for continuance and making perpetuall of an act against rebellious assemblies made *anno primo* Mary and by severall acts continued from tyme to tyme[1] (and lastly unto the ende of the next Parliament after the death of the late Queen Elizabeth[2]) *primo et 2do. lecta* (and committed).[3] It was moved that this bill should sleepe, wherunto was aunswered that the statute endeth with this cession, and is necessarie to be continued: It was replied that it doth not ende with this cession but with the next cession after the death of Queen Elizabeth, and therefore seeing wee know not of the ende of this parliament neither is it likely at this time to ende and for that it is inconvenient to make it perpetuall there[fore] it was moved that the howse maie do well to view it: Mr. Speaker and the Kings councell moved a committement and that it maie be continued only for a time, if it seems not fit to make it perpetuall.

A bill for naturalising John Steward which was yesterday sent from the Lords was now 2do. and 3° *lecta* and passed.

Sir Fra[ncis] Barrington, Sir Ja[mes] Perrot, Mr. Duncombe, Mr. Bowyer, committees for priviledgs being by the rest of that Committee thereunto appointed, went into the Committee chamber and sent for the Clerks booke of dailie enterances to have proceeded in

Marginal notes:

Small presence to read a bill.

Clercks booke of entryes.

---

[1] 1 Mar. Stat. II. c. 12. *Statutes of the Realm*, IV, 211. Continued by *ibid*. IV, 263, 296, 331.

[2] 1 Eliz. c. 16. *Statutes of the Realm*, IV, 377.

[3] The words in parentheses are crossed out.

perusall therof etc. to whom Mr. Speaker sent up aunswere by the Serieant, that setting the howse they might not have it. And *nota* that Mr. Speaker whilest the said fowre committees weare above moved the howse being vearie few to that purpose: namelie that the said booke of enterancs might not be sent up out of the howse. The said Committees came downe and moved the matter *ut supra:* viz. Sir Fra[ncis] Barrington moved it: Mr. Speaker aunsweared that the order is *ut supra*. Mr. Bowyer replied, that the Clerke would not deliver the booke out of the howse and then if Mr. Speaker woulde not permit the Committees to have it setting the howse, then is there no time left, wherefore he desiered that the Committees might be discharged of the service wherof for his owne parte he would be glad to be freed, and such he conceaved to be the desier of the residew, on whome that labor hath ben imposed. Mr. Speaker tooke exceptions that the Committees who now weare mett are but 4 or 5 wheras under 7 as he affirmed is no Committee neither ought by the order of the howse to deale in anie matter. Sir Edwyne Sandys declared that the Committee wherof himselfe was one had made a subcommittee to prepare the busines by perusing the Clerks booke viz. to observe wherabout and which weare matters concerning priviledge, and to be considered of, which saied he maie be well performed by 4 or 3.

Committees Sub-
committee.

f. 49. b] Mr. Speaker saied that the Committee maie make a Subcommittee, but the subcommittee cannot deale in the busines before the howse be therewithall acquainted which most of the howse then present held to be so. *Quod mirandum.*

2. Julii 1607.

Councell, betweene Mrs. Cavendish and Sir Char[les] Cornwallis came to the barre. Counceill against the bill was first herd and after small discorse by counceill on both sides the farther heareing of them was referred to the Committee.

Mr. Speaker declared that whilest manie of this companie weare away the Lords sent 3 bills downe: One formerly sent from hence before to them touching Southampton. The 2d. a bill whereby counterfaiting of the Greate Seale or privie seale of Scotland is made treason. The 3d. for the encrease of Tymber.

The second of theis bills was foorthwith *primo lecta:*

The proviso annexed to the bill of Southampton was reade which proviso was for the cinque Ports. In this bill it was said that when a bill is heare passed and sent to the Lords and by them returned with a proviso, no man may speake to the body of the bill but only to the proviso, *Nota* that the proviso being put to the question for committment was not committed but the third time readde and passed with the bill.

Proviso. Committment.

The bill against the use of Horse hides and hoggs skines etc. by showmakers 3 *lecta:* and reiected uppon argument: *nota* the reason for the bill was yelded to be because such skynnes being put into shoes or bootes will sucke in wett which is against the health of the wearer: Trulie quoth one it sheweth an honorable care in the Lords of the health of us meaner persons, but if this act passe another commoditie will ensue, viz. harneis for coach horses which greate men use wilbe the cheaper.

The bill for preservacion of tymber *primo lecta.*

After dinner in the court of wards divers of the Committees for continuance of the act of *primo* Mary[1] against unlawfull assemblies did meete. After long dispute generallie agreed by all that it shall not be made perpetuall. Allso agreed that unlesse this parliament be now dissolved it doth continue untell a new parliament, for it was in *primo* Elizabeth[2] continued untell the ende of the first parliament after the decease of Queen Elizabeth so now the question grew whether in respect it is doubtfull whether this parliament shalbe now ended or proroged and for that the waunt of this law at this time seemeth not to be without danger (*nota* by reason of the veary late assemblyes in divers counties to lay open inclosures, not yet fully pacified),[3] therefore now this law should be continued untell the ende of the first cession of the next parliament.

Unlawfull Assemblyes.

Sir Edwyne Sandys against anie continuance of this law, for he thought that such continuance woulde woorke in them that shalbe of the next parliament an opinion of the goodnesse of this Lawe as now it standeth, which by the whole committee or the much greater parte was thought dangerous *inter alia* for this reason or

---

[1] 1 Mar. Stat. II. c. 12. *Statutes of the Realm*, IV, 211.

[2] 1 Eliz. c. 16. *Statutes of the Realm*, IV, 377.

[3] See E. F. Gay, "The Midland Revolt and the Inquisitions of Depopulation of 1607," *Transactions of the Royal Historical Society* (*New Series*), XVIII, 195–244.

mischeif in that statut: viz. that heretofore men of greate wisdome and learninge, namelie among others Sir Rog[er] Man-
whood chief Barron came within the compasse of this lawe
unwillinglie before he was warre. Mr. Alford recited a cas of one
condemned in Sussex upon this statute for woords spoken, without anie evill intent. Sir Fra[ncis] Bacon gaine saied the president,
affirming that the Judge saied to the partie suerly when thou
spakest theis woords thou wert droncke to which the prisoner
replied no my Lord I was as sober as I or any man else is now,
wheruppon he was found guilty. But Mr. Alford maintened his
president and the parties iustifieing his inocency, and that he farder saied that he had att the uttering of the woords, druncke with
one other 12 quarts of beare, and this he urged Sir John Shurley
f. 50. a] to testifie, who witnessed it to have benne at Greensted
in Sussex in all points as Mr. Alford had remembered. But quoth
Sir Fra[ncis] Bacon this which I speake of was in Norfolk. And
it was affirmed that 5000 persons in Northamptonshire[1] are by
extremity in the danger of this lawe so divers and intricate are
the points of it, many resting uppon construccion of the Judge to
expound a mans entent in speaking etc. Mr. Bowyer thought
that the preamble of the bill recitinge the lawe to be good and
necessarie, it would adde to much grace to the statute, as now it
standeth, and shew an approbacion of this parliament which might
be to greate an inducement to the next to make it perpetuall being
now since the Kings coming allowed as good and necessary. Mr.
Attorney generally moved that the preamble might be left out and
the law to be continued untell the first cession of the next parliament, who urged it the rather for that (as he said) he had (as by
the howse he was directed) asked of some of the Lords whether
this cession woulde be the ending of the parliament, who aunsweared that it is not resolved: Sir Fra[ncis] Bacon commended
the law as it now is: Then it was putt to the question by the Kings
Serieant whether in anie sort this statut shoulde be continued
wherin the committees weare devided, and because after voices
given neither side woulde yeld to have lost it: therfore the companie was to be devided, viz. the Yea from the No: wher uppon
The Kings Serieant namely Mr. Serieant Doddridge, Mr. Attor-

<hr>

[1] *Ibid.* 215.

ney, Mr. Sollicitor, Mr. Recorder, and the rest which gave affirmative voices for the Continuance requiered the contrary side which
weare against the continuance to arrise out of the Court, and to
draw themselves to the neither end of the roome. But the companie overruled it viz. that the Yea should withdraw themselves
downe and the No to set still as in the division of the howse, and
accordingly the Kings said learned counceill did withdraw themselves to the neither end of the roome, and the other side viz. Mr.
Fuller Sir Edwyne Sandys Mr. Yelverton, Mr. Hyde Sir H[enry]
Neveill: Ro[bert] Bowyer, and others that weare with the No, in
the Negative did sett still, and uppon counting the voices the No
prevailed for they exceeded the affirmative by seaven voices:
Note allso that the Kings counceill would uppon the differinge in
the number of voices have had the names of the affirmative and
likewise of the negative to have ben taken, but it was overruled
that it shold be devided by severance of persons and counting
the poles and not by taking of names, Which was so doon uppon
iust cause least the names should be shewed to high persons and
so some particuler members which with their conscience denied
the continuaunce might have displeasure.

No names to be
taken uppon a
division.

f. 50. b]   3 Julii: 1607.

Sir Edwyn Sandys reported[1] the labor and proceedings of the
Committees of priviledge touching the Clerks booke: and their
opinions to be that the Clerke do before the next cession (according to that which heretofore he affirmed to the howse to be his
purpose) perfect his iournall. And that nothing of anie of theis
three natures following viz: 1. Priviledge, 2. Messages, 3. Conference, be of recorde before the same be perused and perfected
by the Committees and allowed by the howse. And that hereafter, every Satturday the Committees of priviledge peruse the
Clerkes booke and perfect it. And that for his encoragement some
course be taken the next cession for his rewarde. And withall he delivered the draught of an order to the effect aforesaid to be made
by the howse, which he desiered might be readde and put to the
question, and theruppon entered as an order, if the howse should
like thereof and so thincke good: This order so offered and pre-

Clerks booke.

---

[1] Cf. the report and order in *C.J.* I, 390. See p. 343 and note.

sented by Sir Edwyne Sandys was first read by the Clerke and secondlie by Mr. Speaker and then put the question and *Nemine contradicente* allowed and agreed as an order to be entered.

Collecion.   Sir Geo[rge] More, Sir H[enry] Neveill, Sir Edw[ard] Montague Sir Edwyne Sandys appointed to receave the accompt of the Treasurers and to appoint the imploiment and to preferre it to the howse:

Mr. Attorny reported the proceeding of the Committees in Mr. Goods bill and the amendements, which weare 3° *lecta* and passed.[1]

---

[1] The next day the House attended the King in the Upper Chamber. After speeches by the Speaker, the Lord Chancellor, and the King, and the royal assent to bills, Parliament was prorogued.

APPENDIXES

APPENDIX A

[ADDITIONAL MSS 34324, ff. 37–41]

At our last meeting and conference I divided my speech into 3 parts.

The 1 concerned A Declaracion of the present necessities wherewith the Crowne is pressed.

The 2 concerned A Collection of Dyvers iust and urgent causes, wherebie the present necessities of the Crowne are growne so great.

The 3 concerned An answer to certain obiections inferring therebie that there is no necessity of anie support at all.

This order I will still keep, because thereby I shall best deliver unto you both for your memorie to retaine it. And for my better means to expresse it.

Touching the first sorte of necessities, I knowe it is not needful, nor fitt, nor I am sure that you doe not expect that I should particularlie deliver unto you the severall Receipts and payments that belonge unto the Crowne. Therefore in this point I maie onelie trulie affirme thus much that the verie ordinarie present payments, doe far exceed the yearlie ordinarie present Receipts. Which being soe, I hope you maie easily see whether the King's Majestie and the Crown stand pressed with necessitie when wee are dailie cryed and called on, to satisfie even the verie ordinarie it self, And wee have noe sufficient means to paie it.

This part necessarily is of 2 natures. The first. Concerning the want of yearly receits ordin[ary] to answer the due of yearly paym[en]t ordinarie. The second. Concerning the great debts owing by his Majestie without means to paie them.

I call the ordinarie payments theis. The Coferer. The The. of the Ch. The Pencions. The Admiraltie. The Ordinance. The Armorie. The Posts. The workes. The tower, forts etc. Eyers of the Justics; Starchamber, And dyvers others suche setled ordinarie offices belonging to the Crowne.

I call the ordin[ary] Receipts theis. The Revenue under the 7 Auditors. The Revenue in the Pipe Office. The Customes. The Dutchie of Lanc-[aster]. The Court of Wardes.

Thus I have shewed you the first parte of our necessity.

Touching the 2 sorte necessities, the debts nowe owing by his Majestie are of divers natures.

Some are debts of the late Q[ueen] left upon the Crown they are yet. . . . . .387134£

Some arrerags owing uppon the verie ordinarie it self. . . . . . . .117588£

Some particuler debts to particuler persons (of this the K[ing's] love is part). . . . . .196494£

Some are guifts of readie monie by the King. . . . . .4500£

The rest are forreinie payments due Lowe Countries . . . . .4921£

Ireland. . .60400£ 68921£

Some totall 774637 whereof late Q[ueen]'s debt. . . . . .387134£

Kings debt. . . . . .387503£

371

Now if the Lords and you of the Lower House will have me to write unto you, more particuler noates of the debts and more particuler somes due I have it here readie to shewe. But I rather iudge you will hold it bothe nedeles and inconvenient and therfore I forbeare it.

Alwaies I hope you will hold this opinion of me that I would not in this presence willinglie or wittinglie affirme an untruthe no not to gaine all the riches of the world.

And thus I trust I have satisfied the 1 Part.

Touching the 2 Part which concerneth A Collection of dyvers iust and urgent causes wherebie the present necessities of the Crowne are growne so great viz As namely.

The 1 Cause is By reason of a great debt left by the late Quene uppon the K[ing] our Soveraigne.

For although I must confesse that shee was A verie wise warie and reserved Quene bothe in her Guifts and ordinarie expences, yet was she forced to spend in the Warrs of Treasure found in her Receipt 300000£. Besids 14 Subsedies, 28 Fiftenths, 3 Lones. The sale of lande. The burden of the Realme besides, And yet died in debt 400000£ nowe 250,000£. Theis bee the fruites and effects of the warr. And this hathe brought uppon the King this great debt unto which himself was never privie nor partie.

The 2 Cause is By divers extraordinarie but yet most necessarie expences of the King himself.

The K[ing] coming out Scotland as also the Quene; The Duke and La[dy] Eliz[abeth]	10,000£
The funerall of the late Quene	20,000£
The Coronation of the K[ing's] and Quenes Majestie	20,000£
The K[ing's] entrie	10,000£
The defraying of diet, Guifts and rewardes to Forreine Ambassadores and other great personages coming to his Majestie	40,000£
The Charge of newe buildings and alteracions for the K[ing] and Q[ueen] and the P[rince]	2,000£
The redeeming of leases for woodes, And the newe making of seales	2,000£
Debts	504,000£

The 3 Cause is By a necessarie augmentacion of yerely charge which groweth manie wayes.

In the Acco[m]pt of the k[ing's] house hold. Of A k[ing] by himself, Of A Q[ueen] by her self, in state and honor, as is fit litle differen[ce]. Of A Prince by himself. Of two Princesses royall yssews by them selves. Of A Duke A kings Child by himself alsoe. All which you see are not only charges most necessarie but alsoe most comfortable. To this increase of charge is alsoe increased the necessarie increase and charge of many Offices. So as, by this means the k[ing's] house hold necessarie charge is growne to more

then doble, as namely to 55000£ yerly more then in the Quenes
tyme. . . . . 55,000£
    The k[ing's] chamber. The increase of the Board as well in the
Court as the tower. And of footemen bothe for the Quene and
Prince. . . . . 24,000£
    The k[ing's] Receit. The increase of yerlie charges to Ambassa-
dors forreinie as namely, Spaine, Venice, Archduke. . . . . 4,380£
    The increase of intertaynment of one Judge more in dudrie
Court. . . . . 300£
    The 4 Cause is Partly by a necessarie, partly by a gracious
Diminution of the Revenue.
    The Quenes ioynture which hathe diminished the Kings
Revenue yerely. . . . . 10,000£
    The Preemption of tynn released whereby is diminished
yerely. . . . . 2,000£
    The fines for Alienacions pardoned whereby is diminished
yerely, and it is like to continue for 7 years. . . . . 3,000£

                     Revenue. . . . . 77,080£

    The 5 Cause By reason of sundrie gifts and graunts made and passed
by his Majestie since his coming to the Crowne. This 5 Cause I knowe
is the hard and knottie difficulty and exception that troubleth the myndes
of some, And therfore it is necessarie that I devide and distinguishe theis
guifts into their severall natures. For although some of them to A generall
understanding maie bring some question, yet are the most of them free
from all exception. 1. Some have bene suche as even in Justice were to
be graunted. 2. Others suche as in equitie could not be denied. 3. Dyvers
such as were given in recompense of great service. 4. Sundrie others suche
as even in Honnor were fitt for the k[ing] to graunt. 5. And I must confesse some of them suche as were wonn from his Majesty by incessant
importunitie, straynning the gentlenes and bountie of his most benigne
nature and taking advantage of his lacke of knowledge at his first coming
of the state, and course of his affaires. But nowe I protest before god he
begins to have a feeling understanding of the lack of his owne means and
A naturall sense, soe as I verily theis incessant and importunat sutors will
soone vanish awaie, for they will no longer prevaile I doe asure my self,
And yet wee must not denie but that princes at their first entrance have
always extended their guifts, much more amplie then afterwards they
doe.
    So as nowe uppon the whole matter that I have shewed unto you thus
it stands.
    The k[ing's] Majestie found the Crowne in debt. . . . . 400,000£
                     now. . . . . 250,000£
    His Majesties owne extraordinarie but most necessarie ex-
pences amount to. . . . . 104,000£
    The charges as well by augmentation as by diminution in-

creasing. A iust and necessarie yerely expence the one by making
the charge more, the other by making the revenue lesse, hathe
raised in their .3. yeres, since his Majesties Coming in uppon the
king more then was uppon the Quene to the sum of . . . . .231,240£

All which heads make a just and necessarie Debt Cast uppon
the king of . . . . .735,280£

Whereof His owne Debt is only . . . . .335,280£

The other is the late Quenes . . . . .400,000£

Abate . . . . .150,000£

Thus much for the declaration of those iust and urgent Causes whereby
the present necessities of the Crowne are growne so great.

Touching the 3rd parte which contenneth An answer to certain obiections inferring thereby, That there is noe necessity of anie support at all.

Amonge manie false and frivolous obiections I will only remember
.3. wherein my opinion maie seme most materiall.

The .1. is That the k[ing's] Majestie even with his first entrance brought
an universall peace unto us. And what nowe support in tyme of peace.

The .2. is That the late Quene left to the k[ing's] Majestie 2 entire
subsidies and 4 fiftenes. Theis in this tyme of peace have filled his
H[ighness'] Cofers.

The .3. is that the charge of Barwick garison, is likewise ended by the
union, That is alsoe a great saving to his Majestie.

Touching theis .3. I must saie that suche as make theis obiections, are
litle intelligent in the affaires of state matters. For though wee had the
name of peace, yet it is certeyne that the verie necessarie Charge of warr
for Ireland Barwick and the Sea onely hath cost the king since his coming
in verie nere 200,000 pounds.

And to make it plaine and evident I will shewe you some brieff ab-
stracts of the verie accompts themselves in perticuler.

Thus it appeares that the 2 subsidies and the 4 fiftenes which came
into the Receipt Amounting to the some of 242,763£ (for as yet there is
about 14,000£ thereof unlevyed). It appeares I saie, that not onely the
said subsidies and fiftenes are spent uppon the Charge of warr since the
kings coming in, but alsoe more then other .3. subsidies would suffice to
satisffie. I hope then I have by this accompt sufficiently satisfyed those
that persuade them selves so vainely of the said name of peace, before wee
enioye the fruites, as likewise those other two obiections of Barwicke, And
of the 2 subsidies and 4 fiftenes.

And thus it is plaine howe farr of as yet, the kings Majestie hath bene,
from having or enioying the perfect fruites of peace, Beside the name onely.

But nowe on the other syde let me remember unto you howe great
frutes and felicities, wee his Majesties subiects have had and enioyed
even since the first beginning of this happie peace, and the kings coming
to the crowne.

The trade and traffique of our merchants hathe bene open unto us to
the great benefitt even of the whole realme. Their shippes have bene free,
bothe from the danger of taking and from the charge of wasting.

Our tounes and maritime coasts have bene free from the feare of spoiling and burning.

Wee have bene quiet from the continuall toile and charge of trayning.

Wee have not bene charged with the heavie burden of continuall leavying, arming, apparelling and setting forth of soldiers, A burthen more heavie then manie subsidies.

Theis things if wee doe well consider, wee must acknowledge, that howsoever the kings Majesty hath had but the name only, Certenly wee have had the verie fruites, and effects of peace for the which wee can never be to thankfull to our most gracious sovereigne by whose great goodnes next unto God, wee enioye the same.

And thus having declared unto you the kings present great necessities, With the iust and urgent causes that have inforced the same, And with an answer to those strange obiections inferring that there is noe necessitie of support at all. I have nowe noe purpose to proceed anie farther leaving the whole care and consideration (in what meane and measure the same is to be supplied) unto your owne most wise, loving and dutiful respect towards his Majesties service herein. Of which already you have made soe good A beginning as there is noe doubt but that God, and your good endeavours will prosper the same to a happie end.

Only this I will saie, and soe conclude that whatsoever you shall thinke fitt to supplie to his Majesties so great necessity (the which by the grace of god I will religiously observe, Namely that the first frutes thereof what soever it be, shalbee whollie and presently returned unto your selves againe, to satisfy the loane which hathe bene had of you.

The tyme of which repaiement let me alsoe remember unto you, Begins to become due, and payable about Easter next.

And now my Lords and all you the worthie knights and Burgesses, I beseeche you to pardon this my longe and tedious speech, whereunto the necessity of the matter it self, hath constreyned me.

APPENDIX B

The following manuscripts deal with debates between May 5 and May 11, 1607, a period omitted by Robert Bowyer in his diary.

MAY 7. ACCOUNT OF THOMAS WILSON

[ST. P. DOM. XXI, 16]

7 May. 1. The matter was entred into by Sir G[eorge] More whose speech was butt discoursive upon the motion of punishment to mis-reporters which though they cold not be knowne yett they shold not be without *flagrum conscientiae*, and that the kings knowledg of them to be such cold not but add som punishment in ther reputacion with him, but lest by this, men shold be deterred from speaking, and lest it shold be a gappe to open the way to drawe fredome into restraynt he moved that something might be done to skoll it for the conservacion of the liberty of the howse, by a speech to be made by the speaker to the kinge, which liberty notwithstanding he confest he never sawe it less abridged then in this parliament.

2. Heer the speaker reports what he had from his Majesty that to the 3 parts of the Motion made yesterday by Mr. Lewknor the two first he wold be ready to grante upon ther peticion att any tyme viz to suspend his iudgment untill he herd apparant proof of the perticularity of any mans speechs and to be ready to lett explain him selfe before he wold take any aprehension of report. And for the 3d of geveing the ancient liberty to the howse for freedome of speech (soe they kept them selves within the bounds of discretion and modestye) that his Majesty will ever be more iealous of the conservacion therof then our selves and that he accounts him not worthy of that place that (with the limitacions aforesaid) will not freely speake his conscience.

4. Then rose Mr. Brock and comended the graciousness of the kings message, and moved without more words to have the bill comitted.

5. To that Mr. Fuller sayd nay and prosecuted his yesterdayes motion to have it first thorowghly debated. And soe tooke exceptions to divers parts of the bill.

First to the Word, *Continuance* in the title of the bill that it cold not be for the continuance of a thinge but it must have relation to a tyme when the thinge began but this union cold not take his beginninge but from the tyme it was perfected and made. Then he brought in a title as he wold have it.//thus//An Act to make voide certayne hostile lawes for a preparacion to the Union betwixt England and Scotland. Then he tooke exception to that point that a part of the lawe for going out of the land shold be taken away for that they myght thence goe whither they wold, yett wisht that for some respects it might be all taken away that they might not only goe into Scotland but from thence and out of England to what countryes they wold according to the freedome of other kingdomes. He inferd the words of the scripture If you be persecuted in one kingdome flee to an other, heerin he aymed att the puritan ministers that they might

376

have such liberty and alledged that we myght ha[ve] many causes by
affliccions in this kingdom wherby we shold be forced to flee in to others,
he recapitulated many which verry improperly he applyed to be nowe
inflicted upon us as it were for a punishment of suppressing the ministers
(as I understood him) as the innundacons, the smale fruites of our long
consultacons in Parliament, the stricter execucion of lawes etc. and in-
sinuated a prediccion of more to come for which he prayed for a diversion.

Lastly he toke exception to the Comission that by this bill shold be
granted to 20 English and 10 Scottish for the borders, sheweing howe
arbitrary Comissions that have absolute power are the causes of absolute
wronge.

Heer the Speaker answered to the second part of his speech and told
that he had seen yesterday a lawe that the restraynte in Scotland is much
more strict then that of England for subiect, going out of the kingdome,
and that in that case they forfayted lands and goods.

Then rose up Mr. Yelverton to make his apologye which he did
modestly enough, terming him selfe but a worme att the lyons feet; he
submitted him selfe to the ansure and sentence of the kinge with this
sentence *salvi culpa qui talem habuit redemptorem*, out of one of the fathers,
of a sinner to Christ. He taxed those that stryved rather to carry away
words then matter. And then made an apology for his words for which
he was censured, as that of his//fears and hopes//sheweing he ment he
had nether distrust nor feare in the kings beninge interpretacion, nor
Ambition to raise him selfe, his deserts being soe smale. After he had
answered to all those points wherof he thought he was censured (and said
that if he were not iustified by the howse to be condemned without cause
he wold submitt him selfe to be falty) he begann to speake to the bill.
And said that though they wer chidden yett they must not be sullen and
speake noe more, and then shewed that in this bill 3 points of 1 Hostile
lawes 2 Comerce and 3 naturalizacion wer included that this was not to
abrogate hostile lawes but to abrogate all lawes. He shewed that we were
not bound to the comandements of the kinge as he comands by the right
of the crowne of Scottland, and soe repeted that old point of tying allegeance to the lawe and crowne, not to the persone of the king.

He affirmed that if this course of Comission of the 20 English and
10 Scottish shold goe forward ther shold not be in short tyme a man in
Northumberland Cumberland and Westmorland worth a shirt on his
backe for that all the iniuryes that have ben done hertofore shold nowe
be cald in question, which then wer lawfull and iustifiable: his conclusion
was that he was not against the comitting of the bill butt wisht it might
be Comitted and presently therupon the question being made the bill
was comitted, the whole howse Comittees, to morrow in the afternoone
to meet in the parlament howse. After the bill was comitted Mr. hare
rose up and had much a doe to be herd, and it had ben better he had not
ben herd for he renued only the frivolous motion of cleering Mr. yelverton
by voices.

Then Sir W[illiam] Skippwith made a motion to have a petition made to the kinge to lett them knowe who they were that had soe misreported, as if he wold have his Majesty become an accuser, which was generally reclaymed with a Noe Noe.

Sir Ro[bert] Wingfeld ther againe (as he had done yesterday) seemed to accuse him selfe by iustifing first that it was lawfull to tell any thinge to the king, if it wer truth and then mayntayned that, what was told to the kinge was true, and was spoken in the howse, and left the misinterpretacion therof upon his Majesty and notwithstanding he had yesterday said that the kinge had told him that he had herd it reported in severall wayes,//he also might better holden his tonge.

Sir Edw[in] Sands tooke occation upon his speech saying that yesterday he understood him not playnly by reason of his horseness, but nowe that he did understand him, he wold be bold to tell him that he was mistaken and that those things wer not soe spoken in the howse as they wore reported.

Then he defyned what a true reporter is, and what his duty is, viz not to tell the words spoken only, but the ende wherto, and the circumstances and to add nether sugar nor gale. And taxed him for putting an aspertion upon his Majesty by making him to be a misinterpreter, which yett he did verry modestly and in good termes but concluded with this sentence *Nihil est quod male narrando non possit depravier, tu quod mali est excerpis, relinquis quod boni est.*

And soe the howse rose.

May 7. Account of Sir Robert Harley

[Harley Papers]

Thursday May 160[7].

Sir Georg More.

More desirus to be the last yesterda[y] then the first.

Begins with desier to further it.

Matter concerneth the liberty of the hous nay of all subiects.

Fre voyce in making thos lawes under wich they live.

Kings honor to be kings over a fre peple.

As we should be carfull so his maiesty wilbe as a part of his own honor. Whatt the caus.

Speches dutifully deliverd hav bin miscaried to his maies[ty] wich he hath signified to the disgrac of the gentelmen who be in the matter not the gentelmen but all we that sit her.

Who the wronger the reporters.

And the King wronged.

Gentellman yesterday sayd he should hav bin an ill subiect if he should not hav sought means to hav satisfied his maies[ty].

Somthing is to be done for satisfaction of the hous.

But the reporters to be ponished. Ther one [*own* is meant] conscienc will doe it and his Maiesty kno[w]ing them will desern of them herafter.

It is his Maiesty we seek to satisfey and to mayntayn our liberty.

Cours in former parlament. He remembred nether messag by the speker or other sent.

Was ther then never as great an wrong to the hous. As great things hav bin offerd tending to the breach of libertyes.

It is not meet that Chi[l]dren with ther parents or subiec[ts] with ther prince any way to contest.

A member of this hous speking unadvisedly of this house. His Maiesty left to us our liberty both in ponishing and in showing mercy.

His conceat. That as Mr. Speker mencioneth at the begining of the parlam[en]t so at the end to touch thes things passed.

We have iust caus to say that our libertys hav bin less toched then in any the last parlam[en]t of the Queen.

Mr. Speeker.

Remembreth the proiect yesterday offerd to the hous by Lewkner. And hopeth to prevent therby further disput.

Proiect devided into 3 parts.

1. Hous to be petitioners ether by Mr. Speker or som other to desier his Ma[jes]ty to suspend his Jugm[en]t untill Mr. Speker should recave the truthe.

2. That his Maiesty would be pleased to recave graciously the excuses of the gentlem[en] that ther be traduced.

3. That we must wright our ancient priveleges in fre spech.

This spech was delivered with a great deal of Art and reverenc.

His Maiesty hath taken notic and for the .2. first his Ma[jes]ty is pleased when you pleas. For the last his Ma[jes]ty doth marvell that any man shalbe jelious of it. Nether can any [of] you be mor carful to maintany it then [he].

Fre spech fitt for all counsell so it be bounded with Modesty and respect. Nether to tye subiect[?] from speking of the matter in Question.

Now since his Maiesty taketh notic of I desir what you plea[se] to advis of.

Mr. Brock.

This Messang is most honorab[le] and for the bill it is fitt to be committed.

Mr. Fuller.

Allways custom of this house to discus Bill befor committing.

Good satisfaction.

To be locked out of thes doors if speking frely.

If in an[y] matter wher my fayth nay my conscienc lieth in payn to speak my mind freely. But if I be short to doe that that ariseth in my self to doe for the king[?] I should be to blame.

The title is dangerous to us. It is the continuanc and preservation of the union.

Se how we com to be intrapt against a *non possum*.

If then in his maiesti[es] person none be then the hous is in an error.

Som then to tak away thes hostill laws for a preparation.

An act to take away certen hostill lawes to mak a preparation to a perfect un[ion].

No generalty becaus you may by that tak away all laws.

Matter of the bill.

R. 2 act. Not to goe to any other plac but Noblemen. We did all agree that the holl law to be taken away at the commity in the court of W[ards].

The lords wer so at the [*blank*].

Scotland hath liberty. Other nations have the lyk that ar a fre peop[le].

The word of god sayst If you be persecuted ther you may fly into an o[ther].

This king was in fear of a putting out of this kingd[om].

Was ther ever such floods such plages etc.

Excellent men in this hous that on[e] quarter must hav don mor then we have don if we had gods Blessing.

So long as ther is sever ponishment of the sincere men of god what hop can we h[ave].

Jerusalem did have other wal I fear.

Therfor wher very excellent ministers ar ponished we cannot look for Blessing.

Not under one allegienc: we obey by law and ar sworn to that.

Alegianc to England is by reason of the law of England and so of Scotland.

All lawes tending to hostility. He lyketh not that that may subiect any thing to contention and therfore to do it by special wa[*blank*].

Last matter. Border taken away and governed by the lawes respective of the country.

So much as was accounted England to be governed by England. Therfor Berwick to be disput[ed?]. That we loss no part of our ancient borders.

10. by the King nominated for England and 20 Scottland.

What sentenc was formerly given to be by border laws.

But what hath no sentenc as yett to be left to the law of England. He lyketh no arbitrary government.

Mr. Speker.

A law in Scottland to restrayn going out of Scottland more straight then ours. He for tha[t] is loser of lan[d]s gods and chat[tels].

Mr. Yelverton.

Trobuled with carriers of words and not of matter.

Power to tramble uppon myself.

Much mor as a worm befor [*blank*].

Felix culpa quae talem habuit redemptore[m].

So I *felix habere repre[he]nsorem.*

So I say now my words ioyned to the matter.

My grund was that I was voyd of hops and fears. This was from the opinions som of my ambition other of fe[ar].

Under so gratius a princ.

In all humility I doe under go the reprehention.

I shall her confess my faver though I cannot my faultes[?] in conscienc.

Then I am fre by you and that is my course against the reports.

Bills mor easy to se danger as Berwik by rendetion[?] in the un[ion].

Reported that we ar not now sullen but [*blank*].

In this bill is all contayned if we look to it. Hostil lawes Comm[erce] Natur[alization].

Not all lawes hostill but Custome and common lawes.

United under on[e] alleganc but this hous will not [*blank*].

It is *idem persona* but not *eadem rex.*

Ire sub lege is Alleganc.

Under one law not one allegianc.

For that of the borders. To obbollish the nam befor we hav set out the border may greve som.

Though I coud wish all on[e] that desier a fre monarchy.

If we establish the commis[sion] not to Wes[tmoorland] Cumb[erland] Nor[thumberland]. Not a shurt to prove.

On firmament over us.

Bewar of reconciled foes.

No man could hav means to eas him self but by this cours. It wer as piratts uppon the seas. But to give comiss[ion] gives *sustinebit.*

Mak a bill to fre them against the retribution sinc[?] that represed mor by a border.

MAY 8. ACCOUNT OF SIR ROBERT HARLEY

[HARLEY PAPERS]

At the Commity of repealing Hostill Lawes.

Nott to do it in generall words for 2 reasons. 1. We shall repeall lawes we know not for the[y] ar not all printed. 2. Leav to the Exposition of Jugges to say what is repealed what not.

Lawes mad against them as Enimys but thos lawes that hav not mention of being mad against the Scotts as Enimyes ar not repealed by a generall lawes.

The Scotts doe procead by a generall and therfor [*blank*].

Sicut video et audio sic habeo.

My Eye shall lead me. What the Scotts doe I know not nor inquier not.

Danger to us[e] generall words for in a law that may be hostility ther may be som other thing th[at] may be to our good repealed that we would not.

To this last obiection is answered that the word of generality is not named but stattuts. That can not reach ether to Common Law or Custome but only to wrighten lawes as stattutes. And again it reacheth to thos lawes that ar against as Scotland as Enimyes and not as Aliens. And only so much as shall conceave hostility only.

No Mischeiff in perticulers but may be remided in a succeding parlament but not so if we conclud the generall.

If the Scotts Commission[er]s in ther articles hav not concluded a generall repeall lett not us procead.

Enumeratt 1000 and not use generall the Scotts may say the[re] ar
mor obscured but the way to bred love is to take awaye Jelosy.

Cariing in Hors[es] thing in H. 8. tim felony.

So for transporting of Bullion.

To repeall all printed lawes in generall and to direct that any law not
printed shal not be produced against the Scots but not repealed.

Though the Scotts repeall more lawes then we yett many of ther lawes
that they repeall ar to ther o[w]n benifit as going into England, viteling
Berwyk—wich wer mor benificall to vend[?] our vitteyll then thers ther.

What is to be done is to be done mutually. The[y] doe in perticuler
and we have done by our perticulers in perticuler. So have the[y]. If we
alter by sense our perticuler then will the[y] look to doe the lyke and so
it will hinder the work.

Question that as many as will hav all thos Lawes wich shalbe repealed
perticularly enumerated lett them say I.

As many as will have thos and lawes of generall anulled say I. The I
winn it. (Cf. report of Thomas Wilson in Spedding, III, 343–344.)

May 9. Committee Reported by Thomas Wilson

[St. P. Dom. XXI, 21]

Betwixt late cominge and unwilling proceedinge ther hath less been
done this day then yesterday. The point wher we left yesterday was about
repealing all hostile lawes. It was decyded by question that none shold
be repealed by any generale terme but only such as were mentioned in the
bill. To this Mr. Atturney that spoke first to daye said that we must
understand that what soever was done in this kinde his Majesty did
understand of, and soe hee tooke upon him to tell us that the kinge did
aprove our reason that we shold not involve in any generale worde a
repeale of all such lawes as we yett knewe not, yett seemed to desyre that
we wold shewe an inclinacion yea a resolucion to repeale all such lawes
when they apeered unto us.

He moved also a second thinge which yesterday was handled in the preamble viz that wheras we had said the union begone in his Majestyes
royall person, we wold nowe add unto that word begon, some other word
for more strength of the same and that shold be the word, setled, or
grounded, or inherent, or invested or some such.

Thes 2 motions of his were much debated and in the end thus resolved.

That for the first Mr. Atturney shold make a drawght howe he wold
have it brought in and offer it to the Comitte, and then they to consider
of it and soe if it wer thought fitt offer it to the howse.

To the second for adding the word setled or grounded etc. it was
thought to be a matter of great consequence and therfore not fitt to be
debated att soe smale a comitte as that then was, especially the lawyers
being almost all absent, nay if they were present it is of such consequence
said they that it was fitter to be referd to be handled in the howse, and
soe after much canvassing; that point was putt off to the howse.

The greatest opponente was Sir Hen[ry] Poole who said he sawe not howe that word//begone//cold well be used sith we owe not obedience to the kinge as kinge of Scotland but as king of England and that *secundum leges regni stigliae*[?] he was answered with a distinction of an union personal and an union politick and that the union personal was ther ment the words following did explaine viz "the union begone in his Majestys person//and that, that union was begone or consumate noe man wold or cold denye. Notwithstanding, this sound answer wold not geve satisfaccion, but still they wold have it referd to the howse whether any more words shold be added or noe.

Then it was moved to leave thes points and goe forward wher we left, then was redd the clause concerning the Borders wherin ther apeered 3 or 4 such dangerous rocks that they were afrayd to sayle by them unless ther shipp wer better manned. Those which I preceyved apeered most were the words *In one United Alegeance*, and the matter of the *Customes* which was yesterday deferd from the title till they mett with the word in the bill. The third was the leaving indistinguished the bounds of the borders and some other which appered unto them soe dangerous that Mr. Lewknor (which made the first speech somewhat to freely about taking away the freedome of the howse,) moved to have all putt of till Monday by cause they were not ther which he thought had most linces eyes to pearce into those matters and upon his motion the Comitte rose without doing more.

MAY 11. COMMITTEE OF THE WHOLE
[HARLEY PAPERS]

At the conference on Mond[ay].

Nott to agre to a generallyty. It is not fitt for this court to agre uppon that we se not.

Nott to mencion (to commend to posterity to tak away Hostill lawes) in the acte). But to sett down that thes be all the Hostill lawes we can find which may intend our desier to repeall them if we knew them.

The claus put in by Mr. Atturny answereth an obiection: preventeth a question. Obiection. Ar ther no mor lawes etc. Not that we can find.

Saffest to putt all things (only) declaratory in the preamble and not in the body of the act for that doth bind.

Forum Judicii.

Forum Famae.

Principum actiones ad famam componendae sunt. So perticuler repeall serveth for *Judicis* but Intemation of our purposs must be generall and that is *ad famam.*

Jugment of parlament is the fam of parlament.

Small iugment to comend to posterity. It wanteth reason, president, Jugment.

Fitt to mak our will in an act of parlament for this is our last will.

After the lawes repelled in perticuler than to say that if wee found an[y] more we would have repealed them. It is offenc against the crown for the king wareth a severall crowne so that the Jugge may nott wi[th] stand[?] the union nor poster[ity] exicut the lawes of Hostility sinc the king comm[ing].

Ad novas causas duxere Novand[um] concilium.

Ether that before without reason we refused or ells reason to refuss this for this is by the provisions all one as the other.

If future parlament may abrogatt an act binding therfor much mor an intimation of our mind in a declaration.

The only reason the last day against the generall repealle was not to put into the Jugges hand the exposition of what is Hostill lawes but this intention of our desier to repeall if we knewe them doth not inable the Jugges to expound what is a Hostill lawe.

Mr. Crew clause was inserted.

Borders and Border lawes repealled.

1. No borders limited.

2. No remidy for trespases respectivly committed.

3. Customes (in general) may reach further then hostill customes. It may extend to tenant right and so undo the tenants. If you ad a proviso then the lords will say you enact that right which is questionable.

In the parenesys.

Bothe the Kingdoms under one allegianc. Cannot be for *leges* ar the Sinewes of the body and if severall lawes then severall sinewes and so two body[s].

Resolveth that repealed customs and ordinances you tak away teneant right. And it is alredy inforsed by som landlords that the tenent right growing by reson of defenc and danger thos causes being taken away the Custom right is taken away. Therfor to tak away only the Hostill ordinances and customs specaly and not in generall. He desires that the Borders may be first sett downe.

It taketh away suiters and County paliatines and lords leets.

And muche land is possessed by the Scotts that was not in the Borders. First [*word illegible*] of the tennants.

Under one allegiance. This is a playn Jugment in parlament that we ar no more 2. bodys but one and this doth include both fre commerc and Naturalising and Docter and student doth say that it is not ended that an act of parlament doth never mencion untruthes.

To put out thes words (under one allegeance) for if the act of recognition was befor obiected at the conference of the Ante and postnati wher it is sayd united under one imperiall crowne.

Borders do remayn in law so long as the kingdoms ar severall so that it is impropper to tak away the name and the thing remayning. Marches bounds and confines will remayne.

Ob. Tak away names by act of parlament doth no good for so see for purveors so for su[b]scidyes. And benevolence that cam in the plac was malevolous etc.

First question wether to tak away the nam of the borders. But by this we tak not away the limitts but leave the intellectual line. But the name of the borders is the shires that was not decided but claimed by both nations.

No part of the claus for repeall of lawes Border not fitt to pass. The questionable ground is the caus of the name of the border. Therfor tak away the matter befor the name. It is not the nam of the border for that is the erth it self but it was the goods and cattell that was taken away that mad the hostility.

Whosoever offendeth the act doth a contempt as is punishable by the king though ther be penalty and so for the calling of borders when the law is past then if any call it he offendeth the act.

To abbolishe the border nam is worthy a parlament to abollish.

In the book of god few great actions but have in the book of god incepted but a [*blank*]. Acheldama the feild of blood. If then it be a nam of blood it is fitt to be taken away.

Wysdom of parlaments hath bin to alter names.

Purveors nam was changed by parlament.

In this of the border ther is by his majesty a reall takin[g] away of the matter. Not so of purveors, Subsidys.

King a pleasing nam in other places yett not at Rothes.

Borders may have an equivocation nam of *quiddam non quantum*. It is fitt to be altered in bothe.

Whatt points ar to be spoken.

1. Name.

2. Obbolission of Border laws or constitutions. Civill. Hostill.

3. Setting out of boundreys. Becaus so much as is English to be ruled by Englishe and of this the marke ar not Form of Justic. If you tak that away and leav them to the lawe it wilbe inconvenient in the present for a whill and therfor som mor present cours to be taken.

2. Obbolission of Border lawes.

No border lawes but such as ar mad by the two kings or ther com-mission[er]s. As I can observe. Thes border laws ar but in the natur of leages as with franc or Spayn.

Now a question is wether thes be not gone in the person of the king. As if a convention should be mad bettwin the King of England and Scotland severally now com into one person. For I think the[y] ar and thes words to be rather a declaration then an enacting.

All the borders ar ether Civill or criminall. As other laws ar.

The warden hav severall power distinct according to the severall Marches.

March treason for an Englishman to speak with a Scott. The Warden had a power over this man and this is a several power from the mutuall lawes of both borders. This for the warden is by Commission and the commission taken away the law is gon in this so both lawes ar gon.

A Commission now to a warden as afore is voyd now by the law of England.

Not Taken away.

Treateys one thing on other commission to warden and an other thing for Customs.

1. As ther can be no reprehention so no confederation for one King cannot treat with him self.

Suprema potestas or *altera potestas* that is the commission so that if the commission be gon then is the authority gon.

For Custom.

1. *Rectum dominorum a locale* or *feudale* is such as the lords hav over ther tenant and in this plac will com in your tenant right as to do service.

2. *Juridica potestas*. By reason of person. As the lord Marcher hathe a greater commission to comand this over the border then us that dwell [*blank*].

No right of the lords to his tenant is taken away.

Consider how far that Jurisdiction that the King hath over the persons to command them mor then he can over thos further of from the borders.

Tenant right doth aw[ay] with cariag or Escuage.

It is fitt to wip out al that may call in question any mans right of inheritanc though it be for servic. The word usages wilbe dangerous and not to be help[ed] but by an ennacting wich is most suer.

The question then is wither all hostill lawes mad especially for the borders being March laws devised by a discretionary cours to remidy any give redresse unto the English only and that was lost to the wardens. But ther was a wrighten lawe that was bettwene the princes.

The wrighten border lawes ar no mor but the extract of treateys.

Border lawes ar 1. Commission to the warden and ar arbitrary and reach only to the English and deter[mi]ned by Cours. 2. From the Extract of treateys and thes do bind both nations being mad by assent of both princes.

Hostill Customs. 1. *Feudale dominorum*. Tenant right. 2. *Juridica potestas*. 1. Commission England. 1. Treateys.

Fitt rather to grant a commission before them to certify now to whatt commissions shall doe.

Our ac[t] is that when the Scotts have repeled thers we must doe ours and therfor leav this second part first to a Commission and then to enact it after the report as a second work.

Nott fitt to put uppon the Commission that we can do of our selves.

Speech in the Committee of the Whole on May 11 or May 12

[Salisbury MSS]

Seeing it beseemeth every honest member of this House by all means possible to endeavor so to clear our actions, as to make them justifiable to all, that would go about to calumniate our proceedings, that we refuse nothing out of any humour of opposition or contradiction, but out of reason, it is necessary, that we be more careful in the penning of this act of abrogating hostility than in any other bill that can come in question. For although there may be just cause to forbear the repeal of laws unknown for the causes which have been delivered, yet it would be very fit that there be some such word interlaced in the preface or elsewhere which may declare, that we conclude that there can be now no enmity between the two kingdoms, which are subject to one king. And therefore, although the putting in of this be not much material, yet the denial to put it in may be much prejudicial, and conceived that those which have it out, and refuse the general cause of repeal would have it tacitly inferred, that there were some defect in his Majesty's right to both Kingdoms; I could wish that after the clause allowed of yesterday, that if they could have found more laws they would repeal them, these few words (if nothing else will be yielded) might be inserted. "Seeing all that which was enmity in former times between the two kingdoms and people is now taken away and turned into fraturnity," or brotherly friendship as Mr. Fuller hath often said in divers of his speeches. If in this either my speech or my dependency be suspected, for the first, I speak but mine own conscience, which I would not betray for all the world; and for the second I hope that very circumstance may secure all men, that I desire nothing more than to leave no ground for any indisposed persons to move his Majesty to conceive otherwise of our proceedings than we deserve for the great love and duty which we have ever carried and will in all our actions.

INDEX

INDEX

Abbott, Charles, Speaker, notes passage of Bowyer's diary, 343n

Acheldama, 385

Admiral, Lord High, *see* Howard, Charles

Admiralty, expense of, 371; laws of, 336

Albert, Archduke, Regent of Flanders, 29; English ambassador with, 188; expense of ambassador with, 373

Ale, *see* Beer and ale

Alford (Allford, Allforde, Allfoord), Edward, M. P., in debate, 195–196, 251, 267, 332, 340, 342–344, 366; point of order by, 207; motion by, 251, 363; seconds motion, 232; statement by, 100, 232–233; appointed to speak in conference, 232

Allegiance, oath of, 162, 171, 174, 183; to be taken by Catholics, 24; fails to restrain Catholics, 29; to be taken by soldiers, 28; treason to refuse, 30

Allford (Allforde, Allfoord), *see* Alford

Almshouse, 6

Alphonso, King of Spain, law reform under, 268n

Altham (Altom), ——, sergeant, counsel against patent for wool, 141–142

Alum, imposition upon, 118

Ambassadors, members appointed as, 186–188; not factors for merchants, 335; expense of, 372, 373

Anne of Denmark, Queen of James I, attorney for, 89, 315; high steward to, 155; tenant of, 155; expense of journey to England, new establishment, and jointure, 372–373; purveyance for, 40; title of, 325

Apprentices, 25n, 30, 172, 291

Aragon, union with Castile, 271n, 272, 282n

Archbishops, 39, 102; Scots denied office in England, 228, 236; proceedings in courts of, 144–147; in the King's mercy, 146–147; of Canterbury, *see* Bancroft, Islip; of York, *see* Grindal

Archdeacon, right of Scotch to hold position in England, 227n, 228, 236

Archduke, *see* Albert

Arches, court of, right of Scotch to be judges in, 227n

Arkel, Holland, 338

Arms and armour, to be taken from recusants, 19; company of, 323; taken into Scotland, 289. *See also* Ordnance

Articuli super Cartas, 290

Artillery, bill concerning, 137

Artois, exchange of prisoners between Picardy and, 301, 305

Ashley, Sir Anthony, 71n

Ashton (Asheton), *see* Aston, Sir Arthur and Sir Roger

Assemblies, rebellious, debate and committee meeting on bill concerning, 363, 365–367; in midlands, 365–366

Aston (Asheton), Sir Arthur, patentee for logwood, 111

Aston (Ashton), Sir Roger, M. P., sent to James with message, 159–160, 180; sent by James to Salisbury with message, 240n; letters of, 140n, 144n; statement by, 309, 312; private bill concerning, 206; patentee for fines and forfeitures, 114, 126, 127, 131, 154; allowed to remain in House during discussion of patent, 131; speech by, 114

391